# SERMONS ON SECOND TIMOTHY

# THE SERMONS OF IOH

*Caluine vpon the seconde Epistle of S. Paule to Timothie.*

The seconde Epistle of S. Paule to Timothie.
Chapter. 1.

1 *Paule an Apostle of Iesus Christe, by the will of God, according to the promise of life, which is in Iesus Christ.*

2 *To Timothie my verie deare Sonne grace, mercie and peace, fom God the father and from our Lorde Iesus Christ.*

 Hough in all that S. Paule hath left vs in writinges, we haue to confider that it is God that spake to vs by the mouthe of a mortall man, and wee must receiue his doctrine with suche authoritie and reuerence, as if God shewed himselfe from heauen to be sene with our eyes, yet notwithstāding ther is one thing more to be considered off in this Epistle, then in the other, and it is this, that S. Paule beeing now in prison, and seeing his death at hande, meant to confirme his faith in this place, as if he had sealed it with his owne blood. And therefore so oft as we reade this Epistle, let vs lay that stat before our eyes that S. Paule was then in, to wit, that he looked for nothing but to die for the witnes of the Gospell, as he did indeed as bearing ȳ standard before vs, to put vs more out of doubte of his doctrin, and then we shal be touched to the quicke. As no doubte if a man reade this Epistle diligently he shall finde the Spirite of God shewe him selfe in such forte, and in such a maiestie and vertue, that whether hee will or no, he shall bee as it were rauished with it. As for me, I know I haue profited, & do daily profite more by this Epistle, then by any booke of the scripture, and if euerie man wil looke into it diligently, I doubte not but he shall finde the like.

And if wee desire to haue witnesse of G O D S truethe

Tt.ij.     to

Opening page of the first English translation, by Laurence Tomson, of Calvin's *Sermons on Paul's Second Epistle to Timothy* (London, 1579)

# SERMONS
## ON
# SECOND TIMOTHY

## John Calvin

*Newly translated from the French of 1561*

*by*

### Robert White

THE BANNER OF TRUTH TRUST

# THE BANNER OF TRUTH TRUST

*Head Office*
3 Murrayfield Road
Edinburgh
EH12 6EL
UK

*North America Sales*
PO Box 621
Carlisle
PA 17013
USA

banneroftruth.org

First Banner of Truth edition 2018
© Robert White 2018

ISBN
Print: 978 1 84871 840 1
EPUB: 978 1 84871 841 8
Kindle: 978 1 84871 842 5

\*

First published in French by Conrad Badius under the title,
*Sermons de Iean Calvin sur les deux Epistres S. Paul à Timothée et
sur l'Epistre à Tite*, Geneva, 1561

First English edition, translated by Laurence Tomson,
published by G. Bishop and T. Woodcoke in London, 1579, under the title,
*Sermons of M. Iohn Calvin, on the Epistles of S. Paule to Timothie and Titus*

This new translation is based on the French text of 1561 found in
*Calvini opera quae supersunt omnia*, ed. G. Baum, E. Cunitz and E. Reuss
(Brunswick and Berlin: C. A. Schwetschke & Son, 1863–1900), 54:1–370

\*

Typeset in 11/15 pt Adobe Caslon Pro at
The Banner of Truth Trust, Edinburgh

Printed in the USA by
Versa Press, Inc.,
East Peoria, IL

# CONTENTS

Contents

# INTRODUCTION

Preaching was the most public and the most constant of Calvin's duties during his long tenure of office in Geneva (1536–1538, 1541–1564). Health and other commitments permitting, he normally preached twice on Sundays and daily on weekdays in alternate weeks. The Sunday sermons were devoted to a New Testament book and the weekday sermons to an Old Testament text. Exposition was sustained and systematic in the sense that, having selected a book, Calvin would work through it verse by verse, chapter by chapter, until the end had been reached. The preacher is never in a hurry, dwelling on a single verse, or perhaps on two or three related verses, for the time allotted him—rarely less than an hour. Occasionally time does not permit him to conclude, and the congregation is promised a fuller treatment of the text when next it meets.

Calvin began his sermons on the Pastoral Letters—1 and 2 Timothy and Titus—in September 1554. The groundwork for his exposition had been laid some years before, the Reformer having published a commentary on 1 and 2 Timothy in 1548 and another on Titus in 1550. The 1 Timothy sermons occupied Calvin until April 1555; 2 Timothy followed immediately, and was in turn succeeded by Titus in August 1555. The entire series was completed by mid-October of that year. Having been taken down in shorthand and then transcribed, all one hundred and one sermons were published by Genevan printer Conrad Badius in early 1561, under the title *Sermons de Iean Calvin sur les deux Epistres S. Paul à Timothée et sur l'Epistre à Tite*. A second printing from the press-es of Jean Bonnefoy appeared in 1563.[1] Surprisingly, it was Eng-lish readers who were the first to sample the new work, thanks to the appearance of two sermons on 2 Timothy 1:8-10, translated anonymously and published in London in 1560. A full English translation, done by Laurence Tomson, was published in 1579.[2] A much abridged, modernized version of Tomson's text appeared in New York in 1830, and a facsimile reprint of the whole volume was issued by The Banner of Truth Trust in 1983. To date, Tomson's version has been the only one available in English. The time has therefore come for a fresh translation.

\* \* \* \* \*

Paul's letters to Timothy and Titus differ from his customary practice in both nature and purpose. They are addressed not to individual churches or to groups of churches but to men who, as Paul's personal representatives, were required to organize, lead and discipline Christian congregations meeting for the most part as house-churches. The letters touch on doctrine only incidentally, being essentially concerned to strengthen the hand of Timothy and Titus who were meeting worrying and sometimes determined resistance. None of these letters, however, exactly replicates the others. If they are 'pastoral', it is, as was long ago observed, in rather different degrees. 'First Timothy is entirely pastoral, and perhaps intended to be of universal application. Titus is mainly pastoral, but is also a letter of commendation and a letter of recall. Second

---

[1] For bibliographical details on these and related texts, see Rodolphe Peter and Jean-François Gilmont, *Bibliotheca calviniana*, 3 vols. (Geneva: Droz, 1991-2000), II, pp. 584-85, 592-93, 776-77, 857-61, 1038-40.

[2] *Sermons of M. Iohn Calvin on the Epistles of S. Paule to Timothie and Titus* (London: G. Bishop and T. Woodcoke, 1579). See further T. H. L. Parker, *Calvin's Preaching* (Edinburgh: T&T Clark, 1992), pp. 73, 192.

Timothy is mainly personal, a letter of recall and only incidentally pastoral.'[3]

Since writing his first letter to Timothy and his letter to Titus, the apostle's circumstances have dramatically changed. He is no longer free to pursue his mission in the eastern Mediterranean. Once more a prisoner in Rome, but this time closely confined, Paul has undergone a preliminary trial and, with another hearing imminent, he anticipates a sentence of death. Bereft of many of his co-workers, he asks Timothy to come quickly to him, bringing with him books and a cloak and leaving the work in Ephesus to Tychicus. This most personal of Paul's letters is also his most urgent. He has fought the good fight and finished his race (2 Tim. 4:7). Timothy's race, however, is not over. The apostle therefore insists on the need for loyalty and endurance in the face of certain suffering (2 Tim. 1:8; 2:1; 4:5). While Paul is in chains the gospel is not (2 Tim. 2:9). God knows those who are his and will honour the trust they have placed in him (2 Tim. 1:2; 2:19). Present faith is thus buoyed by future hope: Christ who has destroyed death will appear in judgment and glory to complete the work of salvation, and to give to all who love his appearing the crown of righteousness (2 Tim. 4:1, 8).

I have spoken elsewhere of the importance of the Pastoral Letters for Calvin.[4] Together with the Book of Acts, the Pastorals furnished him with a pattern of church governance which took immediate root in the Reformed churches, and which in part constituted them as Reformed. More particularly, the qualities of the Christian minister on which Paul insists, including the competence to teach and the courage to admonish and to discipline, represented a model to which Calvin himself sought to conform

---

[3] Walter Lock, *A Critical Commentary on the Pastoral Epistles* (Edinburgh: T&T Clark, 1924), p. xiii.

[4] Introduction to Calvin, *Sermons on Titus* (Edinburgh: Banner of Truth, 2015), pp. x-xi, and *Sermons on First Timothy* (Edinburgh: Banner of Truth, 2018), p. xv.

and the standard by which ministerial vocations were to be judged. If, in addition, we remember the similarities which the Reformer saw between his own, often difficult, situation in Geneva and that of Timothy in Ephesus and of Titus in Crete, it is not hard to see why the preacher should dwell with such sympathy and at such length on these three texts.

What the Pastorals meant to Calvin may be seen from the unusually frank comment which he makes when introducing his sermon series on 2 Timothy. 'If we read this letter carefully,' he tells his congregation, 'we will see that God's Spirit there reveals himself with such power and majesty that we cannot avoid feeling thrilled. For my part, I know that this letter has done me as much good as any book of Scripture. Every day there is something of value in it. I do not doubt that those who closely study it will feel the same. If we want the kind of testimony to God's truth which will pierce our hearts, we can do no better than tarry here.'[5]

It would of course be surprising if Calvin's exposition of 2 Timothy did not recall themes found in his sermons on 1 Timothy and on Titus. The need to preserve and defend the gospel against error and false teaching, the pursuit of holiness and blamelessness of life, the confident expectation of Christ's return as both Judge and consummate Redeemer—these recur in one form or another in all three sermon series. Issues of church order, above all the provision of a well-trained and vigorous pastorate, are never far from the preacher's mind. Again, in his sermons on the Pastoral Letters, Calvin is acutely conscious of the context in which he is required to work. His ministry in Geneva, as we have said, was fraught with difficulty. He was thought to ask too much of a people resistant to doctrine and wary of ethical challenges. His hortatory style grated on some ears and barely penetrated others. The disciplinary powers of the Consistory, the church court, were frequently contested and

[5] First sermon on 2 Timothy.

its verdicts criticized. Calvin's opponents, the more vocal of whom were grouped in the so-called Libertine party, were in the political ascendancy until the elections of February 1555, and seized every opportunity to discredit the Reformer and to return Geneva to a softer form of Protestantism. The preacher was aware, too, that among his congregation were some who were nostalgic for the past and who would have liked to see an accommodation with Rome, if not a return to Rome itself. Nor could he always count on the support of the many refugees who, for reasons of religion, had sought asylum in Geneva. Not all found the religious settlement to their liking, and many said so openly.

These tensions are apparent in the sermons on 2 Timothy. Along with condemnation of Rome's errors, there are frequent appeals to hearers to embrace the gospel and to profit from its teaching, lest the privilege be taken from them and the opportunity to advance God's word be lost. Neither in Geneva nor anywhere else in sixteenth-century Europe was the Reformation so secure as to be invulnerable to false friends and open foes. If the preacher's tone often seems to us unduly severe and unnecessarily alarmist, it is only because we are privileged to have a larger and longer historical perspective.

Outside of Calvin's major work, the *Institutes of the Christian Religion*, few texts throw more light on his understanding of ministry than the sermons on the Pastoral Letters. The preacher's exegesis of the Pastorals has a great deal to say about the ministerial office. The minister is, in Calvin's thinking, first and foremost a servant and steward of God's word. Without that word he has no message to deliver and no function worth performing. By virtue of God's call, which is sealed by the Holy Spirit and acknowledged by the church, he is God's mouthpiece and herald, appointed to bring to the world 'the infinite treasures of the gospel of grace'. So great a gospel should elicit both our gratitude and our obedience. 'God,' says Calvin, 'will not suffer us to scorn him. When I speak I do so in God's name. All pride must be thrown down, and no creature may lift its eyes to him before whom all, both great and small, must bow.'[6] A bare recital of God's gracious works is not, however, enough. Preaching must stir the conscience, challenge the mind and energize the will. 'We should come to God's school to hear his word, and should let men do a serious work in us. Since we are his vineyard, we must be dug about, pruned and stripped of our leaves and excess growth; we must be harvested or else we will not bear fruit for the Master.'[7] The power of God's word to effect change, however, must never be an excuse for indolence. As teacher, the preacher must himself be teachable: to look into Scripture is a lifetime's study. As teacher, too, he must be sensitive to his hearers' needs, since not all who are in God's school are natural learners. In an arresting image Calvin likens the preacher to an attentive parent: 'If, in a house, there is a loaf of bread and the master has small children who cannot lift the loaf because it is whole and much too big, how can the children get their teeth into it to eat it? The crust will be too tough. Our Lord therefore, like a good father, makes sure that the bread is cut up, and the pieces put in our mouth and well chewed over.'[8] As the shepherd of God's sheep, the preacher must learn to speak with two voices: 'a gentle voice to encourage those who are willing to be taught and to lead them in the right path, and a different voice to cry out against wolves and thieves, to drive them from the flock and to defend God's truth which is the food of life.'[9] The ultimate test, however, of a minister's fidelity is the extent to which his deeds mirror his words. Inconsistency of life is as fatal a flaw as doctrinal error. 'If,' says Calvin, 'I

---

[6] Fourteenth sermon on Titus.
[7] Twelfth sermon on 2 Timothy.
[8] Twelfth sermon on 2 Timothy.
[9] Twentieth sermon on 1 Timothy.

preached about sobriety, but was known to be a drunkard, or about chastity when I was known to be a fornicator—if, in short, my life was inconsistent, what would I achieve by all my preaching except to discredit the doctrine I preached?'[10]

\* \* \* \* \*

The present translation of Calvin's sermons on 2 Timothy is based on the nineteenth-century text published by G. Baum, E. Cunitz and E. Reuss.[11] It has, however, been extensively checked for accuracy against the original edition of 1561 held by the Bibliothèque de Genève. Sermon titles are my own. Modern conventions regarding punctuation and sentence length have been observed, and paragraph divisions, missing in the original text, have been introduced. Scripture references have been moved from the margins to the body of the text, and additional references have been supplied. When Scripture itself is quoted or paraphrased, I have translated directly from Calvin's French. The extempore prayer with which the Reformer concluded each sermon, and which the *CO* editors omitted, has been restored. Some background notes relevant to the content of the sermons have also been included.

The publication of this volume brings the present edition of Calvin's sermons on the Pastoral Letters to an end. I wish to thank the trustees of The Banner of Truth Trust for their willingness to support the project, and to record my deep gratitude to the editor, Jonathan Watson, for his generous counsel, encouragement and constant help throughout.

ROBERT WHITE
Sydney
August 2018

---

[10] Twenty-second sermon on 2 Timothy.

[11] *Calvini opera quae supersunt omnia*, 59 vols. (Brunswick and Berlin: C.A. Schwetschke & Son, 1863-1900), 54: 1-370. (Hereafter cited as *CO*.)

# CALVIN'S OUTLINE OF PAUL'S SECOND LETTER TO TIMOTHY

We cannot determine with any certainty from Luke's narrative when the first letter to Timothy was written. It is clear, however, that Paul knew Timothy personally and that Timothy accompanied him to many places as his fellow-worker. In any case it is easy to see that Timothy was still in Ephesus when Paul addressed this second letter to him, for toward the end he greets Priscilla, Aquila and Onesiphorus. The last-mentioned was a resident of Ephesus, while the others stayed behind in Ephesus when Paul took ship for Judaea.

Here Paul's main concern is to confirm Timothy in the faith of the gospel and to urge him to be steadfast in proclaiming it. We should nevertheless consider Paul's circumstances at the time, in order to give due weight to his exhortations. The apostle was facing death, which he was soon to suffer for his witness to the gospel. What we read here, therefore, must be interpreted in terms of Christ's kingdom, the hope of eternal life, the nature of Christian conflict, steadfast confession of Christ and the certainty of God's truth—things not written in ink but in Paul's own blood. He asserts nothing for which he is not prepared to lay down his life. The letter is thus, in a sense, a solemn endorsement of Paul's own teaching.

As we learned in the previous letter, Paul was not writing for one man only. Through Timothy he lays down teaching of a general nature which is to be handed on to others. Here Paul begins by praising Timothy's faith in which he had been brought up since youth. He tells him to be faithful to the truth he had been taught and to persevere in the duties entrusted to him. At the same time Timothy must not lose heart because of Paul's imprisonment and the defection of others. Paul rejoices in his apostolic labours and in the reward laid up for him. He also praises Onesiphorus for having encouraged others by his example. And because the lot of those who would serve Christ is hard and painful, he likens them to farmers and to soldiers. The first do not hesitate to work hard in tilling the soil before they ever see fruit; the second leave behind their business and concerns, taking up arms in order to serve their commander.

At this point Paul briefly summarizes the gospel, and orders Timothy to instruct others so that the message is passed from hand to hand to those who are yet to be born. Then, having spoken of his chains, he makes a holy boast in order to confirm us all the more by his example and endurance, inviting us to contemplate with him the crown which awaits us in heaven. We are also warned to avoid all quarrels and pointless arguments, and are commanded to strive to edify. And to illustrate the kind of risks we run, we are told of some—two names are mentioned, Hymenaeus and Philetus—who erred so monstrously that they overturned the hope of resurrection, and were severely punished for their recklessness and pride. However, since many often take great offence when they witness such falls, especially where prominent and respected people are involved, Paul warns believers not to be distressed, because those who outwardly profess to be Christians are not necessarily Christ's. The church is bound to suffer the misfortune of living among the wicked and the faithless, yet the Lord will preserve and uphold his elect to the end of time.

Again the apostle urges Timothy to pursue his ministry faithfully and, to ensure that he remains ever vigilant, he predicts that dangerous and distressing times will soon come upon the faithful and that the wicked will make their presence felt. Nevertheless Paul strengthens him by insisting that he may hope for a good and happy outcome. Above all he tells him to train himself in wholesome doctrine and to demonstrate the true and proper use of Scripture, where he will find everything he needs to edify the church effectively.

That said, Paul speaks of his death as imminent, yet he runs to meet it as a victor who is assured of a glorious triumph, and gives proof of a wonderful faith and confidence. Lastly he asks Timothy to come to him soon, and reveals how much he needs him by referring to his present plight. The letter thus concludes on this important note.

# I

---

# LOVED BY GOD

*Paul, an apostle of Jesus Christ by the will of God, according to the promise of life which is in Jesus Christ, ² to Timothy, my very dear son, grace, mercy and peace from God the Father and Jesus Christ our Lord.*

(2 Timothy 1:1-2)

We should always remember that in all the writings left to us by Paul, it is God who speaks to us by the lips of a mortal man, and that we should receive his teaching with reverence and authority as if God himself had visibly appeared from heaven. There is nevertheless something we should especially notice about this letter. Paul is in prison. He believes that death is imminent and seeks to confirm his faith as if sealing it with his own blood. Thus whenever we read this letter we should picture Paul's plight at the time, namely that he was expecting to die for his witness to the gospel, as indeed he did, so that, as our standard-bearer, he might give us greater assurance of his teaching and might touch us to the quick.

In truth, if we read this letter carefully we will see that God's Spirit there reveals himself with such power and majesty that we cannot avoid feeling thrilled. For my part, I know that this letter has done me as much good as any book of Scripture. Every day there is something of value in it. I do not doubt that those who closely study it will feel the same. If we want the kind of testimony to God's truth which will pierce our hearts, we can do no better than tarry here. We would have to be extremely sleepy and utterly mindless for God not to work in us once we hear the truths which will come to light. This is something we should think about before we start our study.

Let us remember what we saw in Paul's first letter. The apostle does not have one man only in mind, but the entire church of God. Hence, if he had been writing privately to Timothy, he would not have needed to call himself *an apostle according to the will of God*. Timothy had long known this and already had proof of it. Nevertheless, although no one denied that Paul was an apostle of Jesus Christ, he sometimes ventured to assure believers of the fact, as he does here. While this letter, then, bears Timothy's name, it is intended for the whole of God's church so that it might be of service to us today. Observe, however, that in calling himself a servant of Jesus Christ he is not seeking authority which would raise him above everyone else. His one aim is to exalt God and to give him obedience. Those who behave responsibly in God's church never try to claim headship for themselves: they want headship for Jesus Christ alone. It is our task to submit to him, since the Father has appointed him our teacher. To his word we must hold fast. All the loftiness of men is thus brought low when his excellence is in view, so that what was said by John the Baptist must be fulfilled: 'All must decrease, and he increase more and more' (John 3:30).

Again, Paul shows us that our trust must not be placed in men. It should always look to God as its goal and to our Lord Jesus Christ, who speaks on God's behalf. So when men exalt themselves and believe anything they like, when they assume the right to forge new articles of faith, they rob the Son of God and deprive him of what is his. As God said, he alone is to be heard (Matt. 17:5; Mark 9:7). Now if today anyone deserves to be heard, is Paul the least worthy? Yet he attributed nothing to himself and claimed no other name than that of Jesus Christ, who had commissioned him to bear the news entrusted to him. Then too, to persuade us that he had not thrust his way in under false pretences, he adds that it was 'according to God's will'. For, as the apostle says in the letter to the Hebrews, no one should intrude of his own accord (Heb. 5:4). To lead God's church is too noble and precious a thing for men to show such boldness. It is for God himself to appoint those he pleases.

He began, then, with Jesus Christ, making him our universal model. Although all majesty and dominion belong to our Lord Jesus Christ, he was content for God his Father to commission him with a solemn oath. Why? To be a mirror to us, so that nothing is done haphazardly in God's church, and that each of us should look to his calling. Here Paul speaks specifically of God's will, for although we sometimes have the power of choice—since God wishes the social order to be preserved—he is nevertheless in control when all is going well.

The office of apostle is admittedly unique, requiring God to speak as it were in person. As for the generality of preachers and the everyday ordering of church affairs, all must attain office by the will of God. His name should be invoked so that it is he who directs men's counsel, and so that whoever is called should have evidence that it is not through men, nor through personal ambition nor through some underhand intrigue. As we see here, it is not for us to put ourselves forward: God must reach out his hand to us. There must be proper order in the church to avoid muddle and confusion. Even so Paul always accords God his rights, making it clear that God has not relinquished control and that his people are still subject to him. Thus we see how special is the love that God bears us, for when he determines the way in which his church is organized, it is a sign that he is present in the church and watches over it. When we see his great concern for us in supplying us with pastors, knowing that it is he who chooses them, we see much more clearly his infinite kindness to us, and we have cause to be comforted and to praise the fatherly goodness he shows us here.

A further point needs to be made. In this passage Paul celebrates God's grace alone, pleading no merits of his own as if he deserved this honour. In speaking of God's will he draws an implicit contrast between God's free choice of us and the merits we might like to claim. We always like to think of ourselves as resourceful, as having something of worth which should put God in our debt. Paul, on the other hand, in calling himself an apostle, does not beat his chest and boast that he did it all by himself. He attributes everything to God's good will and pleasure. He is not concerned to ask whether he was better or fitter than others. (That was true, inasmuch as God had trained him!) Nevertheless he will have none of the credit which people normally take for themselves. He insists that he is not an apostle because he deserved to be one, but because it was God's will. He thus denies us the right to boast about anything, which accords with what he says in each of his letters. He wants God alone to be visible, always and everywhere.

Next he adds a highly significant phrase: *according to the promise of life which is in Jesus Christ*. Paul declares that the apostles were not meant to be like dumb dogs or idols. They were meant to proclaim the news of salvation and were to bear witness to it. This is an important point, for we know that the pope and all his horned beasts are not afraid to call themselves successors to the apostles.[1] But if we try to get them up into the pulpit to do the work of an

---

[1] 'Horned beasts': a pejorative term for bishops in the Roman Catholic Church. The two points of a bishop's ceremonial cap or mitre were called *cornua* ('horns') in Latin.

apostle, such a thing detracts from their episcopal dignity, or so they think! Here Paul shows that there is no prelate, bishop or pastor worthy of the name who does not bring and proclaim the gospel. Thus all who seek any standing in the church should know that God has set them up expressly to preach the message of salvation. Let the pope boast as much as he likes about his hierarchy, and let him say that all his cronies—I mean his attendant bishops—constitute the church. Paul's phrase reveals their insolence and strips away the mask they use as a disguise. If they preached God's truth to us and testified to his salvation, no one could deny the claim they make. As it is, they overturn all order because they do not bother to fulfil the office entrusted to them by God. Indeed they make a mockery of it, believing that it is unbecoming and that it demeans their status.

What need is there for further argument or debate? If they are bishops they must open their mouths and preach. Yet it is not enough merely to preach: men must be genuine messengers from God and must refrain from voicing their own pet opinions and ideas. They must faithfully minister the things they have received, without adding anything else. That is why Paul particularly mentions 'the promise of life', meaning that he does not propose ideas hatched in his own head, nor has he picked up a few odd teachings along the way. He simply preaches in accordance with God's command. Let us be clear, then, that all who want to be acknowledged as pastors in God's church must obey this rule, so that when they make the gospel known nothing evil should be mixed in with it.

Paul further seeks to commend his ministry to us, so as to convince us that the best thing we can do is to heed and accept it. Why, after all, does God raise up teachers who proclaim the gospel to us? Is it for his benefit? No! He does it to secure our salvation. Since God had only our interests at heart when he made known his gospel, we are entirely wicked if we refuse to be led. It is as if we meant to spite him by rejecting the life he offers us. If he were to insist on his rights, like a ruler who demands his tribute, if he treated us as harshly as he might, we would still have to bend our necks. (True, we might then plead that we were willing to obey him if only he were a Father and Saviour to us.) But since there is only fear, it is no wonder we draw back. We are therefore without excuse, because whenever God speaks it is for our benefit.

God intends his love, his mercy and his goodness to be set before us, so that we may receive assurance of our salvation and be saved from everlasting death, delivered from Satan's chains, freed from bondage to death and made heirs of his kingdom. Since this is God's sole purpose, must we not be completely bewitched by Satan if we are not quick to accept God's truth? So when we feel rebellious stirrings in ourselves, when we resist God or are slow to respond, when we are not as prompt as we should be in allowing God to direct us by his word, when we are less fervent and zealous than we would like, let us recall what Paul says here regarding the gospel. God wanted us to hear it preached not for any gain to him: it was all for our benefit. That is one thing we must note.

At the same time Paul rightly points out that the gospel comes to us through Jesus Christ. God has therefore honoured us more than he honoured the fathers of old, and he has raised us one place above them. We deserve the greater condemnation, then, and our thanklessness is all the more unpardonable, if we do not gladly respond to the invitation which God extends when he allows his gospel to be preached to us. It is true that from the very first he promised the faithful the salvation for which we wait today, and which the gospel offers to us as the fruit of our adoption. For what would have been the point of knowing God as our Saviour and Father if we were not destined for the life of heaven? The fathers of old possessed the same hope as we do today, but theirs was in abeyance. They languished, and were so to speak in deep distress until Jesus Christ appeared. It is in him that all of God's promises have their 'Yes' and their assurance, and in him that they are ratified (2 Cor. 1:20). So when Paul speaks of the promise of life, he shows that it is laid before us more directly than it was under the law. We have Jesus Christ who fulfils all that is necessary for our redemption. In him we see what our fathers saw only symbolically and in shadowy form. Thus, as I said, woe to us if our ears are not ready to receive the promise which God makes to us, and which he fulfils in the person of our Lord Jesus Christ.

The apostle continues in the following verse: *To Timothy, my well-loved son, grace, mercy and peace from God the Father and our Lord Jesus Christ.* Now in calling Timothy his 'son', Paul writes as if he had begotten him through the gospel. This does not contradict the saying of our Lord Jesus Christ which forbids us to call anyone 'father' in this world (Matt. 23:9), so that we should all look to God and honour and obey him. If we all made fathers for ourselves God would be robbed of his honour. If, however, we are led to God alone, if we are faithfully taught that all kinship derives from him and that we must pay him due honour, nothing should prevent us from regarding as fathers those who teach us the gospel. Why? Because God is at work in them, putting them, as it were, in his place, while not resigning any of his rights. When God is acknowledged as sovereign Father, men are inferior to him. Yet they are still our fathers and we are their children, especially when they bring us the imperishable seed by which we are reborn as children of God, and when they feed us with the word of truth.

In popery the bishops may well call themselves fathers, but they have nothing which allows them to usurp that honour. Scripture says that we are made children of God by the gospel, which is the imperishable seed (Gal. 3:26; James 1:18; 1 Pet. 1:23). Hence those who fail to preach the gospel cannot claim fatherhood for themselves, or else the children they beget are illegitimate and are disowned and rejected by God. When Paul therefore claims the title 'father' as he does here, it is only because of the gospel he preached and because, as God's servant, he begot souls. Accordingly we see how God works through his word when it is made known to us. Nor is this simply a voice which sounds in the air only to fade away. God adds the power of his Holy Spirit so that we each profit when we place ourselves in God's hands. It is certain that when we come to church it will not be merely the words of a mortal man that we hear: we will feel God speaking to our souls. He is our teacher, and by his secret power he so moves us that the voice of man enters into us and does so much good that we are fed and refreshed.

Paul also seeks to present Timothy as an example to all believers, exhorting us to allow the gospel to bring us in quiet submission to God and to greet as fathers those who preach it to us. We are not to make idols of them, since God has set them apart to serve us. He wishes to display his power in and through them, so that their work is not without effect. Thus Timothy shows us the way. If we want to be considered children of God, we must come in obedience to his word, and we must listen carefully to those who preach the gospel to us, submitting meekly and reverently to what we are told in God's name. This is why the prophet Isaiah says: 'I have put my word in your mouth' (Isa. 51:16). And when God declares that he wishes to be known as Father, he adds that the church is mother of all his children (cf. Psa. 87:5-6).

Again, if Timothy, a rare pearl chosen by God, was content to remain a child, what will they do who still have to work hard at their ABC? Yet nowadays we see such pride that no one speaks of modesty or self-restraint. How shameful it is that those who call themselves Christians refuse to submit to discipline or to control of any kind! At any rate, the example we see here shows that God will not allow such arrogance to go unpunished. So let us remember what we have said. Since God has been pleased to place in men's mouths the seed of life so that it might renew us, let us yield, and once we have received instruction let us honour God by showing that we have accepted his word—a treasure contained, as Paul says, in fragile vessels (2 Cor. 4:7).

As for the rest—'grace, mercy and peace'—'grace' and 'peace' appear as greetings in almost all the apostle's letters. Here he inserts the additional word 'mercy'. By 'grace', Paul means God's love, the favour and acceptance he accords us. Since, however, this is not possible except for his mercy, he rounds out the briefer lists he gives in other texts. Observe, then, that by the word 'mercy' Paul points us to the source of God's grace. Why should God favour us? Why are we acceptable to him? In asking this question we should examine ourselves and confess our wretchedness, the awful depths of misery found in us. How could God love us? How could we find grace in his sight if he did not have pity and compassion on our afflictions? So as I said, God's mercy is the source and fount of the grace he shows us when he sets his love on us and welcomes us as a father does his children. If God is to help us and be favourable to us, he must first love us. But how can he? Only through his goodness, since we are weak and wretched. He sees us as unhappy, doomed creatures who have no hope of salvation. This is why he opens to us what Scripture calls his bowels of mercy (Luke 1:78). He feels true affection for us, forgetting our unworthiness and choosing to love us, for he knows we are lost. 'These are my creatures,' he says, 'yet they lie in Satan's power and are buried deep in death. I must deliver them.' Hence the word 'mercy' which Paul adds here is not redundant, and although he does not always use it, we are warned that it is to mercy that we must look if we would be fully assured of God's fatherly good will.

Likewise we should understand that God does not show himself to be merciful to us once and once only. He continues to be merciful—such is our need—until death. For how does he assist us when we are assailed each day by trials and by adversity? He does it by strengthening us. Why does he strengthen us? Because he has pity on us. Or why does he forgive our sins? For the same reason. God's mercy to us never ceases. We do not only experience it at the beginning when he adopts us as his children; he continually extends it to us day by day, so that it flows endlessly on. Accordingly it always accompanies the grace which is mentioned here.

If we turn now to the two words with which Paul usually begins his letters, there is little need to dwell on them, since we spoke about them earlier. We may, however, briefly recall what was said. We saw first that when God looks on us with favour, he sends us all we need for our happiness. Conversely, if he is against us and rejects us we are lost, even if we have all we could desire. The faithless may feast to their hearts' content and rise high in honour and reputation. They may be healthy, merry and flushed with success; all may go well. Yet everything will become a curse for them. Why? Because the blessings which God showers on us are only hallowed for our use if, above all, we know that he is well-disposed toward us. That is why Paul's first word is 'grace', which shows that we should never be so stupid as to seek the things of earth. That, as we say, would be to put the cart before the horse. We must always lift our heads heavenward. When a pig is looking for its food it sniffs the ground and roots everywhere around. Those who are too earthbound do the same. They have no idea that it is only when God welcomes us and is propitious to us that we know true happiness and perfect bliss. Thus unbelievers, content with their wealth, enjoy their pleasures and delights and follow their inclinations. They are happy to flaunt themselves, to heap up goods and to thrive in the world's eyes. That is the sum total of happiness and good fortune as they see it.

We, however, should be wise enough to see that, while having the good things of this world and enjoying comfort, ease and all the rest, we should make sure we know God as our Father and that he counts us as his children. If we have this assurance, there is one more thing we need to notice: 'peace' which Paul puts after grace. By 'peace' he understands all that is fit and right for us, our prosperity and well-being. Do not think that we can prosper unless we are loved by God. Hence when Paul associates peace with God's love, he intimates that God is rich enough to give us all that we need, as long as we for our part want his love. Then we will have nothing else to fear.

This is an important point to notice. By nature we tend to be distrustful, always thinking that the earth will fail us. How can that be honouring to God? We acknowledge him to be our Father, indeed we glory in the fact! Yet if we lack the slightest thing our distress is pitiful to see. We are thrown into confusion, as if God were powerless, as if he had no means to help us. So because distrust so overwhelms us, we must think particularly hard about this truth and put it into practice. When we are told that God is favourable to us, we cannot doubt that he will help us prosper and that through his blessing he will give us all that we require. Come what may, let us be content simply with his grace.

Of course we are able to ask God for all our necessities, even for a piece of bread to eat. We should cast all our cares on him, but should always start with what comes first, that is, with the love he bears us and with the concern he has for our salvation. This should suffice, even if all else is lacking.

Paul, as we saw, ends his greeting with the words, 'from God the Father and our Lord Jesus Christ'. This simply confirms what we were taught before. If we want what is best for us, we must not turn away from God. Yet how restless and erratic our wishes are! How many are there who truly seek God? Yes, we mention him in passing, but if we looked more closely we would prefer that God were separate from us. Let him mind his own business, as we say, and leave us free to enjoy ourselves! Those are the kinds of mindless fools we are! Therefore Paul urges us to seek no other happiness than in God. We may pile up many possessions; every creature on earth may do our bidding, but instead of moving forward we fall back, until, that is, we come to God. As it is, he tells us that we may ask everything of him in full confidence, expecting that he will grant it to us. Why should we expect this? Because we remember not only God's majesty but also the name of Father with which he clothes himself, so that we have more intimate access to him.

Observe that Paul does not speak of God in bare, blunt terms. If we sought to draw near to him we would be fearful and in terror, knowing our own worthlessness. Yet when we do come God calls himself our Father, testifying that without his mercy none may know him. Hence Paul declares that we must seek our peace in God and in the grace of which he has spoken. How carefully we should meditate upon this word! God's majesty will always fill us with terror if we only think of him as the Creator. Whenever, then, we want God to receive us and are bold enough to come to him, let us fix our eyes on the word 'Father'. However, this cannot be unless we have Jesus Christ as our Mediator. That is why Paul adds 'from our Lord Jesus Christ'. When he says that grace and peace come from him as well as from his Father, Paul demonstrates that he too must be worshipped. He is not merely a created being; he is not the same as men or angels. Here, then, is proof of the deity of our Lord Jesus Christ, whom we must exalt as he deserves. At the same time Paul wants to reinforce what he said earlier, that we should boldly seek from God both grace and peace, since we have a Mediator who gives us confidence to request these things. Again I say that we cannot conceive of God as our Father unless Jesus Christ presents himself as the only-begotten Son, into whom, as members of his body, we are grafted by faith. All that is his he shares with us, out of pure goodness. It is not something we have deserved; it is only because he sets before us the merciful riches of God his Father.

There is nothing superfluous, then, in Paul's greeting, which although addressed to Timothy lays down a rule for all of us to follow. So would we enjoy true rest in this present life? Above all else, we must want to be loved by God, and since we are unworthy we must also know the means: we must come to our Lord Jesus Christ. And if, for this perishable life and for our bodily food, we must first have God's favour, what shall we say when it is a question of our soul's salvation? If we want to eat a piece of bread, to drink or to be clothed according to our need, we must always depend on God's mercy. We must thus begin with his unmerited goodness. To eat, drink or enjoy life's necessities will be to our detriment unless God blesses us with his grace. How much more, then, must we commit ourselves entirely to God for the heavenly life, trusting in the adoption secured for us by our Lord Jesus Christ, and never thinking in our arrogance that we ourselves can attain the salvation which the gospel promises.

Let us forget all about ourselves, and begin with the fact of God's adoption. When God has received us once and for all in his mercy, let us boldly call upon him. Let us not be like the poor unbelievers who are always uncertain as to whether God has heard them. We should take it for granted that, since God loves us, all will be well. Because of his love we can lack nothing, for he holds all things in his hands. He is the fount of all goodness and blessing. Our entire salvation and the praise we owe are enclosed in God's love. So we may heartily rejoice, never doubting our salvation, since God has chosen to love us, unworthy as we are. We may thus hold our heads high, doubting nothing, because God has testified that he will be a Father to us in and through our Lord Jesus Christ. We may bravely overcome all the obstacles which hinder us from coming to our God, until we attain the victory which is laid up for us in heaven.

And although we must fight on until death, and although our life is hidden, we need not doubt that God is our Father, for, as Paul says here, he bears us a father's love.

> Now let us cast ourselves down before the face of our good God, acknowledging our countless faults which we do not cease to commit against him every day, beseeching him to blot them out so that nothing should stop us coming to him and trusting that, for Jesus Christ's sake, they may be put away. May he continue to favour us as his very own children, despite all the wretchedness and weaknesses within us. May we taste his mercy, confident that he truly cares for us and that all will be well. May we learn to trust his providence, so that we are not shaken or blown this way or that, or caught by Satan in the nets he spreads for restless souls. Thus may we walk in this world with our eyes fixed always on the heavenly kingdom. And since our gracious God has given us promises for this life and for the life to come, may we be encouraged to commit ourselves to him, until he frees us from all that distresses and troubles us, and brings us to that rest won by the blood of our Lord Jesus Christ.

# 2

## REMEMBERED IN PRAYER

*I give thanks to God, whom I serve with a clear conscience from the time of my forebears, that without ceasing I remember you in my prayers night and day,* ⁴ *desiring to see you and remembering your tears, that I may be filled with joy;* ⁵ *remembering too your sincere faith which first dwelt in your grandmother Lois and in your mother Eunice. I am certain that it is also in you.* (2 Timothy 1:3-5)

The main thrust of the text we have just read is that Paul's affection for Timothy arose from the fact that he knows him to be a godly man who, since childhood, has had in him a good seed of religion. Nevertheless he says these things not for Timothy's sake, but for the benefit of those for whom the letter was intended, so that all might be edified.

It remains for us to draw the appropriate lesson from our reading. To begin with, we may learn from Paul's concern for Timothy. Since God has joined us one to another, we must all think of our neighbours who are close to us. I do not mean our kinsfolk according to the flesh. Since God is Father to us all, we should nurture the spirit of brotherhood hallowed by the blood of our Lord Jesus Christ. So, to the best of our ability, let us care for the welfare of those who belong to the household of faith. Furthermore, let pastors who hold public office in the church make this their stated aim. Their zeal should surpass that of a private individual who sees himself only as a member of the church. That is why Paul testifies to his concern for Timothy and for his welfare. It is plain, too, that when God brings someone forward and endows him with the gifts of his Holy Spirit, we are not meant to stop remembering him in prayer. None of us in this world is ever so mature that there is no further room for improvement, or that we no longer need God's helping hand. We must always ask him to increase his gifts and to remove the evil in us. Even if a man were quite outstanding, a half-angel even, we would still have cause to give God thanks for having bestowed on him the gifts of his Holy Spirit, and to pray that God might help him grow until he stood complete.

If, therefore, it is necessary for us to pray for those whom God has singularly blessed, what shall we say of those poor souls who have just begun, who are still frail and who have only savoured a little of God's truth? Should we not feel all the more concern for them? Nothing could be clearer! So then, let us understand that no human being ever lived who did not need to be commended to God, so that he might complete what he began. This is because, as long as we live, we are always on our way. We are thus taught to be humble, and not to think well of ourselves or to be happy with our present state, so that we say, 'I've come as far as I need go.' Let us continue to move ahead and pray that God may lead us on, knowing that we have not yet attained the goal, as Paul says in Philippians (Phil. 3:12).

Paul further teaches that we must not only thank God for his personal blessings to us, but that we should also with one accord rejoice and give thanks for the gifts bestowed on our brothers. True, if I know that God has been generous to me, I am more especially in his debt, which should prompt me to give thanks and to praise his name. Nevertheless I should never be so narrow and confined as to think only of myself. I should be mindful of God's goodness to the whole of his church and to all who are part of his flock. And since the diversity of the gifts which he has poured out on his people redounds to his glory, let me be glad that my brothers are equipped to serve him, that he motivates and directs them, and that with unity of purpose they strive to do what is good. We must not look, then, only to ourselves. Let us all share together in the array of gifts which God through his Holy Spirit grants to the faithful, and let us one and all thank him accordingly. We see, therefore, how evil we are when we are jealous of those whom God has adorned with his gifts. How often are we inclined to envy, each of us wanting everything for himself! Yet we are told that if God bestows his gifts on others, we should feel joy in our hearts as if these gifts were ours to enjoy. Indeed, if we knew it, we would see that our brothers possess nothing which does not benefit us and which is not to our advantage. In pouring the gifts of his Spirit on one person or another, God makes sure that we all gain and profit by it. We are therefore duty-bound to give him thanks. That, in sum, is Paul's teaching here.

Greater emphasis is given to Paul's message by the way he phrases it: *I remember you without ceasing in my prayers, night and day*. As we have seen, Paul takes Timothy's welfare very much to heart. He is constantly mindful of him. We notice also how frequently the apostle prayed: 'night and day'. He did not remember Timothy as in a dream, like those who, when thinking casually of absent friends, drink to them or talk about them. Christian friendship is much bigger, as when we come before God and say, 'Father, we remember those who are joined to us in fellowship, and from whom we must not part.' And if we cannot list them all, let us at least think of different categories, praying to God for those busy about his service, or who we know have glorified him by showing zeal or other qualities. We should feel pity for the afflicted, and for those who, like miserable sheep among wolves, are harassed by the enemies of the faith. Let us have compassion on them and on all who we know are suffering want. Let us be stirred up to remember them before God, that he may be pleased to aid them according to their need. This is how we show true friendship. We should not remember as the world does only those who are close to us. We should commend them to God in the way that Paul does here.

This is a hundred thousand times better than all the friendship in the world. Human friendship is mere rubbish when God is not witness to the love that men bear each other, when it is not referred to him and when it has no concern for their salvation.

I repeat the point I made before: if we would apply Paul's lesson to ourselves our prayers must be different, much more fervent than is normal. There are men so cold that they do not know whether they pray once a week! How then could they say with Paul that they remember others night and day? So here we have a notable example. We should not pray to God once a day, merely for form's sake. We need to keep coming back to the practice of prayer and to rouse ourselves since we are so lazy. We must drive ourselves to prayer whenever we feel cold and careless. It is not enough to recognize a failing: we must remedy it. So let us rouse ourselves and spur ourselves on without waiting for someone else to bully us. What else should we do but follow Paul's example?

If, however, we lack the zeal and enthusiasm to pray to God, Paul's testimony serves as a terrible condemnation. None of us, it is true, has received so full a measure of God's Spirit as Paul, and we are not all equal. Even so, we cannot receive so small a portion of God's grace without its being seen in our desire to pray. We must practise prayer often and not merely as a ritual. Let us forget all else as we lift our hearts to God. We have work to do, of course: then let our groans come up to God. When we see the mischief that men do, so much chaos and so much need, we should pray to God that he may put forth his hand to help us. At the very least let us sigh a little and let God answer our prayer. Let us extend the same concern to our neighbours, and not think simply of ourselves but do all we can for the welfare of the whole body of the church. Paul's example is a lesson worth remembering.

When the apostle says that *he remembers Timothy's tears, and the sincere faith which was in him*, he seeks to show that if we know someone who is genuinely good, we ought especially to honour and love him, if, that is, we love God. Now this is a truth which is doubly useful to us. We often love the wrong things. We do not care whether men are really devout—whether, that is, they fear God, live in all purity of conscience and are well-intentioned. None of that interests us; we are fickle in our choice of friends. On the other hand, if we are right-minded, when we see people who are truly guided by God's Spirit and who so bear God's image that it is clear that God dwells in them, we will be moved to love them. And if we do not, are we not utterly devoid of sense and reason? As we read in Psalm 15, 'The man who fears God will love those who also fear him, but he will scorn the wicked and the evildoer' (Psa. 15:4). When we see men who despise God and who do not hesitate to defy him, and who in their depravity do all they can to ruin everything, we should loathe them like the plague and reject them as defiled.

So when we see God-fearers who feel as we do and who are joined in fellowship with us, if we fail to love and honour them we are guilty of despising God. It is he who is wronged and we are held accountable. Let us learn, then, to remedy our faults and to befriend those in whom we see goodness, godliness, faith and integrity. We ourselves are warned to walk uprightly if we want others to befriend us. Thus, if I wish to be commended to the prayers of God's people, I must show myself worthy of their concern. Let us all do the same.

We often feel that we are badly done by when no one thinks of us. Well, if we consider just who we are, we deserve to be forgotten and ignored for our sins! If God is to answer his people's prayers, and if they for their part are to be led to pray for us, we must put this lesson into practice. Let it be known that we love God's kingdom, and that, just as he wants others to think of us, so we must think of him. Then we can be sure of his help in time of need.

Consider now what Paul tells us about himself: *I worship the God of my forefathers with a clear conscience*. Here, undoubtedly, the apostle is seeking to dispel the calumnies and false charges which some among the Jews had brought against him. For many regarded him as an apostate who had risen against the law of Moses, abandoning the God of his fathers and the religion in which he had been brought up. Paul therefore seeks to prove that he worships the God of Israel and persists in the pure, true faith which existed in the days of the law. And by adding 'with a clear conscience', he demonstrates that his motive is neither pride nor ambition nor the foolish itch to know, in the manner of those who are always looking for something new because their consciences are powerless to stop them and to keep them in the fear of God. Paul thus argues that his understanding of the gospel arose not from an empty whim; he stands as it were in the sight of God, having no desire to be conspicuous before men or to think highly of himself. He is content to worship the living God. That is essentially what he wants to say.

At this point we should observe that if so splendid an apostle as Paul was defamed by the wicked, we should not be surprised if God's servants are tried in similar fashion. Observe again that, following Paul's example, we hold in our hand the same shield by which we may parry all the slanders which are heaped on us and which are meant to make us hateful in the eyes of men. We may, I say, always demonstrate, not with lips that boast but in solemn truth, that we serve the living God and that we do so with a clear conscience. As long as we have this witness before God and can prove the same before men, we must bear patiently the complaints, false reports and lies which are spread about us. It is not right that we should be more privileged than Paul! So much, then, for the apostle's personal testimony.

Here too we have a sound rule for serving God. From Paul's words it is clear that his look is directed inwards, not at the outward show which so impresses men. We do not serve God only with our hands and feet: our heart must take the lead. God's true service is service from the heart, just as the law says: 'You shall love the Lord your God and cleave to him with all your heart' (Deut. 6:5; 10:12). God, to be sure, wants us to use all our abilities and all our limbs in his service; all must be dedicated to him. A good tree is always known by its outward fruit. Thus when our heart's desire is to serve God, this must be seen in every department of our lives. All our works must be the fruit of this good root. Nevertheless, to serve God aright we need above all that purity of conscience of which Paul speaks. We must lead sober and upright lives before men and display rare virtues that are above reproach. More, however, is required. We must not be gilded on the outside; there must be gold within. We cannot make do only with appearance: we must be solid through and through; our godliness must be strong and deep within.

If, then, we ask why God should have such hatred of hypocrisy—which is no more than sham, pretence, vice disguised as virtue—we will see that it is justified. Why? Because hypocrisy is a vile corruption of God's service, a sacrilege. If God's service is defiled, his name too is profaned, which is always an offence against him. His truth, too, is turned into a lie, which further mars his glory and distorts his image. That is why hypocrisy is rightly loathed by God. We should be all the more careful therefore to make sincerity and integrity our aim. Let each of us as we come to God look within, forgetting the world of men and finally confessing: 'It is God who must acknowledge me as his. Though all the world should applaud me and find no fault in me, if God my heavenly Judge rejects me, what have I gained?' When in the end we decide that our reputation counts for little unless our conscience is clear and we yearn to grow in godliness—when, I say, that is our aim and purpose, our every service to God will be acceptable to him. Without it, all is smoke. We may put on a superlative display in the eyes of men, but in God's eyes it is filth and rottenness. That is what it means to have a clear conscience.

The apostle protests that it is the God of his forebears whom he worships. As I explained, he was blamed for having arbitrarily invented a new faith. It was said that he had gone so far as to forsake the God of his fathers. Paul insists, however, that he worships the living God who had first chosen Abraham and his lineage, had given the law through Moses and had spoken by his prophets. He had not swerved from the doctrine of old nor had he devised an unknown religion; he continued to follow God's law and the prophets; he still kept to the pure truth which had always existed, and in no way deserved to be considered an apostate. Those, in sum, are the claims he makes.

It is the same with us today, who suffer the same reproach from the papists. They have managed to convince the simple and the ignorant that we have devised a strange mode of living, have abandoned the plain truth and believe nothing which has come down to us from the apostles and martyrs. The opposite, as we know, is true. For why do we fight against the papists, if not because we cannot go along with their deceits? They have constructed in their workshop something called God's worship, along with articles of faith and much else besides. So there you have a medley and a mishmash of lies picked up here and there, while we insist on following the law, the prophets and the gospel. There we find God's full and perfect truth; there is the teaching we must heed and obey. That is what we say.

Paul was thus obliged to make the same defence as we must do today. How comforting it is that we do not have to look around for excuses to shut the papists' mouths and to silence their false charges! It is enough that Paul has replied on our behalf. His cause and ours are identical. Should we not rejoice that God has given us Paul to be our advocate and attorney against the papists? We do not have to rack our brains in order to find an answer. All we need do today is offer and produce the words pronounced by Paul, words uttered moreover under the guidance of God's Spirit. And if we have the apostle as our advocate, the Holy Spirit too affords us his support from heaven. Paul himself had warrant enough to prove that he did not speak merely as a man, a mortal being, but that he spoke in God's name and with his authority. Let us take heart, then, whenever we suffer the papists' false charges. Let us not be unduly distressed, for our God makes our cause his, and provides us with so powerful a defence that even if our mouths are shut, he will make sure that the papists are condemned for their pride and vanity.

We might, however, think that here Paul means that those who bring in changes should be condemned. Now we cannot deny that there is much that we have changed: it was necessary to rescue this poor world from the pit of hell. In popery, as we know, there is nothing that is not corrupt, which is why great changes were needed. There is, in any case, a ready solution to the problem. When Paul speaks of his forebears, he does not mean that he approves of all the superstitions introduced among the Jews, given their very many errors. He is careful not to identify himself with them. He speaks of his forebears in the sense that he belongs to Abraham's line and traces everything back to its point of origin, to the beginning of the covenant which God made with the Jews. So when we say that our faith comes from the holy fathers, we speak the truth. Why? Because, as the Psalm says, our fathers are none other than the apostles and those charged with preaching the gospel in all the world, together with the martyrs who came after them (cf. Psa. 44:1). We confess therefore that we derive our faith from the holy fathers, yet trace it all back to the gospel.

When the papists, on the other hand, boast that they keep to the faith of the fathers, it is all a sham, for they claim as their fathers poor deluded souls who lived in the times of ignorance. They choose as fathers monks who conceived and dreamed up all kinds of nonsense. These are the fathers whom the papists follow. Moreover, when they set out to use the ancient authorities they copy their mistakes. Anything good and wholesome is cast aside. They conspire instead to deny every one of God's gifts, so that if something is badly expressed or if there is a reading that takes their fancy, they seize on it. That is how they cling to their fathers.

Things were no different in the time of Paul. The apostle, therefore, does not intend to condemn changes which are made when religion has been abused or when men have brought in novelties of their own. All this must be cut away. We must return to God's pure and simple truth and keep this as our foundation: God alone is sovereign, and he must lead his people. So in saying that he has worshipped God from the time of his forebears, Paul means that he has never swerved from the faith established by God among the Jews. In addition, however, nothing that he says implies that by appealing to our ancestors we can claim to be justified. The Turks today might well say that they have served God from the time of their ancestors, for it is many years since Mohammed fed them on such illusions. Since their error has persisted for a thousand years or so, they can fairly claim that their religion is not new. Yet even if it had existed from the dawn of time, it would mean nothing. Why? Because idolatry was already in the world.

Idolatry did not come into being when the earth was restored after the Flood. Did men everywhere call upon God's name before that? No! Scripture tells us that God was worshipped only by the descendants of Seth (Gen. 5:22, 24). It was, one might say, a miracle that God's pure worship survived in but a handful of people. Antiquity is therefore not enough to sanction a religion. That would be folly, for on that basis the surest religion would be the religion of the wicked, which God detests! Paul's argument assumes, as we have said, that he comes from Abraham's line and that the God who there was worshipped was no idol, but the Maker of heaven and earth to whom we must come for salvation and who is truly our Father. This too is why our Lord Jesus Christ distinguishes the Jews from all other nations, saying: 'You do not know what you worship' (John 4:22). True, he was addressing a woman of Samaria, but her people were more closely related to the Jews than any other. The Samaritans were circumcised and boasted that they worshipped Abraham's God. They sacrificed in the manner of the Jews, yet they were not recognized according to the law. They were accused of following a spurious religion. Jesus Christ thus tells them that they are wasting their time, not knowing what they do. 'You try hard,' he says, 'to worship God, but he rejects your worship. You do not know what you worship. You have no assured faith, whereas we know whom we worship.' He means of course the Jews. Why does he say that? Because they had the inerrant witness of the law, which was confirmed by the covenant made at a much earlier time with Abraham.

Paul thus does not speak of all who were fathers and forebears, but only of those grounded in God's truth and taught by him. We are warned, then, to be careful and discerning whenever we say, 'our fathers, our fathers'. We should not invoke them thoughtlessly, otherwise we would be like the Turks and the heathen, and though we might win our case in the eyes of men, what advantage would that be? What therefore should we do? We should choose those fathers who were true children of God so that we might have a legitimate line of descent. (I speak of course of spiritual descent.) So, as I say, those who are our fathers should be God's children, and everything should be traced back to him. That will be the case if we follow the pure simplicity of the gospel and of holy Scripture, and if we look for the God who has revealed himself in them. If we do this we cannot fail. And although the world may condemn us, if we are sure that God approves of us in heaven, we need nothing else. That is what Paul means when he speaks of his forebears.

He goes on in the next verse to say: *I give thanks to God for the unfeigned faith which is in you, which already dwelt in your grandmother Lois and in your mother Eunice, and which I am persuaded dwells also in you.* The mention of 'unfeigned faith' further confirms what Paul said earlier about a clear conscience, a term which in his first letter designated faith. This is a point we need to bear in mind. For since we have to behave with integrity toward our neighbours, hypocrisy will always be hateful to God. What will we do when we appear before him? If we seek to deceive a mere man, God will not allow it; but if we set out to deceive him, to mock him and to sport with him as with a little child, where, I ask, will it all end? Do we not mock his very majesty? Faith is thus rightly said to be without hypocrisy and pretence. Would we be full of faith? Then let us first strip away all the pretence and dissembling which we tightly wrap around us. We know what we are by nature. If we continue as we are we will soon become entangled in a thousand tricks and stratagems. We will delude ourselves, thinking that we can do wonders while all the time we are stupid and senseless, for we do not see our faults. We close our eyes to them and want only to feel good about ourselves.

If, then, we would be true believers, here is where we begin. We must get rid of all our worldly fancies and all the deceits we love to practise. This will prove to us that faith is no ordinary thing. We all boast, of course, that we have faith, but in the end we will see how precious it is in God's eyes. We must not lay claim to the word as casually as we do. We protest that we have faith and this is how we want to be known. Yet how full each of us is of hypocrisy! What games we play with God! So while men may count faith cheap, we say that to be faithful is a most difficult thing, because it means being cleansed of all our lies, shifts and evasions. We must learn to hate our sins and to search ourselves so that we are no longer two-faced before God, and so that, in condemning ourselves, we seek only to follow him.

So much, then, for the word 'faith', which was firmly rooted in Timothy. There is a lesson for us all in the fact that Paul further encourages Timothy to continue as he has begun, having had a grandmother and a mother who possessed true faith. Why does he not mention Timothy's father? He could not because, as Luke records in Acts, Timothy's father was a pagan (Acts 16:1). Timothy was born of an unbelieving father. In God's sight his father's line was thus defiled and condemned. On his mother's side, however, he was a Jew, which is why Paul cites the example of his mother. Notice here how human pride is humbled: no personal esteem attaches to earthly rank. True, man comes before woman, and where society is concerned man must always take the lead and have the distinction of being head of the woman. Nevertheless, if a man errs so that he becomes idolatrous, dissolute or wayward, and if at the same time a woman keeps to God's word and has Jesus Christ as her head, before the angels in heaven she is superior to any man who has gone astray. What therefore is said of God's children is true of woman: 'We will walk over all our enemies and will tread their heads into the ground' (Psa. 44:5).

All fleshly pride is here cast down and rightful honour is given to God, when we are told that Timothy's grandmother and mother were dear to God. They are counted worthy to be named, while men are dismissed as unworthy of mention, deserving only to be cast aside and thrown into the bottomless pit. Why so? Because they do not revere the living God. The women, however, are so to speak canonized! God records them in his book and raises them to a place of honour.

Again, notice that what Paul means by faith is the sincere desire the women had to serve God, even though the gospel had not been revealed to them.[2] Thus, although the gospel and our Lord Jesus Christ were not fully known, these women had genuine faith, faith which was acceptable to God. Why was it acceptable? Because they waited for the promised Mediator. Even though he had not been revealed in their lifetime, they were content to live in hope and to call upon God until he should fulfil his promise. And this is no mean compliment, for in Paul's day everything was dreadfully profaned. Among the Jews the common people had no fear of God, and his truth was so much intermixed with human error that it was pitiful to see. Yet he had set aside some small seed for himself. This is why I said it is an outstanding compliment which Paul pays these women, who walked among thorns without getting pricked and who always lived uprightly and in godly fear.

It is as we read in the gospel: 'This man was waiting for the kingdom of God' (Luke 2:25). This is a phrase which we meet only two or three times in Scripture. It was not often used. To wait for the kingdom of God was to hope that God would send our Lord Jesus Christ to be our Redeemer and to put the world to rights. Such were those who waited for God's kingdom. Accordingly they stand apart from all the rest, and because they were so few we have much to learn from the praise which Scripture gives to them.

---

[2] Cf. Calvin's commentary on 2 Tim. 1:5: 'It is uncertain whether these women were converted to Christ, so that what Paul commends here is the beginning of faith, or whether faith is attributed to them apart from Christianity. The latter appears more probable to me. (…) But I make no definite assertion, and it would be rash of me to do so' (*CO* 52: 348).

Nowadays, indeed, the gospel sounds forth everywhere; we hear it loud and clear. Yet, as we know, there are very few who worship God purely. There is in most of us stubborn malice and disobedience. Those who have the gospel preached to them grow bitter against God and show him more hostility than the papists do. That is plain to see. But what is it like among the papists? What a mess there is! We very much need to remember what we are taught here, that faith still dwelt in the hearts of some, so that they were not ashamed. Though all was desolate around them, they hoped patiently in God. Praise is not heaped here on men. Paul speaks not of learned men but of women! We should take heart, then, when all are carried away as if by a flood. Let us learn to look to ourselves and to put away our uncleanness, otherwise we cannot have faith dwelling in us as it dwelt, so says our text, in Timothy's grandmother and mother. Let us make room for God together with his word, that faith may dwell in us however much the whole world shuts it out and banishes it from sight.

To conclude, we note that if the women in this time of darkness, when all was confusion in Judaea, nevertheless clung to faith in God and were so well-disposed as to earn Paul's praise, terrible vengeance will come upon those who persist in their unbelief. Though God appears clear as noonday, and though Jesus Christ, the Sun of righteousness, shines upon us, there are many who still shut their eyes. What condemnation, then, hangs over them, since even in times of confusion those who are far from God cannot be excused? For just as the Holy Spirit commends those who persist in the faith—he himself stokes the flame—so he condemns and detests those who turn from God when they do not get what they want.

Now when Paul tells Timothy that he is sure faith dwells also in him, he is not speaking of his present faith, or of the faith he has had since he was called to the gospel, but of the faith he had possessed since childhood. For God had given him grace to do the right thing by following his mother, given that his father was an unbeliever, as we learn from Acts. Why then does Paul take Timothy back to the faith of his childhood? It was to encourage him all the more to keep to the sound teaching which he had received from the beginning.

From this we see that if we have been raised up from our youth in true religion, we will have much less excuse if we drift away. Someone who only learnt the gospel three days ago and who then abandons it cannot escape condemnation. But when God has called us to his pure truth ever since childhood, and when as adults we change our minds and throw it all away, imagine the condemnation which hangs over our heads! Look at how things are. Today we might expect to see little angels among us, since children have so imbibed the gospel that they might have learnt religion at their mothers' breast! They ought to be pearls in God's church. So what are they like? They have turned out bad and behave like devils! They are much worse than if they had continued to live amid the awful abominations of popery. We must grieve, then, for so wretched an age as ours when we see how spitefully God is used. We should not think it strange if God sends the fearful trials we presently see. We should even expect greater ones, which might in truth sink us without a trace if God were to take revenge for the thanklessness we see on every hand.[3]

Now let us cast ourselves down before the face of our good God, acknowledging our faults and beseeching him so to make us feel them that we may more and more be led to mortify our fleshly

---

[3] Calvin frequently expresses disappointment at the slow progress of the gospel among the people of Geneva, and laments their reluctance to live by the faith they profess. While the preacher's Libertine opponents had lost their majority in the elections of February 1555, later sermons in this series reveal that they were still a cause for worry, not least because of the contagion of their example. See below, Sermons 8, 10, 12, 13, 17, 19, 20, 23, 24, 27, 30.

passions, and to desire the new life promised to the faithful. May he engrave his commandments on our hearts and inner parts, and remake us in the image of his righteousness.

# 3

## FANNING THE FLAME

*For this reason I urge you to stir up the gift of God which is in you by the laying on of my hands. 7 For God has not given us the spirit of fear, but of power, love and sobriety. 8 So do not be ashamed of the testimony of our Lord, or of me his prisoner, but take your part in the afflictions of the gospel, according to the power of God.* (2 Timothy 1:6-8)

We commonly see that men who have led honest lives soon tire of them and think that they deserve to be excused all else. Having done their duty they let others take their place. God, however, is not content with service that lasts but a moment. On the contrary, as Paul teaches us in this passage, the more gifts he has given us in the past, the more we need to press on and to rouse ourselves to do even better. Far from relaxing and slackening off once we have striven to live a good life, we ought to feel more closely bound to God if he has used our labours and enabled us to praise his name. We are quite unworthy of such an honour.

Thus we should all heed the instruction given here. If we have been taught God's truth from our youth up, let us persist to the end; and if we have led upright lives let us keep moving on. As we saw this morning, Paul tells Timothy that he is sure that since childhood he has had the same faith as was in his grandmother and his mother. He says, too, that Timothy took particular care to live a good life, which is why he urges him to do even better. He does not say: 'I absolve you, I release you. You have done enough.' He tells him instead: 'You must finish. Because you have toiled valiantly you are in debt to God who gave you so great a gift. God does not want us to serve him for two or three days, but by our living and our dying. So continue on, and do not grow weary along the way.' This is Paul's meaning.

If we would remedy our coldness and our laziness, knowing that our zeal and devotion are not what they should be, let us tell ourselves: 'Well, God who put me in this world has revealed himself to me, and I have known him these many years. He has honoured me, wretched, useless creature that I am, by using me to exalt his glory and to advance his kingdom. I have served him, but not in my own strength. What must I do? Shall I now rest and idle the hours away? No! Let me be stirred up all the more to finish my race, since God has set me on the right path. He leads me on. I must not fail!'

This is the way to apply Paul's teaching. But to help us do it better, let us look more closely at our text. *Stir up*, writes Paul, *the gift which is in you.* The verb used here has no simple French equivalent.[4] The verb 'to stoke' might do, which is strictly used of stirring a fire. That is more or less Paul's meaning. He uses the metaphor of the fire which is almost out of wood and which is dying down. So we stoke it, raking up the charred wood and blowing on it to revive the fire. Paul therefore urges us to do all we can to revive God's gifts. Each receives them according to his measure. We do not possess them as fully as we would like, not because God is mean toward us, but because he wants to keep us in check. He sees

---

[4] The Greek of 2 Tim. 1:6 has *anazōpureō* ('to rekindle, revive a fire'). Calvin translates *attiser* ('to stir, stoke').

that we are too much given to pride, so gives us what he knows is necessary for our salvation. The truth is we will never have God's gifts in fullest measure; we will only have a small amount of them.

Think now, however, of how Satan contrives to stifle what God has put in us. There are temptations without end which bind us to this world and which quench the flames. Anyone who is consumed with care for worldly things forgets all about God's kingdom. So although the fire was lit some time ago and was good and hot, our vain concerns distract the mind and smother God's grace. That is how it is with everything. And quite unconsciously, without any obvious struggle or resistance on our part, we find to our surprise that the zeal we once had grows cold and slowly dies. The gifts that God has put in us are frittered away. They produce no fruit—why we do not know. Where once we had the Holy Spirit's gifts, now we are dull and stupid. How greatly, then, we need Paul's admonition, that we stir up the dying flames when they are much less hot than they should be! Let us strive to make the most of the gifts we have received. Let them catch fire, and let us be diligent about it!

If Timothy, to whose excellence God himself bore witness, needed to be goaded in this way, how much more do we? Each of us must look carefully to his calling. The man who is in public office must sharpen his wits in order to revive God's gifts and to make best use of them. This of course applies to everyone, but those whom God has raised high and brought to greater eminence must take the lead and set an example for others who are not so far ahead. Whatever the case, know that the Holy Spirit's gifts should so inflame us that we seek God's glory, are zealous to do all that he commands, and are carried beyond this world so that the flesh no longer masters us, nor our vile passions. May the desire to come to God burn hot within us, and let us direct the Holy Spirit's gifts to that end. However, because we are naturally cold, and because Satan has subtle ways of quenching the fire which should burn in us, let us see that we keep it lit, and let each of us be careful to stoke the flames. And if we feel God's gifts waning within us, let us strive to revive them even if we cannot always succeed. That is why God bids us use his word fully, to our best advantage. Enough said, however, on that point.

Now in speaking of the gift in Timothy, Paul says that it was in him *by the laying on of hands*. That is, having been appointed pastor, Timothy had received fresh gifts so that he might better serve the church. This, again, is an important point to notice, for elsewhere we read that when God puts us to work he supplies us with the means to do it (2 Cor. 3:5-6). For example, when he calls ministers he directs them in such a way as to make it absolutely clear that it is not men who have brought them into this work, but that their calling is from God. There are many who might boast of being in the ministry, and who occupy the pulpit which is reserved for those whom God has chosen; yet they have nothing which marks them out as true and worthy servants of God. They are either frivolous or worldly, dissolute or ignorant—men without salt or savour. This is a sure sign that they are disavowed by God and have never been ordained on God's authority. Why is that? It is as I said, when God chooses to make use of someone, he fits him for the work he gives him, and grants him all that his duty requires. Hence pastors who do not owe their calling to ambition and men's favours, who have not crept in through the window but who have been duly called by God, will also be equipped for their responsibilities and will not lack the Holy Spirit's gifts. Of this we can be sure: God pours out his gifts on those he makes ministers of his word. As Paul says, when Timothy took up office he received the gifts he needed for a faithful ministry.

The laying on of hands was a necessary act. This was the normal ceremony by which men were made ministers. The apostles took it over from the ritual of the law, in which after solemn prayer hands were laid on the sacrificial offering, making it an oblation presented to God and dedicated, as it were, to him. By this means those chosen to bear God's word were made to see that they were no longer their own. No longer free and private individuals, they were now bound to God and to his church; and while the offering was being made, all present prayed. Now it is a special blessing from God to have pastors who preach his word and who faithfully do their duty, for the salvation of all believers depends on it. The whole church should therefore pray for those who are appointed pastors. It is for the benefit of every one of us. So God granted the prayers that were made over a man's head. It was solemnly proclaimed that this man was set apart for God so that he might edify the church; and because no one is fit and competent to do even a hundredth part of all that is required, God himself must work.

In the first place, then, it was necessary to ask God in his goodness to give grace to the man who had been chosen, so that he might duly serve the church and bravely persevere to the end. Thus Paul tells Timothy that he received the Holy Spirit's gift when he was made a minister. Proof of this gift was felt by the church in its common prayers, which was why the accompanying rite was not at all superfluous; it was no mere formality performed as it were at will. It bore witness to the fact that God, in receiving those who were presented to him, was guiding them and giving them the means to fulfil their task.

That is the drift of Paul's argument here. Would to God that the church had kept to so simple a practice! If it had simply set aside pastors and ministers to be servants of God's word, we would never have seen the hellish priesthood which is now found among the papists. The accursed sacrifice of the Mass would be unknown, and men would see that all God asks is that ministers of his word should faithfully teach the people in their care and administer the sacraments. As it is, look at the tomfoolery brought in by the papists—all that grease applied to the fingers of those they call priests![5] What is it that they want? To appease God's wrath against men, to offer sacrifice and thus obtain the remission of sins! The office of our Lord Jesus Christ is thus transferred to these greased popish priests—a diabolical sacrilege, for to Jesus Christ alone belongs the title of Mediator between God and man. Satan, however, has defiled the purity of the whole gospel. So let us learn to distinguish between the popish priesthood and that which Jesus Christ approves and which is founded on the gospel.

In the days of the apostles presbyters were chosen and appointed for one thing only: to proclaim the gospel and to administer the sacraments.[6] They were to consecrate themselves to God and to the service of his church by offering up their very selves. But here we have the pope who sets out to make priests by anointing them, as was done under the law of Moses (Exod. 28:41; 29:7). Yet he assigns to them the task of reconciling men to God. What an appalling sacrilege, a novelty forged by Satan! We should look upon such a priesthood with abhorrence, as it richly deserves.

We find, then, that when proper prayer is made, those presented to God as preachers of his word will not lack the grace necessary for their task. This is because God presides over his church and puts forth his power to guide those who represent him, and whose work and calling he approves. Now as we see, well before he was chosen Timothy possessed outstanding gifts. Even so God enhanced those gifts in him when he chose to make him a minister. Those, therefore, whom God chooses must already have given a sign that they are fit for office. No one will randomly choose someone who is ignorant or untutored and who is quite unfit to preach

---

[5] A reference to the Roman Catholic rite of anointing ordinands with holy oil, here called 'grease'.

[6] Calvin here renders the New Testament term 'presbyter' by *prestre* ('priest'). While *prestre* is sometimes used to designate evangelical ministers, his preferred term for the latter is *ministre* or *pasteur*.

God's word. Men must be chosen who are already known to possess certain gifts. Nevertheless God does not fail to work in them. He strengthens and increases the gifts he has already given, and shows us that he means to use those in whom his Spirit appears with greater power.

This is true not only of ministers of God's word but also of magistrates. It would be evil and wrong-headed if we were not discerning in our choice, and failed to accept those whom we judged to be suitable. Yet God too has his work to do once they have been chosen. He must give them fresh gifts, or else they will be too weak. For it is no small thing to deputize for God in this world and to sit in his seat, delivering justice to all men. So much is demanded of magistrates that no mere mortal can suffice. Thus God must put his own hand to the task. Accordingly we should learn to practise what Paul tells us here, which is that when pastors are chosen and specially commissioned to preach the gospel, prayer must be made so that all may be edified. Likewise when magistrates are chosen, we must ask God so to fill them with his grace that they may faithfully discharge their duties, and be ready to answer for them when they come before the great Judge. That, in sum, is what we have to remember about this text.

That said, Paul adds a new idea: *The Lord has not given a spirit of fear to those who are to preach the gospel, but a spirit of power, together with love and sobriety.* What he means is that to prove that we are true servants of God we must not drag our feet, as the saying goes; we must show that we are fired with zeal for God, that it is this which drives us and that we have a spirit not of timidity but of boldness. In his letter to the Romans the apostle contrasts the fathers who lived under the law with Christians (Rom. 8:15). He argues that under the law people lived in such bondage that they did not dare to call upon God so freely. They lived in dread of the law. They were uncertain of their fate, and rightly so, for at that time God had not yet displayed his grace in the same way as it now appears in the gospel. Since the coming of Jesus Christ, however, God has so confirmed his adoption that we can shout aloud, since he is our Father and since he receives us as his children.

While this applies to all the faithful, Paul is speaking here specifically of ministers. He says that if they wish to show that they have been truly called by God, they must be steadfast, invincible, rock-solid, unbending. Whatever happens they must not be like swaying reeds; they must not set out to please men by changing their opinion or by keeping tight-lipped when they ought to speak. They must be alert and vigorous and, when required, must acquit themselves like men. So when they see the wicked rising up against God, they should resist mightily. Let them show themselves good soldiers, so that when God's truth is assailed, when some openly defy God and others dissemble, they must not pretend. Let them take hold of what God has given them and stand against evil. Let them prove, in short, that they have a real concern for God. That is Paul's meaning here.

Alas, today it is all too plain that there are very few who give proof of their mettle and that the word 'minister', 'pastor' and 'presbyter' is much profaned. How many are there who are staunch enough to withstand all men and to press on regardless? No one, as we see, wants to be in people's bad books; to please and gratify is what they are about. Who do they want to please? The worst of evildoers, many of whom would be just as happy to have Mohammed's Koran preached to them as the gospel! As long as their bowl is filled with a good meaty soup, they do not care! That is how it is. Must we, alas, suffer such dishonour to our utter shame? Well then, what do we gain when our wickedness is obvious even to little children, while nothing is said about it from the pulpit? We should look, then, to ourselves, so that those who have been made ministers of the word—myself first of all!—may know that it is useless to glory merely in the title. Jesus Christ will disown us unless we steadfastly defend the truth and ensure that he is honoured, served and worshipped, and that all earth's haughtiness is brought low. We must pay him homage for having called us to so noble an office. If we fail to honour him and to pursue the goal which Paul sets before us, our shame will be all the worse. Of course we are weak and cannot do as much as we would wish. Let us make the attempt nevertheless, otherwise woe to us!

So much, then, for the spirit of boldness, here contrasted with the spirit of timidity. To speak of 'fear' would not be quite right, for there is a wholesome kind of fear. Paul in this text is thinking of faintheartedness, which is the sense of the Greek word he employs. Ministers of the word will therefore be steadfast if possessed of godly fear. For what is it that gives us boldness to withstand all that is opposed to God? What is it that makes us steadfast? It is godly fear. This is fear which does not hold us back; instead it gives us courage to serve God and to honour him. Such fear is sound and holy; it should banish the other—that is, the faintheartedness men feel—so that we are brave enough to say: 'Despite the world we will pursue our calling. Let men rant and roar and act like devils. God bids us preach the gospel, and according to our rule we will not yield whatever happens. God's interests come first; it is to him we owe obedience.' Thus, though Satan may stir up storm and tempest so that all seems lost, this is when true ministers will show their constancy.

Now there are those who, when not under fire, occasionally impress by their firmness and resolution. They do not miss a chance to display their white-hot zeal, though not a blow is struck. When it comes to doing the right thing, however, they soon fold their wings! If we tried to enlist them for some good cause we would quickly see how worthless all their fine show is. These are people who, when safe from blows, are bold and brave, but when battle, as we say, is joined, they show not one drop of the courage and constancy of which Paul speaks.

Along with power, Paul lists sobriety and love, meaning that we must never be careless or impetuous in our zeal, as is the case with some who lack all sensitivity. Their zeal is far too immoderate, although it promises to be effective. 'These people,' we say, 'are truly keen, capable of reforming the world. They cannot abide sin.' Yet they are always prickly, intolerant of everything and contemptuous of everyone; they care nothing for their brethren and exhibit none of the compassion which might gently bring men back to goodness. Lacking moderation, they are impossibly severe.

We note, therefore, that according to Paul ministers of God's word must not only be steadfast and innocent of the fear which breeds timidity; they must also love their fellow-men and be disciplined enough to temper their zeal, so that they do not fret and fume without good cause. As we said, some ministers pick fights for no apparent reason, even growling at their own shadow. But when they need to show displeasure they are nonplussed— defeated without having dealt a single blow! This is not how it should be. I say again, let us give proof of our zeal, displaying it when we must in order to show our love and affection for God's service. We should not slacken, even when our message displeases men and when they grumble and complain. Let us persevere for all that.

If we have to face even fiercer fights and endure the heat and clamour of battle, let us firmly hold our ground and press on despite the enmity of those who rise up against our Lord Jesus Christ. Whatever the threats and dangers, let us demonstrate the courage which Paul urges on us here. Yet let us try as much as we can to lead to Jesus Christ by gentle and kindly means all who are teachable, having pity and compassion on them. It is important that we distinguish those who are surly and stubborn from those who are more even-tempered. If I saw a man who wished only to be taught, but treated him harshly, what would be the point of that? That would be the way to treat someone who was sour and stubborn. According to Scripture, those who are ministers must cure the sick, strengthen the feeble, support the weak and extend a helping hand (1 Thess. 5:14). However, when wolves approach the flock they are to drive them sternly away. They must comfort the desolate and the afflicted, but with sharp threats and rebukes must bring under Christ's yoke those who behave like untamed beasts. If we make this distinction we will be sober in our actions, just as Paul exhorts us to be.

Finally, Timothy is urged *not to be ashamed of the gospel of Jesus Christ, or of him who is his prisoner.* Paul is saying in effect that what we need today is firmness. Since God's name is blasphemed and since men deride the gospel and generally reject it, we must arm ourselves with courage so that we do not waver or go astray. This is a most necessary exhortation, for if we want to continue in the office which is ours we must close our eyes to all the chances and changes which happen in this world. Why? Because men have itching ears and many are looking for something new. We know, too, how hard it is to persevere; even the good are sometimes shaken when everything is so confused. It is not easy, in a word, to serve God without being sorely tried. For there are many worldly people who would gladly do away with the gospel; others would like to see it preached only as a formality and its message rendered lifeless, because they cannot bear to be corrected in any way. Some want preaching which lacks authority so that, when the sermon is over, it is as if they had been listening to a harp or flute. Words will have fallen on their ears, but that is all. Again there are those who seek to mask the truth, and who in their shamelessness mock all sound teaching; like ugly hounds they continually bark against God's word. That is the kind of contempt into which the gospel now has fallen, and the mockery which more and more is heaped upon it. And in the very place, I say, where it is preached, not in that hell-hole we call popery! When things have reached this point, what else is there to do but shut our eyes lest we be ashamed of our witness to Jesus Christ? What I mean is that because our Lord Jesus Christ commends the gospel as a treasure he holds dear, though men may reject it we must magnify it, obeying the commands God gives us there and paying no heed to what the world does.

In the same verse Paul speaks about himself—a prisoner close to death. This might have earned Timothy a reproach: 'A fine teacher you have! A prisoner! It's the gallows soon for him! What's so special about his teaching?' That is how men might judge the matter. Hence Paul tells Timothy not to bother about men's spiteful blather: all they want is an excuse to jeer at God and to deride his truth. When bad things happen they love to add to the confusion. The apostle therefore insists that we should never be ashamed when God's servants suffer persecution and when the gospel is everywhere blasphemed. We should appeal instead to the testimony we have from heaven. There the Son of God acknowledges his gospel, scorned and reviled as it is by men. Let us, then, not be ashamed to acknowledge it, along with him.

For the rest, since he honours us by making us witnesses together with him, how bravely must we toil! Such was his purpose in appointing pastors in his church. As he said, 'You will be witnesses to me' (Acts 1:8). Since this is so, let us recognize how greatly the Son of God has honoured us by using us in so high and noble a work. He has made us witnesses to his truth. Let us not be ashamed to share in something which he holds so dear—his gospel—whatever the world may think of it. We must reckon the world as filth and dung, and hate it if it rises up against the one to whom all glory and majesty belong.

Now let us cast ourselves down before the face of our good God, acknowledging our faults and praying that he may make us feel them more and more, until we are led to true repentance. May we, renouncing all that is our own, submit only to his holy will as it is revealed to us. May he take us out of this evil and perverse world, and graciously keep us from being carried about by every wind that blows. May we hold fast to his truth, and may he give us faith which triumphs over every trial through which we must pass. May we defy all evildoers who furiously raise their horns against our God, never flinching but remaining steadfast in our God, forever fighting under the banner of our Lord Jesus Christ until he brings us to his eternal rest.

# 4

## CALLED AND SAVED

*Do not be ashamed, then, of the testimony of our Lord, or of me his pris-*
*oner; but take your part in the afflictions of the gospel, according to the*
*power of God, ⁹ who saved us and called us with his holy calling, not*
*because of works which we have done but according to his purpose and*
*his grace, which was given to us through our Lord Jesus Christ before*
*time began.* (2 Timothy 1:8-9)

Although in the gospel God displays his glory and majesty so
that all may worship him, our ingratitude is such that
we need to be exhorted not to be ashamed of the gospel. Why?
Because, while God calls all creatures to himself that they might
pay him homage, most refuse him, scorn him and even defy the
truth which was meant to make him known and worshipped. So
although in our wilfulness we rebel against our Creator, let us
nevertheless remember the message of this text. We should never
be ashamed of the gospel, for it is a testimony from God. We are
to proclaim all that comes to us from him, to this one end, that he
should be known and glorified as he deserves. If the gospel is not
preached, Jesus Christ is buried as it were. Faithful witness must

be borne to him, as he himself testifies in this text. Let us honour him by always remaining true to sound teaching.

Paul here draws attention to himself. Not that he cared much for men's approval, but because as soon as we separate ourselves from God's servants we find to our surprise that we have left their Master too. At first sight, when a minister of God's word is troubled and harassed and suffers persecution, if we abandon him in his hour of need we feel that we have only failed a mortal man. God himself is wronged, however, because he who suffers bears the mark of the gospel. It is as if God's cause had been betrayed. That is why Paul urges Timothy *not to be ashamed of him*.

As we have seen, it would have been easy to mock Timothy by reminding him of Paul his teacher. The wicked do just that, seeking to profit whenever God humbles his servants by allowing them to be unjustly afflicted and their followers to be persecuted. 'See,' men cry, 'see how it is!' Timothy might have been badly shaken, which is why Paul says that although everyone reviles him, mocks him or loathes him, Timothy must not be moved. He is a prisoner of Jesus Christ. Paul might therefore have said: 'Let the world abuse me as it will. It is not for any wrong that I have done. God acknowledges my cause, which is also his. I suffer not for my own misdeeds but for having defended God's truth. I am persecuted because I upheld God's word and because I continue to uphold it. Pay no attention to the judgment of men, who are nothing if not evil. It is enough for you to know that I am a hostage for the sake of God's Son, and that he has given lustre to my prison, so that although men may abhor it, it is honourable and noble before God and his angels.'

Let us therefore learn not to rob Jesus Christ of the honour which we owe him, by shutting our mouths when we need to defend his honour and authority in his church. When also we see our brothers suffering for their faith in God, we should unite with them and struggle for their cause as hard as we can. Let us not be shaken by every passing storm, but let us stand firm, even though the devil seems to have a free hand and though all is chaos. Let us remain steadfast in purpose, since we are witnesses to the Son of God who graciously consents to use us in so excellent a work. In the meantime we should consider whether people are suffering for their own sins or for God's truth. If we see someone who is oppressed, we ought not to despise him on that account. We should not be too hasty in such things, otherwise it is God we offend. We must be careful to ask why people are suffering. If we find that they have acted in all good conscience and that they are unfairly blamed and harassed because of their service to God, this more than nullifies whatever men may say against them. Hence Paul goes on to say: *Take your part in the afflictions of the gospel.*

Now there is no one who would not like to be spared, for this is our natural instinct. And although we affirm, quite sincerely, that God is exceptionally gracious when he uses us to defend his cause, we would all dearly love to escape persecution. We heap generous praise on those who take up the fight, and those martyred for the sake of Jesus Christ deserve to be admired and honoured. Even so, who would not like to be out of harm's way? Why? Because we forget the warning which Paul gives us here, that the gospel involves suffering. Jesus Christ, who in his own body endured crucifixion, wills that his message should be inseparable from suffering. It would of course be good if, were he to choose, the gospel were accepted without opposition. Yes, but the Scripture must be fulfilled which says 'He will rule in the midst of his enemies' (Psa. 110:2). We are also meant to come to him only after many conflicts, because the wicked rise up against God when he calls them to himself. The gospel therefore cannot come to us without affliction. Not that the fires of persecution are always lit, but by one means or another we must be tried. We must all, I say, fight under our Lord Jesus Christ. Well then, does not the man who would gladly run from the cross of Jesus Christ renounce his salvation? Where is there hope of life except in the redemption purchased by his sacrifice? The Son of God wills, then, that we be made like him, and that we be transformed according to his image. That being so, let us learn to accept his terms, since it is to this that he calls us, and since this is God's will, as we saw before. We must therefore, without a word, bow our heads.

Here, then, are the steps by which Paul's argument unfolds. We must not be ashamed of our brothers but must always side with them when the world curses and reviles them. For the gospel involves suffering, by which God is pleased to separate one man from another. Not that he does not call all to the unity of faith, for the gospel is the message of reconciliation. Nevertheless the faithful, as we will later see, are drawn by the power of the Holy Spirit, while the faithless remain hardened. So the flame is lit, as when thunder builds up in the sky and heralds great disturbances. It is the same when the gospel is proclaimed. But if the gospel means affliction, if Jesus Christ wills that his members too should suffer as he did, and if he is daily, as it were, the Crucified, is it right for us to refuse his terms? Thus, because the gospel is always about the hope of salvation and because our faith should rest upon it, let us remember Paul's teaching, that we should reach out a hand to our brothers when they are abused and trodden down, when men spit in their face and treat them spitefully. Let us choose to be partners with them in suffering the world's reproaches and wickedness, rather than be held in high repute while turning our backs on those who suffer for our common cause. That is what this passage tells us.

We ourselves are weak. We are afraid that, given the world's power and the furious attacks of our enemies, we will be crushed. Paul therefore says that we will not be without God's help and assistance, so that when he sends us into combat it is not to test our strength, but to arm and equip us with invincible power to endure.

Thus Paul adds the phrase, *according to God's power*, in order to remove any excuse for sloth or lethargy. Now as I said earlier, everyone would welcome an excuse for avoiding persecution. 'Oh,' we might say, 'I would willingly suffer for God's sake if he granted me that grace. That would be the highest honour I could have.' We might all say the same thing, while adding that we are weak, easily discouraged, terrified by tribulation and by the fury and cruelty of our enemies. This is the kind of apology we might make having spoken in glowing terms about affliction. Paul refuses our excuse, however, by promising that God can be relied on to strengthen us, and that it is wrong to think only of our own resources. Long before our enemies attack us, we already baulk at our own shadow! That much is sure. Apprehension makes us turn and run.

Knowing this to be our weakness, let us turn to the remedy. We must certainly consider our frailties and our reluctance to hold out against our enemies. This, however, should lead us to ask God most humbly for his help. Aware that we ourselves can do nothing, let us humble ourselves before him and pray that he might stretch out his hand. In time of utmost need he will not fail us. So even though we are conscious of our utter frailty, we may be at peace, knowing that God is preparing us for whatever happens and that we will be armed whenever he wants to put us to the test. This is the proper way for us to view our weakness. If we know our disability we will come before God so that he may put it right, according as he knows is best for us. That is what we have to remember here.

If this truth were firmly planted in our hearts we would not need much persuading to suffer affliction more readily than we do. Alas, there are very few who remember this lesson. Worse, it seems as if we stop our ears and close our eyes when mention is made of it. We pretend that we want God to strengthen us, but we are incapable of looking far enough ahead to that power of which Paul speaks. We do not think that it has anything to do with us. Yet our

Lord assures us that his power will always be given to us and that it is ours to grasp. So let not our weakness make us back away from the cross or from persecution, since God has undertaken to supply our wants. This is his promise, and he will do it.

Paul's mention of God's power is not made in jest. He points out that it is ready and prepared for believers when needed, if, that is, they want to be armed and equipped with it when the Son of God summons them to battle. Moreover, because we need to be goaded and constantly spurred on, Paul seeks to shame us if we lack the zeal to glorify Jesus Christ by suffering persecution, should that be his will. He therefore reminds us that *God saved us and called us with a holy calling*. Since God has gone before us with his boundless grace, consider whether our thanklessness can be excused if we fail to respond to him. It was when we were lost and damned that God rescued us from the depths of hell. He brought salvation to us. If we turn our backs on him who treated us so generously, and if we fail to accept his offer of salvation, are we not irredeemably evil? So whereas Paul reproaches the fainthearted for failing to resist the enemy's attacks, he seeks to instil into the faithful strong hope for the future by reminding them of what God has already done for them. God's purpose in giving us a token of his goodness is that we should expect more of the same, as we wait for him to finish what he has begun. If he has saved us and called us with a holy calling, do we think that he will abandon us along the way? Since he has revealed our salvation to us and given us legs to walk and the gospel by which he calls us into his kingdom, since he has opened the door and is constantly at work, will he mock us by emptying his grace of its effect? Not at all! We can expect him to bring his work to completion.

We should thus walk boldly on, and since he has already put forth power on our behalf, we cannot doubt that he will continue in the future, giving us full victory over Satan and our enemies.

And all the while we look to Jesus Christ, our head and our commander, to display the power given to him by God his Father, in which we too may share. That, then, is Paul's meaning. So we see that God has in practice and in earnest testified that he will not fail us in time of need. Why? Because he has already saved us. When he called us to the gospel, what else did he do but redeem us when we were lost and perishing? Has he, then, saved us? We may therefore expect, since we are still on our way, that he will bring us to salvation. He has called us with a holy calling; that is, he has chosen us for himself, and has delivered us from the universal plight affecting all mankind. Since our Lord has rescued us, will he not hold us in his hand and guide us to the very end? Here we have sure proof of the power of God, who is always ready to help us when we place our trust in him, and when we recall the help we have had in the past.

The best use we can make of Paul's teaching is to remember that, in granting us knowledge of his truth, God has already given us assurance that we have a heavenly inheritance, that we are his and are members of his flock. Once this is beyond any doubt, we will not hesitate to go steadily on, for we are under his protection. And because he is strong enough to overcome all our enemies, our salvation is secure. We need not fear our weaknesses; we may look to God to make up for them for he has promised us his help. We should think deeply about this, weigh it carefully and resolve to accept what this passage teaches. We need no long or wordy exhortation to fortify us against trials and temptations, as long as we are persuaded that our Lord will complete our salvation as he began it, by aiding us in time of persecution and by giving us the steadfastness to overcome, though in the world's eyes we are like men trodden down and crushed.

We come back, however, to what Paul says about God's holy calling and the salvation he has wrought. He declares that *it was*

*not according to our works but according to God's purpose and his grace.*
Here we are warned that our ingratitude will be all the more condemned because God has opened to us the priceless treasure of his
grace. This was why he drew us to himself. How much less excuse,
then, will we have if we betray our faith, since not only have we
been bought by the blood of Jesus Christ his only Son, but he
made provision for our salvation before the world was made! So
Paul condemns our thanklessness if, when God calls us to maintain a firm witness to his gospel, we prove unfaithful to him. Why?
Because, as our text says, we are saved not by our works but by
God's purpose and grace.

To make his meaning plainer the apostle declares that this was
given to us *before time began*, before, that is, the world came into
being. But now all has been revealed by the coming of our Lord
Jesus Christ. When our great Saviour appeared, the grace which
was hitherto concealed was brought into the light of day. This was
because the Son of God, as Paul says, destroyed death and brought
immortal life (2 Tim. 1:10). We do not need to run about in circles
in order to find him: the gospel leads and directs us to him. So
when God sends us the message of salvation, all we have to do is
accept the inheritance he promises; we do not need to travel very
far, for God is already looking for us. All we need do is open our
mouth so that he may fill it, and open our heart to the witness of
the gospel; then the immortality of the heavenly kingdom will be
ours. And although we are poor, frail vessels, full of corruption and
decay, we may lay hold of this immortality, of which we receive
assurance when we accept the grace offered to us in the gospel.
These are the themes which Paul treats here.

Note, however, by way of further explanation, the word 'purpose'. By this is meant God's eternal decree, which has no dis-
cernible cause. For when we speak of God's counsel, we should
never argue about what it was that moved him, or try to find a

54

reason, saying, 'This is why God has acted thus. This is what he had in mind.' On the contrary, God demands that we be sober and restrained, and that his will be all the reason we require. When it is said, 'God ordained it so', we may be amazed and think it very strange, for we see no rational explanation. Even so we must make up our minds that his will is just and irreproachable. All our wisdom comes down to this: that whatever God ordains and does is right, though we cannot say why. But because we are restless spirits and let our curiosity run wild, Paul seeks to humble our temerity by bringing us back to the purposes of God. We must, he says, consider that God has his own plans. We cannot fathom them or know what his motives are. There is no higher cause than his will, which is both just and the standard by which all justice is judged. We learn, then, that our salvation does not depend on any consideration of our merits. When God chose us for himself he did not enquire what sort of people we were or to what extent we were worthy. He had his purpose—that is, he did not seek the reason for our salvation outside of himself. Because the word 'purpose' signifies God's decree, Paul's point is clear.

Since, however, we are arrogant enough to think that we possess merit of our own, we feel that it is only right that God should seek us out. So to rule out anything that we might claim for ourselves, Paul writes *purpose and grace*. It is the same as saying 'gratuitous purpose', thus dismissing all our works and our stubborn belief that we possessed something of worth which led God to choose us. Observe, then, that God did not go outside of himself when he chose us for salvation. He saw only perdition in us, and thus contented himself with his grace alone and with his infinite mercy. He saw our wretchedness and determined to help us, notwithstanding our demerits.

To emphasize his point the apostle declares that God's grace was given *before time began*. This shows just how senseless people are when they try to flaunt themselves and imagine that salvation is their work, or that they have stolen a march on God by anticipating his goodness! On what does our salvation depend? On God's eternal election! God chose us before we ever existed. What could we have done at that point of time? Were we so clever or so well disposed that we could come to God? No, our salvation did not start when we reached the age of reason and discretion and began to have right feelings. It did not start then, but is grounded in God's everlasting election, made before the world began. What could we have done? Could we have made our presence felt, or induced God to call us to himself and to set us apart from the rest of mankind? Are we not astonishingly stupid if we think that we are deserving, and if we exaggerate our merits so as to cloak God's grace, imagining that they entitle us to come before him?

We see, then, what Paul is driving at when he speaks of grace 'given before time began'. We are duly warned that those who think that they can dispense with the doctrine of election are really intent on subverting our salvation. The devil has no better allies than those who deny the efficacy of the blood of Jesus Christ, who sow confusion, ruin the gospel and wipe from our minds all memory of God's goodness. He has no better allies than those who oppose predestination, and who in their fiendish rage cannot bear to hear it spoken of and preached as it ought to be. If we detest and execrate the papists for profaning all of holy Scripture, for twisting and defiling the truth of the gospel and the worship of God, and for infecting the world with their superstitions and idolatries, how much more should we abhor those people who seek to blot out God's election, and who by underhand and crooked means want to stop it being loudly proclaimed and clearly taught!

Where does our salvation lie if not in God's election? Do we not want to hear the news that God of his free goodness has chosen a people for himself, without any other consideration? Do we not want so high and unfathomable a mystery to be made known, to the extent that God has revealed it to us? We surely conspire with Satan if it is found that Jesus Christ suffered in vain, that the passion he endured benefits no one, and that we are all lost and bound for hell!

This, therefore, is the first thing to bear in mind: if we dispense with God's election there is no gospel to proclaim; in its place is a spurious, worldly gospel—as taught by Mohammed—and both the church and Christianity cease to be. What would happen then? If we cannot accept this truth we will be making the Holy Spirit, who speaks to us here, a liar. So let us be constant in our resolve to fight on, for this is the foundation of our salvation. How can we build, and how can we maintain the building, if the foundation is destroyed? Paul thus appeals to us by showing how bravely we must fight, how we may attain the inheritance so dearly won for us, and how we may enter into God's glory and so complete the building we have begun. 'My friends,' he says, 'we must rely on the grace which was given to us not yesterday or today, but from the creation of the world. Today, it is true, we hear God's call, but his election has gone before. He chose us without regard to our merits or to anything else we might claim, except our need of him. He drew us from the depths of hell where, miserable creatures that we were, we languished without hope. It is only right that we give him full obedience, for we are debtors to his goodness. His grace is all our joy.' These are Paul's words to us. We must, I say again, keep to this foundation if our salvation is not to crumble and disappear.

Think lastly of how useful this teaching is when we apply it to ourselves. Those who will not have a word said about election will protest: 'What's this we hear? It's all a waste of time!' These are people who have never tasted God's goodness or the hope we have as Christians. They barely understand what it means to come to our Lord Jesus Christ. For if we do not know that we are saved only because God was pleased to choose us before the world was made, what sense can we make of Paul's appeal to dedicate ourselves to God and to serve him gladly whether in life or death? How can we praise and magnify his name? How can we confess that our salvation is his work alone, and that he began it with no help from us? We might confess this with our lips, but it will only be a sham unless we are convinced of the message which we have laid before you.

Let us therefore learn that the truth of God's election, by which he has predestined us before the world began—that this truth, I say, must be preached loud and clear, however much the world opposes it. Not only that, but here we have a most important article of faith, without which we cannot consciously appreciate the boundless goodness of our God. For until this point is settled—that God chose us before ever we were born or could seek him out—we will have a false view of God's mercy. Why? Because while we may claim to be redeemed by the blood of Jesus Christ and to be unworthy of God's great mercy, we will nevertheless think to ourselves, 'Who has part and portion in the redemption wrought by God in the person of his Son? Those who, wishing to be redeemed, seek after God and are obedient to him; who mean well, who are not too ignorant, who are good-natured and suitably devout.' Now when we mix in all these things and imagine that we are called to God and his grace because of something we possess, that we can bring an atom of our own and parcel out salvation between us and God, God's grace is veiled and torn indeed to shreds. Such sacrilege is intolerable, which is why I said that we can never truly grasp God's goodness until we face the issue of election. We must see that we are called only because our Lord chose to show us mercy before ever we were born.

This is the lesson we must learn. We must take it further, but we cannot do so now. It must keep till after dinner.

Now let us cast ourselves down before the face of our good God, acknowledging our faults and asking him to make us feel them more and more, so that, being brought to true repentance, we may forsake our evil desires. May he gather us to himself and, having chosen us out of the world, may he keep us always in his power and under his control. And may he so deliver us from this world's corruption and defilement that we may fully give ourselves to serve and honour him.

# 5

## WHY ELECTION MATTERS

*[God] saved us and called us with his holy calling, not according to our works but according to his purpose and his grace, which was given to us through Jesus Christ before time began, <sup>10</sup> and which is now made manifest by the appearing of our Lord Jesus Christ, who destroyed death and brought life and immortality to light through the gospel.*

(2 Timothy 1:9-10)

We pointed out this morning that, according to Paul's text, in order to appreciate fully God's unmerited goodness in saving us, we must go back to his eternal counsel, by which he chose us before the world was made. We learn that he took no account of us as persons, of our inherent worth or of any merits we might claim. Before we were born we were already entered in his book; he had already adopted us as his children. So we must ascribe everything to his mercy, knowing that we ourselves can boast of nothing without robbing him of the honour he deserves.

Now it is true—such is our wickedness—that men have thought up various objections designed to mask God's grace. For example, it is said that, although God chose men before the creation of the world, it was because he foresaw that some would be different from others. Scripture, on the other hand, is very clear that God, before choosing men, did not wait to see whether they would be deserving or not. The Sophists, however, have tried to obscure God's grace by arguing that, while God overlooked our past merits, he took note of those which were to come.[7] 'For,' they say, 'although Jacob and his brother Esau had done neither right nor wrong, God chose one and refused the other, but only because he foresaw—all things being present in his sight—that Esau would be a godless man, a despiser of all goodness, whereas Jacob would prove his worth in time to come, as indeed he did.' This is the kind of edifice these men throw up! It is worthless speculation which plainly contradicts Paul's point that, when God chose us, he did not reward us for our works, since it all happened before the world was made.

Supposing, however, we set aside Paul's authority, we nevertheless see how senseless they are who try to escape by such a trick, and how unskilled not only in Scripture but in their powers of reason. For if we closely examine ourselves, what, tell me, do we find? Is not the whole of humankind under a curse? What else do we bring from our mother's womb but iniquity? Not one of us is different from the other, except that God takes to himself those whom he wills. That is why Paul in another place declares that men have nothing of which to boast, since no one is superior to his neighbour unless God chooses to make a distinction (1 Cor. 4:7). Given, then, that it is for God to distinguish between us and those who remain in their condemnation, we would all be lost if the remedy did not come from somewhere else. So when we declare that God chose us before the creation of the world, it follows that he prepared us to receive his grace, that he put goodness in us

---

[7] The term 'Sophist' was used by both humanists and Reformers to designate the medieval Schoolmen who had systematized and refined Roman Catholic dogma. Their sixteenth-century imitators, entrenched especially in the Sorbonne, were among Calvin's most relentless critics.

where before there was none, and that not only did he choose us to be heirs of his kingdom but he set his mark on us to justify us and to rule us by his Holy Spirit. Christians should be so absolutely convinced of this that if men scorn it, as many shameless people do who want to extinguish God's truth, we must regard them as enemies of the Holy Spirit, as wild bulls and beasts bent on demolishing the whole of Scripture.

The papists are more honourable than these people. Papist teaching is much better, holier and truer to holy Scripture than the doctrine of these miscreants who today deny God's holy election, these curs who bark against it, these swine whose snouts are into everything—so widespread is this wickedness today. Whatever the case, let us remember what we are taught here, that because God chose us before the world began we must attribute our salvation to his free goodness, and recognize that he did not adopt us according to our merits. For we have nothing, and we can bring him nothing of our own: our salvation has its cause and origin in him alone. It is on this that we must build, otherwise all that we do will come to nothing.

Notice, again, how certain things are brought together here. Paul first connects the grace of Jesus Christ with the eternal counsel of God his Father; next he brings us back to our calling, so that we may be assured of God's goodness and of his will, which would have been hidden from us except for the testimony we have received. First, then, Paul teaches that the grace which depends on God's sole purpose and which is enclosed in it, is given through our Lord Jesus Christ. It is as if he said that because we deserved to be rejected and hated by God as his mortal enemies, we had to be grafted as it were into Jesus Christ before God would accept us as his children. As long as God looks on us he is bound to detest us, poor wretches that we are, full of sin and steeped in iniquity. God who is supremely righteous can have no accord or agreement with us as long as he sees us as we really are. So in choosing to adopt us before the world began, it was necessary for Jesus Christ to come between us, so that we might be chosen in him who is the well-loved Son. We are made acceptable to God when he unites us with Jesus Christ.

Thus, in order to be sure of God's election and to benefit from it, we must come straight to Jesus Christ. He is the true mirror in which we may behold our election. Take Jesus Christ away and God becomes for those who sin their Judge. We can expect no grace or favour from him, only retribution. Without Jesus Christ God's majesty would be terrifying; mention of his everlasting purpose would fill us with dread, as if he were ready and waiting to blot us out. But when we know that all goodness is found in Jesus Christ, we can be sure that God has set his love on us, unworthy though we are. That is our first point.

In the second place, Paul does not speak only of God's election, for far from soothing us this would deepen our perplexity and our distress. The apostle therefore speaks of God's calling, by which he reveals to us his counsel which before was unknown to us and beyond our reach. How, then, may we know that God has chosen us and that we can rejoice and glory in his goodness? Those who speak carelessly about election think nothing of the gospel and ignore the means by which God brings us to himself, means which he knows are fit and proper for our use. This is not the thing to do. Let us do as Paul does, and connect election with God's calling. The word 'vocation'—that is, 'calling'—comes from the Latin, but those who are uneducated need to know its meaning.

We have been called by God. How does he call us? He calls us when he chooses to give us assurance of our election, which would otherwise be beyond our comprehension. For who, as the prophet Isaiah says and as Paul repeats, can enter into the counsel of God (Isa. 40:13; Rom. 11:34)? When, however, God is pleased to communicate personally with us, we are given more than human understanding, for we have a good, reliable witness, the Holy Spirit, who lifts us up above the world and reveals to us God's marvellous secrets.

This is why we cannot speak baldly about God's election, so that we can say that we have been predestined. In order to be quite sure of our salvation, we must not ask flippantly and carelessly whether God counts us among the elect. What should we do? We should look to the gospel which is set before us. There God reveals that he is our Father, and that he has marked us as those he seeks to bring to the inheritance of life. This knowledge is the Holy Spirit's seal upon our hearts; it is a sure and certain witness to our salvation if we receive it by faith. The gospel is preached to many who are really reprobate. God shows that he has cursed them and that they have no part or portion in his kingdom, because they oppose the gospel and refuse the grace offered to them. When, however, we receive God's message with obedient faith, when we rely on his promises and accept his offer to be counted among his children, there, I say, we have true assurance of our election.

It should nevertheless be said that although we are saved because God has called us and has so illumined us that we trust in his gospel, this does not cancel out the eternal predestination which has gone before. There are many today who say, 'Has not God chosen only those who have faith?' I quite agree, but then they draw the wrong conclusion, fools that they are: 'Our salvation has faith as its cause—faith first and foremost!' If they called it an intermediate cause, this would be correct as far as it goes, for Scripture says that we are saved through faith (Eph. 2:8). Nevertheless we must go higher, for to attribute faith to men's free will is a wicked blasphemy against God—indeed a sacrilege, worse, as I said, than anything we find among the papists. No, Scripture says the very opposite, that when God grants us faith we can only accept the gospel if the Holy Spirit has prepared us. It is not enough to have heard a human voice sounding in our ears. These are merely words which vanish in the air unless God is at work, speaking secretly to us by his Holy Spirit. This is the source from which faith comes. What is the reason for that? Why is faith given to one and not another? Luke tells us why when he says: 'As many as were ordained to salvation believed Paul's words' (Acts 13:48). There were many who heard him, but only some among them accepted the promise of salvation. And who were they? Those, says Luke, who were ordained to salvation.

Need we go further? Paul also, in the first chapter of Ephesians, goes into such detail that those who oppose God's predestination are struck dumb (Eph. 1:3-14). The devil must have blinded them, robbed them of their wits and entirely bewitched them if they cannot see something so obvious! According to Paul, God who has called us has made us to share in the rich and boundless treasures brought to us by our Lord Jesus Christ. How can this be? Because, says Paul, he chose us before the creation of the world. So in discussing faith, the apostle points to a higher principle, to that first cause which is the real source of our salvation—that is, to God's free grace, of which much has already been said. Thus when we say that we have been called to salvation and that we can be certain of it because of God's gift of faith, we declare that there is a higher cause still: election, which is from eternity. Those who cannot agree, diminish God and belittle his honour by maintaining that he distinguishes between people on the basis of their merits and their willing disposition.

This, then, is how we are to understand the connections which Paul makes in this passage, and which are found throughout all of Scripture. But to recapitulate briefly, this is how we should proceed. In asking whether we are saved, we must never begin with the question, 'Are we elect or not?' No! We can never climb so high, and we would be confounded a hundred thousand times and be thoroughly bemused before we got close to God's strict counsel. How then should we proceed? We should listen to what the gospel has to teach us, and when God graciously enables us to accept the promise he offers, it is as if he had opened his heart to us and had written our election on our consciences. That is how we may be sure that God has adopted us as his children and that the inheritance of the heavenly kingdom is beyond doubt, since God has called us by Jesus Christ. How do we know that this is so? How can we hold to this truth which God lays before us? We must exalt God's grace by confessing that we can bring him nothing that is ours, that we must become as nothing, claiming not a drop of praise for ourselves, but that he calls us to this gospel having chosen us before the beginning of the world. Yes, God's election is as a closed book to us, both in and of itself. Yet we may read it, because God bears witness to it by calling us to him through knowledge of the gospel and of faith.

God's witness is therefore twofold, for just as the original, the basic document, in no way lessens the value of the transcript or copy which is made, but rather confirms it, and just as we need not worry about the original when we have the genuine copy, so we can be assured of our salvation. When God testifies in the gospel that he reckons us among his children, we have a full and accurate transcript of the fact, a transcript signed with the blood of Jesus Christ and sealed by his Holy Spirit. If we have this, should it not suffice? Far from invalidating the witness of the gospel, God's election gives all the more weight to it. We do not have to leaf through the original, God's register, as if anything were in doubt. We have a true and accurate copy. What more could we want? Would it not be rash and arrogant of us to ask, as Moses does, 'Who will go up beyond the clouds when we have the word in our mouth and in our heart?' (Deut. 30:12). True, if we thought this copy untrue to the original, we might regard it as unreliable. When, however, we are certain of its accuracy, what more do we need?

It is the same with God's witness. We cannot doubt that he enrolled us before the world began among his chosen children, but this he kept to himself. Nevertheless we have letters patent of our salvation, a most reliable copy, as has been said. Besides, we must always come to our Lord Jesus Christ when our election is in view, for without him we cannot draw near to God. If we were to enquire into his decree we would be seized with terror like men guilty of death. But with Jesus Christ to guide us we may be bold and rejoice, knowing that he has merit enough to make all his members acceptable to God his Father, and that we need only to be grafted into his body and made one with him. This is how we should read Paul's words if we would profit from them.

The grace of salvation, says Paul, was given to us *before time began*. To know how and why we are saved, and from where salvation comes, we must go well beyond the natural order. God, however, has not left us in suspense, nor has he hidden his counsel so that no one knows whether or not he is saved. He called us to himself, not only when the gospel was preached to us—that would not have been enough—but also when he witnessed to his goodness and fatherly love and sealed that witness in our hearts. Since we have such assurance, let us first praise God for having called us of his free mercy, and let us rest on our Lord Jesus Christ who gave himself to us, as the Holy Spirit testifies. For, as I said before, faith is an unerring mark that God counts us as his children, and from there we are led back to election. As Paul writes in the first chapter of Ephesians, God calls us according to his prior choice (Eph. 1:4). He does not say that God chose us because we paid attention to the gospel. On the contrary he attributes the faith we have been given to the fact that God in his sovereignty had already set us apart for salvation, since in Adam we were lost and perishing.

It is important to notice that Paul is referring here only to believers, for there are fools who try to baffle the ignorant and others like them by objecting that saving grace is given to us because God made his Son the Redeemer of the whole human race, so that salvation is indiscriminate, common to all. Paul, however, has spoken in such a way that his teaching cannot be distorted by such childish interpretations. He had already said explicitly that God saved us. Is that true of everyone in general, without exception? Not at all! It applies only to believers. Did God call everyone? Some were called by the preaching of the gospel, but they were unworthy of the salvation offered. They were therefore reprobate. God left others who had never heard a word of the gospel in their unbelief. Thus Paul is speaking here particularly to those whom God had chosen and set apart for himself. Remember, then, that God's goodness will never have the lustre it deserves unless we recognize that he did not allow us to perish with the rest of humankind, among people who are exactly like us and from whom we in no way differ. We are no better than they, yet such was God's good pleasure. Every mouth, therefore, must be shut; no one can claim credit for himself. Even so, we may open our mouths in praise to God, as we confess that we owe our salvation solely to him. Be sure to remember that fact.

What else does the apostle have to say? He has shown that we can grasp the truth of God's election only as it is revealed to us in the gospel. God accordingly made known what he had kept secret from time immemorial. But to make his meaning clearer Paul injects this thought: God's grace is made manifest to us *by the appearing of our Lord Jesus Christ.* We would thus be worse than thankless if we were not content to rest in the knowledge that the Son of God has given himself to us. What more could we ask? For supposing we could ascend beyond the clouds and probe God's deepest secrets, what would we achieve? What else would we learn

than that we are God's children and heirs? Yet this is abundantly
revealed to us by Jesus Christ, since it is said that all who believe in
him are privileged to become the children of God (John 1:12). To
be fully assured of our election, we must not swerve an inch away
from Jesus Christ.

Now Paul, having already argued that we are loved and chosen
by God in the person of his only Son, goes further and declares
that Jesus Christ, having appeared to us, also revealed to us life
such as we never knew. He conveyed to us God's grace from which
we were otherwise estranged; he made us obedient to God so that,
without having to enquire into things forbidden and beyond our
reach, we should understand God's eternal counsel. For when God
teaches us with his own lips, we must not venture to move too far
ahead, as do those who walk in disobedience. It is presumptuous of us to try to discover more than God allows, but when we
act soberly and reverently in obedience to our God, hearing and
accepting what he says in holy Scripture, the way lies open before
us. Paul thus teaches that now that God's Son has appeared to
men, our eyes are opened. We now know that because of the grace
granted to us before the world was made, God receives us as his
children, welcomes us and reckons us as righteous. We cannot
therefore doubt that our inheritance is prepared for us in the kingdom of heaven. Not that it is ours by reason of our merits, but
because it belongs by right to Jesus Christ, and because he bestows
that right on us.

The fact of Christ's appearing takes us back to the gospel,
for Paul concludes by saying that Jesus Christ *brought life and
immortality to light in the gospel*. For how was it that Jesus Christ
appeared to us? The same way as he appears to us each day! Paul
had no intention of obscuring Scripture's witness to the salvation
which is ours in Jesus Christ. He does not baldly describe him as
the Saviour sent by God his Father to be his representative. We

read that he was sent to be our Mediator, to reconcile us through his sacrificial death. He was sent to us as the spotless Lamb who cleanses us and who makes satisfaction for all our debts. He is our surety who delivers us from the sentence of death which hung over us. He is our righteousness, our Advocate who intercedes on our behalf and who ensures that God hears our prayers. He is the bond of peace between God and us, for he has won for us what does not belong to us by nature. We must ascribe all these merits to Jesus Christ if we would know how he appeared. Simply to take the word 'gospel' and to ignore all that it contains would be to twist and distort everything. We would be making a phantom of Jesus Christ if we merely said that he appeared as our Saviour, but failed to mention and recall all that he endured for our salvation, all that he did to reconcile us to God his Father, to purge us from each spot and stain and to redeem us from bondage to everlasting death. Why say anything if none of this is said? What good is it if we do not know Jesus Christ to be our Advocate, the one who brings our prayers to God so that he does not refuse us? What confidence could we have when we call upon God's name, since as Scripture says he is the fortress of our salvation (Psa. 18:2; 31:3; Jer. 16:19)?

So when Paul writes that Jesus Christ appeared, he means first and foremost that he fulfilled all that was required to redeem the human race. At the same time he shows us the power and glory displayed in his resurrection, and the accompanying benefits which he confers on us. If, however, the gospel were taken from us, what good would it do to know that God's Son suffered so bitter a death and rose on the third day? It would serve little purpose. The gospel therefore puts us in possession of all the blessings which Jesus Christ has obtained for us and which he brings to us. So even though today he is absent in the body and does not live on earth with us, we should not think that we are any worse off.

71

He has not withdrawn from us as if we had to search for him and risked not finding him. For the sun which shines on us is no more visible to the world than Jesus Christ is to those who, with the eye of faith, behold him when the gospel is proclaimed.

Jesus Christ, having thus appeared, brought life and immortality to light. Let us look closely at Paul's exact words, however, so that we may see in them all that I have said. Jesus Christ, he writes, *has destroyed death.* How did he destroy it? If he had not offered an eternal sacrifice to appease God's wrath, if he had not gone down to hell in order to rescue us from it, if he had not taken our curse and removed it from us, if he had not freed us from the burden under which we toiled, what would have become of us? Would death have been destroyed? No, sin would have had dominion over us and death would have prevailed. If we look inward we will see that we were slaves to Satan, the prince of death. So there we would be, trapped in this wretched bondage, if God had not crushed the devil, sin and death. This he has done. How? By the blood of our Lord Jesus Christ, who has cleansed us of all our stains.

Although, then, we are miserable sinners and thus liable to God's judgment, sin cannot harm us. Its venomous sting has been drawn so that it cannot prick us, for Jesus Christ has been victorious. He did not suffer in vain; his blood did not fall needlessly to the ground; it was the means by which the Holy Spirit washed us clean, as Peter says (1 Pet. 1:2). Hence, as Paul shows, it is in the gospel that Jesus Christ appears, and it is there that he appears each and every day. Still, the apostle does not forget his death and passion, and everything else which has to do with our salvation. These two things must thus be borne in mind: that in our Lord Jesus Christ we have all we could desire; in him also we have full and perfect confidence in God's goodness and love. Why? Because while our sins separate us from God and make us his sworn enemies, peace has been made in Jesus Christ. He has shed his blood to make us clean, and has offered himself as a sacrifice to reconcile us to God; he has paid our debts and cancelled the curse so that now we may enjoy God's blessing. He also vanquished death and triumphed over it to free us from its tyranny, which threatened to overwhelm us. He overcame all things by his power. Thus everything related to our salvation was accomplished by our Lord Jesus Christ. To lay hold of all his benefits we need to know that he appears every day to us in the gospel. Of course he dwells in heavenly glory, and he is not visible to us as long as we are on this earth. Yet he has not removed himself from us, and we do not have to run around in endless circles looking for him. Let us open the eyes of faith and we will see how he reveals himself to us.

All that I have been explaining is found in Paul's text. So let us make sure that we do not separate what the Holy Spirit has joined together. Observe also that Paul here suggests a comparison designed to amplify the grace which God showed to the world after the coming of our Lord Jesus Christ. It is as if the apostle meant us to see that the fathers of old were not blessed as we are by having Jesus Christ appear to them. True, they possessed the same faith and they share with us in the same heavenly inheritance, since God revealed his grace to them as he did to us, but not to the same degree. They beheld Jesus Christ from afar and in shadowy form, as Paul says, in the symbols of the law (2 Cor. 3:14-15). The veil was still stretched tight in the temple, so that the Jews could not approach even the material sanctuary. Now that the veil has been torn down, however, we can draw near to the majesty of our God; we have a direct entry into heaven itself, and we have the lively image of God in whom all fullness of glory dwells. In a word, we have the substance while the fathers had only the shadow, as we read in Colossians (Col. 2:17).

What this shows us is that if the fathers of old were steadfast and unfailingly zealous in bearing the sufferings of the Son of God—though he had not yet been revealed to the world—we today should be much more fervent, or else we will be guilty of the vilest indifference. The fathers therefore obediently bore Christ's afflictions, as we read in the eleventh chapter of Hebrews. For it is said of Moses that he bore the reproach not of his father Abraham but of Jesus Christ (Heb. 11:26). In this way the fathers, though living under the law's dark shadows, offered themselves as a sacrifice to God by patiently enduring Christ's afflictions. Now since Jesus Christ has risen from the dead and has brought life to light for us, what must we do? If we are too fainthearted to suffer for the gospel, do we not deserve to be struck out of God's book and disowned by him? Let us take heart, therefore, and suffer with greater steadfastness of faith for the sake of Jesus Christ, whenever God should choose. For life is set before us and we have a closer and more intimate knowledge than the fathers had.

Let us especially consider what the letter to the Hebrews says. We stand amazed when we read that the patriarchs did not flinch but showed outstanding courage. We know how they were persecuted by tyrants and by the enemies of the truth, and how they never ceased to suffer. The state of the church today is no harder or more grievous than it was then. Since this is so, will we hesitate to follow Jesus Christ who has shown us the way? But lest we be too sluggish or too cold, remember that Jesus Christ is said to have brought life and immortality to light through the gospel. Every time God's grace is proclaimed to us, it is as if the kingdom of heaven were opened to us and God were stretching out his hand, testifying that life is near to us and that he wants us to be partakers of his heavenly inheritance. We are told this because, until we behold Jesus Christ who lifts us up on high and leads us to eternal life, we will always be captive to this present life, and so bound to this world that we will have to be forcibly parted from it. When, however, we look to the life won for us by our Lord Jesus Christ, it will cost us nothing to leave all that attracts us here below, and to set our sights on heaven above.

Let us not be wilfully blind, for Jesus Christ daily offers us the life and immortality of which Paul speaks. For mention is made of immortality as well as of life, implying that we already enter the kingdom of God by faith. Although we are strangers on this earth and seemingly subject to death and the curse, the life and grace bestowed on us by our Lord Jesus Christ will bear fruit all in good time, when he comes again to fulfil in truth the things which are daily preached to us, and which he himself accomplished when he took our nature.

> Now let us cast ourselves down before the face of our good God, acknowledging our faults and asking him to make us truly feel our wretchedness, lest in our pride we claim credit for ourselves. Confessing that by nature we are defiled and hateful in his sight, may we therefore seek the cause of our salvation in his will and counsel, which he graciously made known when he called us to his gospel. May he grant us also to look to our Lord Jesus Christ, to rest in him and to trust in the redemption which he won for us. May he reckon us as his children, and make us partakers of the inheritance of life once our fight on earth is done. And since by his leave Satan and many foes, both near and far, assail us, may he give us strength to withstand their attacks, and never to tire until we have run our race and have attained the rest to which he daily calls us.

# 6

---

## GUARDING THE GOSPEL

*Keep the right pattern of sound words which you heard from me in faith and love which are in Jesus Christ. ¹⁴ Guard the good deposit which was entrusted to you by the Holy Spirit who lives within us.*

(2 Timothy 1:13-14)[8]

B ecause Satan knows that the life of our souls lies in God's pure truth, he tries very hard to deprive us of it, and when he cannot turn food into poison he attempts to pervert it by veiling it so that we cannot be fed as we ought to be. The devil is always shown to be the father of lies who distorts God's word as much as he can. He does so, however, in different ways, for if God lets him have his head, he falsifies and spoils everything. Accordingly we see that in popery affairs are so outrageously bad that Satan has clearly had a free hand. God has taken terrible retribution, allowing the world to become utterly blind and devoid of sense and reason. Such madness prevails among the papists that little

---

[8] Most unusually, there is no record of a sermon on 2 Tim. 1:11-12. While the Badius edition of 1561 contains 30 sermons on 2 Timothy, a manuscript catalogue dating from 1557 lists 31. The loss, for whatever reason, of what would have been the sixth sermon in the series would account for the discrepancy.

children can see and judge it. Even the wisest among them are deceived. As I said before, when men are so senseless it is because God has allowed Satan to do as he wills, since the world is so sinful.

Now if the devil realizes that he cannot wholly destroy sound teaching and turn it into a lie, he will try by craft to disguise it so as to make it unrecognizable. It ceases to be real, natural nourishment. It is as when some sharp sauce is added to food to change the taste: it is more like earth than something savoury! That is how the devil treats wholesome teaching. When he cannot suppress it entirely he alters it as he chooses. Paul thus gives Timothy this instruction: *Guard the sound pattern, the manner of teaching which you heard from me.*

The word which is used here for 'pattern' signifies a sketch made from life. Paul is therefore not content for Timothy merely to preserve the substance of what he has learned; he expects him to follow its outline and the form which has been employed. It is as if Paul said: 'This is how the gospel was preached in all its purity. Nothing has been altered, our approach is always the same. It is in this form that it has always been heard.' So that is what Paul means when he tells Timothy to keep to this pattern and style of teaching. There must be no variation: it is to be just as Timothy heard it from Paul at the very first. That is one point. At the same time we must recognize that this was not said for that time only, but that the Holy Spirit wished to show how we should safeguard the hope of salvation, namely by preserving God's message in its original purity and by not altering it in any way at all or by distorting it with outlandish additions. People should know that this is the gospel as the apostles first proclaimed it.

To help us better remember Paul's admonition, recall what I said before, for there are very few who regard God's word as food for their souls. Not that we do not say so with our lips, but we rarely give it any thought. We are naturally more worried about what we eat or drink! If a man sees someone about to steal his dinner, his hand flies to his sword. Yet when it comes to life-giving doctrine, we do not care even when we see the devil trying to poison it, or depriving us of what we need to keep us in God's kingdom. We put up with false prophets and deceivers; we even bid them welcome. This is a well-known fact. Have we not seen among us wicked heretics who found friends prepared to treat them as full cousins and who applauded them? Who do I mean? Those who claimed to be committed to the gospel! It is no secret that the devil raised them up to do more damage than if they had cut our throats![9] There are therefore very few who are willing to follow Paul's instruction, for they do not realize how much they need it.

What then is to be done? First, we must confess that poor souls are without life unless they receive it through the word of God; and as our Lord by this means delivers us from death, so too he confirms us in the hope of salvation and renews our strength. In short, just as our bodies need bread and food to sustain them, so our souls must be nourished by the word of God and by the pure doctrine of holy Scripture. And since we are filled with dread when we find ourselves deprived of food and drink, we ought to think of what is far more vital—our souls, which are more precious than our bodies. We should therefore recognize Satan's wiles when we see them, since it is both his purpose and his natural bent to corrupt everything and to turn light into darkness. He will feed us with his lies if he possibly can, making error abound and spreading his deadly poison. Thus, because Satan is ever watchful and always

---

[9] The preacher has in mind the Spanish savant Michael Servetus, pursued both by Roman Catholic and Protestant authorities for his anti-trinitarian views. Following his unexpected arrival in Geneva in August 1553, Servetus was arrested, tried and finally executed for heresy. Calvin's Libertine opponents used his presence in the city to embarrass the Reformer, and while not endorsing Servetus' ideas they felt sympathy for his plight and gave him their tacit support. The preacher's sense of betrayal is palpable here.

trying to mount an attack to turn us against God's truth, we too must be alert and on our guard.

Nevertheless this is not enough. We have to be wise, so that when we meet some wild and woolly teaching, though it may not be wholly bad or contrary to Scripture, we should reject it if it looks bogus or full of empty words. God's truth is simple and straightforward; nothing in it needs to be changed. This, then, is how we should apply the warning which Paul gives us here.

An illustration, however, may make his meaning clearer. Our Lord, as we know, calls us to himself. Now if we meet doctrine which is quite different from what the law and gospel teach, we must shun it like the plague, since this is the devil's way of murdering our souls. But even when men worm their way in secretly, in subtle, stealthy ways, so that the gospel is not corrupted but some compromise attempted which allows us to sit on the fence, here too we must be prudent and not relax our guard. Why? We would be unpleasantly surprised if the good seed were smothered and if wholesome food so lost its taste that it could no longer nourish us. Both these things have happened in our day. Would to God that was an end to them! Well then, this is God's way of testing our faith. It is as the apostle says: there are bound to be sects, so that those who have walked uprightly may be recognized and approved, having stood firm and having persisted without flinching (1 Cor. 11:19).

Nowadays, alas, there are hypocrites who seek to trample on all good doctrine and who in their haste furiously assail God's word. There are people who are so unstable that if today they accept the gospel, tomorrow they will turn their backs on it. Why? Because they have no root. What we must do is recognize how effectively Satan works, and let God's truth serve not only as our food but as our armour against all that he contrives against us. We see some who, while not openly advocating support for the papacy, look for an intermediate solution, like the diabolical Interim which has been proposed in our own day.[10] Why? In order to provide an excuse for abominations which are not to be tolerated. There are others who try by more subtle means to please everybody, or who are fired with ambition and who seek to impress by adopting a more florid and grandiloquent style, which ruins the gospel and makes it meaningless. What should we do when we see such things? We should heed Paul's advice, and be so steeped in the language of Scripture and so familiar with its terms that, if we are taught in a way which is at variance with it, we should reject what we hear, since its effect will be to make us gradually fall away. We may not jump all at once and break our necks, but without our knowing it Satan is sure to lead us astray. Let us therefore take steps to avoid the danger.

How few there are, alas, who take this lesson seriously, even among those who ought to show others the way! The pity is that not many give Scripture more than a cursory glance or are well versed in it. As a result they can change in the twinkling of an eye, because they have never taken the trouble to learn, as good students should, how the Holy Spirit speaks. If a student is intelligent and has a skilful teacher, he will be sure to remember the subjects he has been taught, but he will also retain something of his teacher's manner, so that people will say, 'He went to such and such a school.' There will always be signs which allow us to make an accurate guess. How could we want a better teacher than the Holy Spirit? Besides, we know that God's will is that the doctrine of holy Scripture should be kept separate from secular learning.

---

[10] The Interim was a document prepared at the instigation of Charles V, the Holy Roman Emperor, in an attempt to secure a provisional settlement between the warring confessions in his German territories. Approved by the Diet of Augsburg in June 1548, it conceded to Protestants the right to clerical marriage and communion in both kinds, but otherwise maintained the *status quo*. Protestant opinion regarding its merits was deeply divided. Calvin remained strongly opposed and severely criticized the Interim in his treatise of 1549, *The True Method of Reforming the Church*.

Imagine a man who has carefully read the Scriptures but who later becomes blind. If something from Isaiah is read to him along with the finest sayings of all the philosophers in the world, he will certainly reply: 'I know which are the Holy Spirit's words!' That is the way to go.

Nevertheless, as I said, there are those even among ministers of the word who hardly bother to train themselves properly or to gain the necessary experience. This is how doctrine is corrupted. So much the worse for them! But let those who have some zeal for God and who are conscious of their responsibilities attend to Paul's warning. To build up God's church and the flock entrusted to them, it is not enough to shun false and misleading ideas; they must ensure that their people know who it is who speaks, and they must get them used to it. Those who hear must be somehow convinced, so that they say: 'This is not a message from mortal men. This is no mere tale we are being told. We are being shown the majesty of God and these are the pure and simple words of holy Scripture.' So let us make sure that those to whom we preach the gospel are convinced in their heart and soul that it is not our pet ideas that they are hearing, but that they are being taught what we ourselves have received from God. However, not only ministers of the word must show others the way; every Christian must do so too. Let us endeavour to be taught so that we can honestly say that we owe nothing to men, but that we have God's plain and simple truth.

Now if we think of how things are today, we will realize that this is more necessary than ever. Nowadays it is a shame to see how fickle people are. There are many who are concerned for their own reputation, but who are so contemptuous of God and so utterly godless that they have no qualms about perverting the message of salvation. The world is worthy of such teachers! How many of us really want to be led straight to God? Almost all of us have itching ears; we are full of vain desires and crave any kind of novelty. That is why our Lord allows us to be filled with wind and smoke! Thus there are many today who twist holy Scripture, who corrupt and veil it if they cannot openly attack it. We must therefore do as Paul says, and since many try to disguise the Holy Spirit's words we should hold to the real-life picture of which the apostle speaks. Let us be familiar with the truth which our Lord teaches us in holy Scripture, so that as soon as something new is laid before us we can recognize it, even from afar, and be on our guard against it.

So that we will not find this difficult to do, Paul adds *in faith and love which are in Jesus Christ*. He had already referred to the words which Timothy had heard from him, for we need to be discerning when there are many who claim to be ministers and teachers—many indeed who arrogantly rise up so that, when they speak, everyone else is expected to be quiet and to shut their mouths. What we must consider, however, is whether or not they have been sent by God. How do we do that? We come to the touchstone of holy Scripture, by which all doctrine must be tested. If we see someone who in his manner of speech conveys the majesty of God's Spirit, and if we are edified as we ought to be, we know that this is no empty eloquence, no affected speech or speculative rant, but a simple proclamation such as we find in the prophets. They should be our models. Nevertheless we are greatly helped when Paul adds 'in faith and love which are in Jesus Christ'. What he means is that if we want to test various teachings to make sure that they have a form or pattern in which God's image is clearly visible, we must turn to faith and love. For what is God's purpose in sending us his word? It is not to throw us in among a large crowd where we are free to wander at will; it is to furnish us with a sure goal so that we cannot miss our mark. We must rely therefore on faith and love, so that we can progress each day and our faith increase and flourish. In the same way we grow in love, so that when this happens God's word does its appointed work in us. But if faith and love are missing, we might be the most sharp-witted creatures on earth, we might argue admirably about God's mysteries, but we would be empty, mere shadows without solidity or substance.

It was not wrong, then, of Paul to add these words. His intention was to give guidance to the weak and ignorant, so that they do not have to enquire anxiously about how they may know that the Holy Spirit is speaking, and what the pure pattern and lifelike picture may be to which we must hold. Paul says that it is quite easy. We know what it is to which God calls us; we know the goal he sets before us—to grow daily in the faith of the gospel, to lead useful, good and holy lives and to go steadily on. When we find these things in anything we are taught, there we have God's testimony drawn, as it were, from life. All doubt is removed.

Something should be said, briefly, about the word 'faith'. There are many who speak about faith but who are ignorant of what it means. Faith consists in knowing first of all who is the true God, so that we are not deceived by our foolish imaginations or drawn into idolatry. We must know the living God, but know him as our Father in whom we can rest and put our trust, to whom we can look for forgiveness of our sins and on whom we can call in all boldness, not doubting that he will hear all our requests. This is what faith means: knowing the true God, claiming him as Father and Saviour and having such assurance of his grace and love that we can call upon him with complete confidence.

Why does Paul mention love along with faith? We might feel that other things are needed, and so they are. Are not sobriety, self-control, chastity and patience also qualities which are taught to us in God's school? Love alone is mentioned here because the person who loves his neighbour has all the other qualities. Scripture when it speaks succinctly uses the word 'love' so as to include everything else. In fact Paul rightly calls love 'the bond of perfection' (Col. 3:14). And if, as he says in the first chapter of Ephesians, we have love, we will be pure and blameless in God's sight (Eph. 1:4). So since we can only love our neighbours as God commands if our wills are trained to obey him, the word 'love' describes the kind of Christian life which is ordered according to God's word. Paul's argument, briefly put, is that when our trust is firmly fixed in God, when we do not doubt that he is a Father and Saviour to us, when we give ourselves to holiness of life and deny ourselves in order to serve our neighbours, this is a sign that we have studied profitably in God's school and that the teaching we follow is the pure, plain truth which God would have us preach. This is what we have to do if we want to avoid being deceived by Satan.

Paul is careful to point out that faith and love are found in Jesus Christ. The Lord Jesus must direct us if we are to be built up in faith and love. We cannot have faith unless we first have knowledge of Jesus Christ. Now faith, as I have said, means that we must have assured evidence of God's love. But how does that come about? Do we deserve to be accepted by God as his children? With what boldness could we come before him? Have we nobility enough to be acceptable to his majesty? Nothing of the sort, alas! On the contrary, God can only be our Judge until our Lord Jesus Christ makes atonement for us and washes our filth away. It would be impossible for us to put our trust in God before we had knowledge of Jesus Christ, otherwise we would shrink from God in dread. Whenever God's name was invoked we would be terrified by his majesty; we would want either to blot it out or to lose ourselves in the deepest hell. That is how it will always be until we come to know Jesus Christ. For only then will we learn that God is propitious to us and that, however miserable we are, he nevertheless has mercy on us. He thinks not of us but of the efficacy of the death and passion suffered by his Son.

If we wish to enter into faith we must begin with Jesus Christ. The same is true of prayer, for if Jesus Christ is not our Advocate, if he does not intercede for us and obtain grace for us so that God answers the requests we make, what will become of us? God is sure to refuse us. When, however, Jesus Christ opens the door and shows us the way, when above all he acts as our Advocate, then we may cast scruples aside and come boldly to God in prayer. It is the same with love. How are we brought to those brotherly ties which we have with all men, except through Jesus Christ who is the bond of peace between us, in whom we are all joined together, of whose body we are members and who, as our head, wants us to live in harmony with each other and to be led and governed by his Holy Spirit? That is why we can never learn to love until we have first known Jesus Christ. Without him we are scattered and divided, and it is no surprise if we fight like cats and dogs and are full of hate. Until we have learned to love one another, we cannot be considered children of God, or have part and portion in our Lord Jesus Christ. That is why Paul says that faith and love are in Jesus Christ.

It is obvious, therefore, that those who have swerved from the pure message of salvation are without excuse. They have had ample warning. The devil is their master, for they have deliberately given themselves to him. Nowadays we know of many who try to excuse themselves when they drift into error and false teaching. 'Oh,' they say, 'I'm not clever enough to take sufficient care.' Yes, but if we tuned our ears so that we obeyed what we are taught here, even the most ignorant and unskilled among us would learn to be cautious! God does not want us to be like reeds which tremble in the wind, or like children who can be easily ensnared, as Paul says in the fourth chapter of Ephesians (Eph. 4:14). He wants us to be fully assured of his truth. And if we think that this is too involved, Paul says it all in just three words: 'let us hold to the faith and love which are in Jesus Christ'. Three words! But if someone should say, 'Oh, these are too obscure!', I say that nothing could be clearer.

Nevertheless, poor wretches like these allow themselves to be led like beasts to the slaughter. Why do they do it? Can they claim that God has not shown them the way, or that they did not know what was right? No! They have no excuses. Let us make sure, then, that if we would be blameless at the last day, we heed what we are told here. And so that, day by day, nothing should shake our faith, let us see that we have these marks which are mentioned here. If, however, we do not have them, it will happen to us as has happened to many others, indeed to almost all. For why is it that those who have tasted the gospel and who seemed furthest ahead turn bad and become renegades and open enemies, or else disguise themselves so that the devil has them in his grip? They would be glad to see God's word buried, if not destroyed. Why is that? It is because they only remember things that have little power to edify, in order to jeer at the papists and to deride popular superstition. Yet they fail to grow in faith and love. God is therefore right to banish them from his word and to deprive them of it. We should fear lest the same should happen to us, and lest we neglect to be strong in faith and love. We must stop the devil finding a way into us and breaking through our defences. We must be well protected on every side. This is the lesson we must learn.

Paul goes on to urge Timothy to *guard the worthy deposit entrusted to him by the Holy Spirit who dwells in him*. The apostle's earlier exhortation is thus confirmed. He tells him in effect: 'I have taught you to keep to the pattern which you saw in me, and to change nothing in this picture made from life. Take every care. Consider all the gifts which God conferred on you when you were made a minister of his word and a pastor of his church. These gifts are necessary for the discharge of your duties. They are a worthy deposit which you must safeguard.'

The word 'deposit' means that those who have received a gift are all the more in debt to God and are bound to him. It is as if a man were to entrust all his goods to a friend for safekeeping, together with the key to the chest containing his treasure. He gives him the deeds to his house, saying, 'These I entrust to you.' In the same way God entrusts us with what he has and with what belongs to him alone. This does not make us owners, even though the gifts which we receive from God are ours, and we can call them so. Yet he does not cede to us any of his rights: all is for his glory, and all must be referred to him. So what Paul does is remind those who have received gifts and who have a given task and charge, that they are answerable to God. They are not to use them any way they please. They must be used to serve our neighbour, to honour God and always to give Jesus Christ pre-eminence. If they do not do this they are guilty of sacrilege and God will argue the case against them. For if a man cheated a friend who had left his goods in his hands, trusting in his loyalty, while the other robbed him, seized his wealth or spent what had been committed to him, would he not be guilty in God's sight of having betrayed his trust?

That is one point. But because we do not think much of a deposit entrusted generally to all, compared with things more precious, Paul describes this deposit as dearer and more estimable than anything else in the world. If we entrust a jar, a dish or something similar to a person, a deposit has been made. We hand it over and think little more about it. But if expensive jewels are handed over we hold them tight, knowing that they are important. Or we may tell ourselves, 'Here are the deeds to a house. A man would be ruined if he lost these.' So we are much more careful to protect what is deposited with us if it is valuable. Accordingly Paul declares that those who have received the Holy Spirit's gifts hold nothing ordinary in trust, but that God has committed to them a priceless treasure which they must make sure they protect.

How do they do that? No, not by hiding it away but, as the whole of Scripture testifies, by making the most of it and by being faithful stewards of it. God does not want his gifts to be shut up in some chest. He wants them openly made known so that everyone may enjoy them. That is how we are to safeguard God's deposit. Ministers of God's word who act as his standard-bearers must see that they dispense what is in their keeping—dispense it so as to secure or promote as much as possible the church's well-being. Each and every Christian should do the same, according to his rank and his ability. Understand that if we cherish earthly treasures, we should cherish still more spiritual treasures which have as their aim God's honour, the advancement of his kingdom and Christ's rule among us, so that great and small may do him homage and all redound to our salvation. When we see something so precious which should kindle such zeal within us, should we not forsake all else which might prevent us from doing our duty? But since none of us can safeguard the precious things which God has committed to us unless he gives us his power, and since we can do nothing of ourselves, Paul adds, 'by the Holy Spirit who dwells in us'.

He might well have said: 'When God pours out his gifts upon us, he does so for the benefit of all believers. He knows that we are frail and that the devil might snatch us at any moment, taking from us what we have received. God, however, is our sovereign keeper. It is true that we are meant to be, to a lesser degree, keepers of his treasures; he is willing to use us for so noble a purpose. Nevertheless he uses us to make known the gifts he has conferred on us. This is where the Holy Spirit's power is made manifest.' Paul thus shows us that to employ God's gifts faithfully as we should, and to enjoy them forever, we must not trust in our own strength as if we were fully competent. No, we are to ask God—since he first chose to endow us with his free gifts—to confirm them in us, lest we lose them or lest they be taken from us. To this end may he equip us with the power we need.

We should be absolutely certain that God will do this, for he is not far from us and makes it possible for our souls to feel him. So we should each look within. Is not the good which God has put in us sure proof that he lives in us by his Holy Spirit? When we know that God has his abode within us and wishes to make us his temples where he dwells through his Holy Spirit, shall we fear that he will not allow us to persevere to the end or to preserve the blessings received from his hand? Admittedly the devil will strive to take them from us, but since our souls, entrusted to Christ's care, will never become his prey, he will never rob us of all that God has ordained for our salvation. Why? Because we have the Spirit who will always defend us against all that he tries to do. And where is the Spirit? We do not have to look for him beyond the clouds. Although he fills the earth and his majesty sits above the heavens, we feel him dwelling in us, for he has been pleased to bestow his power on miserable creatures like us. Be sure, therefore, that this power is sufficient to protect us from all of Satan's assaults, provided we are not ourselves fainthearted. We must not be slack and indulge our weaknesses. We must pray to God, entrusting ourselves wholly to him in the expectation that he will strengthen us more and more. And since he has begun by making us ministers of his grace, we know that he will continue to advance our salvation, and that of our neighbours, for his sole glory.

> Now let us cast ourselves down before the face of our good God, acknowledging our faults and begging him to make us feel them more keenly, so that we strive to pattern our lives on his holy commandments, and more and more struggle to overcome all our fleshly desires. May he also be pleased to uphold us in our weaknesses, until he has fully remade us in his own image.

# 7

## STEADFAST, COME WHAT MAY

*You know that all who are in Asia have turned away from me, among whom are Phygelus and Hermogenes.* <sup>16</sup> *May the Lord grant mercy to the house of Onesiphorus, for he often refreshed me and was not ashamed of my chains;* <sup>17</sup> *but when he was in Rome he carefully sought me out and found me.* <sup>18</sup> *May the Lord grant him to find mercy before the Lord on that day; and you are well aware of all that he did to serve me in Ephesus.* (2 Timothy 1:15-18)

We saw this morning how Paul urged Timothy to guard the worthy deposit which had been entrusted to him. The apostle now adds a word of warning: Timothy must be on his guard. He must be alert, so that this treasure is not taken from him.

Paul tells him that *those who are in Asia*—those who earlier called themselves Christians and believers—*had turned away from him.* He specifically mentions two by name: *Phygelus and Hermogenes.* Such a scandal might upset the sturdiest of men, for if we see someone who turns against the gospel we all think that the same might happen to us. According to Paul it is not two or three only who are involved: all who are from Asia have forsaken him.

Now Asia was an extensive region which had been won for Jesus Christ by Paul's endeavours. It looked as if the gospel might have triumphed there in every place. Its cities were large and prosperous and there were many men of renown. Yet all had come to nothing, for although these people pretended still to believe, by rejecting Paul they rejected Jesus Christ. What a disaster! What a blow to those who were not very strong! Yet even as he relates his news, Paul has not lost heart; he continues on, for his faith does not depend on men but rests on God.

Paul tells Timothy this in order to make him stronger and more steadfast. As we said before, the apostle is not thinking so much of the man to whom he writes as of the whole church. Thus his purpose is to equip the faithful, so that they are not unduly discouraged on hearing that in Asia the work of the gospel has been more or less frustrated. The faithful must know that, though all had turned away, we are to persist in the truth of God which we must never change.

This warning is most useful to us today. As I have often said, we are all rather sensitive. If only one man changes direction we welcome the chance to go astray, and in truth we seize it much too readily. As soon as an opportunity arises we all try to take advantage of it, as if we had something to gain by delivering ourselves into Satan's hands, thinking, 'Since you got the better of one man, you might as well have me!' This happens all too often. Would to God we saw fewer examples than we do! Today, when there is talk of the gospel, we seize on this excuse and cry, 'Look, there is a man who was a pillar of the Christian faith, but who has turned away.' At the very least we feel less confident. When we hear such claims we seem to think we have an honest excuse for giving up on God and for parting company with him. This is what many people do. So the devil seems to have a field day. Many fall away from the gospel, and small wonder, as we said this morning, for where do we find that living root of faith and love which keeps us obedient to sound teaching?

In any case, every day we see dissidents, highly esteemed people of whom great things were expected, but who abandon the gospel and who even become openly hostile, or who at least become worldly and insipid, devoid of salt. What, then, are we to do, except take up the arms which Paul recommends? We must, that is, hold fast to what is permanent and immutable, even though the whole world should change.

This is an idea which is easy to grasp but which is harder to put into practice. That is why we need to remember this lesson. Thus, if today we see some who give way and others who throw the gospel over, we should recognize that we have less reason to be bewildered and dismayed than Paul and his contemporaries had when they saw Asia itself turn against them. For the rest, if the enemies of the gospel throw these things in our face in order to shame us, we should nevertheless be strong. Of course Satan will scheme to bring the gospel into disrepute and to unsettle those whose faith has never been deep-rooted. Even so, considerations of human worth must never deny Jesus Christ his rights. So let us remain resolute when we are told: 'See! There is a man who showed great steadfastness and zeal, an admirable man! Yet look at him today!' Yes, he is human, but God's truth abides forever, as the prophet Isaiah says when he compares our frailty to the flowers and grass which immediately wither; nevertheless, as he says, God's truth endures (Isa. 40:8). We must cling to that idea if we want to rebuff the claims of those whose only wish is to denigrate the gospel.

In the meantime let us learn to condemn men by hallowing God. By 'hallowing God', as Scripture puts it, I mean ascribing to him the praise that he deserves. We should realize that although men may pervert God's truth, it is no worse off for that, nor can they undermine God's authority. His truth owes nothing to anything outside of it; it is self-sufficient. Let us therefore give God the glory even though the whole world should be in turmoil. As we read in the eighth chapter of Isaiah, if unbelievers are restless and rise up in revolt, we should not be fearful on that account. We should hallow the Lord of hosts—that is, attribute to him all that is his due, knowing that those who rise up against him will be finally brought down, while he remains immune (Isa. 8:12-13).

We may take our meaning further, for we can only hallow God by endorsing the truth which comes from him. Just as the faithful always clung to the conviction that Paul was an apostle of Jesus Christ, we must do the same. Do we see scoffers who go badly astray, some out of spite, others because they hate to have the name of Jesus Christ drummed into their ears—do we see them abandoning the faith? Let us nevertheless keep on honouring teaching which we know to be sound and holy, and respecting those who bring it to us, however much the world despises and rejects them. That is what this passage tells us.

Why is Paul led to name both Phygelus and Hermogenes? Doubtless they were men of prominence who were considered pillars of the faith. The apostle, however, shames them and points them out, so that no one should have cause to stumble. Thus he shows that there is no greatness among men which can obscure God's majesty or the reverence which we should have for his word. So when we see a whole country turn against God, we should say, 'God is able all by himself to defend his truth.' When we see famous and respected people fall away, we remember that all haughtiness of men must be brought low, God alone worshipped and exalted, and Satan and his ministers made to bend the knee before him, whether they will or no. That is what we must do.

Consider, however, how ungrateful people are. For as I said, there are many who think they have an honest excuse for forsaking Jesus Christ and his gospel when they see others fall away. They welcome the chance to do the same. There are men, as we know, who watch events closely. If they see that the gospel is in retreat or in difficulties, 'Oh,' they cry, 'it was obvious it couldn't last!' So when a city throws the gospel over or when tyranny or force grind it down, many people who before pretended to believe the gospel are now content, believing that they can turn their backs on Jesus Christ. They are all the same, and they all have good memories. The gospel makes progress for a time and looks likely to prosper; but suddenly a town or city changes: people or their rulers turn away and a whole kingdom is lost. Though these are the facts to which they point, God still upholds his cause. So our first and greatest need is to persevere despite the damage the devil tries to do. When all is confusion, and when provinces and regions turn unexpectedly about, we must press on as before. Why? Because God does not change.

Think too of man's so-called worth. It is hard to conceive what little respect there is for God today. It is not men of standing and high repute who now assail the gospel. Any idle wretch, an urchin, the merest good-for-nothing, a witless fool, will do! 'Oh,' we say, 'here's someone who looks like he's falling away!' Yet who is he? An idiot—one of many whom we see nowadays! Even if they were angels from heaven, we would have to curse them if they rose up against the gospel. Not that they would, but this is the image Paul uses when he cannot adequately exalt the truth of God (Gal. 1:8). So little can men's authority divert us from what is right that even if the angels turned against God we would dismiss them as devils. Yet we are far from having confidence in God's truth, which should be sure and certain for us and which we should defend against its enemies. We make an idol of anyone who comes along and we put him up against God: 'See that man? Who is he? And who are these who are the talk of the town?'

Let us carefully attend, therefore, to what Paul says. When those who are prominent and respected go astray and set a bad example, it should not affect us. We must keep to the path on which God has set us. For while Paul has his reasons for naming Phygelus and Hermogenes, he intends also to demonstrate that we should not spare men or hesitate to shame them when we see them attempting to harm the gospel or creating disunity or tensions. It is said that we should accuse no one, and that is true. But when we see mischief-makers who set out to poison God's church, or ravenous wolves bent on scattering the flock, or thieves and robbers who want to take from Jesus Christ what is his, this is sacrilege whose effect is to pervert the doctrine of salvation. Nevertheless people tolerate them and try to cover up their iniquity. Now where will that get us? It is a terrible kind of morality when we allow poor souls who have been so dearly ransomed to go to their destruction, when we permit God's name to be blasphemed and all order swept away, while we say nothing and put up with men who want to wreck everything and to pull God from his throne, if only they could. Are we to utter not a word while they are free to do as they like? Would we not be traitors, disloyal both to God and men?

Let us follow Paul's example, then, and point the finger at such men. So when we see evildoers intent on ruining everything and especially on attacking sound doctrine, or eager to overthrow what has been built in God's name, they are to be denounced so that all may loathe them and flee far from them. If we hear talk of them we must block our ears, saying, 'We have nothing in common with these devils.' Since they are sworn enemies of Jesus Christ we must have no friendship or dealings of any kind with them. We should detest them as enemies of our salvation. This is something we should note.

It is true that sometimes we must put up with those who like to show off by thumbing their nose at convention, for there are many who try to attract attention by misbehaving. These people are riff-raff, not fit company even for cowherds! Yet they want to be known as pastors of the church, and not content with that they want to subvert everything that is good! They do not care if they are known only for their infamy and evil. We should have nothing to do with scum like that; we should leave these scoundrels well alone. Nevertheless, if we know that as long as they remain unknown they risk doing harm, we must point them out and pay no heed to the good souls who say, 'Is it right to drive a man to despair?' Why then is he in such a hurry to make war on Jesus Christ and to spoil the good work done in his name? Let us not try to be smarter than the Holy Spirit!

At this point Paul introduces a different sort of man. Having spoken of those of Asia and having particularly named two of the leading renegades, he now mentions Onesiphorus who took a different path. *May God*, he says, *grant him to find mercy, him and all his house. May he find mercy before the Lord on that day*. We are thus encouraged to distinguish between different sorts of men. It only takes one bad man to lead us astray, whereas if we see a hundred who set a good example we are so senseless we refuse to copy them. Are we not wilful in the extreme? When God sets before us a good example, it is as if he were sending us a guide, meaning that he does not want us to err or go astray. 'The world,' he says, 'is full of darkness, and there are many crooked paths. To help you go straight to where you have been called, I will direct you.' Should that not do us much more good than if there were a hundred men ready to lead us into mischief? If, on the contrary, we set out to copy a single person who has gone wrong, while we ignore a whole host of people who set us good examples, we are quite unpardonable, given what Paul tells us here.

On the one hand we see the whole of Asia, which was guilty of terrible disaffection involving many people, not just a few. The gospel had been planted in famous and important cities and among multitudes of people. Nevertheless they all turned away from Paul, which is why the apostle says: 'My friends, when you see so great a host of people, do not be alarmed. God remains firm, even though you see men who were leaders of the faithful turn against him. You, however, must remain true to him.' That said, he introduces one man by way of contrast. He thus warns that while God points us to someone who can keep our spirits up, many more will try to lead us astray, so that if we follow evil and forsake the good, we are without excuse. This is worth remembering, for today there are some who through fear of death or through weakness will fall away and deny Jesus Christ.

Do we know of such? Yet we will also see martyrs who go resolutely to their death, fearing nothing, and who even rejoice that they are called to seal the gospel with their blood. If we know of one martyr, should not his steadfastness encourage us much more than the fickleness of the fainthearted fills us with dread? Again, there will be those who out of self-interest, greed or for other worldly motives fail and fall. Still, there will be others who are rock-solid and who remain unshaken; whatever trials the devil makes them endure, they emerge victorious. When we see one person who is tested like a champion, and in whom God visibly displays his power, should we not honour God by making him our model rather than by sinning, since we know that all must end in our destruction?

This is not a lesson which we practise much today. A hundred evildoers are much more likely to have our esteem than one good man is able to influence us for good. And though our eyes are glutted by a host of good examples, the devil has only to put a stumbling-block in our way for everything to be lost and forgotten. Nevertheless the precious gifts God gives us will benefit us much more. Remember, then, this lesson taught by Paul: whenever meddlers contrive to corrupt God's truth or household enemies spread confusion, and when apostates return to popery and others disguise God's word, we should not be troubled. We should look around us, and if our Lord shows us people who can encourage us to be more steadfast, who hold their course in spite of everything, who have God's power in them and are impervious to all assaults—if we see this, let us profit from what God tells us here.

We may be sure that although all around us is decay and we live in an age which is desperate and past hope, God will see that we are not short of good examples. We will certainly see many who go from bad to worse; others will trample on everything they have heard and will deliberately make war on God. This we must expect. Nevertheless God will show that his hand is on those who suffer much for their witness to him; they will put all their enemies to shame. They may suffer the flames and extremes of torture, yet they will triumph in spite of Satan and the world. These are the mirrors which God gives us. Should we not use them to best advantage? Again, we will witness others who, seeing how things stand, could choose to return to popery and, by forsaking Jesus Christ, could lead a life of comfort. Instead they will prefer to die a hundred thousand deaths. When we see such as these who walk in all humility and obedience, their life speaks volumes. They might have attracted attention and cut quite a dash, but they remained humble to the very end. God, we might say, has put them on a stage to edify us. We would be vile and thankless if we could not follow their example. This was the first thing Paul had in mind when he spoke of Onesiphorus.

We ought, however, to weigh carefully the words he writes: *May the Lord grant mercy to his house, for he strengthened me many times, and when he was in Rome he diligently sought me out and found me, and was not ashamed of my fetters.* Although the apostle was maligned by everyone, Onesiphorus sought him out to serve him as a child might serve his father. So when Paul asks God to grant him mercy on account of the faithfulness he showed, we learn that if God rewards the good we do in the power of his Holy Spirit, it is not a payment for our services, as if it were deserved. Why do I say that? Consider how nobly Onesiphorus behaved. But does Paul say anything about merit? Does he say that God was in his debt? Far from it! He asks God to have mercy on him. And what does mercy imply, except that God should show him pity and forgive his faults? It is clear, then, that the rewards which the faithful may expect from God are not payments owed to them, based on a calculation of their merits. It is because God is generous to them and shows them his mercy. In the same way poor sinners are told that whatever their transgressions, they must always have recourse to God's unmerited kindness which is the ground of our salvation. That is one point.

If we took careful note of this, we would not have so much strife and disagreement with the papists concerning reward for works. They believe that our works are meritorious, that they have worth which puts God in our debt. We, on the other hand, know that whatever is in us we owe to God's gifts of grace, so that we cannot call upon him to reward us for our merits and to satisfy our claims. When all is said and done, we need God to forgive our sins, and if he has allowed us to show kindness to those who are in want, we must ask him to show mercy to us. That is another point.

What Paul teaches us is that whatever we do for God's children is never wasted, even if they cannot return the favour. Indeed, when God bids us help and assist our neighbours, he does not offer us payment as the papists imagine. Anyone who thinks this cannot expect a reward in heaven. If I serve someone or do him a favour because he can do the same for me, I am not thinking of God but am striving as much as I can for some earthly advantage. God repudiates that idea. When, however, we do good to those who need our help without worrying whether they can return the favour, God takes note of it, since our acts are directed to him. He takes cognizance of them, as Paul suggests, for although what he utters here is a heartfelt prayer, it amounts in fact to a promise. It is as if the Holy Spirit, speaking through Paul, says: 'Do not fear that, in doing good to the poor who are destitute of help, they can give you neither warmth nor cold. Do not think that you have wasted whatever you have spent in order to aid them. You have a generous debtor—God himself.' God of course is not bound to us in any way, but he is a willing debtor, for he chooses to take the place of those who are otherwise in need and whom the rest of the world ignores.

Since this is so, let us learn not to seek rewards in this world for the good deeds we do. We must not, I say, seek men's compliments or praise. It should be enough that God knows and bears witness that we have striven to show that we are his children. Since his goodness extends over all his creatures, let us resolve to be like him and to conform to his image. Let that be enough for us, however much the world may mock and men prove thankless. Let nothing deter us, but let us press on. In any case, as Paul shows by his own example, if the favours they do are not always returned, believers should at least lay them before our Lord and not forget them. Naturally, if we can do good to those who have been good to us, nature itself teaches us our duty. The heathen, who are without law, prophets and gospel, will surely condemn us if we are ungrateful. But if we are destitute, and with the best will in the world unable to return the favours that others do to us, what should we do? We should remember them in prayer to God, and have this firmly printed on our hearts. We will find when we do this that it will encourage others whom God has more liberally endowed. This is a practice which men have followed since time began. The heathen regarded those who were ungrateful as contemptible, as outcasts among men. They held generosity to be a quality worthy of praise, even though they gave no thought to God as they were bound to do. But if we pray to God for those who have been good to us, they will be stirred up to go on doing good.

Within this verse are words which we should especially observe: 'May the Lord grant him to find mercy on that day.' In expressing himself this way, Paul tells us how we must sow. He makes the same point in Corinthians, saying that if we do someone a good turn by helping him in his need, we must be patient, until the time when our Lord shows that our efforts have not been wasted. Think of the metaphor which Paul employs. A ploughman waits for harvest time. He lets winter go by and all seems lost. Snow, hail and storms come; but when it is time to harvest he finds that his labours have not been wasted (1 Cor. 9:10). We must do the same. We must learn to extend our hope to the coming of our Lord Jesus Christ. True, God promises that if we are kind to the poor and try to help them in their need, the same measure will be given to us, so that if we suffer want we will find favour with men. He has promised that we will be blessed, and that his blessing will be enough not only for us but for others with whom it can be shared (Luke 6:38).

These promises certainly apply to this present life, but we must go further. We must look to the last day, waiting patiently to possess the life which lies ahead. Even though all appears wasted and God may not appear to bless us and give us success, let us always nurture the hope that at the last day, when the books are opened, we will not have lost the good which we entrusted to God when we helped those whose needs he commended to us. This we must do as long as we live, for if this hope is not lodged in our hearts and does not have pre-eminence there, we will continually err. Would we then give God sure and steady service? Would we be steadfast, never failing? Then above all let us learn to set our sights firmly on that last day and on the coming of our Lord Jesus Christ, knowing that a crown is prepared for us.

In the meantime we should not grieve over our many trials and tribulations and the pains of daily living. We should pass over such things as we look to the last day to which God calls us—'that day', as Paul puts it. Every Christian who reads this verse must surely be moved to the quick. The apostle is filled with exultation when he speaks of the coming of Jesus Christ and of the final resurrection. He does not ask the Lord to grant him grace at his coming, on the day of our redemption when he returns to judge the world. He might well have spoken thus. Instead he says 'on that day', as if he were drawing a visible picture of the Lord Jesus, together with his angels. Such was Paul's faith that he did not airily describe Jesus Christ as Judge of all the world, while he himself was rooted to the earth. He did not speak coldly and in human terms about these things. He was so transported beyond this world that he cried out: 'That day! That day!' Where is it, then? Well, those who aspire to be clever in themselves are sure not to find it, for this saying must be fulfilled: 'Eye has not seen, nor ear heard, nor has it entered into the heart of man what God has prepared for those who love him' (Isa. 64:4; 1 Cor. 2:9).

However much we apply our minds to the study of these things, they will remain dark, deep and inaccessible. When, however, we lay hold of the promise we have been given, and when we know that Jesus Christ in rising from the dead displayed his power not for his own sake but to unite all his members in him, then we too may cry: 'That day!' Why? Because if this word leaves us unmoved when it is on our lips and in our heart, it is as if we plucked Jesus Christ from heaven and denied his death, his passion and his descent into hell.

Attend, then, to this word, and note its importance. There is nothing half-hearted about what Paul says. He earnestly points us to the day of Jesus Christ, describing it as if it were present. It is ours by virtue of the promise. Notice also that he prays not only for

Onesiphorus but for his whole house. This again ought to kindle our desire to do good to all who are members of Jesus Christ and to assist them, for God declares that he will have mercy on us and on those who are close to us. Onesiphorus is praised for having sought out Paul in Rome and for having taken pains to serve him. At the same time we learn that although he expected nothing from him and could hope for no earthly payment, there was prepared for him in heaven a reward which could not fail. In addition, for his sake and out of consideration for him, God willed to grant mercy to those who were near and dear to him. So our Lord not only acknowledges the service we render to his people but undertakes to prosper us both in our lineage and in all else that we have. He will extend his fatherly love to those we love and who are joined to us. That being so, how can we fear that he will not be favourable to us as individuals? Is not our reward most sure and certain?

Paul, in sum, shows us that we do God an acceptable service when, among other things, we aid those who suffer for the gospel's sake, who endure the world's insults and abuse and who are persecuted. When we come to their aid God accepts our service as a fragrant and sweet-smelling offering. So when we help those who suffer in order to uphold God's truth, are we not witnesses with them and do we not bear as much of their burden as we can?

From this passage it is clear that when people are unjustly harassed for defending God's truth, when they are slandered or afflicted in any way, we are to stand with them and to share their shame, being willing to bear part of the wrongs and insults suffered by Christ's servants. When we do this, God affirms that he sees us from heaven. And although men may poke out their tongues at us, and although we may seem stupid by blithely provoking the fury of the wicked against us, it is enough that God assures us from heaven that this is the service he requires of us, and that if we are not rewarded here and now, a sure reward awaits us at the coming of our Lord Jesus Christ. We may thus be certain that, as he suffered death for us, he did not ascend to heaven in vain, for his purpose is to gather us to himself and to lead us to that crown of glory which is presently hidden from us.

Now let us cast ourselves down before the face of our good God, acknowledging our faults and begging him to help us feel them more and more, so that we may come to true repentance and may strive to mortify the evil within us, until he makes us new. And since we cannot follow his holy calling unless we look always to his kingdom, may he be pleased to lift our minds on high, and so draw us to our Lord Jesus Christ that we may despise the fleeting things of this world, knowing that he sees every service which we render him. So may we overcome all that threatens to turn us from the right path, until at length we reach our goal.

# 8

## GOD'S STRONG ARM

*Therefore, my son, be strong in the grace which is in Jesus Christ,*
*² and the things which you have heard from me in the presence of many*
*witnesses, deliver to faithful men who will be able to teach others also.*
*³ Take your share of hardship as a good soldier of Jesus Christ.*

(2 Timothy 2:1-3)

As experience amply teaches us, we cannot continue in God's service unless we have more than human strength. We can easily stumble and fall with every step we take, and we know how Satan continually attacks us, so that unless we had strength from on high we would be unable to resist. God, however, knows our weaknesses and does not send us into battle without making provision for us. Our Lord Jesus, too, has received power and might, and does not leave his people without defences. We must nevertheless prepare ourselves to be immeasurably brave if we wish to follow our calling. Above all, those whose task it is to show others the way need help from heaven, for Satan will subject them to the fiercest and severest assaults.

Paul thus exhorts Timothy *to be strong in the grace which is in our Lord Jesus Christ.* He tells him that he cannot fulfil the duties entrusted to him unless he summons up his courage and resolves to fight to the end. The Holy Spirit clearly means by Timothy's example to teach all of us the same lesson. We are not to think that we can serve God in a state of ease and repose. God seeks to test our readiness to labour on his behalf. He therefore leaves the wicked and evildoers free to trouble us. God tries us in many ways. Even so the remedy is at hand for, as Paul writes, the grace which is in our Lord Jesus Christ is available to all of us, provided we do not refuse it out of laziness. Paul's words convey an important message, namely that the grace which is in our Lord Jesus Christ is not so tightly confined or enclosed that it is beyond our reach. God bears witness that Jesus Christ has been given to us with such power that he promises us victory over all our foes.

Here, then, is the essence of what Paul says. In order to give ourselves to God's service it is not enough to have mean or lukewarm motives. Why? Because Satan will do his best to hinder us, as often happens. We ourselves are frail and must gather strength, or else we are beaten. That is one point. Another is that we should not be afraid, for we have God's assurance that he will help us in time of need. Jesus Christ does not lack strength. If we are weak, let us fall back on him, for he has more than enough to sustain us.

This is a truth which needs to be pondered rather than discussed at length. Even so it should be obvious that Paul was right to urge these things on Timothy. For among those who pretend to be zealous in God's service, how many do we see who really persevere? Most give up, because they reckon they can play at serving God. They give no thought to their own weaknesses and ignore the fact that all around are snares and hidden traps, and that Satan is active everywhere. Those who make no attempt to gather their strength are taken unawares at every turn. We should not wonder, for they are without excuse. Since, therefore, God plainly shows that he intends to try us and that the Christian life is no mere game, that we are not here to please ourselves but to fight on—since this is made clear to us, are we not to blame if through our negligence we fail?

How important it is that we heed Paul's exhortation to be strong, and to show no sign of softness or faintheartedness! God's service demands that we be staunch and resolute, which means that we must be helped from heaven, because human strength alone is not enough. Still, what Paul adds is a source of comfort to us. We should not look to our own strength. If we are short of weapons and have neither heart nor legs for the battle, our Lord Jesus stands ready with the remedy and will not be backward in helping us. So if someone finds it hard to withstand attacks because they are too fierce, he is ungrateful for God's goodness and refuses all support when Jesus Christ holds out his hand to him. God does not sport with us when he allows Satan to oppress us and to tread us down. True, he wants us to feel our weakness so that we may weep and, humbling ourselves, may turn to him for aid. Unless necessity presses us hard we incline too much to pride and arrogance. We need, then, to be convinced of our feebleness, so that we learn to call upon God and to hide beneath the shadow of his wings. We must also learn to bow our heads and to walk in fear and trembling.

Now the grace and steadfastness of which I have spoken are always to be found in Jesus Christ. Whenever the gospel sets him before us we are endued with his power and made victorious over Satan and all our enemies. God does not point us to our free will, or say: 'See what you can do. Test your powers.' He knows that we can do nothing at all. Instead he calls us to himself and directs us to his only Son, to whom he has given the task of strengthening us. That is why Paul writes in another place that he can do all things through him who strengthens him (Phil. 4:13). There the apostle boasts that no temptation has overtaken him, but lest he seems to claim credit for himself or to exalt himself, he speaks of the one who strengthens him. He writes this not only for his own sake, but declares that Jesus Christ, as the head of all the faithful, bestows his power on the whole body of the church. This is where we ought to place our trust. We need not fear when we are shaken, when God shows us that we are no better than worms or scarcely worthier than flies: he will make up for all that we lack. Enough said, then, on the first verse of our text.

In the next verse Paul asks Timothy *to entrust to faithful men the things he has heard from him, so that they may teach others.* Again we see what a treasure the gospel is and how much it means to God. The world in its thanklessness takes no account of it. Many people today are glutted with the message of salvation, and others have never savoured it. However much they hear it, they have never felt the effect or power of what it contains. So mindless are they that the gospel and popery are all one to them. Some have grown so hard in their godlessness that they have lost all reason; there is no more religion in them than in dogs or dumb animals. Worse still, others are full of venom; they gnash their teeth and would dearly love to wipe out all remembrance of God. These things are plain to see. Since this is so, let us remember what we are taught here, that God has given us the priceless treasure of his word so that we might preserve it whole and keep it from perishing. Let those especially who have been made preachers of the gospel see that the message of salvation is not lost or extinguished, but is accepted and protected. Each according to his rank and station must work heartily to this end. This is what the apostle has in mind when he urges Timothy to entrust these things to faithful men.

Naturally the first thing we must do is to keep this treasure locked in our hearts, and the key which protects it is a clear conscience. As we saw before, those who have no godly fear are utterly destroyed, as if left a prey to Satan. It is only right that God should be avenged on worldly folk who despise his holy word and who wickedly pervert it. Do we want this treasure to remain with us? Then let us each clasp it to our heart. Yet it is not enough to think only of our salvation. Knowledge of God should shine everywhere throughout the world; all should share in it. Let us try, then, to lead to salvation, along with ourselves, all who have gone astray. And let us not think only of our life now, but of life beyond death, as Peter declares in his second letter (2 Pet. 1:15). Knowing his death to be imminent, he strives to see that the memory of what he taught when he was alive should survive, once God has taken him out of this world. He thus desires that the memory of what he preached should be preserved. That too is Paul's purpose in this text.

So when it is a question of accepting the gospel, our children's children should have access to the same grace as we do, and when God is revealed to a nation, all who come after and who are descended from those now dead should enjoy the same unlooked-for power. The gospel is therefore, first of all, a deposit, something precious which is entrusted to us. God honours us by making us its keepers, and we ought to be aware of how much we owe him. For who are we, that God should place the most precious and worthy thing he has in our hands? The gospel radiates his glory; it is his kingly sceptre by which he governs his people, and yet he hands it over to us! Let us learn, then, not to cast so splendid a thing carelessly to the ground. Though the world may despise it we should appreciate its worth, as is right and proper. As for those who are responsible for preaching the gospel, let them take such deep root that they neither bend nor sway, even though the devil never ceases to throw up obstacles and difficulties to frustrate God's work. Let us instead fight as hard as we can to ensure not only that the gospel grows and flourishes today, but that after our death there should still be people everywhere who worship God and that doctrine should continue to be strong and healthy, so that men should find that what Isaiah says is true: 'God's truth endures forever and will never fail' (Isa. 40:8).

To understand this better, observe that, in referring to 'the things which you have heard from me', Paul distinguishes the gospel from false doctrine. As we saw before, the Antichrist works in secret, underground. Error thus abounded, so that great care was needed to discern God's pure and simple word. Now Paul had already rightly boasted that he was the messenger of Jesus Christ and the Holy Spirit's instrument. Whatever men heard from him was immune to doubt. Here, then, Paul indicates the mark by which we know sound doctrine without question. We ought to note this point, seeing how fickle people are. They lack discernment, accepting anything which is laid before them. So vile is their taste that they immediately accept spurious and false ideas with great enthusiasm. They are unstable, having a foolish and senseless craving for anything that is new. Thus Paul insists that we should be clear about what the faith teaches, and that we should be convinced of its infallible truth. It does not come to us from men, nor does it leave us free to wander at will. God is the true author of our faith, as he is its true defender. That is what Paul means here.

He does not of course supplant Jesus Christ as our teacher. As we noted, the only claim he makes is that he is a servant of Jesus Christ. This is what he assumes in the verse before us. He wants to ensure that Timothy remains strictly obedient to the gospel, as much as to say that we cannot be carried away with every wind of doctrine as long as we look to him whom God has made our teacher. May our faith, then, be properly grounded, as Paul says to Timothy. We are told that this was done *in the presence of many witnesses*. This was not said for Timothy's sake, for he was well aware that Paul had told him no lies. Likewise he was fully persuaded by the Holy Spirit that the teaching he had heard from Paul was from heaven and divine. Knowing this, Timothy needed no other witnesses. His conscience was testimony enough, and printed on his heart was the seal of God's Spirit. This was more than sufficient. Nevertheless Paul wished to silence the malice of those who might accuse Timothy of having made his message up out of his own head. The apostle affirms that there were most reliable witnesses who could confirm that Timothy had invented nothing strange or new, but was faithfully imparting what he had received from the lips of Paul himself.

These witnesses were specially chosen. There would have been no point in having men who appeared to be one-eyed and who, though witnessing a dozen murders, could not be made to utter a single word! It would be useless to look for the kind of witnesses we see today, devils who allow God's name to be blasphemed and torn to shreds, who see God and his gospel openly scorned and such evils as would make one weep. And far from resisting, they seek only to frustrate God if asked to say one word which might serve his cause.[11] No, here Paul is speaking about witnesses who, like Timothy, know their gospel. They were also expected to help him maintain sound teaching, however much it was attacked on every side.

We understand, then, Paul's motive when he says to Timothy: 'Entrust this teaching to faithful men, who can also hand it on to others.' By 'faithful men' he does not only mean those who believe the gospel, but those who strive to serve God reliably and with integrity, and who are not double-minded. In a word, he means men who are loyal and sincere. These he implicitly contrasts with the many who betray God and his word, and who camouflage the truth so that all is confused. 'There are many like this,' says Paul,

---

[11] From time to time Calvin alludes to lapses in Geneva's judicial system, where cases regarded as serious by the church court (Consistory) were thrown out in the civil courts because witnesses proved to be unreliable or corrupt. Magistrates, too, were frequently suspected of bias or collusion. See, for example, Sermon 3 on 1 Tim. 1:5 (*CO* 53: 38-39).

'but what we must do is choose honest men who will serve God, and who are zealous to preserve true doctrine so that it is not impaired in any way.' It is also said of them that they should teach others, so that the seed is further scattered.

Now when the work of preaching is done, it is not enough for us to think only of ourselves; we must labour to make God known throughout the world. To make this possible we must draw one another in, as the prophet Isaiah declares: 'Each will stretch out his hand to his neighbour, saying, "Let us go up to the mountain of the Lord, and he will teach us his ways"' (Isa. 2:3). Lest we be concerned only for ourselves, we should not choose people who cannot pass on what they have received to the ignorant and to those in need of teaching. If ever it was time to apply this lesson, it is now! For although men were once left stupid and steeped in deepest darkness, God has again kindled so bright a light that all is now revealed. Today we are illumined by the light of the gospel, and God shows himself intimately to us, as if face to face. The devil, however, knowing that if God's light continues to shine his kingdom is destroyed, contrives by one means or another to mask or cover up the truth. So we see these canting hypocrites who are in the pope's employ rise up in hellish opposition to sound doctrine. They know full well that they cannot win out, but in their arrogance they spew forth whatever they can to keep poor souls captive to superstition. We all know this. And when they cannot overturn God's truth they make it hateful or suspect, and dress it up in one way or another.

Is not Satan active in our very midst, so that if God's servants had not been sharp and zealous, whatever knowledge we now have would have been swept away? We know the abuse which is heaped upon God's word. It is true that it is men who are attacked, or who appear to be. Nevertheless it is God who is directly assailed, for men cannot bear to see the gospel preached as it ought to be, in all its purity. We have reached the point where the Holy Spirit is being muzzled, and when the various points of holy Scripture are being suppressed if they are not to the liking of those who claim more rights than God himself. All this we see. We see rascals who continually spit out venom and poison so as to make us hate God's teaching. Many are driven by ambition and stir up no end of trouble. How many are there who uphold the truth, and who want to see God honoured and his face so shine upon us that, as Paul says, we are transformed into his image (2 Cor. 3:18)? Those who walk in all sincerity are few and far between.

We must therefore try all the harder to safeguard this deposit, this marvellous and sacred treasure which God has entrusted to us. Let us resolve in all conscience never to bend or sway in every wind. Why is it that nowadays there are so few who persevere, so that as soon as trouble occurs they err and fall away? Is it not because they were never properly built up, and never had a whiff of the gospel, even in passing? Yes, they are veritable pillars; no one can match them, yet they cannot vouch for a single article of faith, less than a child can! These great zealots would have us believe that they can do marvels; they are certainly good at advertising their successes! When, however, we ask them about God, how we should pray to him, or about Jesus Christ, they look bemused. Little wonder, for they have misused the knowledge given to them. They are no more than drunkards, immoral men, dissolute in every way, full of treachery, envy and spite—depraved men who never cease to defy God, and not only in private. They would like to see an end to discipline and probity among men. With their stench they defile and pollute the whole of God's church. Wherever they go they take their filth with them, as is plain to see. We should have no dealings with such as these. So what else can we do but turn to faithful witnesses to help us defend sound doctrine?

Yet we should also recognize that we have reached the time foretold by the prophet Isaiah, when he declares that God bade him seal up his law among his disciples (Isa. 8:16). The prophet had indeed been sent to preach God's word to great and small without distinction, for all of Abraham's race had been chosen by virtue of the promise. What then? Isaiah sees that the majority are rebellious and so hardened that he merely makes them worse. They grow more and more blind and seem to conspire against God. Well might the prophet have lost heart. So our Lord commands him to seal up his law among his disciples. Today, I say, is the day of which Isaiah spoke. Do we not see the world plotting against God? Among the papists we see not only their stubbornness but also their fury. And among ourselves who profess the gospel, where is there godly fear? Where is that humility which makes us receive God's word quietly and with the meekness which James commands (James 1:21)? Many are as fierce as lions, and others behave less decently than swine! In short, we see wolves and foxes but so few sheep as to beggar belief. Wherever we look we see rack and ruin everywhere.

Now in sending us his word God meant to gather us together, but how few there are who cleave to him! So what else can we do but follow Isaiah's example? Whatever happens, and however much men court destruction and willingly submit to Satan's bonds, God will always have his disciples. There will always remain some sound seed, though not as much as might be wished. Nevertheless let that suffice. Let us seal up God's law and keep it as a secret letter which the world does not understand—the world together with the ignorant, the untaught and of course the worldly-wise. For our part, although God's law is as a sealed letter, let us not forget its contents. It is addressed to us, and especially let preachers of God's word say with the prophet Isaiah, 'Here am I, with the servants you have given me' (Isa. 8:18). For it is not enough that we acknowledge God's message to be true; we must offer ourselves as a sacrifice to him. Preachers must make an offering of themselves, since it was on those terms that they were called. Let them say, 'Here am I, Lord, with the servants you have given me.' To help us do this more readily, note that these words were not written for Isaiah's time alone, for the apostle in the letter to the Hebrews describes them as fulfilled in the time of our Lord Jesus Christ and under his rule (Heb. 2:13). Nowadays, although the trumpet sounds forth everywhere and rings loudly in our ears, there are few who give Jesus Christ a hearing. As we read elsewhere in Scripture, 'Who will believe our preaching, and to whom is the arm of the Lord revealed?' (Isa. 53:1; John 12:38). Jesus Christ is thus despised and rejected, and his teaching mocked. Even so he will always have those who are his and whom he sets apart for God his Father. Let us consent, then, to be included in that hiding-place which God has reserved for our salvation, and let us ignore the ill-will of those who choose to perish and who cannot abide the message of the Son of God. Let us instead follow those who show us the right way, knowing that although God's truth is everywhere assailed, so that chaos reigns and destruction seems assured, we need to summon up our spirits and to obey what we are taught here.

There are those, we know, who profess allegiance to the gospel but who have as little kindness in them as a wild beast. No one talks today of brotherly love, and this is true even among ourselves. Yes, things are worse among us than among the heathen and the Turks! We are a good deal worse, and those who now scorn the gospel display that same madness which the prophets themselves decried. We see these scoundrels, as I said before, who have sullied the sacred message of our salvation with their filth, who have laid false claim to God's name and who have brought shame upon the name of our Lord Jesus Christ, even among the papists. They must be truly mad, cast off by God as reprobates and possessed by the devil, as anyone can see. All that remains of their humanity is their face, their outward form, which nevertheless bears the mark of God's wrath and vengeance. Hence, following Paul's instruction, let those entrusted with God's word keep this treasure safe, and hand it on to those fit and equipped to impart it to others. And may we at the very least have courage enough to uphold the rule of our Lord Jesus Christ, even as these wretched madmen do their best to ruin and destroy it. This, then, is how we are to apply Paul's teaching.

Let me repeat a point I made before. It is essential that we remember God who, we may proudly boast, is the author of our faith. It does not come from men. Until we are firmly persuaded of this fact we will flutter aimlessly about; the slightest thing will lead us into error. Nowadays it only takes a few small mishaps to discourage half of those who once seemed likely to go on to the end. They do not have to wait for major shocks: the merest puff of wind will immediately carry them away! Why? Because they were never firmly grounded in God's truth. Let us therefore discern those who faithfully serve God. With Scripture as our touchstone we can judge the doctrine which is preached to us, and knowing that it comes from God we need never be shaken. Again, let us reflect that when God gives us a small number of people who side with us and who agree with us in the unity of faith, it is a great help to us. Admittedly, if we were all alone in the world and without human company, God would still be sovereign and would deserve our undivided loyalty. But since he so supports us that we are not left to wander on our own but have like-minded allies; since, too, the gospel is bearing fruit and prospering, and since those who profess the gospel show by their lives that they have not been taught in vain, when we have such fellowship among us it should strengthen our resolve and help us to follow God. When God thus provides us with sound witnesses, we ought to make the most of them. We should, however, look higher still, to the angels in heaven who bear witness to the teaching which we have received. They are in a sense our brothers and companions, so that when we praise and magnify Jesus Christ they are in full and perfect agreement with us.

Turning now to Paul's concluding verse, we note that this is said: *We must bear affliction patiently like good soldiers of Jesus Christ.* Only so can we finish our race. This is why Timothy is urged to be strong. If there were no conflict and no suffering it would cost us nothing to serve God. We would not need to be strong. But since we must suffer, and since God by this means tests our zeal and our wish to remain true to his word, Paul exhorts us to be soldiers of Jesus Christ. What he means is that God does not leave his people idle, and that we will not enjoy an angelic existence in this world, but that, being mixed in with those who scorn the gospel and who are God's deadly enemies, hypocrites and relentless devils, we must fight on. All the while, however, God comforts us by reminding us that Jesus Christ is our commander. So there are two essential points to bear in mind. First, that in order to serve God we must not count on leading a quiet life. We will be bruised and troubled. We will also need patience if we are to overcome, while practising no evil and bowing our backs to show our humility.

That is the first thing. The second is that since Jesus Christ is our commander and we are under him, we should not fear, however murderous the enemy's intent and however full they are of fury, malice and treachery. Let them do their worst: we will go boldly on. Why? Because we are protected by the hand of him who has promised that nothing which God his Father has given him will perish, but that he will keep it safe and will fully account for it at the last day (John 17:12). If we remember these two points, it will not be hard for us to bear patiently whatever trials God wills to send us. We will stand fast, even though we see such wickedness everywhere in the world, and even among ourselves, that the devil has the upper hand as if we had never heard a word of the gospel. When, therefore, we witness so much mischief that the fiends of hell seem to have been let loose and all is doomed to destruction—when we see such things we must be patient and bow our backs.

Nevertheless in heaven we have a strong defender, so that we can bravely defy those who raise their horns. They think that they have won and that they can already exult at God's expense. We, however, can be sure that victory is ours and that whatever happens we will remain victorious, since God is for us and his hand is strong enough to sustain us. And do we think that God will allow these blasphemies to go unpunished, when under cover of his name men cut the throats of Christians? Do we think that Jesus Christ is in heaven above but does not look as Judge on all that happens in this world, and does not exact vengeance when men falsely claim to defend God's honour and to maintain the gospel? Do we think, I say, that his eyes are covered or that he is blind, so that he does not see the abuse suffered by his own and the contempt in which his word is held? No, no! We must expect God so to work that our endurance will give us the victory as we each battle on, and will bring us to the goal to which God's Son has called us.

Because we are his, let us each dedicate ourselves to him and take heart. It is true that we are sorely tried when we see justice confined as it were in so small a space, and robbery committed in the streets and public squares so that no one dares set foot outside. It is as if a man were at home clutching only the deeds to his house, when thieves broke in to steal his goods and wealth. One might take his property, another his crops and a third the fruit of his vines. He in the meantime remains a prisoner, holding only his deeds in his hands. When there are so few signs of justice, when we see the devil in control and dogs and swine intent on ruining everything, these are grievous trials which might badly lead the weak astray.

Even so, as we are reminded here, we will not lack help as long as we wait patiently for God to put things right. In the meantime let us lead honest lives according to our calling, and if the whole world should rise against us and the devil and his minions contrive to ruin everything, these things are God's just vengeance on those who mock him and his word, and who dare to utter the foul excuse that they do all this for his honour. How can that be? They claim to be the gospel's standard-bearers, yet it is obviously the devil whom they serve. Little children know this to be so—why, the very pavement and walls proclaim the news! There is no one in the world who does not know these things. So when we see them, let us ask God to intervene. Especially let us bear Paul's words in mind. If we are true soldiers of Jesus Christ we must suffer until he puts forth his strong arm and overcomes our enemies. For just as he is called Shepherd of the sheep and has a staff by which he gently leads us and gathers us to himself (Psa. 23:1-4), so, on the other hand, he has a rod of iron, as we read in the second Psalm, to crack and break the heads of all who rebel against him (Psa. 2:9)—and not only the small fry, but kings and rulers, as is said in Psalm 110 (Psa. 110:5). Let us, I say, pray to him, that we may see this come to pass, providing we wait patiently and honour him by entrusting ourselves entirely to his protection.

Now let us cast ourselves down before the face of our good God, acknowledging our faults and asking him so to make us feel them that we may strive to rid ourselves of all the defilements of our flesh, and to give ourselves in full submission to him. May he rule and govern us by his holy commandments, and as we have his truth in written form, may he dispose our hearts to obey it. May he sustain us in all our weaknesses until he clothes us with his perfect righteousness.

# 9

## PRESENT TOIL, FUTURE FRUIT

*No one who fights becomes entangled in the business of this life, so that he may please the one who chose him for the fight. ⁵ And if anyone contends, he is not crowned unless he has contended lawfully. ⁶ The farmer must first labour before he enjoys his fruits. ⁷ Consider what I am saying, and may the Lord grant you understanding in everything.*

(2 Timothy 2:4-7)

We saw this morning why Paul urges Timothy to play the part of a good soldier. It is because God chooses to try us through suffering, which is a fitting test of our desire to obey him in every way and to renounce our own will. We saw also why he directly refers to our Lord Jesus Christ: it is to show us on what terms we are to do battle. It is not by doing wrong, as those do who have the devil as their commander and whose only intention is to injure. We are to possess our souls in patience and to overcome evil with good. Since, moreover, we are under the banner of Jesus Christ, we cannot doubt that in all our struggles the outcome will be good and successful. Though the wicked may exult they will nevertheless be vanquished. We ourselves may be confident, for we can only land on our feet, as the saying goes, since Jesus Christ is one with us, and will never allow us to be oppressed.

However, because this is hard for the flesh to bear, Paul makes use of a metaphor. *A soldier*, he says, *does not become entangled in the business of this life*. He leaves his home and forgets all that he holds dear, in order to do his duty to his commander. If, then, we honour mere men in this way, what do we owe to the Son of God when he graciously takes us into his employ and desires us to serve him? He might easily do without us and is under no necessity to choose us. He does so for our salvation. Is it not shameful, therefore, if wretched soldiers who fight without knowing why, nevertheless honour ordinary human beings by forgetting their interests and their affairs, while we are so soft that we cannot endure anything for the honour of God's Son?

That is the point of Paul's metaphor. There is no need to dwell on what is said about the affairs of this life. We know that in time of war we cease to go about our usual occupations, and all who are fit and active leave life at home behind them. If they are farmers they must abandon their fields and property; if they are traders they must put their merchandise aside. Why? In order, as Paul says, to please the one who has chosen them. Accordingly, let us learn to give ourselves completely to the Son of God and make sure that nothing deters us from serving him.

Now consider how Paul's metaphor relates to his purpose. We know that our Lord Jesus Christ deals with us in such a way that we are normally left free to go about our business. So how much less excuse do we have if we cannot serve him on such lenient terms! Nevertheless we must be ready to abandon everything and to move on for, as Scripture says, he who loves his wife, father or children more than Jesus Christ is not worthy to be his disciple (Matt. 10:37; Luke 14:26). We must make up our minds that, if God chooses, we should not spare ourselves but be prepared to be stripped of our possessions. Nothing, in short, should prevent us from moving once our Lord Jesus Christ summons us. We must follow his call.

But supposing our Lord Jesus Christ deals with us so that he respects our weakness and allows us to keep what we presently have, how can we account for Paul's statement that we must not be entangled in the affairs of this world if we are to serve God's Son? The answer is that we must, first and foremost, consider what it is to which we are called and where our duty lies. We should set aside every prejudice and the objections which we usually raise. For as soon as our attention is drawn to a text of Scripture, we get to thinking, 'If I do this, I'll be putting myself at risk.' If we are to do as we should, we must turn our backs on all that would stop us obeying, calmly and quietly, what our Lord commands. Then too, we should reflect on those things which get in our way and which inhibit us, all of which we must put aside. When God's Son bids us defend the honour of his kingdom, the world presents us with a host of things which would make us do the opposite. We might be less strong as a result, yet we must surmount all obstacles and pass beyond them. That is Paul's meaning.

It should thus be easy to see how Paul's teaching may be applied. First, let us consider the grace which our Lord Jesus shows us in choosing us to fight under him. Who, after all, are we? Nevertheless he is pleased to use us. Since, then, he does us the honour of choosing us, we are no longer free; we must no longer hum and haw, but resolve to get on with our lives according as he has chosen us. How do we do that? We see poor worldly souls who toil hard in the service of mortal men, not knowing what their reward might be, since all the time their hopes are disappointed. It is the prospect of being paid which drives them on and makes them abandon home and family, as we said. We should at least be equally zealous in serving the Son of God.

Next, Paul makes this point: *If someone contends, he is not crowned until he has contended lawfully.* The word he uses means a duty rightly done. Here we appear to have another metaphor. In times past there was wrestling, jousting and similar sports which Paul mentions in the ninth chapter of First Corinthians (1 Cor. 9:24-25). Here anyone who had begun was not given the crown until he had well and truly finished. As in a half-mile race, the course had to be completed, otherwise the runner who had begun would have been disgraced and mocked if he had turned back when only half-way through. The same was true of wrestlers. So here Paul is saying that if someone sets out to gain the prize, it is not enough to put on a burst of speed or to raise his shield when he is being watched. If he turns tail and runs away people will laugh at his timidity. It would be better if he had never entered the race or drawn attention to himself. We, then, must finish the fight. Paul's theme is perseverance.

There are two things to be remembered here. First, since God's Son calls us to be his soldiers, we must at the very least honour him as much as earthly soldiers honour their commanders. We must be free of every hindrance, and not entangled in things which might hold us back. We must press boldly on, determined to do our duty, for we are no longer free. We must especially ponder the truth that our lot in life is to fight, since we are called to be part of the flock of Jesus Christ. Second, we war not against flesh and blood but against the powers of the air, as Paul writes elsewhere (Eph. 6:12), against the desires of the flesh and the temptations of the world. We must be armed in order to do this. And because we must suffer much affliction, let us be ready to endure, knowing that the outcome is sure and certain. We do not fight aimlessly, as Paul says in a text already quoted (1 Cor. 9:26). Nor are we like those who go through agonies in order to win a crown of leaves and who are often disappointed. Many, Paul reminds us, run in a race, but only one can win the prize, thus robbing the others of it (1 Cor. 9:24).

We, for our part, have a much happier lot. All of us, far from preventing our fellows from getting a prize and the promised crown, are able to help each other. The one who arrives first does not edge out the second; the second does not exclude the one who came third. We all receive the prize and crown. We do not run haphazardly, and ours is no mere crown of leaves which quickly withers and fades. Ours is not the petty glory which the world accords. Our Lord Jesus calls us to his glory and wills that we should reign with him. Would we not be utterly feckless, therefore, if our zeal did not at least equal that of earthly soldiers?

It is important that we speak of perseverance, for there are many who bustle about and cut quite a dash but who soon grow cold. It is not enough to have simply begun. What then? Think of the terms under which we were called. Jesus Christ does not count us as his for just a day; he expects us to continue the race as long as we live. We do not, it is true, have to toil as hard as those poor wretches who ran to win a prize, and who ended up battered and bruised. God, who knows what little strength we have, spares us. Even so we must run, not only for a day but for all the days of our life. So we should not lay down rules for our Master; we should not shuffle about and say: 'Look, I'll be happy to toil another day, but right now I'd like time off to rest.' We should not argue with God this way. Understand, then, that our Lord Jesus sets us to run a race, and that we are to keep going until we die. Anyone who does not contend according to the rules will not be crowned.

Jesus Christ is in charge of all our battles and has determined the order and arrangement that he wants. We must therefore submit to his will: there is no question of our retiring whenever we like. Let us arm ourselves, then, for perseverance, and when we feel aggrieved and downhearted let that thought be uppermost.

The Holy Spirit could rightly reproach us for our thanklessness if we failed to fight under Jesus Christ as vigorously as do those who compete for the offer of a prize. So if we esteem the Son of God less than athletes value worldly fame, are we not more than blind? This is why it is said that we must contend lawfully if we want to obtain the promised crown.

Another thing we must note is that those who in time past used to contend were so keen to excel that they went on a diet and gave themselves a hard time. They did not dare to eat—the wrestlers, I mean, who ate only biscuit, abstaining from all delicacies and refusing to eat and drink as they would have liked. Why? To gain a crown of leaves! Since, however, God allows us to enjoy the good things which he liberally bestows on us—provided nothing stops us from looking to him for aid—we should not regret being asked to follow our Lord Jesus Christ and to set aside whatever might get in our way. We must abstain from all that might weaken us and hinder our race. It is as I said earlier: we cannot decide in advance all that God's servants must forsake when called to fight under the banner of Jesus Christ. Why do I say that? Because today we might be free to enjoy something which tomorrow might not be permitted to us. We must thus consider what our circumstances require, as Paul points out in the seventh chapter of First Corinthians (1 Cor. 7:17). Although today God may allow us to rest and to eat and drink as we like, in the twinkling of an eye he might call us to suffer poverty, sickness or other trials and misadventures. Hence it is not possible to determine from one minute to the next what God's servants may be required to abandon. Let us always look to our calling, and whatever happens let nothing delay us when we hear Christ's summons. Let nothing stop us moving forward at his command.

To the metaphors he has already used, the apostle adds another: *A farmer must work hard before he receives the fruit of the earth.* Here we are told that our nature is so slow to do as God asks that he must prod us many times, and spur us on before we are led to do as we should. We ought, then, to be thoroughly displeased with ourselves, for is it not most pitiful that God, who ought to be able to win us by lifting a finger, cannot get us to budge, even though he calls us to come to him and shows his love for us? It does no good: we remain hardened. In vain he urges us a second time: he cannot correct our sloth and lethargy. Thus when we see how often we have to be prodded, are we not right to be displeased with ourselves, since we are so wilfully slow? True, Paul is not here blaming Timothy or anyone else, but he makes it clear that by nature we are never motivated enough to come to God unless we are spurred on, and not just once, but over and over again. Now if Timothy needed to be roused in this way, what of us? We are a long way from being as zealous and as keen as he was. The apostle is not of course thinking only of him, but he was among those whom Paul was addressing.

What, then, are we to do? We must put laziness to flight and take good care that we remember what we are told here. The Holy Spirit was not indulging in useless repetition when he assembled these different metaphors. Here we have proof that if God were to sound the alarm once only, we would immediately grow cold unless he kept on doing it. So when the devil tries to blindfold us, to lull us to sleep or to hinder us by some means or other, we should take the remedies which are offered to us. That is the first thing to notice.

Now in saying that the farmer must first toil before he gathers the harvest from his field, Paul is making use of a homely image in order to rebuke us. He is pointing out that in earthly matters we do not need to be constantly goaded. Nature leads us in such a way that we gladly stir ourselves and do what has to be done. Do preachers have to go from door to door, saying to farmers: 'Now's the time to take your plough into the fields. You don't know what harvest you may get, but you have to sow the seed and wait until the crop is ready'? Do we need to press this point in the case of meadows, vineyards and so on? No! All this we know through experience. We are already aware that we must work hard. We do not mind, nor do we find it strange. Why? Because that is what this fleeting life is all about. If, on the other hand, we have to follow God who calls us to the life of heaven, we cannot bear it. The smallest effort seems to us so heavy a load that we faint! We can hardly lift a finger! Why is that? Is not our stupidity to blame, as is all too evident? What I have said about the farmer and his fields is true of every profession. When a merchant gathers his stock and goes off on business, he knows that he will have to face wind and rain, take many risks and expose his goods to a great deal of danger. No need, as we said, to lecture him! He shuts his eyes to all that might go wrong, otherwise he would starve to death. Do people puzzle about what they might do if there is no other way to earn a living? They make a decision and get on with it. That is the way they reason, which proves that when it comes to this perishable life our minds are made up.

We can only say that we have no conception of the heavenly life if we are tied to this world and to the things which are seen, forgetting that our inheritance is in heaven. If we were convinced of this we would be readier to do battle than we are. So Paul's purpose here is clear. Just as the farmer has to toil before he enjoys the harvest from his field, we too must toil. Why then should we complain if we do not yet see the fruit of our labour? Nevertheless every day there are moans and groans. We all complain if our Lord chooses to use us in his service and if he treats us more roughly than we would like. We get cross, as I said before: 'Is it always going to be like this? Must we put up with it forever? Will there always be hardships and vexations? Will we never have a moment's peace?'

Now think: this is the time for work. A farmer will never ask: 'Will it always be spring?' When spring comes, he knows that he must work; it is time to labour. Does he say: 'Well, the years come and go and I always have to start over again. I worked last year and now I must work harder than ever. I want to be done with it'? Men never speak this way. They know they would be wasting their breath. We would have to be out of our minds, therefore, to complain about God and not to wait patiently for harvest time when we can enjoy the fruit which is prepared for us.

Returning, however, to our metaphor, we note that the hopes of those who have laboured long and hard are often dashed. Frost may carry our vines away, and hail or storm may spoil our grain or other fruits of the earth. Yet farmers do not lose heart when they meet with misadventure: they go back to work. Why? They have to make a living! For our part, although we have unpleasant shocks we lose nothing, because all the afflictions and hardships we bear cannot make our state one bit worse. Our life is kept so safe for us in heaven that it is proof against storm, whirlwind, hail and everything else. So seeing that we do not toil aimlessly but are assured that we will have fruit, should we not have stouter hearts than those who till the ground?

It remains for us to consider the work which we have to do. For just as these good folk have to handle the plough and do all that their task requires, we must ask what it is that our Lord demands of us, otherwise we will toil in vain. Hence we see that those who practise their own forms of piety go to endless pains, yet they are no better for it. When a papist, afire with zeal, becomes badly entangled in superstition, what good does it do him? None at all, for God will spurn him. It is therefore important to know how we should toil. For example, if some ignorant person took it on himself to till the soil, he would spoil everything and impede another's work. Let us weigh up, then, the work God has for us.

We know what seed God would have us sow; we know what work he asks of us; we know everything in fact, providing we pay careful heed to what he teaches us. Thus, in order to do as Paul demands, we must be taught in the school of our Lord Jesus Christ. Recall the words of the prophet Jeremiah, that we must do as the farmer does and clear away the thorns, brambles and weeds in us (Jer. 4:3). How would it be if we sowed seed in soil that had not been ploughed? What would we gain by ploughing among trees where the earth had long remained unbroken and was full of brambles and thorns as thick as hedges? What would be the point of sowing seed in such a place? The ground must first be cleared and broken up. Accordingly Paul points us to something with which we are all familiar. We must not go thoughtlessly about our work but must obey the lesson which our Lord himself has taught us.

Remember also that when Paul speaks of serving our neighbours, he compares alms to seed, and tells us that if we sow sparingly we will reap sparingly, but that if we sow liberally, such abundant fruit is prepared for us that we need fear no loss (2 Cor. 9:6-10). Hence, as I said, we learn not to be careless in what we do, but to toil in such a way that God acknowledges our work and approves of it. This we do when we abide by the teaching which he has given us in his word. We must recognize at any rate that God intends to try us by putting us to work, for it is not yet time to rest. If our flesh protests and if we feel aggrieved and upset, we should realize that it is too early for us to relax. Why? Because this is what God wants, since our life is constrained as in a race, and he desires to test our obedience by finding hard and demanding things for us to do, things we would rather be spared. Here again is a lesson we must learn.

Paul sums it all up in his concluding verse: *Consider the things which I say, and may God give you understanding in everything.* In asking Timothy to heed what has been said to him, the apostle is not suggesting that his words are in any way obscure. The image of the farmer is familiar to even the coarsest and most ignorant of men, and the image of the wrestler or runner calls for no great knowledge. Paul also uses the metaphor of the fighter or soldier who leaves home to serve his commander—a common occurrence. Such everyday ideas can be mastered without any need for schooling! What Paul means is that we fail to profit from the most ordinary things in the world if we do not let them guide us directly to God's kingdom. Where worldly advantage is concerned we are only too canny and sharp-witted. We do not need to be told something twice. When, however, it is a matter of coming to God's kingdom, we are so baffled that we understand nothing: it is entirely beyond our reach. This is why Paul appeals to Timothy to consider these things. It is as if he said: 'Take care. I am telling you something you should surely know, so that you have no excuse.'

As we have seen, Paul had others beside Timothy in mind, yet Timothy is included, to show that if Paul had to tweak his ear, we need to be prodded even more. Otherwise nothing we are told will move us. It will disappear from view before we even think about it. God's Spirit thus shows us just how ignorant we are. We are so mindless where God's spiritual kingdom is concerned that even when he stretches out his hand as if to little children and leads us one step at a time, we are incapable of moving. That is why our Lord Jesus Christ said: 'If you do not understand the earthly things I tell you, how will you understand the heavenly?' (John 3:12). He spoke of things according to the capacity of those who heard him, and perceiving that Nicodemus, who thought he was a great teacher, understood nothing, he reproaches him for knowing less than little children. 'So if,' he says, 'I speak of loftier and deeper things, how will you understand?'

It is the same with this passage. We should not think that we are clever enough to grasp immediately what is necessary for salvation. Although God chews up our food for us so that all we need do is swallow it, we are so dim-witted that we cannot comprehend his teaching. Nevertheless Paul accompanies his command with a prayer, that God may grant Timothy understanding in all things. He might have said that his words were clear enough for anyone, even children, to grasp. The truth is that we do not feel drawn to God when we are asked to serve him. When urged to seek the heavenly life we are so drowsy that nothing can enter our head. God must therefore give us understanding.

Time does not, however, permit a lengthier discussion. The most useful thing to say, then, is this: God has taught us what we are to do, but we cannot do as he commands unless he leads us by his Holy Spirit. Thus when he urges us to distinguish good from evil, we are as ignorant as the blind until he enlightens us and impresses on us the truth proclaimed by human lips. This is most necessary, for if we come to church foolishly trusting in our own unaided efforts and believing that we can understand what we hear, our Lord will mock our pride and send us home more ignorant than when we came. Our minds cannot grasp the things of God's spiritual kingdom unless we allow him to guide us and to give us what we lack. Nevertheless, although we are so dull that we cannot see the ground beneath our feet, we must not lose heart, since our Lord will give us understanding in everything. As he sets his word before us he will open our eyes and ears, so that he will not only give us understanding but will train our hearts to follow him wherever he calls us.

On the one hand, then, we must be humble and lowly, knowing that we can only understand when we are illumined by God's Spirit. Yet we must also resolve to have God as our teacher, so that as we attend earnestly to his word and allow him to make us his pupils, we cannot doubt that by his light we will grasp the heavenly mysteries which would otherwise be beyond us.

Now let us cast ourselves down before the face of our good God, acknowledging our faults and begging him to put them behind him, and to blot out all remembrance of them by the blood of Jesus Christ, his Son our Lord. May he be propitious to us, and henceforth remake us so that, free from all worldly hindrances, we may cling wholly to him and follow the path he sets before us. May we never grow weary, but may we continue to the end in expectation of the heavenly life, knowing that the hope and trust which we have placed in him will not be disappointed.

# 10

---

# RISEN IN GLORY

*Remember that Jesus Christ, who is of the seed of David, has risen from the dead according to my gospel, ⁹ for which I suffer affliction, even unto bonds, as an evildoer; but the word of God is not bound.*

(2 Timothy 2:8-9)

As we saw before, the devil could not inflict a more deadly wound on men than to corrupt the purity of the gospel, for it is there that we find life. Just as man, when deprived of his soul, has neither understanding nor strength, so it is with us. From God's point of view we perish when deprived of his word, because it is his word which gives us life. That is why from time immemorial the devil has contrived to corrupt purity of doctrine. When unable to destroy it completely, he has mixed in other things, perverting it so as to make it unrecognizable. He would like if it were possible to blot out from the earth the name of Jesus Christ so that nothing more was heard of him. When, however, he perceives that God will not allow his Son's rule to be entirely overthrown, what does he do? He tries to do it by craft and cunning, distorting the simple truth so that a phantom is put in place of Jesus Christ.

This is what has happened in popery. The papists indeed confess, as we do, that the Son of God came into our world to be our Redeemer, and that having been baptized in his name we owe him reverence. Even so, they know nothing of his power, and everything they believe is so twisted that there is not one article of faith which they have not obscured in such a way that no one can tell what proceeds from God. If we ask on what grounds we may base the assurance of salvation, see what the devil has achieved! Nothing has been left intact, because instead of knowing that Jesus Christ is our full and perfect righteousness, these poor souls are obsessed by their own merits. And when they feel guilty in God's sight, they plead their works of satisfaction, or anything else which denies the efficacy of the death and passion of our Lord Jesus Christ. What do they do when they set out to worship God? Everyone has his own particular devotions. Then too, they make laws to suit themselves, so that God is only half listened to, or is scarcely heard at all. When it comes to prayer, theirs are defiled. On the one hand holy Scripture describes prayer as our principal act of worship; it is the sacrifice by which we show that God is our refuge, and that we have access to him because Jesus Christ is our Advocate and Defender. The papists on the other hand have recourse to the saints. As for the sacraments, such confusion reigns that they make them into idols. Instead of mirrors reflecting the grace we have in Jesus Christ, they are credited with miraculous powers which make it impossible for Jesus Christ to be known.

Such is Satan's craft. We should therefore arm ourselves with the warning which Paul gives to Timothy and to all Christians generally. Let us carefully guard God's truth as we find it in the gospel and not allow ourselves to swerve from it in any way at all. It should be so imprinted on our heart and memory that when the devil has done his worst, our faith should remain firm and constant, since we know that God is one and that he has revealed himself to us. Let us remain true to his word, understanding who Jesus Christ is, what he means to us and the blessings he has brought. We must be fixed and grounded in him alone. In a word, we should know that through faith and repentance we may call upon God. So when that is the case we need not fear, however troubled and dark things may be. God's truth will give us light so that we continue to follow the right path.

Paul therefore says to Timothy: *Remember what my gospel is about*. Now what is the substance of the gospel? That we should look to our Lord Jesus Christ, in whom we know are hidden all the treasures of wisdom (Col. 2:3); and that to be truly blameless we must cleave to him alone. Once we come to know him we may rest assured that we are beyond reproach. So let us continue to cling to Jesus Christ, despite those who are not content with him, who love their own ideas and anything else man-made. Let them talk as wildly as they like, but let us hear only God and be taught by him, since he points us to Jesus Christ in whom lies every part of our salvation. If we have him we need wish for nothing more.

That is the first thing to be said about this verse. Christians are not to be so fickle or unsure that what they believe today they will change tomorrow. They must persevere to the end in the simple truth of God. We must be true to Jesus Christ or else our faith will be uncertain. And since, as experience shows, the devil does his best to turn us from the truth, let us be armed against him. Let not the knowledge which we have received grow rusty or fade away, but let us engrave its memory on our hearts so that we can withstand all attacks and calamities. Let us press on to wherever our Lord calls us, and stand fast however much the devil assails our faith. We must not fear, for our Lord Jesus Christ will strengthen us in every way.

Note that our text gives him this title: *he is of the seed of David*. The reason for the title is also given, and rightly so. If we want to have victory over all of Satan's temptations, we must be strong and steadfast, knowing that our trust in Jesus Christ is not founded on a whim or on dubious belief, but that he is the one who has come to be our Redeemer. That is why Paul insists that he is of David's seed and line. Remember the promises contained in holy Scripture, that the whole world would be blessed in Abraham's seed (Gen. 12:3; 22:18). God confirmed this promise to David, declaring that the Redeemer would come from the line of Judah and above all from the house of David (2 Sam. 7:12-13, 16). Paul ascribes this title first and foremost to him, so that, having the promise of a Redeemer given earlier to the patriarchs, we should never doubt, but should receive him with full assurance, without wondering whether this is truly he. How can we be certain? Because he is of David's house. And even though the majesty of kingship had ceased to exist, its absence could in no way diminish the glory of Jesus Christ. Rather, this was meant to confirm that he was the one sent. Isaiah the prophet did not say that he would be born in a palace and brought up in the lap of luxury. He foretold that there would come from the stem of Jesse a small shoot (Isa. 11:1), meaning that although from royal stock, Jesus Christ would nevertheless have parents who were poor and who had no standing in the world, people without honour or esteem. It was as if there were a dry or fallen tree, with only a stump or stalk showing, easily trodden underfoot. Nevertheless from there, Isaiah says, a small shoot would come from beneath the earth. Thus Jesus Christ was born just as the prophet testified. When we see that this was how he appeared among men, our faith is greatly strengthened. We can place all our trust in him. That is one point.

At the same time Paul affirms that the Son of God took our nature on himself, and having clothed himself with our frail flesh he rose again in glory, giving us fresh confidence and boldness not to falter when we suffer abuse, persecution or insults of every kind. In short, although God's church might seem to be almost destroyed, we should look upward to behold the glory of the exalted Son of God, knowing that we are partakers of his blessings and that he is one with us. Nor should we forget that he stooped low to accept our poor and wretched lot. Being made a mortal man he suffered and became as nothing, enduring even the shame of the cross. Since, therefore, our Lord Jesus Christ exercised the powers not only of his divine majesty but of the frail human nature which, as servant, he took from us, we may be sure that he will receive us, and that the contempt we presently endure will not stop us running our race, buoyed by the hope we have in him. Let us, in short, remember the words of the prophet Isaiah, that he was lifted out of our sorrow and reproach and was set as it were upon a triumphal chariot (Isa. 53:8, 10). God the Father had chosen to exalt him, rescuing him from such extreme calamity that he seemed as one who was disgraced, a man marred, no longer human, despised and rejected by all (Isa. 53:2-3, 8-10). It is similarly said in Psalm 22 that he suffered the reproach not only of the great but of the common people too (Psa. 22:6-7).

We see, then, that this passage has something else to teach us, namely that if God's church is scorned in this world and seems doomed to perish, we must not allow ourselves to be discouraged. We must turn to the resurrection of our Lord Jesus Christ, knowing that when the head of this body which suffers here on earth was raised in glory, it was to strengthen us so that we might withstand every tribulation. Let us, moreover, hold to these two things. First, that the Son of God took all our infirmities upon himself and willingly bore them, taking what was ours but giving us what, as God's Son, was uniquely his. With this thought we may resist all of Satan's assaults. Second, that we must acknowledge him to be beyond any doubt the promised Redeemer who fulfils all that is needful for our salvation. Let us not savour these things coldly so that they worry or bemuse us. Let us heartily believe them, for God is faithful, having done all that he promised the fathers of old in sending his only Son to be men's Saviour.

If ever this doctrine was necessary for believers, it is especially so today. For although what the Psalm says has always been true, that God's church is like a ploughed field and that the plough is drawn across our backs (Psa. 129:3), the persecutions which we see today are awful beyond belief. We see all the mighty of this world conspiring to wreck the gospel. We see their fury and their cruelty toward God's children. We see the arrogance of the faithless and of all those so-called Christians who will not do homage to the Son of God. They are sworn enemies of all that is good and they pervert the gospel in order to suit themselves. All these things we see. Even in those places where the sword is not unsheathed or fires lit, it is only too plain that men are intent on corrupting the gospel, on pushing against it and on bringing all to ruin. What else, then, can we do, but heed what Paul says here and take comfort in the fact that, despite all his foes, the Son of God is established as God's agent who must rule the world and have dominion over it? Let men then rage as much as they please, he will display his power despite all who stand against him. Unless we allow this truth to strengthen us, what else will we be but desperate and defeated? When, however, we look to the resurrection of our Lord Jesus Christ, we will be brave enough to defy all that the devil strives to do. Our troubles may be so severe that heaven and earth may seem confounded, yet we will stand our ground as long as we fix our eyes on what Paul tells us in this text, as long, that is, as we behold our Lord Jesus Christ in all his majesty.

In addition, let us allow the bond of faith to unite us with Jesus Christ. Unless we know that we are members of his body, and that what he has is not for himself alone but for us to share in, we may indeed worship him but will be separated and distant from him; we will be worried and perplexed and able only to lament our wretchedness. If we thought that our Lord Jesus Christ knew nothing of the shame and persecution which the faithful suffer, while forcing them to undergo them, this would make us all the worse. We would lose heart if we forgot Paul's words that Jesus Christ was of human seed and was made like us. He did not honour angels by taking their nature, as the apostle writes in the letter to the Hebrews (Heb. 2:16); he took our nature in order to have the closest affinity with us, to be our brother and our companion as it were. He took our weaknesses and did not scorn the bondage which was ours.

Since the Son of God has made himself our partner, let us boldly gaze upon his glory, having the assurance that we too will attain it. He did not ascend to heaven to leave us to rot feebly upon earth. He rose instead to open the door to us, and having entered in for our sake he will gather us to himself. This is what we must bear in mind whenever men despise us, spit in our face or curse us. For so arrogant are the papists that they think we are not worth feeding to the dogs, as they say. Let us dismiss this nonsense, so that when we think of God's Son who so humbled himself as to endure such reproaches, we may take heart and follow the path he has shown us, being conformed to his image, as we read in the eighth chapter of Romans (Rom. 8:29). Let us remember, then, the bondage borne by our Lord Jesus Christ, and his assurance that, having entered into glory, he has nothing which he calls his own, but only what he shares with us.

When he is said to be of the seed of David, we should also recall the promises given to us in holy Scripture. It is not enough to call him the world's Redeemer, for that is a title which the papists also carelessly ascribe to him. We must also know his power, and what it is that Scripture says he brought us. The title 'he who was of David's seed' is meant to convey all the riches that are his. We are not to make him into an idol or something equally empty. We must know that all that was necessary for our salvation was given and committed to him, so that we might all receive of his fullness, and grace upon grace, as is said in the first chapter of John (John 1:16). This is how we are to understand this passage and to profit from it, as the Holy Spirit intended.

Note also Paul's phrase, *according to my gospel*. This is to emphasize the point made earlier, that Timothy and all believers should stick to the pure and simple word which they heard from him— even in the detail of its language, as a portrait made from life. That was the image which Paul used to show that once we swerve, however little, from the simple gospel, the devil will put obstacles in our way, leading us astray and concealing our goal from us. So Paul speaks of 'my gospel', as much as to say: 'My friends, those who have been faithfully instructed in God's word should make sure they do not turn from it in any way at all, or change or falter. They must hold always to the pure doctrine on which faith rests, and must keep on growing.' We too are well advised to heed this exhortation, so that we learn to distinguish one kind of teaching from another. There is little point in saying, 'This is what I was taught, and my fathers and forefathers were taught the same. Most people think this way.' True, the ignorant use this argument as a shield, but it is no better than straw. A spark is all it takes to consume the lot! Our faith must be made of sterner stuff. We must know that it is based on God's authority, and that those who teach have themselves been taught by God.

Paul's intention was never to invent a body of doctrine which he himself devised. Being an apostle entrusted with the task of preaching, he saw many who thrust their way in but who proved to be false teachers, and who so disguised the truth that Jesus Christ ceased to be known as he should have been. The apostle therefore, to avoid the malicious accusation that men might unwisely and thoughtlessly commit themselves to anything, urges us to consider him in whom we trust, to submit to God's rule and to make Jesus Christ our teacher and instructor, since that is his office. We must thus be sure that those by whom we are brought to faith have been taught from heaven, that God has given them this task and that they have his authority. Without that we have opinion instead of faith, and we are likely to be swept away at any moment. For a time we were stubborn and unyielding, like the papists who are content to mouth the word 'faith' but who are full of doubt and indecision, and who know nothing except what men tell them. For our part, let us learn to take our stand on God's pure truth, and may we boast that the faith proclaimed to us is not from men but is indeed the word of God.

This is Paul's message. Today we must lay hold of it, since there are many meddlers who are bent on making mischief. What then should we do? We should be discerning so that we recognize the simple, straightforward gospel. The papists loudly protest that they are perfect Christians, yet they do their best to deny the power of our Lord Jesus Christ. Let them play their silly games and wear whatever disguises they like; let the devil teach them every piece of craft and cunning in order to dazzle our minds—we must nevertheless hold to the gospel. Even among us there will be mischief-makers, men who, worse than Turks or pagans, want to root out all religion from the world—accursed villains who would love to remove all traces of the gospel. We will also see firebrands whom Satan raises up on every side. When these combine to attack our faith, let it not be overthrown, but let it rather be proof that God's truth has power to sustain us against all of Satan's assaults. This is how we are to interpret Paul's reference to the gospel which he preached.

Accordingly he insists on the need for believers in those days to be well armed. He himself was a prisoner, during which time the wicked seized the opportunity to abuse and malign his teaching. Can we imagine his situation? He is in prison, where he lies languishing as he has done for many a day, having first been detained in Judaea for months on end, before being taken, still in fetters, to Rome. The wicked were therefore free to open their mouths and to denigrate both him and the message he preached. As a result weak Christians might have felt unsettled, and all would have been dismayed if they had not had this shield to withstand their many trials. Paul's imprisonment and bonds could not be allowed to bring his gospel into disrepute. He thus explains that he is not concerned: *I suffer in myself, even unto bonds; but the word of God is not bound.* For we learn that despite all opposition the word continued to advance, as God added to his church and as the life-giving seed was spread further and further afield. Paul tells his friends that they should not lose heart since God was at work, nor should they forget that he had been sent as a minister of Jesus Christ, even though he was now a prisoner and was reviled by the great and the powerful. He had faithfully done what God had asked of him, and the message of salvation which he had preached was food for the soul. It contained the hope, glory and blessedness of all who would reign in the kingdom of heaven.

How right the apostle was to urge Timothy and, through him, all the faithful, to remember Jesus Christ who had risen from the dead! For Christians in those days saw the shepherd who had led them to faith in Christ, oppressed, rejected and hated by the Jews, treated as an enemy by the heathen and despised as the lowest of the low among the prisoners. Paul, it is true, had some freedom, as Luke tells us in Acts (Acts 28:30), but he remained in fetters, which was a mark of disgrace, and was regarded as a criminal, no better than a thief or murderer. Given, then, that unhappy believers might find him a great embarrassment, Paul exhorts them to look to our Lord Jesus Christ and to the glory of his exaltation, which wipes away any shame we may suffer in this world. Elsewhere in Scripture he rightly boasts of his bonds (Eph. 6:20; Phil. 1:7); they are far dearer to him than every sceptre of every king on earth, dearer than the crowns and decorations of dukes, kings and princes. His bonds are the badge of office which Jesus Christ has conferred on him (Gal. 6:17). Admittedly he calls them brands or stigmas, as one might brand a criminal; but they are more precious before the angels in heaven than all the princely coats of arms, however splendidly embellished.

What may we learn from all of this? First, we learn that we must carefully distinguish the cause of the Christian martyrs from that of evildoers. We cannot tell the difference between the martyrs and thieves, robbers or murderers in terms of the shame, torture, imprisonment and so on that they endure. We know that Christians are sometimes made to die a more ignominious death than robbers. The punishment inflicted is thus the same, but the reason is very different. Thieves, like murderers and robbers, deserve their punishment; they rightly suffer disgrace, so that even if they were highly esteemed and exalted above the clouds they wear the mark of shame. Their very consciences condemn them, says Paul, who speaks of the iron which sears them to the bone and scorches even the heart. Hence the wicked and those who mock God and who give themselves to all iniquity may be as richly adorned and as grandly titled as anyone can be. It is only a disguise, however: they end up as objects of contempt, as men who are abhorrent to God and to his angels.

Conversely, when God's servants suffer, they endure contempt only outwardly, but this is a brand which the wicked will always bear. Their punishment means that they will always be hated, and their suffering will only ever earn them ignominy and blame. We must therefore learn to discern the cause, otherwise we will be like idiots and our blindness will be inexcusable. To close our eyes so that we do not see the light would be to erase the image which God has impressed on all who are his; it would dishonour him. In a word, it would make no distinction between Satan and Jesus Christ.

So when Paul likens himself to a criminal, he sets out to counter all the wrong ideas we might carry in our head. 'It's inconceivable,' we say, 'that God should let his people suffer this way and to descend to the very depths!' We should not be surprised. Why not? Because God continues to bear witness to his truth, Jesus Christ still defends his cause and we have a faithful protector in heaven. All who suffer for his sake will always know his help and favour whatever troubles they may face. That is why Peter says: 'My friends, let none of you suffer as a fornicator or adulterer, a thief, an evildoer or transgressor. Do not wrong your Master by bringing shame upon yourselves and by suffering for your misdeeds. Instead, let your boast be that you suffer as Christians' (1 Pet. 4:15-16).

What we see, then, is that the worldly and those who do not know what it is to serve God will hate and despise the gospel, and will seek to persecute God's servants in some form or another. We should learn not to take offence at this, as if it were something new. This is how it has been from the beginning! Let us continue our race, looking to the resurrection of our Lord Jesus Christ and knowing that those who today so cruelly persecute wretched believers and who behave more brutally than wild animals, must come before the judgment seat of the Son of God. Today they rise up furiously against him and against those who defend his teaching; but in the end he will sit in condemnation over them. They will have to answer for their godlessness and temerity, their tyranny, cruelty and stubbornness, since they refuse to obey the gospel and to humble themselves under his word.

Now to make practical use of this passage, let us bravely withstand the whole world, both great and small, whenever men stubbornly resolve to attack the Son of God. Let those who are but miserable worms, mere trash, dare to do battle with the one who holds all power in his hand. And let us not be greatly worried by the reproaches we have to suffer, since in the sight of God and his angels these are far more worthy than all the honours of this world.

Since time does not allow us to say more, we must put off the rest until after dinner. To sum up, Paul brings us to this point, that the bond of fellowship which we have with the Son of God affords us full and perfect comfort, both in what he suffered for us and in the glory of his resurrection. I say this because next Sunday we are to receive the Supper of our Lord Jesus Christ.[12] How fitting it is to know that he is united with the whole body of the church! If that were not so, what good would it do to believe that he was glorified and that dominion was given to him so that every knee should bow and even the devils should tremble before his majesty? What good would it do us if we did not know that he is entirely one with us? For not only did he become a mortal man like us, in order to be brother to all who yield to him in faith; he also feeds us with his substance, he is our head, and through the power of his Holy Spirit we draw our life from him.

To this he bears witness in his holy Supper, which is his pledge and guarantee to us. Whenever we come to this holy table, we ought to be strengthened by the knowledge that our Lord Jesus Christ is one with us and that we can never be parted from him. If he is rich, we need not fear our poverty; if he is strong, we need not fear our weakness; if he is God's righteousness, we need not fear our sins; if he is the wisdom of God, we may come boldly to him so that we can be made new. These are the things to remember

---

[12] The Lord's Supper was celebrated in Geneva four times yearly, at Easter, Pentecost, the first Sunday in September and the Sunday nearest Christmas. Ministers were required to give a week's advance notice of the sacrament. Sermon 10 was preached on 26 May 1555, the Sunday preceding Pentecost (Parker, *Calvin's Preaching*, p. 168).

when we come to this holy table which is set before us. Here, our Lord Jesus Christ testifies that he receives us to himself and desires to feed us on his very substance. We must only approach his table if we remember the things of which Paul speaks. We must first be instructed in the truth. It is not enough, however, to have been taught; his truth must also do its work in us. Though we may daily look into it, it is a lifetime's study.

There are many, alas, who are far from remembering that Jesus Christ is risen. They have never savoured the first principles of the faith but have remained ignorant. Some, to begin with, lent a willing ear and pretended to believe the gospel, but they turned away so that, compared with the papists, they are devils, while the papists are more like angels! God will surely be avenged on their thanklessness, because they made light of him and of the splendid treasure of the gospel which they have wickedly profaned. Yet, as we see, they still mix with God's children, to their own condemnation. Such things ought to make us weep. Not that we should give up trying to guard this holy sacrament from such vile pollution, and when we try to put things right we should pray that God will cleanse his church of such abominable scandals. As for ourselves, let none come to receive our Lord's Supper who does not see before him the Son of God who, for our sake, became as nothing, who endured unutterable abuse and descended to the depths of hell, and who from there was lifted up to glory, so that we too might be gathered in, as Paul goes on to say. When we see men who openly oppose his majesty, let us contemplate their imminent destruction. And however hard Satan fights against us, let us press on, confident of victory.

May we, in humility and fear, aim for such steadfastness of faith that we may rise to heaven above, beholding Jesus Christ who reigns supreme and to whom all creatures owe obedience. May we always set our sights on the heavenly life, so that, passing through this world as strangers, we find our rest only in the heavenly inheritance which is prepared for us, and where we await the crown of glory which the Son of God has won for us.

Now let us cast ourselves down before the face of our good God, acknowledging our faults and asking him graciously to cleanse us of them more and more, and to renew us in true repentance, that we may seek to give ourselves wholly to him. May he wipe away all the sins we have committed and make us acceptable to him, not for the sake of our worthiness but of his sheer mercy, and for the love he bears us in our Lord Jesus Christ.

# I I

---

# GOD EVER FAITHFUL

*For this reason I suffer all things for the sake of the elect, that they too
may obtain the salvation which is in Jesus Christ, with eternal glory.
[11] This is a sure saying, that if we die with him, we will also live with
him. [12] If we suffer, we will also reign with him; if we deny him, he also
will deny us. [13] If we are faithless, he remains faithful: he cannot deny
himself.* (2 Timothy 2:10-13)

Paul, having spoken of the afflictions which he suffered for the
gospel's sake, comforts himself and rejoices, because God's
word is not fettered as he is. It is enough that Jesus Christ is glorified, that the gospel is going forward, that the church is growing
and that many are being brought to the obedience of faith. It is
clear, then, that Paul sought nothing which would personally benefit him. He laboured only to ensure that Jesus Christ was served
and honoured everywhere, that God was known as Father and
Saviour, and that lost and miserable souls were brought back to the
way of salvation. This was his aim. Consequently, all whose task
it is to proclaim God's word are reminded of the care they should
have for the whole church. They must forget themselves where the

salvation of all is concerned. We are all reminded, too, that we need not lose heart if one of God's servants suffers affliction, nor should we think that God's word no longer prevails. Rather, we must not forget that God's word is not bound even though a man may be in prison. The fact is that God allows one or other of his people to suffer, but he nevertheless opens the door to his gospel in spite of his enemies.

Naturally the purpose of Satan and his servants is to stop God's word advancing, to obstruct it in every way and to see it trampled down. Yet God makes sure that his word remains invincible, that it flourishes when men attempt to suppress it, and that despite everything it goes from strength to strength. Thus Paul's imprisonment caused God's word to be preached with even greater authority, for as he says in the first chapter of Philippians, his imprisonment was vindicated both in the Emperor's palace and everywhere, for the name of Jesus Christ sounded forth among unbelievers where it had not been heard before (Phil. 1:12-14). Even when the wicked with their slanders sought to vilify Paul's teaching, their efforts caused many to open their ears and to inquire about what up until then was unknown to them and hidden from them. This is how God multiplied his church through the apostle's preaching; although Paul was in chains his message was freer to run its course. That is what this text tells us.

Paul, then, by his own example, shows all who are charged with preaching the gospel that they must aim above all to edify the church, while giving little thought to themselves. Nor should we become discouraged when we see some of God's servants suffering affliction, since our hope is that the gospel will progress and that God will overcome all the hindrances and difficulties which we so much dread. Unfortunately we are far from doing as we should. Many people make up reasons for hindering God's word. Quite unjustifiably they imagine one thing or another which, they believe, will limit the gospel's spread. Such obvious ingratitude shows just how far we are from the courage and constancy displayed by Paul, and which he urges on all the faithful. Let us leave the gospel free to run its course, and however much the wicked try to lessen its honour and authority, we should know that whatever God's ministers suffer serves as a fitting proof that the gospel should be all the more precious to us. So when we see someone who, having neither influence nor reputation, resists attacks without flinching, or when we see God's servants standing fast, unafraid of what is done to them, what better proof could there be that what God has affirmed is true? Let us learn, then, that for all their scheming the wicked cannot by their attacks stop God's word from advancing, or God from increasing the number of his people and causing his seed to prosper throughout the world.

Paul now adds this remark: *I suffer all things for the sake of the elect*. That is, he has no thought for himself, but is thinking of all of God's children. He does so, as he says, *that they also may obtain the salvation which is in Jesus Christ, with eternal glory*. Here Paul contrasts salvation with the afflictions he presently endures; glory is contrasted with the reproaches and humiliation he is suffering. In effect he is saying: 'I am well rewarded. I am content to know that, although I suffer affliction and see death close at hand, this serves to advance the salvation of God's children. This is more than sufficient for me. And if I am reviled and if unbelievers cast me out, God will make it work for the glory of all the faithful. So neither suffering nor shame can trouble me when God brings such good out of them that all his people profit.'

We might perhaps ask why he did not have God's glory in mind, since it is infinitely superior to man's salvation. There is an easy answer. The apostle is setting out to exhort and encourage God's children, so he speaks only of them and of what will advantage them. He might well have said: 'My friends, humanly speaking you may have been upset when you heard bad reports about me. You may have thought that I had done wrong and that God had abandoned me; that, if I was innocent, God would not have left me to rot in prison. You may have been outwardly alarmed by hearing lies like that. Know, then, that it is for your good that I am suffering. May you grow stronger, and may my imprisonment testify that as I freely and boldly proclaimed God's word to you, so now I do not spare my life. I am blind to my own predicament and I do not worry about being in prison. I do not mind, as long as it is for your benefit. So do not be thankless where God is concerned. He wishes to strengthen your trust in the teaching you have received. It was not preached to you thoughtlessly or in vain. And since you see me persevering even unto death, you will know that I have served God faithfully. Let this greatly fortify your faith.' So we see why Paul here speaks of the children of God rather than of the kingdom of our Lord Jesus Christ. His aim was to encourage believers with the knowledge that his suffering was for their good and their salvation.

The objection might perhaps be made that it was pointless for Paul to suffer for the sake of the elect. Does God need human help to save those he chose and adopted before the creation of the world? Does his immutable counsel require the aid of man or of any other creature? Why does Paul say that he is suffering for the sake of the elect? Of course it is God who brings his people to the heavenly inheritance prepared for them. Nevertheless he is pleased to give effect to men's efforts. Not that he needs to borrow anything from us; it is an honour which he does us out of his free goodness, for he chooses to make us instruments which work for him. Paul is not boasting that the salvation of God's children depends on his endurance or on the afflictions he has suffered. All he means is that God wills to lead his people by means of his word, and that to this end he uses the men whom he has chosen, making them instruments of the Holy Spirit's power. We must understand that God alone who began our salvation will also finish it, but that he freely employs the means he has ordained, not of necessity but of his good pleasure.

Let us acknowledge, then, how good God is to make such worthy use of us, so that our task is to see that his children are saved. This naturally applies to ministers of the gospel, but it extends to all believers, both great and small. Every one of us ought to work to the best of his ability for the salvation of his neighbours. Not that we can do anything by ourselves, as I said before, but God confers such honour and distinction on us that we, who by nature are lost and condemned, are allowed to be ministers of salvation to those who might otherwise perish. We should be encouraged when we see that to suffer for the gospel is a service acceptable to God and an honour we render him; but it is also a service which benefits the entire church, since it helps to confirm the salvation of believers. When we understand these things, should we not be better motivated to do the work committed to us, and to which God in his goodness has called us?

Accordingly Paul writes that he suffers *so that they too may obtain the salvation which is in Jesus Christ*. By saying 'they too', he teaches us that we are not to be concerned only for ourselves, but that we must endeavour to draw in as many as we can. So if God has honoured someone by placing him at the front, he should not disregard any he might win over; he should gather in as many as he can. We need not fear that there will be less for us to enjoy! In this world, if we come into an inheritance which has to be divided many times over, everyone gets only a little. But where the heavenly inheritance is concerned we can be sure that we will lose nothing and that we will not get less. If we gather many others in—an infinite number, even—they will be our glory and our joy. When God calls us to himself he does not work by portions, in the way that things either increase or diminish in this world. We will have so much that our salvation will be all the greater, and our glory too, when we win many for our God. It is important that we remember this.

Notice also that Paul does not suggest that salvation is something which he has obtained by his own efforts. This salvation, he says, is in Jesus Christ. That is, nothing which we do detracts in any way from the grace brought to us by the Son of God. Instead Paul seeks to give it greater lustre, so that we may better see its splendour and its power.

That said, Paul writes as follows: *This is a sure saying: if we die with Jesus Christ we will also live with him. If we suffer in this world, we will have the inheritance of his heavenly kingdom.* Here he shows us that we should not be troubled when we see how the devil stirs up persecutions in this world, how unbelievers rage and how wolves come in to scatter the whole flock. We should not let such trials defeat us, for we must die if we would live in Jesus Christ. If we want to enter his kingdom we must walk amid affliction and suffering, in order to be conformed to his image. However, because the idea seems strange at first glance and is hard for our minds to grasp, Paul prefaces this verse by saying: 'This is a sure and certain word.' This is the formula he uses whenever he wants to convince us of something really difficult, or which is so important that it needs to be pondered and remembered.

Now as I said, we cannot get it into our heads that we must die in order to live, and that the way we attain God's glory is through shame and reproach. These things are against nature, yet such is the church's condition. Paul therefore writes that this is a sure saying in order to help us do battle with our own understanding, and to accept God's decision by denying our own powers of reason. Thus we honour God by quietly submitting to his decree. Paul might therefore have said: 'My friends, if we listened to our own feelings we would think it impossible that, once dead, we might come back to life again, and that we should only reign with Jesus Christ if the world hates us, spits in our face and curses us. We might think all such things a fantasy. Nevertheless, putting all argument aside, let us not rely on mere opinion or appearance, since this is God's appointed order. Let us accept his judgment and be guided by him.' That is the significance of Paul's expression.

We return, however, to the statement that we must die with Jesus Christ before we can live with him. By 'death', the apostle does not mean our decease, when God takes us out of the world. He has in mind what he says in the fourth chapter of Second Corinthians and in the third chapter of Colossians. That is, we must bear in our flesh the death of Jesus Christ so that his life may be manifest in us (2 Cor. 4:11; Col. 3:3-4). In saying this Paul points to what he says in the second passage I have mentioned, that as long as we live in this world our life is hidden, just as in winter the life of a tree is hidden. It seems dry and without vigour; the wood appears dead, yet growth returns in the spring. It is the same with believers. In this world their life is wrapped up in hope, and what we hope for cannot be seen, as Paul declares in the eighth chapter of Romans (Rom. 8:24). It is invisible to the eye. Consequently in living we must die, but not in any mundane sense: we must die daily and the outward man must decay.

Illness, misery, disgrace and suchlike help us to forsake the world and to regard our life as a shadow, a mere nothing. We receive similar intimations of death whenever things do not go our way. We see, then, that Paul does not mean that we must die only once in order to live. As long as we live let us remain as it were buried, viewing death as ever present and ourselves as sheep who feel the knife at their throats, as we read in the eighth chapter of Romans (Rom. 8:36). For it is not enough to die in this way; we must follow the banner of the Son of God and look to his resurrection, which serves to soften the rigours of death. The wicked, on the other hand, can only see death as a constant menace which beckons every minute of the day. Although they seem perfectly at ease they suffer much, more than God's children do, for they have a worm within them which gnaws at their hearts and torments them. And although the world may leave them in peace, God's judgment will pursue them so that, already stung by remorse, they can never be at rest. What the prophet Isaiah says is fulfilled in them: 'Their sins are like waves which crash one upon the other' (Isa. 17:12). Admittedly they put their consciences to sleep as long as they can; but like it or not, God will awaken them.

That, then, is how the wicked suffer. They have neither part nor portion in Jesus Christ because they are under the curse pronounced on all who do evil. The tribulations and punishments they suffer are for them the gate to hell. They can expect no happy outcome, since all they have is sin which leads them to destruction. For our part, in suffering and dying we are made partners with Jesus Christ. Let us therefore resolve to cleave to our God and to give him our service, striving to live so that when men afflict or trouble us, it should not be for the wrongs which we have done them but for our service to God. So when the world is hostile to us because of our blamelessness, we are said to suffer with Jesus Christ. We fight under his banner and we want him to have the glory. When, without provocation, men persecute and harass us, they cannot claim, humanly speaking, to be seeking retribution. We are therefore taught that, if we would share in the life and rule of our Lord Jesus Christ, we must be made like him in our suffering, and must truly testify that our one desire has been to serve God.

Nevertheless it might be said that the faithful often suffer for their sins. Despite serving God they frequently do wrong and deserve to be punished. God himself applies the rod to them in order to humble them and call them to account. That is true, but

Paul is speaking here of the afflictions suffered by those whom God graciously allows to be persecuted for his name's sake and for their witness to his truth. If we are punished for our faults of course we must bow our heads, calmly accept the chastisement God sends and recognize that we are not worthy to suffer for his sake. Even so, we should take comfort from knowing that God is concerned for our salvation, since he will not let us stray like lost beasts but will bring us back to himself. So although we are punished for our sins we have reason to be comforted. When, however, men persecute us, let us consider why and on what grounds we are being made to suffer. Remember Peter's exhortation, that we should suffer as Christians in order to glorify God, and not as evildoers (1 Pet. 3:17). Although the world may blame and condemn us, and although we often seem to suffer worse disgrace than the wickedest men on earth, it is enough that God approves of us.

Moreover when he honours us by letting us suffer for his sake, we should reflect that he could justly punish us for our transgressions. Instead he spares us and permits us to suffer in a most worthy cause. The martyrs, for example, who suffered for their witness to God might well have been chastised for their offences, for there was never anyone so perfect whom God could not have removed from the face of the earth. Nevertheless he pretends not to see his people's trespasses, and he honours them by letting them suffer for him and his cause, as if they were acting in his defence. So we should learn to praise God when he does not allow us to suffer for our misdeeds, but for having upheld his cause and borne witness to his gospel. When Paul, then, speaks of dying with Jesus Christ in order to share his life, this is what he means.

In the same verse he writes that *if we deny him, he will deny us*. To gentle words of encouragement Paul thus adds a threat, for God has the habit of prodding us when too much leniency makes us lazy. When he cannot draw us immediately to himself he uses harsher means. Paul employs the same device, telling us: 'We are assured of life if we are conformed to Jesus Christ by passing through this world like men who face a hundred deaths. But if we forsake Jesus Christ he will deny us, as he himself has said: "Whoever confesses me before men, I will confess before my Father in heaven; but whoever denies me before men, I will deny before God and his angels" (Matt. 10:32-33).' We are thus reminded of this terrible saying of our Lord Jesus Christ. It ought to make the hairs of our head stand on end, if we are too timid to confess his name and to uphold his truth before men when it is attacked. We must not dissemble, as many do who imagine that they can still be Christians while betraying Jesus Christ. They take to disguising themselves and think that it is of no concern to God. Paul, on the other hand, shows that God expects us to serve him by defending his truth and that, if our life is threatened, we should not spare it. It ought not to be as precious to us as the truth which is the ground of our salvation and the instrument of God's rule.

Those, therefore, who look for pretexts in order to avoid the sufferings which God ordains for his people, are entirely without excuse. There are so many sensitive souls who want the right not to suffer for God's sake! That cannot be, says Paul, for we have a master who demands that we worship and confess him. Whoever is ashamed to uphold his name before men should know that his name will be struck out of the book of salvation. He must not think that Jesus Christ counts him as one of his.

The apostle concludes this passage by saying this: *If we are faithless, he remains faithful, for he cannot deny himself.* Thus, even if the whole world were to go astray, God's truth would remain untouched. We are not to think that it depends on us or relies on our testimony. This is a most useful message. It first challenges all those—there are many of them today—who are in two minds and who, to save their lives, would betray Jesus Christ and blaspheme his holy truth. Paul challenges them by saying: 'You think that God's Son cannot do without you. Off with you! Leave him, however many you are. He still remains King of heaven and earth.' In addition Paul had in mind the needs of those who were weak and troubled. When they saw someone who had stumbled or lost his way, they might think that all was lost. Today this exhortation is even more necessary to us than to those of Paul's day. Although there were many then who were weak, nowadays we are delicate beyond belief. A leaf has only to flutter for us to fear that the end of the world has come! What is worse, we so often feel this way that we actively look for reasons to worry. If we hear of a disaster which has overtaken someone, many of us with fiendish glee use it as an excuse to turn our backs on the gospel. As well, the devil cunningly contrives to worm his way in surreptitiously, by crooked means. At any rate, most people lose heart the moment someone forsakes the truth, or when a person who has been on the right path goes awry. 'What are we to make of this?' we ask. 'Is God's word shakier than we thought?' Think of this person, however, as a poor frail vessel which is easily broken. If he falls apart, are we to think that God's eternal truth has ceased to be? Must Jesus Christ be taken from the seat to which God his Father raised him? Must the salvation of men and of angels perish because of one man's weakness?

We therefore see why Paul should say that if we are untrue to God, he nevertheless remains faithful. Already he had said that if we deny Jesus Christ, he can manage without us. A clearer explanation, however, was required. Paul now provides it by pointing out that God borrows nothing from us as though he needed anything, but that his truth is enough for him. Even if the whole world rejected him he would be none the worse for that. 'God,' says Paul, 'remains faithful.' Consider what is said here, for Paul repeats the same idea in Romans, where he writes: 'What if some Jews were faithless? Is God therefore a liar?' 'God forbid,' he replies, 'for it is written that though every man be a liar, God is always true' (Rom. 3:3-4). Furthermore men's unbelief gives greater lustre to God's goodness, for although we break our pledged word he continues unchanged as before. Is it not clear, then, that his truth is mightier than our falsehoods and our sheer futility? We therefore see how well these sayings match. Whatever the world's disarray, our faith should never be overthrown. It must look to God who remains true to his nature and who is ever faithful, however much we change.

A moment ago I quoted the text where Paul declares that God called the Jews to be his flock, chosen and sanctified among all earth's nations. There the apostle shows that the Jews had become estranged from the hope of salvation, that God's worship had been marred and religion hopelessly confused. Nevertheless Jesus Christ appeared and God remained true, although the Jews in no way deserved the redemption promised to them. The Saviour of the world thus offered himself to the Jews who were like lost sheep, as Scripture says (Matt. 15:24), for such was their plight that no one understood the law, the promises or anything else. When Jesus Christ appeared among them, the Jews were so far from confessing their wretchedness and seeking the remedy always promised to them, that they provoked God's wrath and vengeance by rejecting the offer of salvation. They were not content to despise Jesus Christ but, having put him to a shameful death on the cross, they subjected his gospel to increasing persecution. The people whom God had chosen refused to believe. This was a dreadful stumbling-block to believers in those days.

Nevertheless Paul declares that God's faith, that is, his truth, could not be measured by their faithlessness and unbelief, since it remained whole and untouched. He also adds that by way of further confirmation God had reserved some seed from among this people who deliberately sought their own destruction. God, remembering that he had said that Jerusalem would be like Sodom and Gomorrah, apart from a small number who would be saved, preserved them as by a miracle. He thus fulfilled what he had foretold through Isaiah, that there would be a remnant whom he would gather to himself, and that from this seed would come an abundance which would spread over the world (Isa. 1:9; 11:11-12). When these things came to pass, was this not more certain proof which God provided of his truth? In vanquishing men's lies, in overcoming the Jews' unbelief and rebellion and in revealing the salvation he had promised, he showed that his promises did not depend on men but that he would accomplish them and bring them to fulfilment in a way mysterious to men.

Let us apply these things to our instruction. For today how many kinds of unbelief do we see? Some people stubbornly persist in their blindness—the papists, for example, who ruthlessly oppose the gospel and who are so driven by the devil that, though more than convinced by reasoned argument, they will not budge; like wild beasts they lash out and bite. Such is the faithlessness of those who claim to be Christians and who have even been baptized. There are also the Jews to whom the promises belong and who are in a sense the elder sons of God's family, yet they persist in their devilish obstinacy. Not content to close the door to themselves and to forgo the kingdom of God, they blaspheme the gospel in every way and deny all human feeling in their battle against God. The Turks too have been cut off, seeing that they follow Mohammed's false teaching, or rather his delusions, whose errors they might see if their minds were not so closed. What then? God reveals his vengeance by rejecting them because of their ingratitude. Like the papists they were false believers. As for ourselves, how many do we know who have turned from the path of the gospel, who choose to sit on the fence or to meet the enemy half-way for the sake of some hybrid gospel? Have we not recently seen, and do we not still see, that those who designed this vile Interim aim to mix up God and the devil?[13] Have they not gone badly wrong? Such are the different faces of unbelief.

Nevertheless, however much chaos may prevail and unbelief abound, God remains faithful. We must not judge God by human standards or perceptions. It would be dishonouring to God to claim that, as man is faithful, so too is God. To weigh his faithfulness by human measure would be to deny his truth. We are only vanity and lies, but God is true. Indeed he is truth itself. So let us take to heart what we are taught here and use it as the Holy Spirit intended. Though this world were turned on its head a hundred thousand times, we must remain staunch, grounded in God's truth which does not change to suit men's fickleness and whims. Why does God not change? Because he cannot deny himself. We may thus defy all who today forsake the truth and who seek to take many simple souls with them to destruction. Let us defy them, for though they are traitorous and disloyal they cannot diminish God in any way.

Here Paul is not thinking of God's essence. He is not saying: 'Let us hope that God above remains true to himself.' No, he means that we should be true to him. God's word is an imperishable seed. It must bear fruit, and when the devil tries to root it out and kill it he can do nothing against us, for we have the victory which overcomes the world. If the devil stirs up trouble against us, let us triumph over him. Thus God not only remains true to himself, but because he stamps his truth on our hearts by his Holy Spirit he also ensures that his word endures, so that we may press on despite the wicked who would bring us down with them.

Since God cannot deny himself, we can know him as he is. To do this we must hold fast to his word. If we tried to imagine God

<hr />

[13] See above, p. 81, note 10.

as we would like, we would always be dreaming up phantoms and idols. We must know God as he has revealed himself in his word. Do we know him this way? He cannot deny himself, and will never change his nature or his purpose. We should therefore be fully strengthened against all the trials in the world and against all the chances and changes which might occur, as long as we maintain our trust and belief that God can be known by the revelation he has given of himself. How do we know him? Through his law, his prophets and his gospel. Let men err and stray as they will, God will not fail to be true. He does not change. And when we fix our trust in him we can be victorious over all of Satan's attacks, and can steadfastly endure until we come to that eternal rest made ready for us in heaven.

Now let us cast ourselves down before the face of our good God, acknowledging our faults and begging him to give to each the grace to examine himself. And since our iniquity is so great, may we learn to take no pleasure in ourselves but to weep until we find our medicine in him. May he cleanse us by his Holy Spirit, not only of all the sins which have ruled us in the past but of the root of all evil, our unbelief and rebelliousness. May he therefore so instruct us in his word that we may willingly do as he commands, withstanding both the trials which beset us and the obstacles which the devil puts in our way. And whatever the turmoil in this world, may our trust be strong and steadfast, since God is faithful and unchanging, for all men's wickedness and unbelief.

# 12

---

# RIGHTLY HANDLING THE TRUTH

*Remind them of these things, and urge them before the Lord not to argue about words which do no good and which are harmful to those who hear. ¹⁵ See that you present yourself to God as one approved, a workman who is not ashamed but who rightly dispenses the word of truth.* (2 Timothy 2:14-15)

Earlier we saw that Paul urged Timothy to make especially sure that the church was built up. If we use the doctrine we preach for other ends, we profane it and distort the purpose which God meant it to serve. He does not want his word to beat vainly on our ears; it must serve the cause of our salvation. So if a preacher sets out merely to please, to show off or to pursue some pet idea which has nothing to do with the salvation of those who hear, he is guilty of sacrilege, because he is evilly using God's word for illegitimate ends. It is true that men have itching ears. We are all driven by curiosity, and are so fond of novelty that those whose task is to teach try to impress their audience and seek applause by concentrating on trivial questions which nevertheless appear profound. That is all they care about. To edify is the last thing on their mind.

Now Paul makes it clear to Timothy that those who want to be faithful teachers must always strive to confirm men in their trust in God and in godly living. And although such teaching may upset people who prefer a more speculative kind of preaching, ministers must not swerve from the right path; they must persevere. All of us, then, are urged gladly to accept what is useful for our salvation, for although Paul is speaking particularly to Timothy about the office of a good teacher, he nevertheless is trying to curb our foolish appetites. Thus when we come to church we should not want to hear an agreeable message which will tickle our ears and give us pleasure. We should want to grow in godliness and in humility, to be encouraged to pray to God and to become more patient. If we hear an appeal today which is repeated tomorrow, we should not be vexed or think it unnecessary. If we examine ourselves we will recognize that we have not learned the lesson so well that we can put it into practice. God therefore does us a great favour by refreshing our memory.

This is what Paul means when he says to Timothy, *Remind them of these things*. He most certainly anticipated the usual reaction of those who say, 'We've heard all this before. Doesn't everybody know it, even little children?' That is what we hear from people who want to be fed on trivialities. The Holy Spirit, however, wants us to be reminded, day by day, of all that is useful to us but which we have not fully understood. We need to put it into practice.

Now an idea which suddenly springs to mind does not amount to much. It must be firmly rooted in the heart and its fruit must be evident in our lives. Paul's next words are therefore most important: *Urge them as before the Lord*—as if you had them in a court of law and they were called to bear witness on oath—*that they avoid arguments about words*. Here we have a clearer explanation of the point I made before, that Paul is seeking to correct those who, out of self-interest, love to debate in order to win esteem and reputation for themselves. They are keen to sift through things about which nothing further needs to be said. Every syllable is like a straw over which they stumble, and they make a terrible fuss as if to confound heaven and earth. If they come across a statement which suits their purpose, they think they have triumphed, even though their hopes and efforts are mere smoke. In this way most people who have intelligence and learning set out not to serve God, but to distinguish themselves in the eyes of men. It is very hard to curb them. The apostle therefore writes that those who go in for pointless speculations should be summoned before God and solemnly warned that they are answerable for making God's word a matter of dispute and argument, contrary to its real purpose. By 'arguments about words' Paul means what we might call artificial or baseless quarrels. We must indeed toil hard and bravely where God's honour or the very basis of the faith is concerned. Would we not stand condemned if we allowed God's word to be obscured or falsified, or superstition and error to be taught? When it comes to his truth, God expects us to be valiant in his defence. We must not spare ourselves or act half-heartedly. In defending God's truth it is much better to turn the world upside down and to risk destroying it, than to dissemble and to let bad things happen. So as we see, when some are content, as we say, to sit on the fence or to take the middle ground, our Lord laughs them to scorn, and their foolish pride brings them only ignominy and shame.

What then must we do? We must sincerely do as God commands, so that if the devil tries to hinder our freedom by masking the purity of God's word and by spreading errors to deceive poor souls and to lead them to perdition, we must bravely take up arms and not hang back. Whatever men may say, let us press on, blind to all that may happen and confident that all will end well, provided we keep within our bounds and do all we can according to our station. This is worth noting, because sometimes God's good servants are seen to falter when they meet difficulties and much trouble. They fail when under pressure. We should thus be doubly conscious of what our duties are. Whatever our difficulties we should always stick to the pure and simple gospel and persevere in it. Again, when we see that God's truth is secure and that his people are truly being edified, if, in our foolish vanity we stir up needless disputes in order to win a reputation for cleverness or for learning, woe to us if we distort the message of salvation and look for men's applause! This is how arguments arise, for we are too much given to that infernal pride which itches to be respected and admired.

Let us be all the readier, then, to weigh Paul's words when we see braggarts who are keen to draw attention to themselves. If we cannot win them back by simple warning or reproach, we should summon them, as it were, to appear before God, to whom they are answerable for disturbing the church and for raising issues so trivial that they seem bent on blotting out the sun and covering it in darkness. So let us bring these people up before God and consign them to that day when they will be judged. Bear this in mind. Remember, too, that just as we should detest hotheads who stir up disputes in the church, we should also learn to be peaceable and to clamp down on idle speculation. Let us be sober, wishing only to be taught for the sake of our salvation, so that God is honoured among us and that we seek all the time to grow in his love and fear, humbly bearing his yoke and all that he cares to lay upon us. These are the things we should strive to do if we do not want to see the gospel and God's word profaned because of us, or pointless conflicts arise which, as Paul says, can only harm those who hear.

Observe also the two reasons which the apostle gives when he reproves useless quarrels and controversies. First, he says that *they do no one any good*, and second, that *they unsettle the hearers*. The first point, as we have seen, is that what God's word contains should benefit us for, as Paul goes on to say, all Scripture is useful (2 Tim. 3:16). Experience tells us that this is true, unless we ourselves are at fault! For why is it that we cannot read holy Scripture without wondering whether we have wasted our time or used it well? It is because we come to it carelessly. We do not come before God asking to receive what might really profit us. Now Scripture asserts that God will instruct the humble and the meek (Psa. 25:9). But quite apart from that we should know him to be a good and faithful teacher. Accordingly we should look to him for sound instruction which will be useful and of help to us. So if we thrust our nose into holy Scripture but handle it amiss, or if we search for what will satisfy our prejudices, we should not be surprised if we are fed on wind and if God leaves us no better off than before. If, however, we are truly minded to be taught for the sake of our salvation, we will most certainly find in Scripture nothing that is not good. We will draw from it nothing that does not assist our faith, that does not encourage us to fear God and to obey him, and that does not teach us to call upon him in prayer and to be more patient. Whether it be the books of history or the prophets, all will prove useful.

In denouncing, then, those things which benefit no one, Paul is implying that all who have no concern for the salvation of their hearers profane God's word. Yet we must also think about ourselves. If we are content to listen to what we are told but cannot work out how to apply the message we have heard, we sin against God. Let all of us, in short, strive with heart and mind to seek only what we know will strengthen us in faith, in godliness and in everything else.

As to Paul's second reason, the apostle stresses just how much harm is done by needless controversy. It upsets those who hear. Why? Because, as we well know, we are feeble: we need no outside force to unsettle us. Even without storm or tempest we stagger, and we falter still more when affliction comes. We are fickle by nature and always prone to tremble. Moreover Satan is sure to put many obstacles in our way. Even if there were no disputes or controversies we are exceedingly weak and unable to live as we should. We cannot trust God's truth so firmly that our hearts are calm and settled. So how will we fare when the bellows are used to fan the flames much more? Already we have within us a seed of faithlessness. Then here come the scoffers who want to use God's word for their own ambition and vainglory! They stir up controversies: 'What are we to make of this?' People become alarmed: 'I used to be convinced of this, but now I don't know where I am!' Or again we hear this said: 'If I've got this point wrong, what about the rest?' Satan has no easier or more effective way to undermine our faith than by embroiling us in silly and speculative disputes.

What are we to do? We are to keep to the simple gospel and to go no further. And having learned that our God has shown himself to be a Father and Saviour to us, we must see that the way to find grace in his sight is through our Lord Jesus Christ. We must further learn what his will is for us, how we may call upon him in confidence and how he draws us to himself. We are to dwell on his promises and to learn how the sacraments can serve us as an additional seal. We must further understand that all this comes from the unmerited goodness of our God and from his kindness in making us one with him. And all the time we hope in him, that he will lead us to the end. These are the things that we must ponder. Here we have so complete a statement that, providing we have learnt it well, we need not envy the wisdom of the cleverest people on earth. For here is the ultimate truth, that from the creation of the world—and earlier still, from all eternity—our salvation has been founded on God's goodness and his immutable counsel.

We know also that he has called us personally to himself. In the person of Jesus Christ he has been reconciled to us; in him we have remission for our sins and fullness of grace. As we said this morning, it is he who generously bestows on us the gifts of his Holy Spirit. We are further shown how to order our lives and how to offer ourselves to God by purging our earthly appetites, by looking to God as we pass through this world and by fixing our eyes on the immortal glory which he has promised us. Again, we learn how to approach God in prayer and how to use the sacraments profitably. What more could we ask? We might all like to climb high above the clouds. Though we break our necks a hundred thousand times we cannot advance an inch unless God guides us.

Let us therefore hold to the simplicity of the gospel if we do not want to be accused of bringing destruction on ourselves. Since God's Spirit has given us due warning there is no excuse for us if we do the opposite. If we took this more to heart we would handle God's word more reverently than we do. As it is we see how reckless people are and, as the proverb says, there are none so bold as the ignorant. We should in any case think hard about this passage. If we have been built up in God, let us see that we make all possible progress. We should make sure that we are not puffed up with foolish pride, or that we desire things which only serve to ruin us.

Having spoken thus, the apostle adds another exhortation: *Endeavour to show yourself as one approved by God, a workman who has no need to be ashamed, rightly dispensing the word of truth.* While urging Timothy to offer himself to God, Paul at the same time reveals the remedy of which I spoke. I briefly summarized what Paul had in mind, but more detail is now required. How, then, can those who are responsible for teaching God's people be kept from futile and useless inquiry? How can they resist those who want to meddle with the gospel? They must offer themselves to God and must do so in real earnest. As long as our sights are set on the world we are bound to go wrong. Our vanity will deceive us and lead us into all sorts of error. Any man, I say, who goes up into the pulpit merely to impress his hearers cannot avoid profaning God's word and obscuring it. So the first thing to do when we approach the pulpit—those of us, I mean, who are charged with preaching—is to arraign ourselves before God and to know that, since he has assigned to us this office, we are accountable to him. If, therefore, as his representatives, we have not spoken truthfully as though our eyes beheld his majesty, all the angels of heaven will gather to witness our utter and most awful condemnation.

Accordingly Paul reminds Timothy of God's presence. 'Imagine,' he says, 'that you have been summoned to appear before him.' Now because we are inclined by nature to earthly things, Paul suggests that it is not enough to begin carelessly, with the vague idea that God has a right to be served. We must make up our minds to serve him each and every day. Otherwise our thoughts will turn to men; we will forget about God and will turn aside at once from his pure and simple word. Would we therefore refrain from idle, pointless questions? Then let us teach as if God were present before us, or as if an emissary, the instrument of one who wields supreme power, were speaking in the presence of a ruler or of someone in high office. We must be fully conscious of our role if we wish faithfully to proclaim God's word. Yet because the devil is astonishingly clever and because it takes almost nothing to put us off our stroke, it is not enough to speak well once. We must be careful never to approach the pulpit without solemnly arraigning ourselves before God, saying, 'I am in God's presence, and I am as it were his mouth. I must be made anew, and all that is human in me must be set aside, so that I may truly confess that my message is from God and that I have received it from him.'

All of us, however, without exception, are warned that when we come to be instructed in God's word we gather together in his presence. Let us give up trying to hide, like those who come to church for appearance's sake, and who merely go through the motions. They are only mocking God, some through indolence or indifference, others through hardness of heart which refuses all admonition. It is pitiful to see how obdurate they are. The devil so possesses their souls that they have no taste for anything they are taught. Let us guard against such carelessness, knowing that we come before God's presence. Let this be our resolve, since we are all too conscious of our lethargy and coldness.

Timothy is told to show himself 'as one approved by God', for those speculative teachers Paul mentioned, who only want to please, do not toil to achieve a worthy end. It is enough if they put on an impressive show, like someone who works at this or that but who finally achieves nothing. He does not set his hand to the plough, but thinks his field looks fine when all he has done is scratch the surface of the soil.[14] Weeds are sure to spring up when the plough has not been driven deep enough. Anyone who seriously sets about a work will not see immediate results. Our work, we think, is no more than mediocre. Those, on the other hand, who decide on worthless tasks merely to impress have only to lift a little finger to create new worlds, or so they think! That is how it is with those poor braggarts who aim to please with their oratory, their bombast and their speculative flights of fancy. Only when we look at what they are within do we find that they have done no work at all. What then must we do? We must follow the plain teaching of holy Scripture, knowing that all who pretend to be preachers of the gospel are men without substance or steadiness. All they do is muddle us with their useless questions; they deserve only our contempt.

Thus Paul asks, 'Who are preachers of the gospel? What is it to which we have been called? Is it to display our eloquence? To

---

[14] The metaphor of the plough is derived from Paul's use in 2 Timothy 2:15 of the verb *orthotomeō*, 'to cut straight' (KJV: 'rightly dividing'). The verb may refer to the art of the stonemason or the roadbuilder, but Chrysostom's picture of the ploughman cutting a straight furrow is the metaphor preferred by Calvin.

gratify our hearers in order to earn their admiration?' No! We have been called to work for the Lord. We are summoned to his vineyard, so let us be good workers. Let us build up the people in our care and prove that our teaching has been effective, so that we can at least be said to have done all we could to lead men to the fear of God, and to give full authority to his commandments. It is expected of us, too, that we reveal the service which God asks of us, the ground of our salvation and the way by which we gain eternal life. If we do this we will truly be good workmen, for we will have been earnest labourers in the church of God. But if God's word is no more than an occasion for pretty words, brash display or something similar, we are not workmen: it has all been a foolish game and a farcical performance.

These are Paul's words to Timothy. All believers, however, are reminded that, when faithfully taught God's word, they must see that their souls are well worked over. Do we come here, therefore, to be true learners in God's school? Let us allow the plough of his word to pass over us, and the brambles, thorns and weeds to be torn from us. Hence the image which we find in the prophet Jeremiah: we must break up the waste and fallow ground (Jer. 4:3). For ground which has been left waste or fallow must be cleared and dug over until all the weeds are removed. God must therefore plumb the very depths of our hearts, must cleanse them of every evil impulse and thought, and the plough of his word must pass over us.

We ought also to know that the gospel is, as Paul writes, a sword which is meant to mortify us (Eph. 6:17). We can only be offered and dedicated as a sacrifice to God if we have denied ourselves and are no longer rebels against him. Let us thus come here and receive the teaching which by God's command is to be presented to us, and which requires us to renounce all that belongs to our nature. Moreover, when we are rebuked for our faults and made to feel ashamed of them, or when we are criticized and threatened with God's judgment, we should not be aggrieved; instead we should be abased and thoroughly humbled. This is how we will be good scholars for God. Otherwise we will be waste ground, and whatever else is done to us will be unprofitable. This is why there are so few who allow the husbandman to work them as he should. We would prefer labourers who lull us to sleep, as the prophet Ezekiel says (cf. Ezek. 13:10; 22:28). So the warning given to us here, to both great and small, is that we should come to God's school to hear his word and should let men do a serious work in us. Since we are God's vineyard we must be dug about, pruned, stripped of our leaves and excess growth; we must be harvested or else we will never bear fruit for the Master.

To further emphasize this point Paul speaks of a workman 'who does not need to be ashamed'. Here he counsels us against the embarrassment felt by those who think too much of worldly reputation. They are not evil men, admittedly, but they are much too sensitive and thin-skinned, so that when they see people tiring of the simple gospel they are tempted to dissemble; they trim their sails, as we say. Paul therefore tells us not to be ashamed but to hold our ground. Though some may sneer at our teaching because it is too plain and less attractive than they would wish, and though others may be offended by it, we must press on. Let men want whatever they will, we should always do as God commands. What Paul says is therefore true: all who aim to please men are incapable of serving Jesus Christ.

Think of how it is with doctors. If a doctor attends a patient who is bent on getting his own way, all around will do their best to gratify him. But if the doctor is led to please both the patient and those around him instead of doing what is best for the sufferer, might he not kill him? It is the same with those whose task it is to preach God's word. Those who are rebuked feel angry and upset and want to be treated very differently. And though they may be quite well taught, all are bound to have their own solution and to prefer something else. Now how could we possibly agree with such silly thinking? We might feel only a small tinge of shame; even so it is enough to mar our service to God. Accordingly, in order not to offend the Master whom we are required to serve, let us not be ashamed. That is, let us not be distressed if we see that we are not appreciated, that no one seeks us out or even that we are rebuffed, so that people say: 'Here's someone who says nothing nice to people. I don't approve of what he does. I'd be happy to listen to him, except that when I turn up I find nothing to my taste.' If we ourselves give way to shame we will be hopelessly confused. God will disown us. The world might admire us, but the shame we feel will cost us dear.

Paul's final instruction to Timothy is 'to rightly divide the word of truth'. Here we are told that God will have his gospel preached and that teaching should follow a certain order. Some are called to this task while others are called to listen, so that the word of truth is properly dispensed. This is an important point to notice, for there are extremists who think that it is a waste of time to come to church to be taught. 'What? Doesn't the Bible contain all of God's truth? What more can anyone say?' As long as they have the Bible they believe they are exempt and bound by no particular order. Children, they argue, are expected to come to church to be taught, but adults can do without. So there are these extremists who say such things, not out of ignorance or stupidity but out of spite for God. They would dearly love to do away with all order in the church. 'Why,' they ask, 'do we need all this preaching? There are only two things which Scripture teaches: love of God and love of neighbour.' These are not comments which others have reported to us. The main defenders of those who spew forth such blasphemies have said so openly. I know the exact day when this was said, the hour, the location and the names of those present. These villains have spat out their venom and poison against God in order to overturn all religion and to wipe it out, if only they could! This is a matter of common knowledge.

Paul, on the other hand, tells us that if we have Scripture it is not enough to read it privately at home. We must have the doctrine which it contains drummed into our ears and preached to us, so that we may be instructed. Why? If, in a house, there is a loaf of bread and the master has small children who cannot lift the loaf because it is whole and much too big, how can the children get their teeth into it to eat it? The crust will be too tough, so they will not get much to eat and will be hungry.[15] Or if a servant carves off a piece of bread for his master's soup, thinking, 'There's the bread. Let him eat it if he wants', but leaves everything in disorder and fails to lay the table, is he doing his job? If, however, he cuts up the bread, brings meat to the table and tidies everything up, does he not serve his master well? In this way our Lord condescends to us in our weakness, giving our souls the true food of his word which contains all that is necessary for our salvation, and much else besides. He is more than generous to us. He demonstrates his concern for our salvation, for like a good father he makes sure that the bread is cut up and the pieces put in our mouth and well chewed over.

So when we see how greatly our God loves us, should we grumble when he does all this for our good? Must we bark and snarl like dogs? As it is, we are so ungrateful that we need to take Paul's words to heart, so that those charged with bringing us God's word and with teaching the church must never devise anything of their own, but must wisely and rightly dispense the word of truth. By 'word of truth', Paul makes it quite clear that we should never

---

[15] The image of the loaf, like that of the plough, is suggested by the verb *orthotomeō*, which Calvin here translates as *couper* or *tailler* ('to cut'), or as *trancher* ('to slice').

propose our own ideas. We are not made preachers in order to set forth whatever takes our fancy or to regale people with our own theories. The word of truth binds both him who speaks and him who hears. God desires to have dominion over us, and Jesus Christ alone must be master. When we have the word of truth we must not depart from it in any way, nor be so fickle that we are driven first one way then another. We must be able to dispense the word well and rightly so that our people are fed.

There are many who find in holy Scripture much that is obscure, but when it is faithfully explained to them light dawns where before they could see nothing. Those who dutifully read Scripture before coming to church know from experience that this is true. Let them read the passage which will be expounded in the sermon. If the preacher is true to his task he will chew the pieces over and will fulfil his duty. No one will have any excuse since needy souls will have been nourished by God's word. In short, anyone able to read the text will, before returning home, discover that God has given him knowledge of things which earlier were unclear. Scripture further shows us that the function of preaching is to help us, when we come humbly to God in order to be taught, not to return home empty-handed from God's school. If, however, we are disposed to be arrogant, we profane the bread which God gives us. We should not therefore be surprised if we go back to our homes having received nothing from God's word and no less hungry than before. Such is the recompense our thanklessness deserves.

Ministers of the gospel should understand what Paul means by 'rightly cutting' or 'rightly dividing' the word of God. By 'rightly' the apostle has this to say to those whom God has made his messengers: 'Think of the people whom we are meant to edify. We are to order God's word in such a way that we show men and women, both great and small, what God is telling them, why he does so, and how his message is framed.' This is what it means to handle God's word aright. We must admonish our hearers in a way appropriate to their understanding, so that each receives his part and portion, as when a father feeds his children, giving to each his share. That, I say, is how God deals with us, and how ministers of his word are meant to do their duty. We should make sure we benefit by having God's word divided for us, so that we may digest it more easily and be correctly fed. Let us come here as to a table, just as this morning we came to the Lord's Supper which points to all of this.

True, the table is not always set before us so that we can share in the sacrament of the Supper. The word of God in any case remains our food. When we come here, therefore, let us receive the food God has for us and which he dispenses through his servants. Let us ask to be given the word of truth and let us never borrow anything from men. Let men instead serve us and feed us on God's word. May we allow it to do us good, as Paul exhorts us to do in First Corinthians (cf. 1 Cor. 3:9-10).

> Now let us cast ourselves down before the face of our good God, acknowledging our faults and begging him to make us feel them better than before, so that, learning to hate them, we may heartily desire to be cleansed and rid of them. May he so enlighten us that he may see that we have made good progress in his school, and that we are truly temples in which his Holy Spirit may dwell. May we glorify him as we ought, in both body and soul.

# 13

## HOW TO COMBAT ERROR

*Shun also all profane babbling, which leads people to greater evil. [17] Their talk will spread like gangrene; such are Hymenaeus and Philetus, [18] who have swerved from the truth, claiming that the resurrection is already passed; they have overturned the faith of some.* (2 Timothy 2:16-18)

W e noted previously that Paul rightly took care to urge Timothy to follow the pure simplicity of God's word without disguising it. For the devil knows that the teaching we receive in God's name is food for our souls, which is why he does his best to spoil it. And since he cannot completely ruin it, he throws in things which will make us weary of it and which stop us discovering as fully and as clearly as we ought God's will and purpose for us.

Experience tells us this is so. How many are there nowadays who undertake to preach the plain, unalloyed truth? And why is that? Ambition leads some to veil God's truth, but we should look further, to Satan, who seeks to deprive us of the spiritual life. This he can do only if God's truth is discredited. Paul therefore is not content to have warned us once against useless babble, and to have urged us to stick to a plain, sound, robust style of teaching. He repeats his exhortation. He does not merely condemn obvious errors like superstition and falsehood; he also condemns those who, in their desire to please, disguise God's word and advance theories which tickle the ears but fail to feed the soul or to build up hearers in God's faith and fear.

When he speaks of *futile babbling*, Paul means anything which pleases the inquisitive. There are many people, as we know, who are fond of pointless questions which give them a flutter of excitement as they grapple with some new idea or other. They are ecstatic and they revel in it. It is not that they openly oppose God's truth, but they dismiss it as if it were commonplace or trite, suitable only for the humble and the ignorant. They want something higher and deeper, and they have no time for anything which might be useful. Why? Because they are driven by the itch to know, and do not care whether or not it does them any good.

So let us carefully consider Paul's warning about useless babble. In effect he calls it window-dressing, a choice display of rhetoric designed to exalt the speaker and to demonstrate his learning. None of that, I say, has any place in the church. It must be banished, for God demands that his people be edified and he has appointed his word for that purpose. So if we do not work for the salvation of our people by offering them sound and solid instruction, we are guilty of sacrilege, for we are distorting the purpose for which God's word was given.

The apostle further describes such talk as *profane*, which is the opposite of what is sacred and dedicated to God. All is sacred, therefore, which serves to magnify God, so that when we know his majesty we may worship him and give him full obedience. Sacred, too, are those things which draw us to the heavenly kingdom, which turn us from this world and lead us to Jesus Christ, making us one with him. Conversely when we have no concept of God's glory and so cannot submit to it, when we are not conscious of the riches of his heavenly kingdom, when we are not led to serve him and to live in all purity of conscience, when we know nothing of the salvation won for us by our Lord Jesus Christ, we are captive to this world and thus profane. And any teaching which leads us into errors of this kind is also profane.

Paul's meaning then is perfectly clear. When we gather together in God's name it is not to hear sweet singing or to be fed with wind, that is, with idle, worthless speculation. We gather to receive wholesome food, for God desires that nothing be preached in his name which does not benefit and edify the hearers, and which does not offer them substantial nourishment. Our natural inclination is of course to like novelties and speculative ideas which we think are clever; they suit us very well. We should nevertheless be on our guard since these things profane God's word. Let us look instead to what will edify, and let us not be deceived by things which have no substance or solidity in them.

However, because it is hard to wean us off such foolishness to which we are instinctively disposed, Paul shows how utterly wretched is the itch to know. *Those*, he says, *who give themselves to such things always go on to even greater wickedness.* It is as if he said: 'My friends, at first glance you do not see how evil these deceivers are who seek to earn your admiration. In order to impress you they go in for pleasantries which put you at your ease. Know, however, that they are ministers of Satan, and that far from serving God they grow more and more godless. If we leave them alone they will corrupt the whole Christian faith: nothing pure or wholesome will remain. Shun them, then, like the plague, even though you may not at first perceive their venom.'

Thus, in judging doctrine we must first be suspicious of ourselves. Why? As I said before, we are all weak, or else we have restless minds which draw us toward unprofitable things. To do this is to risk going to extremes or losing our bearings. Though for a time we were well instructed in God's word, we now turn our back on it. Let us take care, therefore, not to gratify our natural desires, but to see that, even when what we are taught does not immediately seem wrong, if it does not serve to lead us to God, to strengthen us in his service, to confirm us in the faith or to deepen the hope we have of the heavenly life, such teaching will deceive us in the end. It is a hotchpotch of error which will rob us of whatever blessing we may have had before. In short, those who do not try to draw people to God and to help build the kingdom of our Lord Jesus Christ so that he may reign among us, are seen to be bent on ruin and to grow ever more godless. If they are allowed a free hand, the door will be open to Satan to wreak fearful havoc and to frustrate more or less whatever is of God. This may not happen on the very first day, but that is what we will ultimately see.

Paul makes his meaning clearer by saying that their talk will thrive, *and will spread like gangrene*. The word is not to be understood in its ordinary sense; it is what the surgeons call 'creeping sepsis', or what is also termed Saint Anthony's fire. It is an extensive inflammation in the body which keeps on spreading, so that it increasingly consumes not only the flesh and sinews but the bones as well. It is like a fire which devours everything, so that a diseased hand will lead to the loss of an arm, and a diseased foot to the loss of a leg, if the affected part is not amputated early enough. Without appropriate treatment a patient risks losing the use of every limb once he has the illness in his body. Nothing must be spared. The infection must be removed once it has set in; it must be got rid of if the rest is to be saved. This, then, is the image which Paul uses here.

The apostle explains that although we may have been soundly instructed in doctrine, it is all lost if we pursue pointless questions or make light of good teaching in order to please our hearers and to pander to their foolish tastes. We do not at first perceive the harm that is done, but it will end up devouring everything and extinguishing the last spark of life. So since Paul's meaning is plain, let us make sure that we obey his exhortation. As soon as we see people who would have us abandon sound teaching we should avoid them and close the door to them. For what will become of us if we tolerate them or pretend not to see? It will be too late to find a remedy when we finally decide to act. As with a stubborn disease, we must amputate at the earliest opportunity. Let us not, then, be lulled into sleep. Paul is quite serious when he describes this disease as deadly unless immediate steps are taken.

If men had carefully observed Paul's warning, affairs in Christendom today would be far better than they are. But from the corruption which has ensued we see how right the Holy Spirit was to warn believers in good time, well before the event. All the nonsense which we see in popery is nothing less than the godless folly to which Paul refers. Those among the papists who aspire to be expert theologians spend twelve years—no, an entire lifetime!—studying, yet their sole ambition is to master a form of words which is outwardly impressive but which no one can understand! They are as little fond of leading men to God as they are of dung or trash! The devil, it seems, has cleverly forged this form of words for them, in order to sow terrible confusion and to bring all teaching to an end. In short, they appear to have openly conspired to do the opposite of what Paul bids us do in God's name. How right the Holy Spirit was to speak this way by the mouth of Paul, for those who have turned God's word into a strange and foreign jargon are all the less excusable. Nevertheless this is a fault which is still with us. How many there are who only want to hear pleasant news! They would like God's word to be a sort of hobby or entertainment. This is what they are after. It is no wonder, then, if our Lord allows the simplicity of his word to be corrupted, in order to punish the evil tastes of those who cannot bear to be purely taught by him. How many, I ask, are there who seek—I do not say some useless, empty form of teaching—but clear and manifest errors, arguments and disputes in order to upset the church, to question the faith we hold and to conceal God's word, so that we cannot tell white from black?

Given that these people are a growing plague, what steps do we take to resist them? On the contrary, do we not see that those who ought to be armed against these ravenous wolves feed them, clasp them to their bosom and fully endorse their cause? Accordingly we should try to serve God all the more and to remain faithful to the purity of his gospel. If we really want to obey our God as we should, let us attend to what we are asked to do here, that is, to shun these people like the plague and not to wait until they have defiled the church of God. Let us do all we can to counter them, knowing that this disease will prove incurable if we delay too long. Let us detest those who support these people, who would like to see this ill fester here and who would encourage it still more. And let us pray that God may cleanse his church of such as these, for they are tools of the devil, whatever their winning ways.

This is of course what we should always do whenever the devil contrives to pervert God's truth and to stir up trouble for us. But it is especially true of doctrine, which is the means by which we are given life and our souls truly fed.

The apostle proceeds to single out *Hymenaeus and Philetus*, who are among the people he is speaking of. *They have*, he writes, *departed from the truth, claiming that the resurrection is already past, and they undermine the faith of some*. In naming Hymenaeus and Philetus, Paul shows that we should not spare those who, like scabby sheep, infect the flock. Rather each of us is warned to keep clear of them. Do we not betray our neighbours when we see them in danger of being alienated from God, but act as if nothing were amiss? Is not someone who tries to spread false teaching or to make trouble in the church no better than a poisoner? If I pretended not to notice, would I not be like someone who saw his neighbour in peril but gave no word of warning? Would that not be an act of base betrayal? Now if the life of the body should be so precious to us that we do our best to preserve it, what shall we say about the life of the soul? We all acknowledge the truth of the proverb which says that one scabby sheep is enough to ruin the whole flock, but we seem incapable of applying it so that the church remains whole and pure. Worse still, these evil rascals who are intent on overturning everything promote their false ideas in order to foster contempt for God. So as these curs snap and snarl and seek to wipe out all religion, should we call them scabby sheep? No! They are filthy, stinking goats or ravenous wolves who come to scatter and destroy.

And yet we put up with them! True, we make the fine excuse that it is wrong to confront men outright, to reject them and thus to drive them to despair. This is what we hear from those who argue for leniency whenever God's church is threatened by scandal and error. Tell me, what kind of mercy is it when we spare one man but allow a thousand souls to perish because we failed to warn them? We know the apostle's teaching. Weeds must not be allowed to grow among us for they will very soon win out, and whatever good seed there is will be choked or entirely lost. What we see is not only weeds but Satan's venom which like some plague mars everything. God's flock will be troubled and harassed by goats which will run full tilt against them with their horns and will infect them all. Or like ravenous wolves they will tear all to pieces and wreak as much destruction as they can. Should we be touched by pity for a wolf, yet abandon the poor sheep and lambs for whom our Lord has a special concern?

When, therefore, we see evildoers troubling the church either by causing offence or by teaching error, we should do all we can to curb their activity and to warn simple souls not to be deceived. That, I say, is what we must do. So if someone objects, or if others who do not want anyone to be named get angry and upset, let us not try to be wiser than the Holy Spirit has made us. Let dogs and swine grumble as they will, the lesson which Paul teaches us is that, if God wishes the wicked to be named, identified and their shame made known to all, we should be content. We must, in any case, avoid them.

Earlier we pointed out that Paul urges us to mark and shun those who have erred and strayed—not as adulterers, thieves and blasphemers, but as idlers who will not earn a living and who are unruly, busybodies and lazy. Such people may not be criminals, yet we are to take note of them and avoid them. What, then, shall we say of those who have the sword in their hand but who behave like demons, who cannot live in peace and harmony but who are driven by the devil to pull everything down? Should we be silent when we see such things? Let us therefore learn to mark those who disturb the church of God, to resist them and to bring them to heel so that they can do no harm.

How few there are who are truly zealous for God's church! We all know the identity of those who would dearly love to ruin everything. I do not only mean the obvious enemies. The papists, I confess, deserve to be marked and known, so that we are not entangled in their errors and superstitions. As well, however, there are those who would be glad to see us lay aside the pure and simple gospel, who seek to undermine all established order and who sow tares in order to discredit doctrine and make us tire of it. These things are plain to all of us. There are those who want to be left free to do whatever mischief they like, and little by little to throw off the yoke of our Lord Jesus Christ. Some who want an end to godliness spew forth their blasphemies and foul talk in order to trample down all reverence for God. Others are blatant drunkards and filthy beasts who want to throw all into disarray, so that nothing matters any more and religion serves only as a shadow. Yet who stands against them, and who calls anyone to account? Who says, 'Let us be careful, let us be on our guard'? On the contrary, those who ought to undertake to curb these evils not only shut their eyes and let things be, they actually encourage them!

There is no need to bring these things to light, for they are well known and plain to see. No one, however, takes any notice of them. We think to ourselves: 'What a disaster! This person is an obvious enemy of God. He is out to ruin everything.' Nevertheless we put up with him. You can see the mischief that is done, how all that concerns your salvation and the church's welfare is twisted and perverted. Yet you pretend not to notice and you behave as if nothing was wrong! What cowardice is this! Yet it happens all the time. We can boast as loud as we like that we are Christians, but we are more devils than Christians when we act this way! Look, then, at what we are taught here. If we see people who set out to corrupt God's church, to obscure sound teaching or to cheapen it, they must be pilloried and marked, and we must all beware of them. We must do the same when there are those who sow discord and make trouble in the church. If we do not do our duty, each in his own way, we are traitors to God, having no zeal for his honour or for the church's welfare. We may protest our loyalty as much as we like. God will reprove us in the presence of his angels and of all his creatures, because we failed to defend his cause when he called us to so noble a work. If we would serve God we must be sworn enemies of evil. It is not enough that we do no evil ourselves; we must denounce it as much as possible so that it does not prevail and overpower us.

Having identified these two men by name, Paul records that 'they have swerved from the faith to the point of saying that the resurrection is past'. Here we discover just how dreadful was their downfall. These men were not at all unknown. Although Timothy was far away in Ephesus, when Paul names them he expects him to recognize them. They can only have been men of prominence. For a time they must have been respected as pillars—leaders, even—of the church. Yet we see how far they fell by denying the eternal salvation purchased for us by our Lord Jesus Christ. If we have no expectation of resurrection, what is the point of being told that we have a Redeemer who has saved us from bondage to death? How can Jesus Christ's death and passion benefit us if we cannot expect the fruit promised to us at his coming, on the last day? These men had fallen into the deepest pit of hell, yet they had been numbered for a time among the faithful and were regarded by them as leaders.

Thus in these two men God chose to display his vengeance on those who wrongly use his gospel. At first they did not think that they were doing any harm by their clever teaching. But being ambitious they craved men's applause, disguised the simplicity of God's word and sought to prove how much better they were as scholars. They flattered themselves and had no idea that God might let them fall. God's word, however, is much more precious to him than it is to us. He will not allow us to refuse it and to make light of it. Now what this passage especially makes clear is that those who were half-angels became utter demons, who in their blindness forgot the principles and rudiments of the faith. No longer content with the ABC of doctrine they aspired to be learned teachers. Paul tells us that, as to these men's standing, they were not ordinary or ignorant individuals; they were men of repute, known throughout all the churches and even overseas. Nevertheless they were so smitten by blindness that they denied the resurrection of the dead, thus abandoning the first article of our faith and depriving themselves of all hope of salvation. What was the point of that? How was it possible? We might think it a monstrous aberration that people whose task was to teach others should end in such abysmal ignorance. The fact is that God takes retribution on scoffers who corrupt his word; he casts them off so that they are incapable of understanding and no longer even have the use of reason. That is the message of this text.

Consequently, if today we see some who, having known God's truth, become stupid and brutish like dogs, it is because God chooses thus to exalt his word and to make us feel its majesty. Why? It is his way of punishing our contempt of it. He hands such people over to the devil, giving him licence and authority to seize them and to carry them off so that they cease even to look like men, so mindless are they. We should never, then, stumble when we see those who have tasted the gospel refusing to yield God obedience; rather it should confirm our faith. For God is showing that he so much values and cherishes his word that he will not allow us to misuse it in any way by emptying it of its meaning, or by masking or profaning it. That is one point.

In addition, however, we are exhorted to walk in fear and trembling. Each of us must think, 'Alas, since God sets such mirrors before our eyes, when we see those who pretended to be faithful swerve from the faith, utter curses and blasphemies, openly defy God, lead thoroughly dissolute and evil lives and cast reverence aside—when God sets such examples before us, does he not mean to rouse us so that we may walk in all simplicity, being gathered to him and kept from falling prey to Satan?'

This is the sense of Paul's reference to resurrection. It is true that Hymenaeus and Philetus conceived of an imaginary resurrection, just as in our own day there have been madmen who have taught that we are raised once we become Christians. Scripture, on the other hand, points us to the coming of our Lord Jesus Christ and tells us to be always ready and prepared. But Jesus Christ must first be revealed. Until then, our life is hidden and we live under the shadow of death, as Paul writes in the third chapter of Colossians (Col. 3:3). Scripture thus points us to our Lord Jesus Christ, whereas these madmen declare that we can imagine no other resurrection than that which takes place when God illumines us by his gospel.[16] On the contrary, we must lie buried in this world, knowing that Jesus Christ is not our resurrection until we are changed fully into his image. Our old man, I say, must first be crucified if we would know the glory of our Lord Jesus Christ and be raised with him. Paul had already made this point when he said that it is a sure saying and certain fact that in order to be part of the kingdom of Jesus Christ, we must even now share in his cross and walk amid death before attaining life. How long does our death last? As long as we are in this world. Thus Peter calls baptism a representation of Noah's ark (1 Pet. 3:20-21), for we must be enclosed in it as in a tomb, like those who have perished on earth, if we would be made alive by the touch of Jesus Christ. So do not those who seek for resurrection while still in mid-course falsify the nature of baptism and the entire pattern which God has appointed for us? Until God takes us out of this world we must always know that we are pilgrims in a foreign land, and that our salvation will not be revealed until the coming of our Lord Jesus Christ.

Therefore he is called the first-born of those who rise from the dead (1 Cor. 15:20; Col. 1:18; Rev. 1:5). The head must assuredly precede the members and must take the lead. Jesus Christ is indeed risen, but he must appear to us, and his life and glory must be revealed to us before we can reach him. In the same vein John writes that we know that we are children of God, but that this

---

[16] The 'madmen' to whom the preacher refers are contemporaries whom he elsewhere calls Spiritual Libertines, members of an influential sect who held among other things that man is possessed of an immortal spirit which lives in heaven in union with God. Those enlightened by the gospel are no longer prisoners of *le cuider* (the world and the flesh): already they live the resurrection life. See Calvin's treatise of 1545, *Against the Sect of the Libertines Called Spiritual*, XVIII, XXII.

is not yet revealed. We will see him, he says, when we are made like him (1 John 3:2). Now it is true that God is made known to us when he remakes us in his own likeness, but what we grasp by faith we do not yet see; it is something for which we hope at the coming of our Lord Jesus Christ.

Absurd though these men's error was, they nevertheless undermined the faith of some, says Paul. This should make us tremble, for two reasons. First, as has already been said, it is so foolish an idea that it ought to be immediately dismissed. The resurrection already past? How can that be? God's children are wretched in this world; their lot is pitiable to see. If we compare them with unbelievers, we see that they languish here below while those who despise God live a life of ease and pleasure. They exult, while the others are, in Paul's words, like the filth of the world (1 Cor. 4:13). So how could anyone imagine such a heresy, affirming that the resurrection is already past? Yet this was believed by some, even in the early church, in the days of the apostles! At a time when those chosen by Jesus Christ to proclaim his truth were still alive, there were people who turned aside. To what? To a diabolical error, a mindless fantasy! Should we not, then, be alarmed and disposed to walk in fear when we see such a thing? Not that we should doubt that God will aid and guide us, but we should be well armed. But how? By prayer and by the contemplation of God's promises, as we will later see.

Here we see an error so monstrous as to make the hairs of our head stand on end! That God should allow the faith of some to be ruined and changed into a thing so vile and accursed! And that men should be so wicked! Now if the apostles, though exercising the power given them by God to defend his truth, could not prevent some from falling away, how is it with us today? Let us be doubly afraid. I do not mean overcome with terror—as, God willing, we will see after dinner. We should, however, be driven to prayer, asking God to be our refuge and to preserve us by his Holy Spirit. Let none of us be puffed up with pride, for we are nothing and we would soon be defeated if God did not sustain us.

Paul's warnings, in any case, are not given without good cause. Although Hymenaeus and Philetus are no longer with us, it is clear that through them the Holy Spirit means to discredit all who seek to mar our faith. Let nothing which may happen distress us or turn us from the right path. Let us arm ourselves so that we can overcome every obstacle, but let none of us become so self-assured that we allow our foolish thoughts to lead us astray. Let us resolve to remain obedient to God's word, and to trust it more and more until God in his goodness brings us to that eternal rest to which he calls us.

> Now let us cast ourselves down before the face of our good God, acknowledging our faults and praying that he may bring us to true repentance, and that we may so profit every day that our life may be lived according to his commandments. And although our ways are so evil that he might justly cast us off, may he in his mercy sustain us until he takes us from this mortal life, and transforms us after the pattern of his heavenly glory.

# 14

## A SURE FOUNDATION

*Nevertheless God's foundation remains firm, having this seal: The Lord knows those who are his; and whoever calls on the name of the Lord, let him depart from iniquity.* (2 Timothy 2:19)

As we saw in part this morning, Paul's aim in mentioning the example of those who had gone astray was to warn believers not to be unduly alarmed. Here he takes further steps to resolve the problem, urging us not to falter when we see those who were pillars of the church stumble and fall. That men are frail, prone to error and full of sin is nothing new. Such is their natural inclination, and we should not wonder if they turn to evil rather than good. Our salvation depends on the grace of our God, who has been pleased to choose us before the world was made and to mark us as his children and his elect.

So if we are alarmed when those who appeared to promise much go the other way, that is all to the good. It should make us more zealous to see that God's church grows and increases rather than shrinks. Moreover we should feel greater concern for our brethren, so that we would be sad if they perished. It is no small thing if souls redeemed by the blood of Jesus Christ were to be lost. At any rate we should be comforted by the knowledge that God will uphold his church, however small it is—smaller indeed than we might wish! Nevertheless it is enough to know that God will preserve all whom he has chosen for himself. As for those who err, as for those apostates who deny Jesus Christ, even though they kept company with us we must conclude that they were never part of us since, as John writes, they went out from us (1 John 2:19). As for those whom God has truly claimed for himself, the world would have to turn over and over a thousand times before any of God's elect should perish. Such a thing can never be, for God is the keeper of our salvation, as he promised. It is our Lord Jesus Christ's special office to safeguard all those chosen by God his Father.

This is the message which Paul conveys when now he writes: *The foundation remains firm, having this seal: God knows those who are his.* Here Paul includes two things which we should heed. The first is that, when those who seemed the most mature in the faith change unexpectedly, depart from us and in their unbelief become total strangers to God's kingdom, we must not think that the church is in decline. True, the number of those whom we thought were believers will diminish. Even so the foundation is firm—that is, God will always maintain his church, and there will always be those who call upon him and who worship him. Let that suffice, for he has sworn that as long as the sun and moon shine in the sky, there will be a people here below who worship him as Lord (Psa. 72:5). Do we see, then, the devil scattering the flock of our Lord Jesus Christ? Do we see those who looked like believers falling away and being finally cut off? Yet the building survives, even though it is hidden underground. The fountainhead remains, as experience teaches us, even though one believing man is scarcely to be seen. What was it like forty years ago, before God restored to us the light of his gospel? Did not the whole of Christendom seem finished in men's eyes, with no building visible from afar? There was nevertheless a hidden foundation. God, that is, had set apart in a miraculous and incomprehensible way those he wanted, few though they were in number. This, then, is one of the things the apostle mentions here: God's foundation remains secure.

We are therefore taught that when troubles abound and when we think all is lost, we must look—by faith, of course—to the unseen foundation. Otherwise there is no way that we can discern the church of God; it will cease to exist for us. Remember what befell the prophet Elijah, who thought that he was alone in the world and that only in that one place was God worshipped; he could not see three or four men who were united with him in faith. Nevertheless God rebuked him, telling him that he still had seven thousand men whom he had kept safe in his hand (1 Kings 19:14, 18). That is how it is every time we imagine that the church has been wiped from the face of the earth. God preserves his foundation underground.

We note, in the second place, the image of the seal. While, as Paul says, God's foundation endures, it is like a letter which has been closed and sealed. Why closed and sealed? Because God knows those who are his. The reason why we cannot identify them and decide that this one or that is God's, is because God desires to humble us so that our eyes are either blind or dazzled. We must be content to know that God's election is secure; although concealed from us and not first of all divulged, it lies within his private counsel. If, therefore, God knows his own, we should not be surprised if we are often deceived when people fall away. Why? Because they were not known to us. God, however, is not deceived: he brings to pass whatever he has decided in his counsel. This is Paul's second point.

The apostle meanwhile utters a solemn warning: we must not be lazy or neglectful. Whenever we hear of some who err but who before were almost seated with the angels, we must resolve to walk in fear and trembling, not falsely swearing by God's name or calling ourselves Christians as the hypocrites do who have God's name on their tongues, but who clearly scorn him and abuse the holy name which once they bore. Let us then put into practice what is added here, so that if we invoke the name of our Lord Jesus Christ and profess to be his, we must cease to do wrong. We can only belong to the church if we are separated from the world and from its deceits. Let us recognize, then, the purpose of our calling and what our manner of life should be. Let us be true to God, for he might well cast us out of his church if, being warned by these examples, we fail to learn from them.

To get most benefit from this text we should first return to what Paul says regarding God's eternal counsel, which is the very basis of our election. Admittedly, as Scripture says, we are saved by faith (Eph. 2:8). We do not know that God is our Father or that we are reconciled to him except by faith, as we lay hold of the promises of the gospel. There God assures us that we are acceptable to him for the sake of our Lord Jesus Christ. We must thus accept this gift or else we will forfeit it. Salvation is therefore ours by faith. But who grants us faith if not God? Why does he grant it to us, if not because he was pleased to choose us before we were born, before, even, the creation of the world? Paul explains these things especially in the first chapter of Ephesians (Eph. 1:4-12). There too he outlines for us the more familiar truths, that we are made to share in the heavenly blessings in Jesus Christ, that having pardoned our sins God makes us acceptable to him, and that we are his by adoption. The gospel teaches all of this. Paul, however, takes us higher, declaring that all this is ours because God chose us before the world began, having loved us in our Lord Jesus Christ before ever we were capable of good or evil.

It is to this that we must keep coming back. God draws us to himself by the gospel, and by faith we receive the righteousness of our Lord Jesus Christ who is the cause of our salvation. Nevertheless before all this there was God's secret love, love so hidden that though he had already chosen us he was in no great hurry to bring us to himself! This is the real sense of Paul's words concerning the firmness of God's foundation. Here God's foundation is contrasted with whatever strength there is in men and with whatever they choose to build. God's firmness is contrasted with our perishable state. Since we are changeable, since we so quickly fail and ebb away like water, Paul urges us to find our stability in God, for it is not to be found in us or in our human nature.

There are two useful lessons to be learned from this. When we see the disobedient and the faithless forsaking God's church, we might be tempted to think, 'Well, aren't all men weak? Everyone else is no different from me.' Experience tells us this is true. Thus, if we hear that the gospel is no longer being preached in a certain place and that the work is being ruined, we think that all is lost. If we hear of troubles and unexpected changes we tell ourselves, 'Why should things not be as stable there as they are here?' Now we must dismiss this temptation, using as our shield what Paul tells us here, that the church is grounded in God and not in any quality of man. If, then, we can find no firmness on earth, be sure that God has made our salvation secure, and that he maintains it so that it cannot pass away.

That is one lesson for us to ponder. The other concerns ourselves and is much weightier. If I see someone going wrong, what does that tell me about myself? That I am like him. Nevertheless I must keep coming back to this, that weak though I am God himself is steadfast. Thus our Lord Jesus Christ says in the tenth chapter of John that nothing that the Father has given him will be lost. Why? 'Because,' he says, 'God my Father is greater and mightier than all who would frustrate his will' (John 10:29). With these words he makes it clear that if we think of our condition we may well feel desperate. Indeed we would perish every minute of the day if we were not upheld by a power greater than our own. But since God's power is invincible, our salvation is assured for God is its keeper. Remember also that Jesus Christ has pledged to care for our souls; he will not permit us to be plucked from his hand. However hard the devil tries and however many his resources, though we may seem likely to be snatched a hundred thousand times from the hands of our Lord Jesus Christ, we are nevertheless safe with him, since our election depends on God and on his unchanging counsel. To this thought we must cling, and although we may fear to stumble when we see others abandoning the gospel, let us recall the words of John which we quoted before: 'They went out from us, but they were not of us, otherwise they would never have left us' (1 John 2:19).

We should recognize that for a time God allows hypocrites to mix with us, even though he knows them to be reprobate. And although they appear to be sheep, in the end they do not have hide thick enough to cover their wickedness. The Lord Jesus Christ thought similarly, teaching that the faithful should not be upset by the ingratitude shown when men resist the gospel. For they detest sound teaching and choose to defy God on some pretext or another, or because of a preconceived idea they have. Jesus Christ speaks of such when he declares: 'Every tree which God my Father has not planted will be torn up' (Matt. 15:13). There he compares those who appear to be believers to trees planted in a field or garden. Open enemies of God in no way resemble trees, but hypocrites who look the part and who want to be thought of as God's children do seem to be like trees planted in a field or in God's house. Yet they have not taken root, for God did not plant them—that is, they were not chosen by him.

It is true that, in order to test our faith, God allows them to claim his name falsely, despite the fact that he has not reserved them for his own or chosen them for the inheritance of life. They must thus be rooted up. Jesus Christ's disciples often made the same complaint to him as we do. If someone turns against the gospel, people come to us and say: 'Look, so-and-so has thrown the whole thing over!' So if some trouble erupts—I do not mean those who are sworn enemies of God and despisers of his word, but those arrogant individuals who cannot abide sound teaching but who for a time pretend to accept it—if they tire of it or dislike it, then there are problems. In the same way the disciples inquired of Jesus Christ why the scribes and Pharisees were so little edified. 'Leave them alone,' he said, 'for they are blind. Take care that you do not go to destruction with them, but know that they are not my Father's chosen and elect' (Matt. 15:14). Everyone of course saw nothing but holiness in them. It was all a mask. For our part we see that they never truly feared God. They could not receive his truth, for they were hypocrites. Do not be alarmed, therefore, if you see people who rise up against God: not all have been planted by his hand.

We benefit most from what Paul teaches if we understand, first of all, that faith is given to us from on high, since God has enlightened us by his Holy Spirit. We have accepted the gospel not by our own efforts or in our own strength. God, who graciously chose us to be his children and adopted us before the creation of the world, did not do the same for all. So it is a special and priceless privilege which he has granted us, for he is free to choose whomever he pleases, yet he chose to regard us as his. How much, then, do we owe him, who saved us from the ruin common to all mankind! Observe, too, how useful it is to know about election, which allows us to judge God's children from the reprobate. We must return to this truth every time the church is faced with scandals and troubles, every time, that is, when those who began so well fail to go on but instead turn tail and run. We are naturally frail, but we will find firmness enough in our God, since in his goodness he is pleased to adopt us as his own and to defend us. Since, above all, he has assigned to Jesus Christ the task of keeping and sustaining us, be sure that he will faithfully do his work as he has promised.

Let us therefore come back to the fact of God's election when we see someone we formerly respected fall. And if the whole of God's church should come to grief—well, God's foundation is sure, for the church does not depend on the will of men. Men did not make themselves nor can they remake themselves: it all comes from God's sheer goodness and mercy. Even if the building above ground has completely disappeared, having neither columns nor shape nor form, God will still preserve its foundation which is immovable. Judge, then, whether what we teach concerning God's election is unimportant.

We do not of course presume to enter into God's secret counsel in order to fathom his extraordinary mysteries. Though they are hidden from us, not to know that God chose us before the world began would be to deprive ourselves of much helpful and necessary comfort. The best means of destroying our faith that the devil could find would be to conceal this truth from us. For what would become of us? Nowadays especially when we see so many dissidents and hypocrites—people who promised miracles—might we not fear that the same could happen to us? In that case how could we remain firm in our trust in God, earnestly committing ourselves to him, not doubting that he will care for us to the very end—how could we do this if we did not believe in his election as our only refuge? It would seem as if God had broken the promise made to us in his gospel, and that Jesus Christ had been banished from the world.

This, accordingly, would be the chief reason and best means that Satan could use to turn us against the gospel. So, defying Satan and all his acolytes, let us keep hold of the arms we have for our defence. Let us, I say again, grow in our confidence in God's election. Let us affirm it loud and clear so that it is not taken from us, if we truly hold dear the salvation of our souls. We must regard as deadly enemies all who would hide this doctrine from us, knowing that the devil has raised them up to rob us of the comfort without which, as we have said, we have no assurance of salvation, which we should desire above all. That is how we are to apply the message of this text.

Let us attend also to Paul's final appeal: *Let those who call on the name of the Lord depart from all iniquity*. For just as God's election serves to make us steadfast and unyielding, and to cheer us in the midst of all our worries and troubles, so too we must not cease to call upon God, to turn to him for help and to follow carefully that to which he calls us. There is an enormous difference between the sure confidence which believers have in their salvation and in their peace with God, and the unconcern felt by those who think of nothing, but who, as we say, trust to luck and hope that no harm will come their way. Men are much too negligent; they are forever mindless of the dangers which surround them, so that they fail to call upon God and to hide beneath the shelter of his wings. On the strength of having been instructed once, they show no interest in good teaching.

The faithful, on the other hand, do not cease to fear. Even though they rely on God's goodness and resolve never to let storm or whirlwind carry them away, they are alert to Satan's every move. They know moreover how frail they are and are driven to turn to God, asking him not to forsake them in time of need but to preserve them with outstretched hand. They are conscious of their calling and they rouse themselves to repentance, calling upon God to increase in them the Holy Spirit's gifts and to rid them of their fleshly desires. This is how the faithful, though having assurance, do not cease to fear. By contrast the faithless do not fear God, but they lack assurance. Hence if a leaf should fall or some small shadow should surprise them, they are dismayed. Why? Because they have no firm trust in God; they are heavy with sleep like drunkards. God most justly mocks their folly. That is why, when speaking of the Jews' downfall and ruin, Paul says that those who think that they stand should take heed lest they fall (1 Cor. 10:12). Not that the apostle means to leave us hesitant, anxious or uncertain, wondering what might happen or whether God will lead us to the end. We must be absolutely sure of this, that God begins nothing that he will not complete, as we read in the first chapter of Philippians and in other places (Phil. 1:6). Nevertheless we must always be instant in prayer and supplication. We must not misuse God's grace. Since we are consecrated to him, let us walk in fear and trembling, and let us make sure that we are not caught up in the condemnation of the wicked. If they are poor blind souls, we should not be surprised when they err and stray. Since we, however, have God's light, should we not tread a straight and proper path? And seeing that he has adopted us as his children, should we not serve and honour him as our Father? That is the point of Paul's appeal.

To call upon God's name is to confess that we are his. Sometimes by 'invocation' Scripture means turning to God in prayer. The word, however, has at times a wider sense. We therefore call upon Christ's name when we profess to be part of his people and his church. To call ourselves Christians is to claim Jesus Christ as ours. It is as if someone said: 'So-and-so is my master: I therefore take his name for myself.' We cannot lay claim to the name 'Christian' or protest that we belong to the fellowship, household and church of God's Son—we cannot, that is, be part of Jesus Christ—unless we are freed from all our uncleanness. Otherwise do we not do him an intolerable dishonour? If someone boasted that he served a prince but was in fact a robber, he would be doubly punished because he had falsely claimed a name to which he had no right.

Here, then, is God's Son, the source of all holiness and righteousness. Shall we hide ourselves under his shadow and with it cover all our iniquities, however foul they may be? Is not this a sacrilege which deserves the very worst punishment?

Paul's meaning, then, should be perfectly clear. It is true that however hard we try to serve God purely we do not cease to be miserable sinners, marred by many blemishes and harbouring many imperfections in ourselves. Nevertheless, when we make it our aim to seek to do good and to hate evil, although we may limp along, since our goal is good and since we endeavour to grow in the fear of God and in obedience to him, our impulse is sincere and Jesus Christ accepts us as if we were righteous. He absolves us of all our faults so that they are not imputed to us. Hence believers, although by no means perfect, still subject to many sins and not above reproach, are nevertheless accepted by God as his children, and Jesus Christ does not think it a dishonour if they lay claim to him. By his grace he causes what good there is in them to be pleasing to God. If, however, we falsely claim his name and try to use it as a cover for our transgressions, does not Jesus Christ have every right to range himself against us, because we have sinned against his majesty, taking his name and his armour under false pretences?

We must therefore understand all that the word 'Christianity' implies. It means that we are members of God's Son. Since he was pleased to accept us as members of his body, we must cleave to him in all righteousness, for he has received all fullness of grace in order to share it with us. True, he shares it only in part and only in small measure. Even so the Spirit of God must reign in us if we would be counted as God's children and as members of our Lord Jesus Christ. It follows, then, that all who give themselves to evil and who make no effort to obey God's will in order to mortify their sinful appetites, are counterfeiters who falsely claim to be Christians. When we see many people abandoning God's church, people who began well but who did not go on, remember this, that however frail men are God's foundation is always firm. Why? Because God knows those whom he has chosen for himself; he will sustain them. We should not doubt that we are included among them. The fact that our Lord has called us to himself solidly testifies that he marked us out before ever we were born. Let us be content with his holy calling.

Further, we should hope that since God always keeps us in his care and since we have a form of church among us, God will not allow his people to perish, even though the world tries hard to thin their ranks. We need never be alarmed by whatever obstacles we may have to face. In the meantime let us walk in fear, not abusing God's goodness but recognizing that he has separated us from the rest of the world, and that we must live as those who are of his house. May we continue to be his, according as he gave us the outward sign of baptism and sealed us with his Holy Spirit, who is, as Paul says, the guarantee of our election (Eph. 1:14). He is our pledge that we are called to the inheritance of heaven.

Let us therefore pray that God may by his Holy Spirit sign and seal his free election in our hearts. May he continue to keep us hidden and enclosed as under the shadow of his wings. And if poor lost souls should stray and vanish away, or if the devil should carry them off so that they do not rise when they fall but rush headlong to destruction, let us for our part pray that God may keep us under his protection. May we know what it means to obey his will and to be upheld by him. However much the world tries to shake us, let us stand firm on this foundation: the Lord knows those who are his. May nothing turn us aside but may we continue always to advance, until God draws us into his kingdom which knows no change.

Now let us cast ourselves down before the face of our good God, acknowledging our faults and asking him so to make us feel them that we learn to like them less and less. Knowing how frail we are, and how quickly we would fall if we were not supported by another power, may our good God strengthen us, so that we are daily led to follow his holy calling. And since he has united us with his beloved Son, our Lord Jesus Christ, and since we rest content in the salvation won once and for all by him, may we grow ever more in confidence, according as the gospel is proclaimed to us each day.

# 15

## FIT FOR GOD'S USE

*Now in a large household there are not only vessels of gold or silver but of wood and clay, some to honour, and some to dishonour. ²¹ If a man therefore cleanses himself of the latter kind he will be a vessel sanctified to honourable use, fit for the Lord and ready for every good work.*

(2 Timothy 2:20-21)

If we see men who scorn God, and evildoers who set a bad example, we welcome the opportunity to stray from the proper path having, as we think, a ready-made excuse to absolve ourselves in God's sight. It never occurs to us that these are the means by which God seeks to train us, so that our faith may be better tested before he sends us into battle. Thus Paul not only exhorts us here to depart from all iniquity and to show that we are not like the scornful; he also warns us not to stumble when we see such mischief-makers. Their actions should not alarm us or lead us astray.

This is a point which Paul had already made, but which he now confirms by means of an appropriate metaphor. To stop us blaming our sins on the example of those who despise God, the apostle speaks of *a large house in which there are different kinds of vessels.* While a sideboard or table may be decked with vessels of silver and gold, in the kitchen there will be vessels of wood in which offal or rubbish is thrown, anything indeed which is to be swept out of the house. There will also be vessels of clay. The difference does not strike us as strange, for how would it be if we threw out gold or silver along with the household refuse? Would men not call us mad? If, then, no one sees anything wrong in a great house where there are vessels intended for mean or ignoble use, why should the same not be true of the house of God? Will we allow mere men, created beings, greater privileges than we allow the living God? Paul therefore urges all of God's children, mixed in as they are with the wicked, not to allow themselves to be corrupted by their company or to be defiled by their filth. Rather they are encouraged to be careful to avoid their bad examples and to cease to keep company with them. In a word, they are to give themselves more earnestly to God. Such is the general tenor of this verse.

Now as we have said, Paul's warning is one which is most useful to us. If there are evildoers and hypocrites who for a time are in God's church, and who even set out to be admired more than the rest, we should not be dismayed. God's house is large. Some, admittedly, take the word to include everybody. This meaning is possible, but we will say more about it directly. Here it is Paul's theme we need to consider. He spoke, first, of apostates who for a time professed the gospel but then rebelled and drew apart. Now come words of comfort, as if Paul were saying: 'Since God's church is spread throughout the world and since many are called to the gospel, they are gathered together, just as in a large house there are vessels of silver and gold which are used to adorn a sideboard or table. There are also vessels of clay and wood which are left lying around the house and which, after a time, when no longer needed, are burnt or else thrown out, as objects of no value.' Thus, although we might dearly wish that everything in God's church was pure and above reproach, we must nevertheless concede that scandals will arise and that there will be much confusion.

Why so? God has brought together many vessels and all of different kinds. As Scripture says elsewhere, God's church is like a draw-net cast into the sea, gathering all sorts of fish, both good and bad (Matt. 13:47). The gospel cannot be preached without many going along with it and pretending for a time to be among the faithful. But then—these fish—off they go. God's church is similarly likened to a threshing-floor where the wheat is beaten and mixes with the chaff. No one can distinguish the good grain from the chaff, which will later be thrown on to the dung heap (Matt. 3:12; Luke 3:17). All of this is intended to show that during this present life God's church will not be unmixed. There will always be hypocrites who accept that the faith should be taught or who at least want to be known and thought of as Christians. In the end, however, they turn out to be illegitimate offspring who will be disowned. Their type is represented by Ishmael (Gen. 21:14). There was a time when he was the first-born of the house. He was superior to Isaac, but Abraham was obliged to cut him off and to drive him out. That is how it is, and that is Paul's meaning here.

Before going any further, however, there is a problem which we must address. In Psalm 15 and again in Psalm 24, it is said that those who come to the mountain of the Lord and who dwell in it must be clean, walking in all integrity (Psa. 15:1-2; 24:3-4). Paul's text seems to contradict this, for he speaks of vessels for dishonourable use. All must be employed to serve God and all must be set apart to obey him. To what does God call us if not to holiness, as Scripture says (Eph. 1:4)? Are we not vessels in his temple? Are we not, each of us, part of his sanctuary? Should we not therefore be consecrated to him, cleansed of every spot and defilement?

Now in the passages which we have cited we are told what kind of people they must be whom God calls to himself. Not all, however, are said to be like this. There are many who are not in accord with God's will. Although commanded to dedicate themselves to him in all purity, they remain defiled. Indeed, when it is said that those who dwell in God's holy mountain must be pure and clean of heart and have washed their hands of all filthiness, we understand that although many claim to be God's children and boast of being believers, they do not deserve to be reckoned by God as members of his house. In the end they will be expelled from the place they have wrongly occupied. Having wickedly abused God's name they must be banished, as happened to Ishmael.

This is the meaning of the two Psalms to which I have drawn attention. As we see every day, there are those who for a time are members of God's church and who appear to belong to his family; yet they prove to be wicked and sinful, despising God and acting deceitfully and with malice toward their neighbours, whom they attack, rob or ill-treat. We see it all the time. Despite this they always fancy themselves as closest to God. It cannot of course last, and finally God will separate the goats from the lambs, showing who it is he calls his own. This exactly corresponds to Paul's teaching here.

In the second place the apostle appeals to us to cleanse ourselves of the filthiness of the wicked, so that we are not like them. If we are tainted by their defilement God will bring shame upon us. If we would be vessels of honour, it must be more than a matter of outward reputation. Our practice must match our calling so that we can demonstrate that God has not chosen us for himself in vain. Remember, in any case, what we are told here, that if evil men are mixed in with the good, we should not be unduly distressed— not like those sensitive souls who, noticing that there are faults in the church and that it is not as reformed and as perfect as we would wish, ask: 'Can this be God's church?' They are disposed to leave it, thinking that they will be defiled by associating with those who cannot fully remedy the faults we see among us.

I confess that we ought to be extremely zealous in doing all we can to put an end to scandals in our midst. Each of us must try to do his best. If we see something wrong it should be cleansed, removed and quickly forestalled so that it does not get worse. We all ought to be zealous in seeing that God's church remains pure. Nevertheless we must put up with many things which we are unable to correct, and if we cannot remedy them we should weep. Even so this is no excuse for us to leave God's church on the grounds that all are not living as they should. Why? Because, supposing we enter a large house by the kitchen, we do not worry if we see vessels which have been left aside and which are for mundane use. It is not as if they should stand as ornaments on a sideboard or table: they are merely there to receive the household waste and smelly scraps. They play their part in keeping the house decent. So if a man were so upset that he resolved to leave and never come back to a house where there were vessels intended only for rubbish—would such a man, I ask, be so silly as to take offence? On the contrary he would realize that people were keen to serve him better. When, therefore, we see such vessels in God's church, we should not be so aggrieved that we abandon it. We should instead continue on.

What Paul sought to show in this verse was that while the wicked try to bring God's name into disrepute, they nevertheless serve his glory despite themselves, for God will turn their evil into good. At first glance the wicked seem bent on discrediting God, denying his majesty and abolishing his righteousness, so that the world is turned upside down and God ceases to be known. This is their objective, and the devil drives them to it. For all that they are vessels whom God contrives to use so that he is glorified through them. Not that this excuses them or serves them as an alibi. They have failed to serve God, nor did they intend to do so. Nevertheless God makes use of them. For our part, if we cannot submit to God's providence we should not think that we are excused when, disappointed or distressed, we plead that all is so confused that we must wait for God to correct what is amiss.

Let us be absolutely sure in any case that God will be glorified in spite of Satan. In the meantime let us put this teaching to good use, so that when we see so much mischief among us, and when offences are not suppressed as they ought to be, when honesty is ignored and lawlessness allowed, when eyes are shut so that nothing is seen or noticed, and when no one is severe or strict enough to curb wrong conduct—when, I say, we see such things, we should weep and, if possible, strive to put them right. Yet we should not think that God's kingdom has been destroyed, that our Lord Jesus Christ has lost his power or that his church is scattered and close to perishing. We should dismiss such idle thoughts, knowing that although the wicked mar the church's beauty and do all they can to tarnish and spoil it, ultimately God will be glorified. He will bring them to their end, and when they have had their way and stirred up a great deal of trouble, God will be their judge and our faith will be all the stronger.

In the meantime we are to be patient, knowing full well that God is a wonderful workman who, by the choicest of means, is able to bring glory to himself, whether through the devil or through the wicked. Naturally the devil will always prove to be the deadly enemy of God's glory and he will attempt to tread it underfoot. But even when he has done all he can, God will turn evil into good. The same is true of all evildoers who plot and scheme to make all possible mischief, to end God's sovereign rule and to erase even the memory of his name. When, however, they have done their very worst, they still remain vessels. Thus Paul, in the ninth chapter of Romans, although pursuing a more general theme than the one we have here, shows that the reprobate—not only those who profess to be Christians but those who are openly hostile—are nevertheless God's vessels and tools in whom he displays his glory, though that was never their intention; they were driven to it all the same (Rom. 9:22). Here Paul has in mind both those who never confessed God or pretended to be members of his house, as well as hypocrites who appeared to be pious for a time until they were unmasked by God. All of them, the apostle declares, are God's instruments. Do you see an evildoer who is bent on mixing heaven and earth? He is in God's hands. Satan will carry him this way and that, and he will come close to achieving all manner of marvels; yet God will show that he has kept him under tight control and has used him as his instrument.

God's Spirit, it is true, never impels the wicked to do evil. It would be blasphemous to suggest such a thing, for the Spirit leads us to righteousness and to integrity. While the devil drives the wicked to do wrong, God remains supreme, though how he does so we cannot comprehend. In any case he knows how to use the wicked and to make them serve him, so that through them his glory is made known. Thus when in the church troubles arise which cause offence, let us learn to be patient, but not so as to encourage evil for, as I said, we must each according to our role try hard to see that the church is rid of all uncleanliness. When, however, we are not able to do better, let us sigh and weep and wait in all patience for God to bring good out of evil. Bear in mind, then, the lesson we are given here, that the wicked are vessels—they are obliged, that is, to serve God. They strain not a muscle to that end, but God is able to drag them after him as if by force, and to dispose of them according to his counsel which is beyond our understanding. In God's house they are not appointed for honourable use, yet the master's rights are not impaired: God's name does not cease to be glorified, his righteousness is not diminished, nor is his wisdom, power and goodness. This is how we may apply Paul's teaching.

In the next verse Paul says that *if anyone cleanses himself of this kind, he will be a vessel for honourable use.* This is the second point to which reference has been made. In the first place, we said, the apostle wants to avoid those things which cause offence and which so incense and distress us. When we see that God's church is not as reformed as we would like, we think that all is lost and that God has ceased to rule the world. No, says Paul, we should not feel too discouraged, but should wait patiently for God to use men's malice to his glory. The outcome will inevitably be good, provided we are resolute and unmoved by the turmoil we see around us. We should not, however, while living among the wicked copy their ways or ally ourselves with them. We must be separate from them, which is what Paul means by 'someone who cleanses himself of this kind'. He does not simply say, 'if someone cleanses himself, let him dedicate himself to God.' We read that we must cleanse ourselves of the evil which the apostle has in mind.

Now it is not easy to walk through the mud and mire and not to sully ourselves. It would be remarkable if we went into some filthy place and emerged unspotted! When we live among those who scoff at God, among hypocrites and the dissolute, we must be all the more careful to remain pure and clean. Nothing could be simpler than to be caught up in the general corruption and to let it infect us. So, says Paul, let us be vigilant. His advice was not meant for one time only, but for all time. Let us therefore learn that, although there must be discipline in the church so that wrongs are punished and the people kept in godliness and integrity of life, we are bound to witness many things which, unless we guard against them, could harm us and turn us from the proper path. Hence while in this present life we have to associate with the wicked, we must endeavour to cleanse ourselves of their defilement. And while Satan desires to mix and muddle everything, let us ask God to protect us and to keep us by his Holy Spirit in all purity, so that his righteousness may shine in us and always reign supreme.

When Paul urges us to cleanse ourselves of evil, he means that we have no excuse for copying the wicked among whom we live and who want our company, for God did not sanctify us in vain when he called us to himself. Not that we have strength enough to cleanse ourselves as we are asked to do. God's intention is that we each do our best to dedicate ourselves to his service. There are some who, on the pretext of this statement, have tried to prove that it is in our power to cause God to choose and predestine us. This, however, is to overturn the very foundations of the faith. It is utter folly to maintain that, if we want God to choose us, we must separate ourselves from the wicked. This is the same as saying that before we were born and before the world was made, we had to ensure that we were worthy of God's adoption! On the contrary, God did not weigh up our merits when he elected us before the world began. This is pure madness, and deserves no further comment.

Others, again, have tried to make a case for free will by claiming that we are commanded here to cleanse ourselves. Such a thing must therefore require effort on our part. These people, however, make their ignorance and stupidity all too plain. They are abysmally unskilled in holy Scripture, for when God shows us what our duty and calling are he does not say that these lie within our power and our capacity. All he does is show us what is sound and good. Yet all the while it is he who works in us, especially since he knows how prone we are to fail, and how incapable of doing what he asks of us. What this text teaches us is that we must cleanse ourselves so that we do not become like the wicked. More than that, however, God tells us through Ezekiel that he will provide pure, clean water in order to wash us—in other words, his Holy Spirit (Ezek. 36:25). Hence we are commanded to cleanse ourselves, but it is all God's doing, for it comes from the unmerited grace of his Holy Spirit.

Why, then, did Paul speak this way? Because although our Lord alone works all that is good in us, so that nothing comes from any impulse of our own, he does not treat us like blocks of wood, but gives us the will, the intention and the strength to fight against every obstacle. He thus attributes to us what is really his. He works so effectively in us that we appear to do the work! Those who believe will therefore strive—with utmost difficulty—to cleanse themselves of the world's filth, so as not to be defiled by the iniquity of evil men. We will take pains to achieve that end and the struggle will be long. God, however, urges us on, and he is the one who gives us strength. In short, he enables us both to will and to do, as Paul writes, all of his own free grace (Phil. 2:13). But because we should never be idle he rightly exhorts us, as we see him doing in this passage, and his exhortation is by no means needless.

So much, then, for Paul's command to cleanse ourselves. He then explains why: *so that we may be honourable vessels, fit for the master's use and given to good works.* When Paul speaks of vessels of honour, he shows that it is not enough to have a place in God's church and to bear the name 'Christian', unless we have been also, as it were, set apart. True, all who have been baptized, all who take part in the Lord's Supper and who mix with believers are already separated from the faithless. No one would call them Turks or heathen. Yet we must be sanctified even more, in another and higher sense. We must be marked not only outwardly so that we can claim to be baptized and can profess to be willing to serve God. Our life too must demonstrate that we are truly God's children, and when we are governed by his Holy Spirit this must further testify to the reality of our adoption. This is what Paul means to imply when he says that we must be vessels of honour. Why? Because it may well be that, although members of God's church, and mature members too, we will finally be discarded like a broken jar, or set aside like a wooden bowl which has no further use. Such is the fate of hypocrites who boast that they are reckoned among God's children. To be sure they are vessels that God employs, but they will be disgraced and God will bring them to destruction.

Let us therefore make sure that we are honourable vessels, known as God's children not merely outwardly or fleetingly, but as children chosen and set apart by him as his permanent inheritance. Let this be the way in which we draw near to our God. Thus we will be not only household vessels but vessels in God's temple employed for sacrificial offerings, honouring to God. For when God is glorified even by the wicked, as is said of Pharaoh both in Exodus and in Romans (Exod. 9:16; Rom. 9:17), this seems quite contrary to nature, as if fire could be got from water. God indeed must work a miracle, as we said, whenever men's evil, which is totally opposed, is made to serve his glory. Here we have a work too involved and too exalted for us to understand. Strictly speaking we cannot say that the wicked glorify God. We glorify him when we give ourselves to him and ask only that his name be honoured. This we do when we are his true children, and when with body and soul we endeavour to be useful to him. Has God not called us to this very thing?

At the same time Paul suggests that we are not only vessels in God's temple but the priests who bear them. God therefore honours us by choosing to make us worthy vessels, and by consecrating our bodies and souls to his service. We are to be vessels in his temple put to holy use, so that he may have dominion over us. Accordingly we should strive even more to sanctify ourselves, as we read in the prophet Isaiah: 'Be clean, you who bear the vessels of the Lord' (Isa. 52:11). We read too that God commanded the vessels to be pure and clean and not to be defiled. Since, then, we are vessels in his temple, since we are their bearers and keepers, let us see that we dedicate ourselves to God's use. May that use be honourable. Again, since we are God's temple, whether as individuals or all together, let us keep ourselves pure.

In order to prove that the verse which I quoted from Isaiah concerns us and is addressed to us, let us heed Paul's exhortation in the sixth chapter of Second Corinthians, which shows that Isaiah's words are meant as much for us as for the priests of old (2 Cor.

6:17). Why? Because, says Paul, we have the promises. Seeing, then, that God honours us by accepting us as vessels in his temple, and especially by dedicating us to his use and choosing to live in us by his Holy Spirit, ought we not to be cleansed of all filthiness? It would not be right for God to dwell in a foul or dirty place: his dwelling must be pure and holy. All that touches or comes close to him must be sanctified, otherwise he will not draw near to us. Hence Paul urges us to sanctify ourselves, so that we may be fit for God's use. Not that he cannot turn the hostile acts of the wicked to his advantage but, as I said, he does so by force. We, however, cannot be fit to serve our God, who is the master of the house, unless we are vessels of honour, that is, as Paul goes on to explain, 'given to every good work'.

This is the way we become fit and honourable vessels. For as I said, the disobedient—yes, even the most evil, the most villainous of men—are used by God as his tools, so that they are finally made to glorify him, or else God himself is glorified through them. But because their intention is not to do good but rather to do evil, to impugn God's righteousness, to abolish all law and, in a word, to create chaos in the world, God must keep them in check and use them as he pleases. If we, on the other hand, want to be fit for his service, we must devote ourselves to good works, which means obeying him and following his holy calling. Then we will not only be instruments in the hands of our God but also vessels of honour. Being led by his Holy Spirit we will be fit for his service, that is, eager to see that he is exalted and that we, first and foremost, should serve him with body and soul, for this is the ministry to which he has called us and the service by which we may glorify him. That is the main thrust of this passage.

Briefly to conclude, let us learn not to go astray, whatever troubles the devil may stir up and however many waves and tempests there may be. Though we do not see the order and the discipline which we think are needful, we should press on. Let us not think that this in any way impairs God's majesty. Remember that, as in a large house, there are bound to be vessels meant for unclean use. We should not think that we are excused, however, for mixing with the defiled. Let us be all the more alert. Since God wishes to test our feelings for him, let each be on his guard, so that when we see the wicked enjoying themselves and making mischief, we should go the other way. When evil is rife and when men are out to drag their friends with them to destruction, let us turn to God and ask him to bring us under the Holy Spirit's control. May we strive after the purity of which Paul speaks. We realize nevertheless that we are not equal to the task. Being both weak and sinful, let us pray that God will pour out on us his pure water, as Ezekiel says (Ezek. 36:25). Then we will be fit for his service, desiring only to give ourselves in obedience to him, freely, not out of compulsion or constraint. When God is glorified through the wicked whom he has appointed for his glory's sake, know that it is not of their volition but that it is a wonderful act of providence which demands our worship. For God works to such effect that he brings good out of evil, just as when he made the world he turned darkness into light, according to the image used by Paul in Second Corinthians (2 Cor. 4:6).

Now let us cast ourselves down before the face of our good God, acknowledging our faults and praying that he may make us feel them more, lest we presume on his goodness. Since he has made us his household servants, may he give us grace to serve him and to keep ourselves from this world's uncleanness and corruption. And although we cannot avoid the taint of the iniquity around us, may he defend us so that we have no part in the works of the wicked, but may be cleansed of them. May his church, too, be cleansed, until the day when Jesus Christ appears to restore what now is broken and to bring all things to completion. Then may he acknowledge us as honourable vessels who bear the mark of his Holy Spirit, that we may live forever with him in the glory which he won for us and which is prepared for us in heaven.

# 16

---

# STRIVING FOR MATURITY

*Shun also youthful desires; instead follow righteousness, faith, love and*
*peace with those who with pure hearts call upon the Lord.*

(2 Timothy 2:22)

I f we were more conscious of our faults and imperfections, we
would be led at any time of life to humble ourselves before God,
to detest ourselves and to be on our guard, since the smallest thing
will trip us up. When we have lived in this world to the age of
thirty, although God may have graciously blessed us with his word,
provided the means for our instruction and given us a liking for it,
we are still far from being mature or rounded off. Have we gone
beyond the age of thirty? In that case we begin to fall away, and
there are weaknesses which pull us in the opposite direction. If
we consider someone in his youth, he is not yet fully formed. And
once past the age of thirty, he begins to acquire different faults. In
short, there are neither young nor old who do not need to be told
humbly to recognize their failings, and to take care so to walk that,
if there is evil in them, it should never have the upper hand.

An excellent example of this is found here in Paul's exhortation.
If ever there was an outstanding man, it was Timothy. He was one

of those who by God's hand had been placed in the church as a mirror of every virtue. We know the testimony which Scripture bears him. Nevertheless this is Paul's solemn warning to him: *Shun youthful passions.*

Timothy was not like a young man of twenty. He was an experienced preacher of God's word. He was also a recognized teacher not of one church only but of the whole surrounding region, for Paul had appointed him not to preach in one place only but to have a larger oversight, so that he might counsel bishops and those who had responsibilities similar to his. Here then is a man of some years' standing and who is certainly mature. We saw already that the Lord chose him over others and endowed him with remarkable gifts. He not only had a sound command of doctrine and prophecy; his life too was consistent, and he was most zealous to promote God's honour. He was, in a word, an example to all. For all that he needed to be disciplined, which is why the apostle urges him not to lose control, as sometimes happens when youthful passions simmer.

How old was Timothy? He must have been more than thirty. However, as I said, God's Spirit means to show us by the mouth of Paul and by Timothy's own example that, even though we have progressed in God's school and have long been governed by his Holy Spirit, we are still not fully formed or rounded off. And even when we reach the age of forty can we demonstrate that we are really adults? We are disposed to resist everything we are taught, especially when it is a question of God's service. We still steam and simmer! So until we reach our declining years we are rough and ill-finished. God must continue to touch us with the plane and hammer us once or twice, or else sand us down, otherwise we leave much to be desired. We begin to grow old before God has made us fully ready for his service. The fault lies with our frailties, since before we are even moderately prepared we are already, as it were, half broken! Let us learn, then, not to presume anything of ourselves or to become drunk with pride and vainglory, for we are never above reproach.

In the light of what is said specifically about the young, let each of us look to himself, far though we are from possessing the holiness and maturity of Timothy. The young are positive and energetic, having a certain ardour which excites them to commit many follies. They do not yet have enough skill or experience to be prudent. They do not foresee things from afar; nothing is too hard for them; they are bold and reckless and have other failings too. Admittedly Paul does not speak here of youthful lusts which lead to unruliness or bad behaviour, such as fornication, gambling or drunkenness. No such thing applied to Timothy, who was expected to teach and to instruct men who might have been his fathers where the gospel was concerned. Here, then, was a man who needed no one to save him from the follies of the young. Nevertheless he does not escape the limitations of his age, as if our Lord humbles his own by not making them immediately mature, but allows them to drag a leg or a wing after them, so that they may sigh and humble themselves and never dare to boast without feeling shame.

Our Lord does not leave those to whom he has been most gracious without some imperfections. Thus Timothy is commanded here to shun youthful desires. What, then, shall we say of those who follow far behind? Although God grants them, as I said before, a measure of his gifts, they may still simmer. They must be brought to see that they are not mature enough to be as prudent as they ought to be. They lack seriousness; they do not see all that passes before their face; they are too impetuous, given to too much boldness, too self-confident, too complacent.

The young should therefore learn from Timothy's example to cease from their faults and to be sober, for it is a duty strictly enjoined on children and on the young to submit to discipline, since they are not yet capable of judging as they should and of knowing what is in their own interests. If this is lacking in young people, whatever virtues they may have are turned to vices, vices so hateful that this one spot or blemish is enough to spoil all the goodness they may have. They will be so arrogant that they will stubbornly refuse to heed or calmly to accept what is said to them. So let the young especially respect the quality of moderation, for if those who are decent and who do not lead bad or disorderly lives need this word of warning, how much more do those who behave like runaway calves? They are beyond control, these greedy, promiscuous young people, drunkards or despisers of God and of all religion! Paul's warning to Timothy is needed not only to keep them in check but to chain them down!

Nowadays, alas, the world has become so bad that we find most young people a great disappointment. Where is that humility which makes them manageable and which teaches them self-control? If they have one small virtue given them by God, they refuse to accept a single word of advice; they fancy that, as wisdom goes, they are better than the ancients. Or else they are so excessively foolish and dissolute that it is pitiful to see. There is no getting near them, so proud and presumptuous are they. If someone utters a word of rebuke they immediately gnash their teeth and spit out their venom. They heap insults and abuse on those whose age ought to earn them their respect. They will not listen to either father or mother, nor do they have any consideration for their pastors. Today's youth are so beyond the pale that the hairs of our head should stand on end. I mean most youth, since here those who are not fully grown and mature should learn that God offers them an effective remedy by condemning their simmering passions and their unruly cravings. They should all understand, then, that these words are addressed to them. They would have to be mad if they thought they could compare themselves with Timothy. And even if they were exactly like him, the Holy Spirit makes it clear that they are still not above reproach. In fact they are so much more imperfect. Let them be sure, then, that they keep all youthful excesses under control, and instead of being hotheads let them douse the fire of youth with water, so that all may see that they follow good counsel, reason and wisdom.

Now if this is Paul's message to the young, how much more shameful is it for those who are already old to be much too impetuous, to go too far and to give no sign of being serious or self-controlled? If the age which is subject to excessive bouts of temper offers adults no excuse, what shall we say when the elderly, who should have left skirmishing behind, remain unchanged and will not correct themselves? Is this not disreputable and almost contrary to nature? Scripture tells us that the young particularly need God's word so as to order their ways (Psa. 119:9). But the elderly also are included, for God rightly insists that as long as we live we should profit from the teaching he provides. The old must therefore be scholars in God's school, but since they are not beginners they must give proof that they have matured. They must show that they have not begun only today to be earnest and sober, and to have left behind the ebullience of youth.

Let us come back in any case to the point made earlier. Whatever a man's age he must recognize that he is never blameless. For if old age does not favour quickness of temper or excessive enthusiasm, if it removes pride or else moderates it, it brings greater problems so that the old are heard to say: 'When we were at our peak we were able to accomplish worthwhile things, but we did them badly and we misspent our time. Today we are half dead, and although by God's grace we still survive and are free to do the things we must, we are half broken and just about all up.' In short, how true the proverb is: 'Youth knows not, old age cannot.'

Those who think they are infinitely wise are full of arrogance and have no idea which path to take. They are like half-trained horses; they run and frisk about because they have not learned to be controlled. That is how the young are. By the time, however, they begin to grasp what virtue and decency are, they cannot manage either because of their declining strength and ability.

We must therefore learn to like ourselves less and to humble ourselves before God. Let all of us be conscious of our own failings so that we condemn them and, in condemning them, let us determine to resist them as much as possible by God's grace. Here, however, Paul indicates the appropriate remedies which help to correct the excitability which affects almost all young people. *Follow righteousness*, he says, *with faith, love and peace, along with all those who with a pure heart call upon the Lord.* In urging Timothy to follow righteousness, faith and love, the apostle seeks to show that when we err and stray or are too impetuous, too undisciplined or extreme, it is a sign that we are not properly rooted in God's faith and fear, and that we are too heedless of our duties. Those who are somewhat superstitious or who are reckless in their zeal demonstrate that they do not know themselves or look closely enough at what lies within. That is why they go astray. Paul thus prescribes a remedy which is the very opposite of the things he spoke about before. So if we want to correct the faults which hinder us, let us consider Paul's solution. We must, that is, acknowledge the evil passions which we harbour, given that we have not been careful enough to grow in faith and love. We fly off the handle, so to speak, since our conscience is not sharp enough. In sum, if we go much too far it is because we are vain and futile. We are too immature and empty within, which leads us into error and makes us vulnerable to our feelings. One fault points to another so that, knowing the reality of our plight, we must turn to the remedy which is set before us. This is what Paul means, and this is how we can profit from what he says.

Timothy, to be sure, did not need to be told to follow faith and love. He was, as we have seen, no novice in such things. The Holy Spirit bore witness that he was not only praised by men but was declared by God to excel all others. Even so Paul sometimes urges him to follow integrity, love and faith. Thus we should all acknowledge that even the most mature have not yet reached their goal; they are still on their way, which is why they need encouragement. This is a point well worth noting, for when we find that we have made some progress and are different from what we were before, we fancy that we are already almost better than the angels in paradise! So any warning we receive is quite superfluous and is wasted on us. Why is this so? Because we do not see that, as long as we live in this world, our journey is not ended. We are not conscious enough of our feebleness and of how far we are from being fully righteous and blameless in faith and love, as God commands. We are oblivious of this and we fail to live accordingly. None of us thinks to arraign himself before God to see whether he has grown in any way—even half grown! Solomon says as much when he declares: 'A man's ways are right in his own sight, but God values the heart' (Prov. 21:2). When we fall into error and think that there is nothing wrong with us, do we not flatter ourselves? We must all appear before the Judge who has a different set of scales. He plumbs the most secret of our thoughts and will bring our emptiness to light.

So where do all these simmering passions come from, these seething emotions, this turbulence which we experience? It is because we are not alert enough and because God's fear has not taken vital root, is not so deeply attached as it ought to be. This should teach us not to shut our eyes to our failings, and if we are not conscious of them let us ask God to enlighten us, so that we may be led to weep, to condemn ourselves and to turn always to him.

For the rest, it is important to remember the contrast which I drew between Timothy and ourselves. Here we have Timothy, a mirror of holiness and righteousness, a true model of love and faith. Yet he is told to give himself to them better than before. What, alas, are we compared with him? So let us not be like those madmen who think that they know exactly how they ought to live. If we tell them what it means to live decently and fairly in obedience to God, and how to grow in faith, 'Who,' they cry, 'doesn't know that? There's nothing new there!' Let us not give in, I say, to such foolishness, and let us keep on learning the lesson daily taught to us by God. And if someone speaks to us of righteousness, whereas these rascals think they know it all already, let us learn to examine ourselves, as our text suggests. When we look carefully at what we are within, what wisdom and prudence do we find? We come back to the fact that our sin is the common one of ignorance. Yet we are full of pride, believing that we know everything.

Turning to the word 'faith', we all regard ourselves as faithful. It is commonplace—the Christian ABC—to speak of faith. Yet a simple leaf falling from a tree, or a small shadow passing before us, is more than enough to discourage and dismay us. Even when there is no obvious danger we are prone to conjure up a thousand thoughts which make us nervous and distrustful. Thus when we do not call upon God with steadfast hearts, when tribulation upsets us and when all strength fails, be sure that the faith we have is very poor and meagre. Paul's exhortation, then, is by no means needless. It is worth remembering.

Timothy is expressly asked 'to follow peace with all who with a pure heart call upon the Lord'. This is meant to suppress the strong assertiveness which Paul had earlier condemned. For when we go about things thoughtlessly we risk destroying all friendship and stirring up fights. Much quickness of temper in a man serves as a trumpet or a drum to sound the alarm. Peace should therefore be particularly dear to us, so that God may dwell and reign among us. This, then, is the fault which the apostle has in mind when he counsels Timothy to keep the peace with all who with pure hearts call upon the Lord. When this is true of us, no better curb could be found to keep us under control. Although we may still have cause to feel indignant, our desire to preserve the peace will restrain us. 'Peace,' Paul says, 'with all true believers.' Not that God's children should not strive as much as possible to be at peace with everyone, as the apostle writes in the twelfth chapter of Romans (Rom. 12:18). He does, however, add this proviso: 'so far as you are able'. Why? Because although we give the wicked and God's enemies no reason to attack us or to feel angry over some slight or other, we are bound to be in conflict with them as long as Satan is the enemy of our Lord Jesus Christ. It is he who leads them and inspires them to do all kinds of mischief. How, then, could we be of one mind with them except by totally sharing in their sin? Anyone who seeks to please the wicked by taking their part denies God and forsakes his righteousness. As we all know, if there are evil and wilful men, as soon as we associate with them we learn to support them in their sinful ways; we soon become their accomplices and are caught up with them in their contempt for God. Would to God we saw fewer instances of this than we do! True, such people complain that we are not their friends, but what they want is for us to side with them by taking up arms against God. This we cannot do.

We should certainly try, therefore, to the best of our ability to live in peace and harmony with everyone. Yet we must not forget that the wicked will never agree with us, and that we must do battle with them if we would fight under the banner of our Lord Jesus Christ. On that point we should all be resolved.

What, then, remains? We must be at peace with those who call upon God. This calls for unity and brotherhood, for if we are on bad terms or in dispute with genuine believers, with whom are we in conflict? We think that we are only dealing with mortal men, but it is God we grieve, as if we had deliberately set out to provoke him. In short, we cannot separate ourselves from the faithful nor quarrel with them without God taking sides against us. So we should try all the harder to be at peace with those who call upon him. Be sure that faith and love are lacking unless we are so united with the brethren as to be bound to them by ties of fellowship, so that we give our neighbours a helping hand and encourage each other in our service to God. Let us all endeavour to serve those who need our aid, and let us especially fear lest the devil kindle among us the flame of conflict. That would be like banishing God from our midst, since he has promised to dwell only with those who live in peace. That is why, if we want to be seen as God's church and as the flock of our Lord Jesus Christ, our brotherliness must be visible and known.

However, because many claim God's name but show scant signs that they are his, Paul adds the words, 'with a pure heart'. Now to call upon God can mean two things, though they are part of the same truth. Sometimes Scripture speaks of calling upon God's name in the sense intended by Paul when, as we saw, he writes, 'Let those who call upon the Lord's name depart from evil' (2 Tim. 2:19). Thus to call upon the Lord's name is to bear that name oneself. Hence when we are called Christians we are said to claim God's name and to carry the mark of his Son. That may be what is meant in this passage. There is, however, a prior meaning intended by Paul. By calling upon God he means that we turn to him and petition him in time of need. And because prayer is our principal service and, according to Psalm 50, the supreme offering which God demands (Psa. 50:14-15), sometimes under one category Scripture includes all the rest. So to call upon the Lord implies that we love him, serve him and do him homage as is our duty.

God is not worshipped by ceremonies. While we may make a fine show we should not think that we have done all that is required in order to serve God. God's main requirement is that we confess, by prayer and supplication, that we are empty of all goodness, that we are utterly wretched, that we look to him alone for refuge and praise him for all his benefits. Thus, since the true service which God asks of us is prayer, to call upon his name is to honour and serve him. That is why it is said that we blaspheme his name whenever we cease to serve him.

Those, writes Paul, who call upon the Lord's name must do so with pure hearts. The fact is that there are many hypocrites who mingle with the flock; they use it as a cover to hide their contempt for God. Can we be at peace with such as these? They are far worse enemies than those who reject the gospel outright. The prophets, we know, often had to struggle against idolaters, as did the apostles and martyrs. Yet they had most trouble from the enemies within, who belonged to God's house and who loudly boasted that they were God's people. Nevertheless they were wicked and perverse. There is no way that we can be at peace with people like that. They protest long and loud as if they had no peer and were pillars of the Christian faith. They are bound to be our enemies and we must fight against them. More than anyone else they disturb God's church, and since they have the means they do more harm. An abscess is much more dangerous when inside the body than others which are visible and which can be cured more easily. It is the same with those who are mixed in with the faithful but who make light of God, scorn him and reject his word.

We must always therefore be involved in conflict. We are given due warning of this in our text, so that the weak should have no reason to stumble. Thus when God's servants, and particularly ministers who preach the word, have to respond sharply to those who resist them and to stand against them, we should not be surprised. We should consider it inevitable and regard it as God's way of testing us. On the other hand, when someone calls upon God with purity of heart, we should resolve to support him and to give him no cause to stumble or to be grieved by our outspokenness. We should try rather to pursue peace and unity with him. That is Paul's message to us here.

There is a general lesson also which we may gather from this verse. To call upon God is not a matter of lips alone, lest Isaiah's reproach be addressed to us: 'This people honours me with their lips, but their heart is far from me' (Isa. 29:13). Let us make sure, I say, that God does not accuse us of such pretence. When we call upon his name let us learn, as was said a moment ago, to depart from iniquity. While sin assails us on all sides and while the devil spreads his infection in our midst in order to ruin everything, let us remain apart from the wicked. Although we may be in their company for a time—that is, we may, humanly speaking, live alongside them—we should avoid intimacy with them so that we are not yoked together, so to speak, with them.

Consider also that it is not enough to lead an honest life in the eyes of men. The main thing is that our heart should be pure, for God does not look on the outward appearance, as we say, and as we read in Samuel (1 Sam. 16:7). He looks on the heart. Above all, let us learn to cleanse ourselves of all our sham and evil whenever we call upon God's name. Then we may truly say that we are Christians and that God acknowledges us as his people, provided we are not two-faced and do not falsely disguise ourselves in order to win esteem. Let us walk uprightly, in full integrity of life, calling upon God purely even if he is our only witness. When he acknowledges us as his we will be free of all deceit and evil.

Again, as we saw, controversies lead to conflict and to any amount of quarrelling. Paul therefore instructs Timothy to edify and to think of what will help God's people. His command is not new, but we may gather from it that the chief duty of ministers of the word is to resist the urge to show off, and not to try to impress men by fanciful or pompous display. Let them be content to serve God and their neighbour, and to provide appropriate instruction for those to whom they have been sent. It is of this, then, that Paul reminds Timothy, as he did before. We cannot discuss the whole text now, but we will keep the rest until after dinner. At any rate, let us—I mean we who are charged with preaching God's word— avoid all futile arguments and endeavour to proclaim only good, sound doctrine which will continually edify our people in godliness and faith, and will stir them up to prayer and supplication, teaching them that the whole of their salvation comes from above, and that all human boasting must be brought low. On this we must insist and this is what we must labour to accomplish.

If this is a lesson for us, it is a lesson too for the whole company of believers. All must desire only such teaching as serves to build us up in faith, in repentance and in godly fear. This should be our purpose when we come to church. We should not come from fickle motives, for that would be to profane God's word. To come in that mood would mean that we did not deserve to hear anything helpful to our salvation. So are we truly ready to learn in the school of God and of our Lord Jesus Christ? Then let us desire teaching which will really edify. And while our flesh may prompt us to pursue utterly useless questions, we should resist it as something harmful and injurious, and we should do the same when we read Scripture privately at home. For whenever we treat God's word lightly and speak carelessly about him, we are reminded that God's name conveys such majesty that every knee must duly bow before him, not only outwardly but in our souls. We must strive with heart and mind to submit to him alone. May we learn to serve and honour him, and may we pray all the more earnestly for his kingdom to prosper and flourish until it is complete.

Now let us cast ourselves down before the face of our good God, acknowledging our faults and begging him to make us truly feel them. May we so repent that, turning to him, we renounce all our affections and desires and are conformed to his righteousness. And although all that we do to serve him falls far short, may he graciously uphold us until he draws us to himself, frees us from the law's demands and grants us to learn faith and repentance. May we walk in purity of life, showing that the light of his glory shines in us, and that his image is remade in us by our Lord Jesus Christ.

# 17

## THE LORD'S SERVANT

*But reject foolish controversies which are devoid of instruction, know-*
*ing that they breed quarrels. <sup>24</sup> For the Lord's servant must not engage*
*in disputes, but let him be mild-mannered toward all, an apt teacher,*
*patiently bearing with the wicked, <sup>25</sup> gently teaching those who resist,*
*to see whether at any time God may grant them repentance so that they*
*may know the truth.* (2 Timothy 2:23-25)

We began this morning to expound Paul's statement that we should not pursue questions which do nothing to advance our salvation. We are to have no liking for them. Indeed we are asked *to reject foolish arguments which are devoid of instruction.* Paul calls them foolish, but most people do not judge them that way, for they regard as clever and sharp-witted anyone who raises problems which cloud their minds and which torment them when they cannot find a solution. In the long run we see no point in all these disputes and arguments. Nevertheless many of us are highly impressed when people bring up futile matters for discussion.

True wisdom for God's children consists in godly fear. Anything which does not serve that purpose is condemned by the Holy Spirit as a waste of time. A fine text it is when someone quotes the statement—reflected everywhere in Scripture—that to fear God is true wisdom (Prov. 1:7; 9:10). We all agree, yet we do not grasp what is meant, for instead of concentrating on the things which lead us to fear God, we give ourselves to things which do not matter. This is what occupies almost all our lives, and our minds are naturally inclined this way. We love only vanity, so that many are content to feed on air. Moreover the greatest minds which might have been of service to God's church throw caution to the winds and pursue worthless irrelevancies; they therefore neglect what might have provided sound, worthwhile teaching. Let us remember, then, what Paul tells us here: any idea which serves no purpose, however lofty and admirable it may seem to us, is mere foolishness. Why foolish? It is as I said: our one thought should be to fear God.

When Paul speaks of instruction, he does not mean that we should be thought of as intelligent or learned, but that we should be profitably taught. As well as the knowledge we have and the things we have heard, practice too must follow. See how deservedly this wretched world gropes blindly about! Men are always tickled by curiosity, wanting to know more than is permissible and wasting their time on silly trifles. True, they insist that these are deep mysteries, but in fact they are completely useless. God is therefore right to punish such ambition, since men have only ever had ears for foolishness; they have never been interested in what might build them up in godly fear. God therefore left Satan free to trick and deceive them, and was justly avenged on men for their thanklessness when he allowed folly and superstition to prevail, and all truth to be turned into a lie.

When, on the other hand, we come into God's school, we must be ready to accept teaching which is useful to us, and be resolved to walk as we ought in holiness of life. If that is not the case, we make poor use of God's word and we do our best to profane it. Accordingly God pays us the wages we deserve: we are fed on lies, since we did not choose as we should to be edified by God. Since, then, God visited so dreadful a judgment on the world, instruction ceased to be and in its place came falsehood and delusion. Those who were reputed to be theologians and to possess all the wisdom in the world were drunk on their own lies. That being so, let us heed Paul's warning all the more, so that we follow what will profitably lead us to fear God and to obey him. And although the world applauds these pointless disputes, as the Holy Spirit tells us here we must view them as madness and vanity, since they do not edify or benefit anyone.

Furthermore Paul, who knows how hard it is to keep us from engaging in such idle business, seeks to turn us from things that cannot edify by adding that *they only breed strife and quarrels*. As we know, men itch to show their worth in clever, subtle debate; the world flocks to listen and cannot get enough of it. Since we are prone to turn aside, let us remember what we read here, that not only will we have wasted our time, we will have run the deadlier risk of being hurt by our quarrelling and bickering. We ought to live in peace with all the faithful. For as we said this morning, if it is pitiful to see conflict in God's church, we should learn not only to shun pointless controversies but to remove and banish them from our midst. Otherwise we deliberately poison ourselves when we welcome and allow such things among us. Paul thus speaks of controversies which engender strife in order to reinforce the instruction that we shun them. Unless we learn that they will harm us we will never avoid them, because it is to this that our nature leads us. This accursed disposition is so deeply rooted in us that we will never come to hate it unless we regard it as a poison or as something equally fatal.

In the light of what he has just said about arguments and strife, the apostle continues: *No servant of the Lord should be quarrelsome; he should be mild-mannered, patient and an apt teacher*. Paul's conclusion therefore is that all who go in for useless arguments clearly show that they have neither the wish nor the zeal to serve God. For although someone may be the most learned man imaginable, we must nevertheless consider him to be a hopeless devil if he has no desire to serve God or to see him honoured. The ancient proverb is right when it says that knowledge in a man who is a villain is like a sword in the hand of a lunatic or madman. Paul's aim here is to shame all who insist on quarrelling. We are to loathe and abominate them as people who refuse to serve God. Why loathe them? Because serving God and loving quarrels which engender strife are as incompatible as fire and water.

We may gather from this passage that there are very few who deserve to be considered true servants of God. How many there are who are bent on provoking needless controversy in order to disturb the church! How many firebrands there are nowadays—ignorant though they are and almost entirely stupid—who continually try to attract attention by stirring up trouble! More particularly, however, we see from this passage how necessary it is for ministers of God's word to know that they can never faithfully fulfil their office unless, in keeping with Paul's teaching here, they shun all contention and strife.

There is, however, a message here for every member of God's church. We must carefully distinguish between those who are God's servants and the hypocrites who misuse his name. Here is an infallible mark: when we see a quarrelsome man who insists, as we say, that sheep have five legs not four, we must reject him like a deadly plague, knowing that whatever he may say it is Satan he means to serve, and that to edify God's church was never his aim. This is Paul's message to us.

He explains how conflict may be avoided by urging us to be 'mild-mannered toward all, apt teachers and patient with evildoers'. In saying that we must treat all men gently the apostle means that we should be amiable and easy-going when we welcome those who come to be instructed in the gospel. If we do not let them in, it is as if we were shutting the door to them and stopping them from ever drawing near to God. We must, then, be kind and gentle, willing to receive all who want to be taught. Hence Paul adds the words, 'apt teachers', as if gentleness and what we call skill in teaching go together. This is because no one can be taught by someone who is prickly and stand-offish. A good teacher must therefore be mild-mannered; he must be able to attract those who come and to win them over. This cannot happen without that affability which Paul mentions here. He thus insists that no quarrelsome or contentious man can be God's servant. Why? Surely it is only as we strive to win the ignorant that we can serve God. And this is only possible when we are calm and peaceable, so that we listen to what men have to say and bear with their infirmities, until little by little they are built up in the faith. Not to do that is to turn our backs on them.

Now it is a fact that those who want only to argue disturb our minds. They do not care about bringing others closer to God; instead they scare them away. It is thus absolutely clear that when someone is over-curious and given to quarrelling, he does nothing but pull down instead of building up. He has no concern for God's reverence and honour, nor does he wish to see him served— the opposite is true. Hence we infer that no one who is unfit to teach should be accorded the name, title, rank or honour of prelate, bishop, minister or pastor. From Paul's point of view those who are not apt to teach must be cast out from the company of God's servants. We therefore see that the pope and all his villainous clergy (as they are called) have no cause to boast brazenly of their heavenly hierarchy, claiming that they constitute God's church and that they are its shepherds and its prelates. We would not envy them this claim if they had anything to back it up. But if they want to be believed, let them give evidence of the mark which Paul describes here and which is the genuine token which will prove that they are servants of God. The truth is that they are dumb dogs. They are good at biting and devouring and, as we well know, at scattering God's flock. If all they did was swallow up the goods and substance of the poor, that would be bad enough; but they suck people into hell and destroy miserable souls. As for uttering one word of doctrine, that would diminish the episcopal dignity: they have more to do than preach God's word!

As a result, those who call themselves prelates and bishops in the papal church are incapable of teaching, and they are even less concerned to edify the people. So as we see from this passage, the Holy Spirit condemns them and declares that no one should take them for the men they proudly claim to be. For to be a pastor of the church and a preacher are related tasks and can never be separated, which is what Paul teaches. Again, if we are to teach as God commands, we must do so with the intention of winning over those who hear us. For how would it be if we were content merely to speak, without seeking to lead the erring to the way of salvation? Shame on the title and rank of bishop if we do not make every effort to win for God those who are estranged from him! So far as preaching is concerned, our lips should not utter one word unless, at the same time, we aim to instruct our hearers and to do them good. This is the reason why people today are so little edified. Where are those who desire their people to benefit from the preaching of God's word? There must be some, but they are few and far between! All our teaching is mostly wasted because it fails to edify. Let us therefore take Paul's words to heart, and remember that real teachers are those who do their very best to win the ignorant for God, and to bring the fallen, the wandering and the lost back to the proper path.

Now this we cannot do, this cannot be our main endeavour, unless we are patient. Many people say the most foolish things.

When we try to give them some instruction they come out with all sorts of nonsense. It is sad to see how silly and frivolous they are. Others talk their heads off, pretending to be knowledgeable without ever having read one word of Scripture! Yet they chatter on and will not yield an inch in argument. The most ignorant are the boldest. So we cannot have the zeal which Paul asks of us if we are not patient in the face of evil, and if we cannot put up with all the foolishness we see in those who have not yet savoured the truth, or who, with only a fleeting taste of it, still do not respect God's word. We must thus tolerate the fickle, the ignorant, the dull and the erring who have not yet learned what it is to obey God. We must, I say, be patient with all such people, otherwise we will not succeed in drawing them to God. That is Paul's lesson for us here.

Nevertheless, because evildoers, including those who scoff at God, cite the word 'patience', expecting us to bear with them and to forgive them when they mock Scripture, make light of all our exhortations and scorn even God's threats, Paul clarifies his meaning, so that while bearing evil patiently we must not encourage it by our indulgence. We are to teach, he says, *and to admonish in a kindly way those who contradict*. This is an excellent means which we do well to note, for there are two extreme faults which cannot be condoned. First, if we are too permissive, closing our eyes when God is mocked and pretending that nothing is amiss, and if we allow men to ridicule all that is taught in God's name, such leniency is wrong. Then there is the opposite fault, when someone who says something out of place is rebuked at once and so severely that he is terrified. He feels cast out and no longer has any way of drawing near to God. We must guard against both of these errors. Paul's remedy is thus to teach 'with kindliness'. That is true, but we must also teach with a view to correcting what is wrong. The word the apostle uses does not simply mean to teach, but to instruct in order to improve, as when we teach those who have fallen in such a way that they learn to bear the yoke and to realize that they cannot sport with God.[17] This is the sort of instruction which Paul has in mind.

Paul's intention therefore was not to give a free hand to those scoffers who want to be allowed to grin and guffaw whenever they are told about God's mysteries. He will not have us tolerate such things or turn a blind eye to them. Truth to tell, the world today is full of such mockery. How many are there who, in seeking to know God's will, are humble enough to think that God must be worshipped through his word, and that the least they can do is submit when they are told the things which come from him? How many, I ask, think this way? On the contrary we see holy Scripture held up to ridicule, and those who speak about it attach no more importance to it than to a fairy-tale! It is awful to see how wickedly God's name is profaned. Yet these scoundrels expect the word 'kindliness' to inform our dealings with them! No compromise is possible. If we become annoyed when God's name is trodden underfoot and when so little honour is paid to his word, 'Oh,' they ask, 'where's the patience which Paul spoke about?' As if we were meant to shrug our shoulders and not to get upset when abuse is hurled at God! If any one of us saw his father vilified, he would take it terribly to heart. So when we see God torn from his throne by these rascals who scoff at the message of salvation, shall we pretend that nothing is amiss? Where would our zeal be? And what cowards we would be! So when these louts who are intent on mocking God want us to put up with their blasphemies, let it be clear that Paul never meant us to encourage their vileness by showing them patience. He meant only that we should not close the door to the ignorant, nor rebuff them too smartly without seeing whether they can somehow be corrected.

[17] The Greek verb used by Paul is *paideuō*, 'to instruct, educate' or, alternatively, 'to correct, discipline'. Calvin leans here toward the second sense.

So whenever it is said that we must bear patiently with evil men, must put up with their mischief and must treat them with mildness and gentleness, there is an exception we must add. Nothing should stop us from sharply admonishing those who resist God, and from making them see how wretched it is for them to remove the yoke which God has laid on their shoulders. The recalcitrant should be taught to submit. For as Paul says, all of men's loftiness which exalts itself against Jesus Christ must be brought low (2 Cor. 10:5), otherwise the gospel is not preached in all its majesty.

In sum, the Holy Spirit here clearly demonstrates that ministers of God's word, while bearing patiently with those who cannot quickly be brought to obey the gospel, must not fail to correct them, to reveal to them their faults and to show them that there is a discipline which is binding on all creatures. That is one point. Another is that all of us are instructed not to seek men's flattery of which the world is far too fond. As I said, it serves our purpose admirably to be told that ministers must correct us in a kindly way. But we forget the word 'correct' and we emphasize only kindliness! We would rather indeed the word was not mentioned, or if it were, that our feelings were spared and that we were not hit where it hurts! The patience of which the apostle speaks, however, always accompanies correction. That is why in the preceding verse he says that God's servant must be mild-mannered. But why? Must he shut his eyes when he sees wrongs being done? Must he speak only honeyed words? Not at all! He must correct at the same time. Such is the tenor of this passage.

Observe now Paul's closing words: *to see whether God may at any time grant them repentance.* It is plain, therefore, that we should not be discouraged if, first of all, we see such hardness in men. Though it seems difficult to bring them to the right way, we must endeavour as much as we can to conquer them with kindness. True, we are told not to cast our pearls before swine and dogs (Matt. 7:6).

But how do we know whether someone is a dog or a pig until we have tested him? I will not call some ignorant person I see a pig, for who among us has not been a poor blind soul, buried in popish unbelief? What would have become of us if God had not sown the seed of his word for us? Instead he sought us when we were like wild beasts. So it is right that we should do the same for those who still languish in the darkness and tyranny of popery, where we too once lived in brutish ignorance.

However, just as we must win over if we can those whom we do not yet know to be dogs and swine, so too, if having tested someone we find him rebellious, having the marks of a reprobate, refusing all medicine and turning good into evil—when we see someone thus hardened, what else can we do but leave him be, since he does not deserve to have the message of salvation put before him? This is how we are to interpret our Lord Jesus Christ's prohibition. We are not to cast precious pearls before dogs or swine, but those who have not yet shown such stubbornness and who err through lack of understanding should not be rebuffed before God has humbled them. And although they seem not to feel the spur, we must persevere to the end. For how can we know whether God will extend his mercy to those whom we think of as condemned? This is something we need to note, for when Scripture says that God's mercy is higher than the clouds and deeper than every depth (Psa. 36:5), it is so that we will not limit it as we think fit. We are so twisted by nature that when we dislike someone we want God immediately to strike him with a thunderbolt! God therefore shows that he is not like us, declaring through his prophet Isaiah: 'As far as the heavens are from the earth, so are my thoughts from your thoughts' (Isa. 55:9). 'For,' God says, 'I am kind, mild and full of pity; you cannot comprehend my mercy.' We must therefore beware lest we measure God's mercy by our own standards. Rather, while we may regard a person as lost and incapable of being won, let us wait patiently for God to do his work. And if it takes longer than we would like, we should grieve and feel sorry, but in any case we should struggle on, in keeping with God's command that we win others for him.

Thus Paul writes that we should wait to see whether God will grant them repentance. It is as if he said: 'My friends, it is hard and upsetting to bear with those who resist God, who withstand his grace and who will not at first heed sound teaching which is meant for their salvation. We lose patience with them and cast them off. Nevertheless we should be kind to them, and though for a time we see them going badly wrong, we should try to bring them round and tame them, unless they are so wilful and so implacably opposed to God that we must judge them past correction. They are in God's hand.' Further, Paul writes 'if at any time', meaning that if unbelievers are not converted as soon as could be wished, we should not let them drop, for God has them in his hand. Then too, although today a person may be obstinate, we do not know how he will be tomorrow. Now why is that? It is because men's conversion does not depend on them, their strength or motivation. It is God who refashions them and who makes them new creatures. Shall we stop God, then, from working a miracle which far exceeds our understanding? Let us expect more from God's grace than we can ever conceive. That is Paul's meaning.

We cannot conclude all that should be said today. This, however, should be the point we finish on. We must never reject the ignorant as dogs or swine. However much they resist God and go against him, until we have proved that they are past correction and that they are stubbornly set in their opposition, we must not close the door to them but must try instead to win them over. Our method must be to distinguish carefully between those who resist God out of unbelief or ignorance, and those who, knowing that it is God who speaks, are so embittered that they refuse all sound teaching and will not reform, having forsaken goodness once and for all. With those who are beyond hope there is nothing we can do. They do not deserve to be offered the word of life; that would be to profane it. However, when people are ignorant we should bear with them and continue to draw them in, until we know whether God is pleased to bring them to himself. Paul reasons that men's conversion is not something they can do in their own strength. Therefore though they may seem to be past correction, and though they may daily grow worse and worse, God can still set to work and accomplish amazing miracles. Accordingly since God, who does what he wills, reserves men's conversion for himself, let us learn to leave everything in his hands, and to make sure that we fulfil our obligation by drawing others to salvation so far as we are able.

Now let us cast ourselves down before the face of our good God, acknowledging our faults and praying that he may make us feel them better than before, so that, being humbled in ourselves, we may both confess our sins and learn to hate them and the wickedness within us. May we devote ourselves to doing God's will and continue to grow each day in obedience and righteousness, until we are free of every evil and rebellious desire. In the meantime may he support us in our weakness, that we may be delivered from the iniquity of this world and be gathered at last into his heavenly kingdom.

# 18

---

# IN AND OUT OF SATAN'S SNARE

*The Lord's servant must teach patiently those who resist, to see whether at any time God may grant them repentance so that they may know the truth,* [26] *and may escape from the snares of the devil, who has taken them captive as he wills.* (2 Timothy 2:25-26)

Earlier we noticed the sort of people to whom, Paul says, we ought to be kind and courteous—to those who resist God out of ignorance. We should feel pity for them, because they are poor blind souls who in their foolish devotion believe that they are doing right. Although this does not excuse them in God's eyes, we should have compassion on them and try to put them on the path to salvation. Since, however, it is not easy to tolerate those who oppose God's truth, and since, as we said before, it seems that we are wasting our time, Paul points out that change lies in God's hand. We may think that all hope is lost, but God is able to work today in ways unknown to us. Let us learn, then, not to judge God's power by our own understanding. When we see wretched unbelievers who are exceedingly hardened and obstinate, let us wait to see whether God will have mercy on them. Meanwhile we must do our duty to them, that is, win them over if we can.

That these are the people the apostle has in mind is shown by the statement that *God may enable them to know his truth*. He is clearly not thinking of those who in their malice rise up to trouble God's church and who reject what they know to be good; nor is he thinking of apostates who, having tasted the gospel, take up arms to fight against God, his word and his church. No, he is not thinking of such people, for they are quite unworthy. Instead, he wants us for a time to bear with those who have no idea of what truth is, and to wait patiently to see whether God will stretch out his hand to them and bring them into his flock.

It is important to note, however, that when he speaks of knowing God's truth, Paul begins with *repentance*. He therefore suggests that it is no small or ordinary thing to know God's truth. We should never say that someone knows God who, when God's name is set before him, mentally acknowledges that God exists, for knowledge must have its roots in the heart. What, then, does it mean to know God's word? It means first that we give God our worship and that we submit to him and to all that he tells us. It means also that we seek to know what he wishes to teach us, and that we try to obey fully and without protest. Now this is a task so great that it exceeds all the powers in the world. No wonder Paul says that we cannot know the truth without repentance! Why? Because, first and foremost, men are so wicked and wilful that they are only too happy to be rid of God's yoke and discipline, and to refuse all that he teaches. They want God to ask nothing of them and to let the reins fall loose. God must therefore tame our inborn pride or we will never draw near to him and be good scholars in his school. Humility is the first thing we need if we are quietly to accept what he teaches us.

Yet we behave like wild animals; we are full of arrogance and overweening pride. We are a long way from submitting to God's word, by which he seeks to test whether we are willing to let him lead us. God, for his part, humbles man's reason and every impulse of the flesh, which is why the gospel is called a sword by which we are offered as a sacrifice to him (Rom. 12:1; Eph. 6:17). We, however, want to be left whole and untouched, but God would reduce us to nothing! What agreement can there be between us unless we are brought low? As long as we are ruled by our thoughts and inclinations God can make no impression on us. We will continue to be blind, to have hearts of stone, to be hard and unyielding. God, however, wants us to be as sheep and lambs who hear his voice and follow his commands. Hence men must be tamed before they can come to know God's truth.

We should not be surprised, then, if most people resist the gospel and cannot be drawn by any means at all. As long as men continue to live as they do, they must always move further and further away from God. To come near to him is out of the question. We should not be shocked when we see most people opposing God's truth, for that is their natural inclination. So when we observe a small number of believers who allow themselves to be ruled by God's hand, we should regard it as a miracle! They have become new creatures; their conversion is an unexpected work of God. So if we would celebrate God's goodness, let each of us begin with himself. Let us first know with certainty that if God had left us to live the way we wanted, we would have been his mortal enemies and would never have tasted anything of his word. Our faith is the particular gift of his Holy Spirit who has enlightened us. Otherwise we would still be blind; nothing would have touched our hearts in which there is only rebellion. No one should boast as if faith were his own doing. Let us give God the honour he deserves for having brought us to know him, even when by nature we were alienated from him.

What this passage tells us is that faith cannot exist without repentance. That is one thing. The second is that both faith and repentance are given to us by God, and that it is not for us to change our hearts and wills. God must do this work, though in a hidden way which exceeds anything we could do.

As to the first point, that faith cannot exist without repentance, there are many unstable people who, on hearing these words, think that they have faith, but they are still in sin. They happily assent to the idea that God's word is true, but they do not stick to it. Such people may call themselves believers but they are really faithless, because, as we said, faith has its roots in the heart of man, inasmuch as he submits to God and knows that it is God who governs him. Now this mask or rather this pretence of faith which we see in hypocrites must be viewed as God's doing, insofar as we cannot rise so high as to have the slightest notion of what Scripture contains. Yet these men are not made new as believers ought to be; they have not received the Spirit of adoption which makes them children of God. Such is the faith of the hypocrites, as we read in the letter to the Hebrews (Heb. 6:4).[18] There the knowledge of those who have rebelled and gone astray is said to have been a 'heavenly gift', but they were never deeply or consciously touched. That is why I said that to have even a fleeting notion of God's truth, God must work in us. When, however, it comes to true faith, by which we believe the gospel and are made to share in Jesus Christ and in all his benefits, faith must be combined with repentance. Why? Because we cannot yield obedience to God without denying ourselves, our reason, our wisdom and every yearning in us. Thus those who give no evidence of change but who want to be thought of as believers and as children of God are in fact faithless. They take God's name in vain when they claim to be Christians, for repentance is needed

---

[18] Calvin here addresses the problem of transient belief. In the light of Heb. 6:4 he attributes to God's working a sufficient knowledge of the gospel as would suggest real faith on the part of the 'hypocrite'. Such faith is, however, false. God's gift does not confer saving grace; only a fleeting and superficial change is effected. A fuller discussion will be found in *Inst*. III.2.11 and 3.23.

in order to know the truth. Let us resolve, then, to have done with our human nature, so that, in sacrificing ourselves, our souls and our bodies to God, we may give him dominion over us.

Repentance for Paul is a first step which leads to the knowledge of truth and faith. We recall what is said elsewhere, that in order to attain God's wisdom we must become as fools (1 Cor. 3:18). We must, in other words, confess that we are nothing but falsehood and vanity. No mortal man is capable of creating life for himself in this world. How could he remake himself so as to be equal to the angels in heaven? Faith and repentance mean that once we are freed from the curse inherited from our father Adam, we can be adopted as heirs of the heavenly life and made to share in God's glory. How, then, would it be if such a thing lay in our power, or if we were able to bestow so great and excellent a gift on ourselves? We would have cause to feel immense pride, as is our natural inclination. Let us therefore learn that we can never draw near to God, think one good thought or feel one good impulse, unless they are given to us from on high and unless God works in us by his Holy Spirit.

It is entirely appropriate, then, that Paul should speak of God's gift of repentance by which men may know the truth. He might have said that perhaps men may change, and that if today they are past correction they may improve tomorrow. He does not, however, speak this way, but brings us back to God. His purpose was, as has been said, to urge us to be patient when people are less receptive than we would like. Yet he makes it very clear that conversion is not something we can do for ourselves. The idea does not appeal to us, and it only attracts us when God wins us for himself. We cannot open the eyes of our mind to understand the mysteries of the gospel unless our Lord puts forth his hand and changes us. He must, that is, make new creatures of us. That is our debt of honour to God.

It is as I have said: when we compare ourselves with the ignorant and the faithless, we should all think: 'Alas, here is a mirror in which God shows me the kind of person I was and would have continued to be, if he had not remade me by his Holy Spirit. By nature I was no better than those I see around me who are opposed to God. I too was his mortal enemy: not a single nerve in me was disposed to obey him. I was full of infernal pride, malice, arrogance and obstinacy which were arrayed against him and which could have consigned me to everlasting death. That would have been my fate if God had not taken pity on me, and had not poured out on me the infinite treasures of his mercy.' We should learn, then, to compare ourselves with the faithless, so that seeing them we may be filled with horror that mere creatures should rebel against the one who made them. But let us also remember that we would be exactly like them if our Lord had not had pity on us.

More light is thrown on this idea by Paul's next words: *Let them escape from the bonds—or nets—of Satan, by which they are kept captive according to his will.* This verse tells us a great deal more and confirms the point which I made a moment ago. For if we think that we can come to faith and to knowledge of the truth without God having to change us, we would need to be strong enough to free ourselves from Satan's bonds. But until God has rescued us from the devil's nets we will never draw near to him. We remain slaves to sin, having death as our inheritance. Who is the man clever enough to free himself and to be his own redeemer? Will we really dare to claim what God reserves for himself? Is this not a sacrilege which God rightly detests? If we were asked, 'Can you be your own redeemer?', we would answer, 'Of course not, for that would be to usurp the office of the Son of God.' So if someone thinks that he can trust in his own strength and can contrive his own conversion, he is taking the place of Jesus Christ and robbing him of the office of Redeemer. Why? Because Paul is very definite that we cannot have the light of faith or be converted until we are delivered from the devil's bonds.

Let us, then, be all the more sure to do as I have said, and to exalt God for the grace so freely given when he allowed us to share in the faith of his gospel and when he confirmed our trust in it. We should therefore loathe the presumptuousness of those who trust in free will, who flaunt themselves and who in their blindness foolishly believe in their own merits. Let us tread all such nonsense underfoot.

At the same time, just as we are meant to honour God for all that he has already given us, so also, for the future, we should look to his sheer mercy to strengthen our faith, to lead us forward and to help us continue in repentance. The fact that we have faith does not mean that it is complete in us. We may see some small spark of brightness, but only in part, as Paul tells us (1 Cor. 13:12). We must thus ask God to increase our faith, and we must not think that we can achieve it by our own hard work or intelligence. What God has begun, he must also finish.

So far as repentance is concerned, although we may have a sincere and zealous wish to draw near to God, we nevertheless drag our feet and limp along, and there is so much impatience in our flesh that it is pitiful to see. We therefore need to pray to God that he may daily give us strength until he finally removes us from this world. In battling our sinful desires we cannot win of our own volition or in our own strength. God must give us the victory. We are therefore exhorted not only to glorify God for his past blessings but to turn to him in prayer, that he may supply our wants until he brings us to true perfection, from which we are still a long way off.

Since this verse speaks of unbelievers who are held captive by Satan's bonds, it ought to lead us to humility. What else were we in the past, and what would have become of us if our Lord had not been merciful to us? Were we not raised in that blindness which the ignorant still suffer? Would we not have remained blind if God had not set us free? So when we are tempted to make much of ourselves, let us bear these things in mind. It is true that by nature you are Satan's slaves. A horse, an ox or an ass is no more its own master than you were. So go ahead and flaunt yourselves, believe that you can do marvels! God covers your head with shame, and says that you are a miserable cur controlled by Satan and enslaved to him. That is what you are, and you will stay that way until God breaks the cords which bind you. When, therefore, we are told that unbelievers are kept in cursed bondage to Satan, are we not worse than mad if we still feel that we are somehow deserving, if we plead a measure of free will and if we proclaim our virtues and our merits? The Holy Spirit could not thunder more loudly, or challenge and shame us more plainly, than by saying that Satan has us in his grip, that we are under his tyranny and that he masters us as he wills until God delivers us.

For the rest, let us try to grasp how dreadful is God's curse upon the human race when it is said that Satan has dominion over us, both great and small, without exception. For we were made in God's image and the world was created for our sake. When God placed his stamp upon us it was to make us as it were his children. So is it not awful if the devil holds us in his bonds and nets? Should not the hairs of our head stand up in horror? Consider our original creation. God made us to be his children and desired his glory to shine forth in us. He placed us in this world so that we might be the living images of him. We therefore say that sin came at an appalling cost: the devil took possession of us, and so noble, fine and excellent a nature as man's was so destroyed that Satan took him in his snare. This ought to make us hate sin all the more, since while God created us in his image that we might be partners with the angels, we have been cast headlong into hell, and from our mother's womb we all bring this curse with us. Where will it end? And from where does it come if not from sin?

Sin should thus be hateful to us when we understand that it has so ruined us as to make us slaves to Satan. Furthermore we ought to learn to fear God and his judgment. We know how unconcerned men are, and how when drunk with empty pride they forget what it is to be accountable to God. And although they hear every day that God regards them as his deadly foes, that he is armed and ready to visit them with retribution, they do not care. They must not be merely drunk but bewitched, reeking of their filth, if they do not fear God's wrath which is prepared for them and with which Scripture threatens them. Because we are so confused, we should attend all the more carefully to those passages which show us as we are as long as we remain in our sins. They show us, that is, that God disowns us, that he no longer reckons us—I do not say, as his children, but as his creatures. Since he consigns us to Satan's bondage he no longer likes us; we are outcasts from his kingdom. He no longer has any dealings with us. That being so, we should be moved to fear God when we see that all men stand condemned before him. We have all the more reason, then, to magnify the goodness God has shown us in taking us out of the pit where Satan held us captive, and in choosing not only to govern us but to guide us by his Holy Spirit and to illumine us so that our hearts and wills are changed. So when we witness God working in this way, does it not give greater lustre to his mercy and encourage us to praise him as he deserves? That, in sum, is what this passage teaches us.

There is nevertheless more that needs to be said. If the devil possesses poor ignorant souls who have never known the gospel, what will happen to those who give themselves to him and refuse the knowledge granted to them, as if they deliberately set out to provoke God's wrath against them? Here Paul has in mind the unhappy heathen who have never heard one word of the law, the prophets or the gospel. Think of these poor wretches who have been born and raised in superstition, and who believe that in practising their foolish rites they are doing good. If they truly knew about God they might be expected to obey him, for the reverence they show their idols is evidence that they are willing to fear God. Even so Paul declares that because they are ignorant they are in the devil's power. They are his captives, so that he draws them after him and drives them as he wills. Thus, if the unbelieving who have never known anything are in so wretched a state, what of those to whom God has stretched out his hand, to whom he has opened the door of his church, saying 'Enter', and whom he has signed with his own mark of baptism? When they rebel after knowing all about the gospel, when they reject the knowledge they have received, when they bury God's gifts and profane the blood of Jesus Christ—when, in a word, they throw to the ground all that has been given them, must not Satan have claimed them twice over? Must he not have mastered them more thoroughly than he does the ignorant? Of course he must!

The devil indeed exerts his rule over all who do not believe, as Paul says elsewhere (Eph. 2:2). In speaking to believers, he says: 'Be careful, my friends. God has chosen you as his inheritance. Do not give yourselves to Satan who has power and authority over the faithless.' This is by and large true. Observe, however, that if the miserable heathen and the blind who have never been able to draw near to God are under Satan's tyranny, how much more are those who turn away from God and who, having been brought to God, become apostates, fearful monsters! When we see them so full of fury we must regard them as demons in human form, as the devil's own possession. God clearly shows how severe he is toward such hapless souls. Can we find among the papists such spite against God and such impiousness as we can among these apostates who know the gospel but who end up forsaking it? Can we find such cruelty among the Turks and heathen as we do among the papists? So step by step, as men got closer to God and became ever more vicious, and as they profaned this splendid gift of knowledge of the truth and abused it shamefully, God was bound to show himself their judge and to take double vengeance on them. Should not something so monstrous strike fear in all of us? Remember, then, Paul's message: until our Lord Jesus Christ has done his work as our Redeemer, we are held fast in Satan's bonds. As Jesus Christ says in the eighth chapter of John, his work is to deliver us (John 8:36). We are all in bondage to the devil until Jesus Christ makes us free. So let us walk in all humility, with fear and trembling, if we want to possess and fully enjoy the freedom won for us by the blood of God's Son, and given to us by the Holy Spirit. To retain possession of this blessing we must be vigilant, making sure that we do not knowingly throw ourselves into Satan's nets and snares.

In saying that Satan keeps them captive as he wills, the apostle warns us yet again to open our eyes when we are fast asleep, and to recognize that the devil is drawing us after him, that he drives us as he wills and does whatever he pleases with us. And if this is true of the heathen, what shall we say of those who deserve to be doubly and more severely chastised? Now although the devil draws the faithless after him, they are not blameless on that account—an excuse which those who scoff at God would love to use in order to escape his hand. 'Look,' they say, 'if it is Satan who drives us, should sin be imputed to us?' Others blaspheme against holy Scripture, thinking that God ought to shoulder the blame for sin since he leaves us in bondage to it. Know, therefore, that unbelievers are not absolved even though it is the devil who leads them on and who fills them with such frenzy that he is obviously in control. When heinous acts are done, our Lord shows us that Satan is the master of men. Sometimes men think that they are clever, resourceful and smart, but they are wrong. They make such gross mistakes that even little children laugh at their stupidity which is plain to see. How can it come to this? Such foul deeds are done that everyone curses the doer. It is as if men have conspired to earn the censure and contempt of both great and small. We witness such horrendous things that we are forced to say, 'The devil is behind it.' However, if we pause to ask whether evil is unpalatable to those who do it, we discover that they have a treacherous heart which resists God. They are wilful and wanton, determined to use every limb and all the powers of mind, soul and feeling to offend God and to harm their neighbour.

Now when we are Satan's prisoners and when we deliberately do wrong, not out of constraint but because every impulse urges us to it, are we to be excused? No! So the captivity of which Paul speaks is, humanly speaking, voluntary. We are not obliged to accept it. Yet while it is Satan who carries us off, God's vengeance, as I have said, can also be discerned. One word would be enough to make this plain if we understood God's judgments as we ought. What then? Because we forget that God blinds men and that in his just vengeance he cuts them off, we do not see how men can be captive to the devil and yet subject also to God's condemnation. We must hold to these two truths all the same. The first is that when we see people going to extremes, acting senselessly and with such frenzy that they seem lost to reason and decency, it is because the devil is in control. People defy God so openly that they seem bent on opposing all sound doctrine and on infecting the whole world with their corruption. If we try to win them over with gentleness they laugh and jeer at us; and if we threaten and rebuke them, their only thought is to plot whatever mischief they can. Such people conspire with the devil who holds them fast and claims them for his own. Let us therefore learn to submit to God and to give ourselves to him. May he keep us from provoking him to the point that he abandons us and allows Satan to master us.

That is one point. The other is that when Satan carries people off, although he controls them, drives them, stirs them up and uses them for his various ends, they are not exempt from sin. They are not compelled to do wrong, but do so voluntarily. True, they are bereft of reason and understanding but the root of evil lies within them, and they are seen to have conspired and plotted with Satan. So although he controls them and makes them his slaves, they are perfectly willing to please him and to ally themselves with him, in order to do battle with God and to attack all that is good and honourable. This, as we know, is the way of the wicked. What excuse, then, do they have? And must not those who try to shift the blame onto God feel his awful vengeance for having lied? Must not what the prophet Isaiah said be fulfilled in them: 'Woe to you who call evil good' (Isa. 5:20)?

Once we have learned these two things we should be moved to glorify God and to condemn men, for it is chiefly to this that Paul's teaching leads. Although it is a fearful thing to see people being swept up by the devil, we must acknowledge God to be a righteous judge and to be just when he brings mortal creatures to their ruin. As Paul says, when we refuse to obey the one who made us, do we not deserve to become the devil's prey (Rom. 1:28)? And despite the fact that God did not give the heathen knowledge of his word, they are inexcusable once he has brought them into this world. They all knowingly give themselves to evil rather than to good. Thus, on the one hand, we are to glorify God when he justly rejects them and deprives them of reason, by sending blindness upon them so that they are filled with rage or mindless stupor. Here he shows himself as judge, as indeed he ought to be. And on the other hand let us learn to hate sin and to be always on our guard.

If those who are carried off by Satan are meant to be mirrors, what should be said of us? We would be just like them if God had not preserved us, continually stretching forth his hand to keep us safe. But if hapless unbelievers and those who know nothing of God are thus swept away, what will become of us? If we do not live humbly, meekly and soberly and in God's fear, what do we deserve? We know the threats he makes against those who have had intimate knowledge of his word. The prophets, it is true, proclaim like a herald at arms that God will blind the world and that the devil will rule upon earth; but in speaking of those who have been closely taught and to whom God directly shows himself, what do they say? That their iniquity exceeds that of all other men. Hence the most terrible retribution is reserved for those whom God has called to himself. He has cast them off. Not only so, but he gives Satan greater licence to drive them mad, so that all may see the vengeance he takes on them for scorning the treasure of his word and for their thanklessness.

This is what we must remember whenever we see the devil pushing and propelling those he means to destroy. Let us learn to turn to God for protection. Let us ask him to hold the reins tight so that we do not err or stray. Whatever the devil does, may we not yield to his will or give him entry or access to us; may he not get the better of us. This we can do provided we remain in the care of our Lord Jesus Christ and make him our guide. He will faithfully perform the work entrusted to him by God his Father. He will, that is, ensure that nothing which has been given to him will perish, but will be kept safe until the last day.

Now let us cast ourselves down before the face of our good God, acknowledging our faults and praying that he may make us feel them better than before, so that we may be brought to genuine repentance and may grow more and more in grace. May he bear with us in our infirmities until he has remedied them and has rid us of them all.

# 19

## HARD TIMES AHEAD

*But know that in the last days there will come dangerous times.*
*² For men will be lovers of self, covetous, boastful, proud, blasphemers,*
*disobedient to mother and father, ungrateful, despisers of God, ³ with-*
*out natural affection, disloyal, evildoers, intemperate, cruel, hating the*
*good, ⁴ traitors, insolent, conceited, lovers of pleasure more than of God,*
*⁵ having a form of honesty but denying its power. Turn away from such*
*as these.* (2 Timothy 3:1-5)

If evil is done around us, we think that this gives us an excuse
for being as dissolute and as bad as the rest. For there are many
who, when wrong things happen, take advantage of them, or who
even go looking for them and who, if they fail to find them, make
them up! As long as they have partners in sin they do not care,
but use them as a shield to hide behind. Even people who are not
ill-intentioned are troubled when things go badly and when they
are no longer sure of what to do. Nevertheless God has supplied
us with enough protection to stop us straying from the right path,
however confusing things may seem. We do not, alas, heed the
warnings given us from heaven, which is why the devil so easily
upsets us. Still, God continues to remind us that however bad the

world is, we should hold fast to him. Woe to us if we do not, for there will be no excuse for us if we ignore the one who would have amply armed us if we had listened to his warnings.

It is as Paul tells us in this text: *In these last days dangerous times will come.* We must not think that until the world ends all will be well ordered in the church of God, that nothing untoward will happen and that men will be like little angels, zealous in serving God. On the contrary there will be conceited and disloyal people, traitors full of cruelty and malice and savage like wild beasts. Men will have contempt for God; others will be unrestrained, leading dissolute, vile and callous lives. Yet they will call themselves Christians! In short, says Paul, while they may appear to be God's children not one drop of virtue will be found in them. In saying this, did the Holy Spirit give us leave to do evil, so that we are free to run with the rest of the pack? No, it is so that we should be watchful, lest we think we can rest easy as if this were paradise. We must be all the stronger, for there are battles which await us and Satan endeavours to seduce us. That is the point of Paul's warning to us here.

What then? We turn a deaf ear, so that God has to speak this way to us. Many people fall away who seemed to live as Christians. They change in the twinkling of an eye. Why? Because they do not deign to listen to what God tells them through the lips of his apostle. They deserve to have the devil steal up to them, subdue them easily and immediately trap them. We should therefore pay the closest attention to what this passage teaches us, for Paul did not speak only for his own time; he tells us of what will happen in the last days. Now what exactly is his meaning? He is referring to the whole state of the Christian church. When Scripture speaks of the last days, it is comparing the shadows of the law with the fulfilment which was hoped for at the coming of the Redeemer. The fathers were poised as it were between the two until the gospel came. The world was changed when Jesus Christ appeared for our salvation. For this reason the faithful always looked with expectation to what had been promised under the law, that is, that God would bring things to greater perfection than we see them now. We have been in the last days ever since our Lord Jesus did all that was necessary for our salvation. Thus the apostle writes in the first chapter of Hebrews that God, who had earlier spoken in different ways and at different times to our fathers, has in these last days fulfilled all things by making known his gospel through our Lord Jesus Christ (Heb. 1:1-2). Hence Paul declares that we have reached the last times and that the end of the ages has come upon us (1 Cor. 10:11). So now we must run quickly in order to finish what remains of our life in this world. We need no longer hesitate, wondering what will happen. Jesus Christ has brought us everything that was promised to the fathers. All we need do now is walk until God ends our earthly pilgrimage.

In the meantime let us learn to look to the final appearing of our Lord Jesus Christ, when he will gather his people in and destroy his enemies. The last days, therefore, began with the age of the apostles; they continue to the present and will last until the end of the world. But why does Paul, both here and elsewhere, speak of the last days when he warns believers to be ready for trials and for suffering? It is because there was a fairly popular belief abroad that things would get better than they had ever been. Previously the prophets, in speaking of the kingdom of Jesus Christ, had said that all would be miraculously restored, that the world would submit to God, that great and small would worship his majesty, that every mouth would sing his praise and every knee bow before him. With such promises we ought to have been, one would think, as holy as the angels since Christ's appearing! That is the picture many people conjured up, but they were mistaken in believing that since the advent of the Redeemer all would be decent and honourable, and that things would so improve that iniquity would cease among us.

The opposite, Paul says, is true. Change has begun, but its true perfection is not apparent from the very first. Those, he says, who call themselves Christian are far from being the people they profess to be. They will be full of pride, malice, bad faith and treachery; full of covetousness, of contempt for God and of wickedness in every form. They will lead evil and unruly lives: some will be womanizers, others drunkards and still others slanderers who never stop telling tales. This, I say, is the kind of Christianity typical of many. It is obvious, then, why Paul should speak of the last days. It is as Peter says in his second letter: there will always be deceivers and false prophets as there were among the Jews (2 Pet. 2:1). What he means is that as God sought to test the faithful under the law by allowing the wicked to mar the pure truth, so today there will be scoundrels intent on perverting the gospel, on ruining everything, on veiling God's light and on turning his truth into a lie. In short, Paul's description shows that although our Lord Jesus Christ is seen to be the Saviour of the world, and although he has done all that was needful for our salvation, we must continue to tread this earth. As we are not yet perfect we must struggle on, walking amid the thorns. On the one hand we are assailed by the wickedness men do when sin prevails; on the other we must be on our guard, lest the troubles we endure lead us into error. When there are dissensions and false teaching, and when Satan seeks to wreck everything, to scatter the church and to throw down what God has built up, let us ask God to help us rise above it all.

We see, then, that it is not enough for Christians to jog happily along and to be willing to obey God; they must also withstand trials of every kind. Although we meet problems on every side, we should be equipped to face them and not be like reeds which tremble in the wind. A pool of water when undisturbed by gale or storm is calm and placid, but what good is that when it takes only a gust of wind to churn it up? So if we are like pools of water, if, that is, we are neither steady nor stable, and if as soon as Satan summons up a gale we are tossed about, not knowing which way to go, has not our faith been overthrown? Thus it is not enough for those who want to be reckoned as God's children to be disposed to do their duty. However much they are beset by troubles which threaten to bring them down, and providing they are determined to go on and never to alter course, let them continue in the faith despite Satan and his lackeys, and let them maintain their integrity. Lies and deceit may be all around, and the world may be full of corruption and uncleanness. They must nevertheless, I repeat, hold their ground, for God has sanctified them once and for all, and they must persevere.

Observe how appropriate it is for Paul to use the word '*know*'. It is to Timothy that he speaks, but through him he exhorts both pastors who are in charge of churches and the faithful not to lose sight of this most useful truth. That is why I said that we will be easily led astray unless we are armed in advance. For if we are careless the devil will soon find a breach in our defences and will use it to find a way in. Hence Paul deliberately prefaces his remarks this way in order to drive his point home.

When all is said and done, what sort of Christians are they who decide to forsake the gospel or to speak out against it when things do not go as they would like? Everywhere the complaint is heard: 'I would have thought that people who professed the gospel would be spotless and without fault. Yet I see that they are the very worst of men. Those who speak endlessly about God turn out to be absolutely evil—immoral, covetous, callous, given to trickery and deceit. What am I to do when I see such things? I'd do better to make no commitment at all!' This is the sort of talk we hear. How can we explain such foolishness except to say that people forget the lesson we are taught here? 'Know this for a fact,' says Paul. Yet we affect to ignore him! And even though experience—which, as the proverb says, teaches even fools—proves that this is so, we nevertheless shut our eyes and prefer to know nothing about it. Therefore if those who want to perish do indeed perish, let us for our part open our minds to what our Lord teaches us. He bids us commit it to memory so that no one can deceive us.

Let us also weigh up what is said about the dangerous and trying times to come. The word Paul uses has all these meanings: dreadful, difficult, fearful, vexing, troublesome, perilous. God's children must thus be prepared for these things. Paul might well have said: 'My friends, God could have brought us together in some retreat where we all with one mind might honour and serve him. Nothing could be more desirable. If God had chosen, such a condition could have been ours. The fact is that he wishes to test us, to mix us as wheat among the chaff, to place us indeed among thorns which sting and scratch us so that we fight and struggle day by day. No sooner do we escape one danger than we face another. Our life is like armed combat to the very end. We are attacked on all sides; the devil plots and schemes and has the means to seduce us. God wills that these things should be, to see whether or not we serve him in truth and to reveal hypocrites for what they are.'

So let us be warned that if God gives us some respite, allowing us to live in peace for a time, we must always be aware that dangerous times are not far off—terrible and trying times, for those are the Holy Spirit's words. It is pointless for men to promise the opposite. What will we gain by hoping for the best if we do not have God's promise to guide us? It is true that we cannot overrely on God's promises, but we are sure to make mistakes if in our heads we make up things which God has never said. Since, then, God is preparing us for dreadful and distressing times, we ought not to dream of resting, nor should we expect to be at ease. We cannot sing as if we were already in the kingdom of heaven. These are times of conflict. We must be ready and armed with sword in hand; we must take our shield and helmet. In a word, we must be equipped from head to toe, as Paul writes in the sixth chapter of Ephesians (Eph. 6:13-17).

Notice what is said: these are hard and dangerous times *because men will be lovers of self, covetous, evil, treacherous and so on*. We speak of trying and terrible times only when there is famine, war, pestilence or other ills, only when things are not going our way and when we are afflicted. These are what we call hard and painful times. 'Alas,' we say, 'times are bad.' Why? Because we are short of wheat or wine. 'Times are bad' because war has come. 'Times are bad' because plague is about. Life hangs by a thread and each day threatens to carry us off. Those are what we think of as hard, worrying or troublesome times. This is not what Paul means, however. He says that times will be distressing because evil and transgression will abound; iniquity will engulf us like a flood. Remember therefore that when we are abundantly supplied with wheat and wine and when each of us is comfortable, at peace and seemingly beset by no great ills—when God thus spares us, we should not let prosperity lull us to sleep. The main thing is for us to make sure that we are living soberly, and that we are all agreed in seeking to honour God and to bring an end to evil talk, drunkenness, immorality, theft, cruelty, deceit and false witness, so that God's word is both heard and honoured.

Consequently if we want to know what 'good times' really are, we should not ask whether the vines are healthy and the harvest plentiful, or whether things are going our way. We should not focus on these things for they are little more than trifles. Of course if God gives us enough to live on, this is a blessing which testifies to his fatherly love and which encourages us to turn all the more to him. It is not, however, our final goal. We must look higher, hoping to see that wrongs are put right. This is Paul's message to us here. But as it is, we are such earthly creatures that we do not care as long as there is nothing which upsets us, or which inconveniences us from a worldly point of view. When we live quietly at home and are free of trouble and annoyance, none of us thinks that times are bad. Yet God continues to be blasphemed, heinous wrongs are done and the world is full of trickery, theft, ill-will and all the things the apostle mentions here. For our part we say nothing about them unless we personally suffer. We only make a fuss if harm is done to us. If someone wrongs us or cheats us out of a penny we are quick to cry, 'What's the world coming to?' We give voice to our complaints and grievances. If, however, we have all that we want and if no one troubles or vexes us, we think that all is well. Though God's honour is trampled down and goodness put to flight, and though order and good government are absent and men behave like mindless beasts, we do not care as long as we sustain no loss or injury.

Be that as it may, if we are God's children we should appreciate what his Holy Spirit tells us here. Although all may be going just as we would like, although we may be enjoying every comfort imaginable, we ought nevertheless to sigh in deep distress if God is not being served. This should be the rule for all: let good be done, and let evil disappear as is right and proper. If this were the case we would all be doing our duty. Thus those who hold public office would know that it was not enough for no one to have been beaten up, for no house to have been robbed or for law and order to have been so well maintained that nothing amiss had occurred. Those, I say, who hold the sword in their hand and who occupy the seat of justice would not think it enough that they had kept the public peace and given no one cause to complain. They would look further ahead, to see that faithfulness, probity, religion especially and the virtues basic to good living flourished and were preserved.

Ministers of God's word and preachers of the gospel should like-wise understand that although there may be no obvious problems, it matters little if we do not live decently, if God is not honoured and if all is not well. Let them at least strive with that aim in view. Even someone who has no public duties should tell himself that if he has children who have been poorly taught, or serving men and women who do wrong, he cannot be at rest. While he may not per-sonally suffer loss he should grieve and worry, knowing that God is not being honoured in his house.

Again, if those who try hard to manage their household well go out into the street and see mischief, shameful wrongs or mis-demeanours being done, they should not fail to grieve and to lament. Thus we read of Lot, that he felt anguish of heart and deep distress while living in Sodom (Gen. 19:1-22; 2 Pet. 2:7). True, in those days there was such an abundance of goods as to fill men to bursting. But we know that the inhabitants of Sodom had thrown off all restraint and had grown so arrogant that they were as hard and pitiless as wild beasts. Could not Lot have enjoyed himself like everyone else? Yes, he could! Yet when he saw how greatly God was offended and how bad things were, he wept and suffered terrible torment. We should do the same. If we would prove that we are God's children, let us feel just how painful and trying the times are, however much we prosper and however safe we are from abuse and earthly harm. If God is not honoured and if things are all awry, we should be troubled just as Paul says here.

In addition he tells us that men will be lovers of self, proud, covetous, full of slander and falsehoods, disobedient to father and mother, thankless, irrational, disloyal and devoid of kindness. The lengthy list of sins which Paul assembles here seems like the furthest reaches of hell, or like some towering mountain which overshadows the whole world. How then can those of whom he speaks still appear to be believers and to bear that name? Paul is forced to conclude that they give signs of being sincere: *they have a form of godliness*, that is, an outward appearance.

Is there not some contradiction here? If someone is so depraved that he scorns God or slanders others, is greedy for gain or utterly cruel, should we not say that he has given himself entirely to evil? Paul is nevertheless right to say what he does, as experience shows. Men, as we know, are so insolent that they boast they are believers, even though their wickedness is so extreme that they are more like devils. Nevertheless they falsely claim God's name, so brazen are they. Nor should we be thinking only of the papists, who naturally confirm the truth of what Paul says. The greatest devotees among them are also the most cunning and the most evil. They mumble their prayers from morning to night, trot off after images from one shrine to another and pay for Masses to be sung. Despite their many devotions, if we ask about their life and character we find that those who are fondest of ceremonies are the worst usurers, the basest and most faithless of men, the biggest traitors and the vilest despisers of God. We see and know this to be true. Yet though we ourselves avoid all such pretence—these rituals, this sprinkling of holy water, all this spectacle and nonsense by which God is said to owe the papists something for their accursed worship—although, I say, we do none of this, judge how things really are among us.

The dearest wish of some is to see God's word abolished, or to have a more congenial gospel at which they can sneer. Some prefer a gospel made up in their heads but which leaves them free to sin as much as they like. There are others who oppose all law and order. They refuse to bear any yoke and continually stir up strife in the church, causing such grievous offence as is sad to see. In short, they would love to ruin God's church! Nevertheless they boast aloud that they are good Christians and marvellously zealous. Yet we know that they despise God; their life is so vile and dissolute that the whole town talks of it. So when we see the world determined to profane God's gifts, and when those who have not a shred of self-control call themselves good Christians, know that Paul was right to say that the most stupid of men, the despisers of God, the wicked, the greedy, the disobedient, the immoral, slanderers and all the rest whom he names, will somehow disguise themselves and adopt some sign to show that they too are members of God's flock and church. We know the tricks that they get up to.

Having attended, then, to what God tells us, let us heed the warning that those who pretend to be what they are not forsake all goodness and purity of religion. For what do we mean when we profess to belong to God? We mean that Jesus Christ is our head, that we are joined to him and are wholly one with him. And if we are bound to God's Son by sacred ties, we must first and foremost be made like God his Father, who is the source of all righteousness. This we can only do if we have offered ourselves as a sacrifice to him, leading a pure life and turning to him for refuge. Thus we are united with Jesus Christ our head; he in turn unites us with God his Father. Moreover we must be joined to one another. How? In uprightness, in equity and in love, living as brothers who are mindful of their neighbours' welfare. We must not be like wild animals, but must try to work for the good of those who, like us, are God's children and members of the body of our Lord Jesus Christ. This is the sort of godliness we mean.

We are thus devoid of religion if, when God gives us his gospel and when it is preached to us, we do not accept it, not in pretence or in any formal way but in purity of life. We are without religion if we deny God his rights and the worship which is his due, or if, estranged from our neighbours, we fail to help the needy and to toil on their behalf. Hence all who are not devoted to God and to their neighbour are shown to be faithless and apostate, having in fact renounced true religion. They may still pay lip-service to it, but

God condemns them, banishes them from his kingdom and casts them out of his church.

Let us bear these things in mind if we would be armed against the troubles which come to us from every side. Yet each must also appropriate this teaching for himself. So although we see the wicked blaspheming God's name, we should hold it in such reverence that our lives may testify that we rightly call him Father. May we do this not only to honour him but to serve one another, and may his adoption of us be all the more confirmed by the life we live as brethren.

> Now let us cast ourselves down before the face of our good God, acknowledging our faults and asking him to make us truly feel them, so that all may learn to condemn themselves and to hate their sins and offences. May we strive also to serve him in all purity of life. And although many things conspire to make us stumble and go astray, may we not be corrupted or defiled, but may we be strengthened by the grace of our God to pursue our calling. While the devil also tries to seduce us and to turn us aside, may we go steadily on until we reach the goal to which God calls us, when, free from sin, we are made anew according to his righteousness.

## 20

---

# ALWAYS LEARNING,
# NEVER KNOWING

*Among them are those who steal into houses and take captive simple
women who are burdened with sin and who are driven by various
desires, ⁷ always learning but never being able to come to knowledge of
the truth.* (2 Timothy 3:6-7)

We might well tremble when we see what bad lives some
lead who appear to be believers and who boast of following God's word. Instead they are dissolute and greedy, intent on
dishonest gain and trickery and wicked through and through. All
have nothing but contempt for God. That God's name should be
profaned in this way is monstrous and unnatural. We can only
wonder at such shamelessness when men who insist that they are
children of God in fact defy him and live like devils. Yet however
much they stand condemned as strangers to the flock of Jesus
Christ, they nevertheless worm their way in. When, however, such
things are seen in pastors and in those charged with the care of
others, it is an even worse offence.

Here Paul makes it clear that it is not only among ordinary folk
that the wicked and the depraved are found. They are found among

those who claim to be teachers, men of authority and repute. So since we have the Holy Spirit's warning, let us learn to keep our eyes open so that we can judge aright. We see just how cautious and alert we must be, for although we may be in a church where God's word is proclaimed and where there is discipline and good order, we are nevertheless mixed in with utterly worthless people, among whom much might happen to offend us if we did not have the Holy Spirit's power to strengthen us. Not only among the flock will there be goats which may infect the sheep. Even among those who work as pastors and ministers there will be those who misbehave and who are bent on ruining everything. What was foretold must come to pass. Let us be on our guard, then, and however fearful we may be let us press on and take heart, for we are forewarned by God. Provided we heed his admonition he will not leave us helpless, but will stretch out his hand and give us strength to overcome all these trials. We will not be put to shame. In any case we should stick to the path of salvation until we reach our goal.

We need to keep our eyes open if we would be wary. When we see riff-raff who try to slip in among us and to curry favour as preachers of God's word, let us take thought and judge them as they really are. It is not enough to claim the name; what matters is performance. Let those who call themselves God's servants give actual proof that this is what they are. That is the true touchstone by which we are to test and know them.

In this text Paul speaks explicitly about false teachers who can do much more harm than private individuals. His purpose was not just to prod those who were worthy teachers: he had in mind the welfare of all of God's people. If the wicked could do no harm by their bad behaviour, they might be left alone to stew in their own juice without a further word. Of course in God's eyes they have no excuse. Their evil should be exposed and they should know of the condemnation which awaits them; but if the rest of the congregation were not threatened they might safely be ignored. When, however, evil flares up like a fire and threatens to devour everything if action is not taken, or when like a poison it spreads if sins are left unchecked, we should all resist or else we have no zeal for God or any concern for our salvation. We will also be traitors to God's church and to all our neighbours.

Notice, then, that Paul would not have pointed these people out if he had not seen the great harm they could do unless they were stopped or reined in. As he says elsewhere, people should be identified if they are likely to corrupt God's church; they must not be spared (Rom. 16:17). We are cruel indeed if, when we see the poor sheep exposed to harm, we close our eyes and utter not a word. A good pastor, in particular, must cry out loud when he sees the flock being attacked. If a shepherd, catching sight of a wolf or of thieves, left his flock to graze while he said nothing and ran off to hide, pretending that nothing was wrong, what would we think? Thus, if we would faithfully fulfil our duties, we must, when we see wrongs done in God's church, clamour for them to be remedied and removed. For, as we already said, when Paul saw that those in public office who were meant to lead others could seriously harm the flock and scatter it, he put on public view as it were preachers who, pretending to speak for God and for his word, deceived the simple and masked the truth, falsifying it and putting God's word up for sale for their own personal profit.

The apostle therefore singles them out and denounces them, so that all may loathe them, avoid them like poison and not foolishly put themselves in harm's way. We are thus taught that if we really desire our neighbours to be saved, when we see rogues who want to ruin everything and to spread their infection, we should not ignore them but should do our best to get everyone away from them. They might possibly be shamed, and if there is hope that they are not beyond recovery let them return to the right path. But if they are completely hopeless and hardened by their sin, at the very least let them be kept apart, so that when they are known no one risks being deceived. If any who side with them should perish, they will do so knowingly and of their own volition.

This is the sort of action we must take. However much people may complain—some, as we know, would love us to keep quiet about their villainies—and however much they may disapprove, let us unmask the wicked and keep clear of them. We must at any rate continue on, for it is God we serve. It is not for mortal men to criticize God's Spirit or to change the rule given to us in holy Scripture. That is one point. A second is that we should always keep a close watch on those appointed to proclaim God's word, to see how they behave. For just as the choicest blessing God gives us in this world is to have his pure word preached to us and to have men who earnestly strive to do it, so, conversely, there is no more deadly plague than to see men occupying the pulpit of truth but defiling everything, seeking their own gain and caring nothing for the flock or for God's service. This is Paul's warning to us here.

Observe also that here Paul gives us a few examples to help us understand the kind of people he wishes to single out. He says that among them are those who despise God and who love themselves, arrogant individuals who scorn everything, provided their own life is easy. *Among them*, Paul writes, *are those who steal into houses or who worm their way in.* In other words, they find crafty ways of slipping into a house and of sneaking further in than anyone would like; and having boldly secured a place, *they take simple women captive.* He deliberately refers not to 'women' but to the diminutive, 'simple women'. By this he means exceptionally pious women who, as we say, would devour the crucifix, such is their show of devotion. They are taken captive, he says, by fanatics and by those who misuse God's word. But why? Should not God pity these poor naïve women who are tricked in the name of piety? Should not God send them people who can faithfully guide them? How can he allow them to stray from the path of salvation? We might think that God failed to be merciful to these poor women who were thus deceived.

Yes, but remember what Paul says: *they are laden with sins*. They are therefore hypocrites who want to wallow in their sins, but who also want to be thought of as holy and as thoroughly steeped in religion. They are guilty of wanting to show off, yet for all that they are worthless. So God justly punishes them by allowing them to be deceived and to be taken captive. They will not let God guide them by his pure word. They thus pretend to be close to God. They have their holy trinkets; they do this and that, all their little rituals, to show how much more devout they are than others. Yet they can never arrive at knowledge of the truth; unable to keep to the right path they go round in circles.

In this passage Paul speaks of women rather than men, because they are more prone to the kind of deception which is described here. Admittedly deception is common to men and women alike when they have no wish to obey God or even to try. So God leaves Satan free to act, giving him power to lead into error those who go round in circles or who wander up hill and down dale. Nevertheless if we compare the two, women will be found to be fonder of these foolish devotions than men. That is why Paul particularly mentions them. Thus these fine fellows who misuse God's name see women as their rightful prey, and they concentrate on those who fancy themselves as devout.

These women are said to be burdened with sins. Now both men and women are sinners, so that when we come to God we must feel our vileness and our misery and must hate them, for we get nothing from the gospel unless we are touched by the awareness of our faults and are ashamed of them. Thus Jesus Christ says to us: 'Come to me, all you who are burdened and afflicted. I will refresh you and you will find rest for your souls' (Matt. 11:28-29). If we would come to the Son of God and find rest in him and in his grace, we must be burdened by sin. That is true. Some, however, who are burdened sigh and look for relief, while others simply wallow in their filth. Paul is therefore speaking of women who are content to remain in their sin and wickedness, and who want to be indulged so that their evil is concealed. To such as these God sends false teachers, just as they deserve, for they will not ask Jesus Christ to take their burden from them and to free them from Satan's bonds. They must, then, be held captive, since they will not come to him who is able to give us liberty.

When the devil plants his foot on our throats and makes us suffer the bondage of sin, if we do not ask our Lord Jesus Christ to deliver us, are we not captives twice over? God thus takes rightful vengeance on us. To illustrate this point, think of the church-going women who are to be seen among the papists and who boast that they are especially holy. Some are full of pride and ambition. Sharp-eyed, they make sure that they are always out in front, ahead of all the rest. When present at some elaborate ceremony or at some other worldly display, they have got to be first. And although known to be exceedingly devout they are riddled with sin, mistresses of evil, well qualified to open a school for pride, vanity and contempt of neighbour! Others are greedy or cruel, feeling no tenderness for their family or neighbours. Or else they are shamefully promiscuous, but as long as they gabble their prayers, trot from altar to altar, shower themselves with holy water and do their many devotions, they are sanctified, or so they think. In short, when we see all these devout souls among the papists we will not find one who, to use Paul's phrase, is not laden with sins, and who does not grow worse and worse in her resistance to God and in malice and hypocrisy. The devil therefore has them on a leash, and drives them this way and that because they will not bear the yoke of our Lord Jesus Christ. Satan's ministers must make them captive to their will. This is Paul's plain meaning.

There are lessons here which we will all find useful. First, since explicit mention is made of women, Christian women should first see that, to avoid being trapped in Satan's nets and becoming his willing prey, they must not be complacent about their sins but must expect to be freely corrected when they do wrong. They must not lull themselves to sleep or hope to be indulged. God will never allow any woman to be led astray who is willing to be corrected for her faults. Consider, however, the reward that comes to women who want their sins to go unnoticed and who try to sport with God, as if there were some way of deceiving him. They are hypocrites, who go so far astray that the devil holds them in his bonds and makes them his miserable captives. This is Paul's lesson for women eager to avoid the curse of which he speaks.

The same applies to men, whoever they may be. Why, after all, is our poor world so blind? God has given us his word; our Lord Jesus Christ is the Sun of righteousness who illumines us; the gospel which is preached to us clearly shows us the way. Why then is the world so deceived? When people are asked if they hope for salvation, all answer 'Yes'. Yet all are rushing to destruction! Why? Because men and women are not worthy that God should give them wisdom and discernment to avoid evil. Evil is what we naturally love. How many are there who come before God asking to be made free of sin? On the contrary, we would all gladly extinguish the light so that nothing could be seen. The reason why so few are taught by God and why most are going to their doom is because we cannot bear to be taught. We ask for darkness, and darkness is what we get. It is as our Lord Jesus says: we should not wonder if the gospel is so poorly received by men, for evildoers are always looking for a place to hide (John 3:20). We are therefore given to evil and we try to hide as long as we can. We refuse the pure truth which God offers us. If we are to be faithfully taught and to enjoy God's grace when his word is truly preached to us, we must ask not to bear our accursed load of sin, but must come to our Lord Jesus Christ who will free us from it. Then we may be sure that all of Satan's bonds have been broken. As long as we flatter ourselves, turn a deaf ear to rebukes and let no one touch a raw spot, we may feel relaxed for a time, but it will come at a very high price. We will finally be so tightly bound that escape will be impossible, for we will have refused the grace of God's Son. His grace would have set us free, since it is offered to all who are not content to wallow in their sins.

Paul has more to say about these women: *They are always learning, but can never come to knowledge of the truth.* At first glance we might think this a strange remark to make. God declares through his prophet Isaiah that he has not spoken in secret, but that his words are clear (Isa. 45:19). So if we make every effort to learn, we ought surely to arrive at knowledge of the truth, otherwise God would withdraw from us when we sought to draw near, and that is against his nature. 'Seek, and you will find,' he says (Matt. 7:7). How is it possible, then, for a man or woman to do their best to learn, and yet remain sadly ignorant and blind? The only explanation seems to be that God will not give them the chance to know, however much they try.

What we must understand is that the learning to which Paul refers does not come from a genuine desire in men and women to study hard in God's school. They are curious to know in order to draw attention to themselves. So we find these highly devout women asking questions. What sort of questions? Not 'What is real repentance?', for that would mean approaching God honestly and sincerely and thinking hard about human nature. They would then discover that we are accursed and defiled, rebels against God;

that our reason is blind and that we cannot trust our own understanding, but that all our wisdom is to be found in the word of God. They would discover also that all our thoughts and feelings are at enmity with God (Rom. 8:7), and that in order to come to God men and women must deny themselves, condemn their sins and be conscious of their faults, saying: 'Alas, how can we be sure of our salvation since we are so full of misery? We deserve to be cast off and cursed by God. Yet we must be reconciled to him if we are to call upon him. How can it be done? How can we be bold enough to come to him and to hope that he will be merciful to us, and will help us pass through the trials of this world? What confidence do we have that he will guide us until we reach the inheritance of our salvation?'

Now the sanctimonious souls whom Paul describes never get that far. They are nevertheless full of all sorts of questions. This, for example: 'Good father, what should I do on the eve of such and such a saint's day? I fast, of course, but should I miss out supper or dinner?' Or this: 'What should I do when it comes to the other fasts?' Or this: 'What must I do on such and such a pilgrimage?' Or this: 'What must I do when I come to worship such and such a saint?' Or this: 'To which saint should I pay greater devotion, this one or that?' Or this: 'How can I tell the difference between the Virgin Mary, St Agatha and St Gertrude?' Or this: 'What must I do when I go to confession? I've forgotten which sins are mortal, so should I own up to this or that?' Such are the questions posed by these devotees! There are of course others. 'What is it like to be in paradise? When I get there, will I be put among the martyrs or the confessors?' 'To what saint should I go to be cured of such and such an illness?' This is how these pious women, while pretending that they want to learn, show how little they care for knowledge of the truth. They avoid it rather and try to stamp it out. It is hardly surprising if they do not reach it. Paul however says not only that they do not reach it, but that they cannot. They have a different aim and they go in quite the wrong direction.

There are devotees, both men and women, who having poured forth all they want into the ears of a monk or priest, can never be prised off. But why do that? Supposing confession in the papal church was laudable. (It is not, of course, being an invention of the devil. Men claim to have this right over poor souls. They bind forgiveness of sins to this accursed piece of sorcery by which the pope ensnares men's consciences, thus defying the power and efficacy of the death and passion of God's Son.) Supposing, however, that confession was basically sound, the hypocrisy of these people can be clearly seen. Amid the darkness of popery and out of malice and treachery they merely sport with God. They feign sanctity by going to confession, often returning because three hours is not enough to rattle off half of what they want to say. And what do they confess? Piffling stuff! If a confessor comes along who will not humour them and who asks awkward questions, he might well say: 'Come now, I've listened patiently to you. You've drummed a whole lot of rubbish into my ears, but you've said nothing that really matters.' If he therefore sounds them out and takes a scalpel to cut into their quick; if, that is, he happens to uncover their real infamy, you can be sure they will be in no hurry to return! Instead of confessing once a week they will not be back within the year, because they have not been treated as they would like. Such people, it is clear, have no desire to draw near to God, so we should not wonder that God leaves them to their shame, and that Satan carries them off and keeps them captive in his bonds. It is a just reward for their hypocrisy.

Thus when it comes to knowledge of the truth, we must keep to the proper path. First, we must beg God to be our teacher and to let us learn in his school. We should be meek enough to submit fully to his word, so that we do not answer back if we do not like his teaching, or proudly retort: 'I don't agree!' No! Let God have full authority over us, and let us calmly allow him to instruct us, just as sheep follow their shepherd's voice, as Jesus Christ says (John 10:27). That is one point. In the second place we should not be so madly curious that we flutter aimlessly about, resolved to learn something which proves to be quite useless. We must dismiss as dangerous all that does not serve to build us up in faith and godly fear, for the devil is quite clever at diverting us so that we wander from the way. If someone has a day's work to do but instead strolls off into a meadow, crossing it from end to end and picking flowers as he goes, his day is wasted. He has hardly done a hand's turn. Why? Because he forgot all about his day. So we should not allow ourselves to be diverted from coming to God, but should head straight for the goal to which he calls us. Let us see that we seek only those things which serve our salvation. Let us, for example, condemn our sins so that we are brought to true repentance, and heed those threats which are meant to help us grow in godliness. Let us heed the exhortations we are given to do good, to strive with all our might and to be attentive to God's teaching, so that we live wisely and honestly. Let us know what it is to endure patiently the sufferings which God is pleased to send us, knowing that they are sent not only on account of sin but to humble us, so that with head and shoulders bowed we receive all that God chooses to lay on us. May we learn what it is to pass through this earthly, fleeting life as we strain toward the heavenly life, for we are pilgrims in this world. Let us mortify our fleshly lusts and learn to call upon God in absolute trust, relying on the death and passion of our Lord Jesus Christ. He is all our righteousness; for his sake we are acceptable to God the Father and are received by him in mercy.

If we make this our aim we will come to knowledge of the truth. We will discover that God did not speak in vain when he promised

289

that by seeking we will find. We must, however, seek, as Isaiah says: 'This is the way: follow it' (Isa. 30:21). We are not free to wander as we like. This is Paul's word to us.

A more general lesson is that when God sends us false prophets, as he says through Moses in the thirteenth chapter of Deuteronomy, he does so to test whether or not we love him (Deut. 13:1-3). For when we lend an ear to false teachers and are deceived by their flatteries, God surely uncovers our hypocrisy, for despite our display of piety it is all just a sham. Accordingly God will never permit us to be deceived by false teachers if we seek him in truth. If we come to his school for instruction and if we are willing to be taught and to accept his word, we will attain knowledge of the truth right away. Not that we will be perfect, but God will not hide from us; we will know as much of him as is necessary for our salvation. He will become more and more familiar to us and we will grow in knowledge until we are entirely free of the darkness of ignorance. We may be sure that God will not allow us to go astray, provided we do not do so wilfully.

It is not surprising if many are disappointed who, despite their desire to learn, remain sadly blind and are entangled by the devil in many errors. The fact is that they were not seeking God, so they received the reward which they deserved. This is not something we should forget today. We see what evil Satan works in the world when those who think that they are truly learned and intelligent, geniuses who soar above the clouds and who seem to carry all the world's wisdom in their heads, are brutishly ignorant. Why? Because, as we said, there is not one of them who does not freely sport with God or try to pay him in counterfeit coin. God must thus give them up to a reprobate mind and must send them a spirit of drunkenness, as the prophets say, so that they are deprived of judgment and discernment (Isa. 19:14; 29:9; Jer. 13:13). Attend, then, to what this passages teaches.

One small comment should be made about Paul's reference to 'truth'. Here he shows that knowledge is not everything: we must have sound and dependable teaching. What does the word 'truth' imply? It is there that we find the substance of our salvation and the means by which God is to be glorified. We may therefore be skilled in many branches of knowledge; we may indulge in all manner of speculation and our tongues may chatter endlessly about it; we may be thought of as miracles of science—but it all comes to nothing if we lack the true foundation, which is to glorify God, to serve him and to depend for our salvation on the assurance that what he has promised he will fulfil. This is the truth of which Paul speaks, as he explains in other parts of Scripture. Moreover if God blinds those who in their hypocrisy do not seek him but continue with their foolish devotions, what will he do to those who rise furiously against him and run at him like an angry bull, showing their contempt for all religion? Do they not deserve to drink in even more lies and to be so blinded by Satan that they have no more sense or taste than a dog or an ass?

Here Paul gives us to understand that the devil holds captive simple women who are hypocrites at heart, even though they have some desire to serve God and apparently want to learn. This is their just reward, whatever excuses are made for them, for God judges rightly when he allows Satan and false teachers to bind them fast. If women—even the simplest of women—are treated so severely, what shall we say of men? How much less can they be excused! Man is head of the woman, so he ought to be more sensible and cautious. Thus when men set out to mock God by remaining entangled in their sin, do they not deserve to be so thoroughly imprisoned that they can never escape from Satan's bonds? That is surely the case. Now if there are men who are piously inclined, sanctimonious perhaps, and who among other things mumble their prayers and fast—if God gives them as slaves to Satan because their conscience is not clear, what will he do to those we see today who plainly despise him?

Open your eyes and tell me if people today, whether great or small, rich or poor, do not openly defy God! The great of course are giants spoiling for a fight! And do not those with ability and wit use them to make fun of all religion? To look no further afield, think of what happens here where the gospel is proclaimed, not only in the towns but in the villages too. Look at how people live. I am not speaking about two or three, but of most people's manner of life. Is it not clear that there is open revolt? Nowadays men and women are not simply bad toward each other, they would like to pitch God out of heaven! True, they want to be thought respectable, so they look for ways to cover themselves and to escape the hand of the Judge. Yet they have no reverence for his word because they all want to do as they like. Drunkards want to swill as much as they like, like swine; the immoral want to wallow in their filth and perversion; the greedy want to snatch other people's goods right and left; blasphemers want to be free to bawl out loud without being rebuked for their faults. No one is prepared to submit to God. Is it any wonder, then, that God permits so many troubles and offences, and that even ministers and preachers fail to do their duty? It is extraordinary, or rather miraculous, that God should leave us with some seed of his word, since we are so ungrateful. If God were to treat us as harshly as we deserve, devils would climb up into the pulpit and take on human flesh, in order to deceive the wicked and the disobedient who are continually at war with God. So when troubles arise and when wrongs are done, when we see scoundrels who seek to spread their poison, to infect everything and to pervert the truth, it is to show that this is a just reward for all who wilfully stray from the proper path.

As for us, let us thank our gracious God for warning us so that we are not deceived. Know that amid all our struggles we can follow the right path, provided it is Jesus Christ who leads us and provided we are obedient to him. And when we see that God still leaves us with his word and that, for all our thanklessness, he does not deprive us of the gospel, let us allow him to teach us faithfully and to confirm us in the truth that we have learned. Let us continue to work hard, as God wants us to do throughout our lives, and may we receive his teaching in such humility that all may see that, having beheld his face, we are being transformed into his image, from glory to glory.

> Now let us cast ourselves down before the face of our good God, acknowledging our faults and beseeching him to make us feel them better than before. And since he has given us the special privilege of being taught the truth of his gospel, may he not allow it to be extinguished through our thanklessness, but may we so grow and be strengthened by it that it takes ever deeper root within us. May it bear fruit and spread more and more, to the glory of his name and the increase of the kingdom of Jesus Christ his Son.

# 21

---

# GOD VINDICATES HIS OWN

*Just as Jannes and Jambres resisted Moses, so also these resist the truth,*
*men who are corrupt in mind and reprobate concerning the faith.*
*⁹ But they will gain nothing more, for their folly will be plain to all, as*
*theirs was.* (2 Timothy 3:8-9)

It is hard and frustrating when, wishing to serve God and to
promote his word, we meet with opposition. Those who are
sorely tried by conflict need to be comforted, otherwise they might
give up, believing that it is intolerable that men should fight God,
should undermine his truth and work against it in order to destroy
it. Thus Paul, having described the plight of all gospel preachers,
informs us that their suffering is not new. The same happened to
Moses and to all the prophets. It is only Moses' example, however,
that the apostle cites.

Now Timothy was well placed to remember all that had occurred
since Moses' time. It was the prophets' experience to always meet
resistance. They were never left to serve God quietly without Satan
doing all he could to hinder their message. So, Paul says, if we
see people contending against God's truth, it has always been this
way. There were Pharaoh's magicians who withstood Moses (Exod.

7:11-12). This then was the pattern established by God to show what must be done by those who seek to proclaim his truth. They need to be armed for battle, for Satan will fight against them and will contrive by one means or another to impede the progress of the truth. This is the first consolation which Paul offers Timothy, and through him he gives heart to all who serve God and who minister his word.

He adds a second consolation. God will work to see that the truth will not always be oppressed. It may be veiled for a time, but in the end God will make it triumph. Satan and his minions, having tried to do their worst, will be defeated. So through the lips of Paul the Holy Spirit gives us two reasons which should make us strong. When Satan resists, and when we see that not all accept God's truth and that there are evildoers bent on defaming and defiling it, this is our reason for comfort. First, our Lord is treating us as he has always treated his church, for those who lived before us had no easier time than we do. God tested them by sending them false shepherds or by leaving Satan free to raise them up.

To show that this is true, let us see what happened once the law had been published. Moses came first, before the other prophets. He was already under attack and was never free of trouble. So today if we endure similar suffering we should be patient. It would not be right if we were better off than he, or than all who followed him. That is one point. The second is that the outcome will always be successful. Although we find it painful to fight and although God's truth might seem close to vanishing, let us wait for God to provide. He will work in such a way that the wicked will earn only shame. If they triumph God will uncover their depravity, and we will see how firmly he defends his cause, even if it is not at first apparent.

What, then, may we learn from this truth? We are greatly comforted when we are not separated from the company of God's children, but when we do as they do and when God makes us one with them. This is a source of strength. Now if trouble was afoot and we thought of how God treated those who have gone before, we might be alarmed if we believed that they had had a better time of it. However, when we see that we are exactly like God's servants of old, that we are trained, as it were, in the same arena, and that they faced similar hardships—when we see this, should it not comfort and encourage us to follow Moses, all of God's prophets and the apostles? When we suffer all the trials which God sends us, let us always bear in mind the state of the ancient church. For our instruction it is written that the church is like a field over which the plough has passed (Psa. 129:3). From start to finish it endures continual affliction. All this happened to our fathers and we must take their place, especially when we see enemies of the truth being allowed favours and a free hand, enjoying themselves and strutting about like victors. All the while men complain, blaspheme and act as if God did not exist. If we feel distressed, let us recall the example mentioned by Paul. These things have been happening since Moses' time, and the prophets experienced the same. We must bow our heads if we want to be like them, for this is what God expects his church to be.

*Jannes and Jambres*, Paul writes, *resisted Moses*. The two magicians he names were not enemies within God's household, like those who counterfeit the gospel and falsify God's word. But because Moses was already used to fighting and because the prophets followed his example, we too should prepare ourselves. When action is required we should not think it new or strange; we should have seen it well in advance. It is something to be suffered meekly and without faltering.

If we ask where Paul found these two names which are not mentioned in Exodus, we answer that the fathers of old not only had their writings, but that they also faithfully remembered what had gone before, so that the Jews inherited a greater knowledge of past history than we possess today. Paul may have drawn upon this when he wrote this text, calling Pharaoh's magicians by the names he gives them here. The fact that there were two of them was probably because of Moses and Aaron. Here, then, are two prophets sent by God, while Pharaoh, at the instigation of the devil, sets two men against them, one against Moses, the other against Aaron, to show that he is not inferior to them. Although Moses does not name the magicians or say how many there were, Paul's information is so certain as to be now beyond dispute. In any case we should not think it dubious or strange that the fathers carefully preserved these things, and that what had not been written down was nevertheless known and kept, so that up to Paul's time the magicians' names were remembered.

Note that in this passage the devil is seen to battle it out with God by counterfeiting what is good. He can be truly said to ape God. He takes care, of course, to leave God's truth well alone, but he so disguises God's works that he transforms himself. Being the prince of darkness, he will appear in the guise of light to deceive the ignorant, as we see from Paul's statement here. Just as God sends Moses and Aaron, Pharaoh, inspired by the devil, sends two magicians to oppose them. He cannot give them the spirit of prophecy, and his aim is not to defend the truth but to destroy it if he can and thus to oppress God's church, to abolish the covenant of salvation and every promise given to the patriarchs. Pharaoh endeavours to make his deception credible, so much so that when we see the magicians counterfeiting God's signs and miracles there seems nothing to choose between them.

Satan has many tricks and he assumes different poses, but always he tries to muddle everything so that we cannot tell God's truth from the devil's lies. We do well to remember this fact, for if we are ignorant of his wiles how can we guard against them? What

Paul wants is for us to think hard about ourselves. 'My friends,' he says, 'we know our enemy's guile and cunning. So when we see teachers who falsely claim God's name, and when they contrive to mask their words so as to make them appear truthful, do not be too concerned, for this is an old trick of Satan's.' Since the devil knows that he cannot completely turn us against all religion, he does not begin by saying that God does not exist and that it is folly to serve him. What he does is to take the word 'religion' and to use it as a shield, or rather he turns it into a deadly sword aimed at all who are not as prepared and as armed as they should be. This is how in every age people have been deceived in the false name of religion. True, as we said this morning, those who with pure hearts seek God will never be led astray, for God will keep and guide them by his Spirit. However many untruths the devil may invent he will never get the better of them. For that is how he usually works: in the name of religion he does all he can to dupe the ignorant.

Furthermore, as soon as we try to establish God's worship, Satan does not cease to spread his corruption among us. If we listened to him the good seed would never remain sound for long! We ought, then, to make sure that God's teaching is kept pure and that we reject the message of false prophets and deceivers. They must never be let in but must be sharply rebuffed, while we must stay within the space which God has made for us by his word. If we heed him who has taken us into his care, we cannot fail. Our Lord Jesus Christ will not allow us to stray, however much Satan entreats us and sweetly whispers in our ears. We have to be vigilant all the same, and never think that Satan is asleep or that God does not allow him to test our faith, for it has always been like this. Be sure that we will find especially puzzling the resemblance between what God has ordained and what Satan has added of his own accord.

What do I mean? When today the papists set out to justify the devilish abomination of the Mass, they will never say that it was invented to suit men's tastes or that it was devised with no good end in view. They say that the Last Supper was in remembrance of our Lord Jesus' death and passion, and was meant to nourish our faith in the hope of salvation, to which the Son of God himself bore witness. The Supper thus came first, and the Mass arose from it. The Supper was its source—that is the excuse they offer. In this way the devil tries plausibly to take God's mantle to himself, but all he does is snatch a piece from it! It is all so foul and sordid that we wonder how the devil could have taken us in at the first attempt, and how we could have failed to see his malice. If we look further, we will find that everything the papists do in the name of God is at variance with what he has appointed, however much they boast that they are simply following the pattern set by Jesus Christ and the apostles. Thus their holy water is a denial of baptism, but they disguise it as something else, claiming that it does not do away with baptism to which they owe the forgiveness of their sins. 'Because,' they say, 'we do not think of baptism as often as we should, and because when we transgress we cannot be sure that God will pardon us, it is good to refresh our memory and to have a second, auxiliary witness. Baptism is preserved and is still effective, but holy water is an additional aid, testifying to the forgiveness of sins.' Holy water nevertheless abolishes baptism, yet the devil so cleverly worms his way in that we might suppose that it matches God's ordinance.

I speak here of things with which we are most familiar. But if we were to run through all the abominations in popery and all the corruptions which Satan has brought in, we will see that he has always used craft to meddle in the order sanctioned by God's word, so that everything appears to be in place. Yet it is just as it was with Pharaoh's magicians. They performed the same signs as Moses and Aaron, but they were openly contending with God. They came to an accursed and unhappy end, for they were free only until God had tested his people and had confirmed that it was his hand and strong arm which brought them redemption. Thus he shamed those who for a time had wickedly resisted Moses and Aaron. Let us learn, then, to consider things carefully, and when the devil mixes tares and corruption with God's pure truth, we should beg him who has the Spirit of wisdom to direct us so that we are not deceived. For the rest, let us turn to the touchstone of the word of God. He will not let us fall away. This is what we learn from the story of Moses' conflict with Jannes and Jambres.

In citing the example of Moses, Paul wants us to see, too, that the prophets followed in his steps. They were also required constantly to fight. We should therefore count it a blessing when God makes us do the same. If today we have to resist those who distort God's truth and who turn it into a lie, let us ask him who is strong and steadfast to uphold us, and let us fight under his banner just as Moses did. We will not suffer defeat in the end. Think also of how grieved Moses must have been to see that Jannes and Jambres had power to perform miracles. God, it seemed, was against him, or else the devil was almost as mighty as he. So though God does his signs in Egypt, turning water into blood and day into night, sending vermin to ravage the fields and the whole country, similar things are done by Pharaoh's wizards and magicians. If God is active in both camps, is he not somehow divided and in conflict with himself? Or if it is the devil who works through the hand of the magicians, might we not say that God is struggling, so to speak, to overcome Satan? What a terrible dilemma not only for ordinary folk but for Moses and Aaron! They might well have gone under, lost heart and doubted their calling.

Today, therefore, when we see evil men whose cunning suggests that God is giving them the means to attack his truth—evil men who before were awkward and ignorant, but who now are skilled in mischief-making—when we see such men, let us persevere nevertheless, and let us not fear, knowing that Moses overcame this very problem. That is one point. When, moreover, we see how highly this world esteems lies and trickery, and that those who fight against God and his truth do so in perfect freedom, and are fêted and welcomed while we have neither equity nor right to defend our cause, with everyone turning a deaf ear when we appeal for help to combat evil—when these things happen, let us press on all the same, remembering that Moses endured such worries for a time. Let us look to the outcome which God has always given his servants and which is promised here by Paul. For he not only asks us to think of what occurred in earlier days, but tells us that when we experience the same we will not fail if we are firmly resolved to serve God always. Although the whole world may quake and fierce storms and whirlwinds arise to terrify us, if we hold fast and remain true to the teaching which we know comes from God, after darkness light will come.[19]

Now while this might not happen as quickly as we would wish, let us leave everything to God. Our task is to remain calm and patient, and not to flinch whatever happens. Let us defy the devil and all his ministers and keep on fighting for what we know is right. If we do this we will be victorious as Moses was over Jannes and Jambres. Nor was this a victory won only once. There God bore witness that his truth will always prevail, and that those who defend it will triumph even though for a time the enemy may be winning. If such things distress us, let us recall the example which Paul sets before us. We must hold fast the promise that our fight will end successfully, provided we do not fail or falter.

Next Paul speaks of *those who are corrupt in mind and reprobate concerning the faith*. He has good reason to call them corrupt in mind. What else are we to think of a mortal man whose anger is kindled against God and who dares to oppose his truth? It is

---

[19] An exact reminiscence of Geneva's motto, *Post tenebras lux*: 'After darkness, light.'

as if someone in a fit of madness sought to war against heaven itself. We could more easily snatch the sun from its place than blot out God's truth! Though the whole world should vanish, his truth endures forever. How can mere creatures behave so shamelessly and in such a frenzied way? The reason, Paul says, is that their depravity has made them blind and robbed them of their senses. Thus he makes it clear that those who go to war with God have already been blinded by Satan and deprived by him of reason and self-control. They are out of their minds. In this way Paul answers the problem we face when we wonder how men can bring themselves to fight against God. He calls them mad so that we might find the enemies of the truth all the more abhorrent. We are to shun them like the plague, for poisoners can do less harm than these miscreants, whose filth could by its very smell or odour cost us our lives. If poison is so strong that it can kill men from a distance, Satan's lies are, without a doubt, stronger still, for they defile so completely that we are amazed to see how quickly they wreak destruction. Paul's message, then, is that we should flee, cursing as we go, those who try to muddle us and who only want to mix tares in with the good seed of God's word.

These men, Paul declares, are reprobate concerning the faith. The word he uses can have two meanings. It is used either of people who lack discernment and judgment, or of the reprobate, that is, vile and detestable people as to the faith.[20] I do not doubt that Paul means to describe them as apostates, as people who have completely fallen away. They may for a time have given signs of belief, yet now they are cast out as rotten members cut off from God's kingdom and from his church. This further confirms what we have said, that we cannot have too great a loathing of the enemies of God's truth. We must in fact avoid them and keep clear of them,

---

[20] The word is *adokimos*, meaning 'unsatisfactory, unconvincing' (of a statement), or 'reprobate, discredited' (of persons).

since if we come close to them we will be at once infected by their poison and their filth. Let us also personally try to practise what we have been taught. Here is a highly useful warning, for the health of our souls and minds depends on our having God's pure word. Thus Paul describes as true chastity our union with the Son of God, similar to the union between wife and husband (Eph. 5:25-30).

The true bond of the spiritual marriage which Jesus Christ has contracted with us is that we cleave purely to God's word and to the message of the gospel. This is what gives health and wholeness to the soul, for as soon as we give Satan the tiniest opening he has only to distil one small drop of false doctrine and we are infected. Our disease is secret, and is thus all the worse. We are like a woman who, having listened to a rake or pimp, is led astray. She makes it clear that she is not particularly modest and that she is ready to give herself. The same would happen to us if God did not graciously give us his pure word to help us lead good lives and to keep us faithful, so that we opposed all that is contrary to the gospel in which we have been raised. When we read of those who are reprobate as to the faith, let us resolve not to go the same way to destruction. What then should we do? Let us walk in all purity of conscience, for as Paul said earlier, those who renounce a clear conscience sink like a ship at sea (1 Tim. 1:19). If, then, we misuse God's word or take no notice of it, this treasure will be snatched from us; God will cast us off and send us to the bottom of the sea. So let us learn to walk in fear and to pray that God may keep us in the faith which we received from the gospel. If we see many falling away, let them be mirrors to us so that we learn from them, knowing that if God is punishing their hypocrisy we must not copy them. If we do this, the punishments which God sends upon those who deserve them will serve to confirm us in his fear.

Further assurance that all will end happily for us is provided by Paul's next comment: *The wicked will get no further, for their folly will be known to all, as theirs was*—meaning Pharaoh's magicians, Jannes and Jambres. At first glance this might seem to contradict the point the apostle made before, and which he repeats: the wicked do make progress. As experience also shows, the enemies of the truth are continually interfering and never stop gaining strength. It would seem that victory is theirs. Now what should we say to that? When Paul declares that all who attempt to pervert God's truth will get no further, he means that although God allows his church to fight new battles, the faithful will always win the day, for God will shed his light on them. Those who serve him purely will have special cause to rejoice when they see that their labour is not in vain.

For example, Satan uses all his wiles to stir up trouble, and there are arrogant individuals who are out to attract attention and to corrupt all goodness. The truth we teach will be resisted, decried and slandered, and as God's servants continue to strive with all their might they will be vilified, and will risk being torn limb from limb. There are many who go astray, and who because the world is fickle and unstable lend an ear to teachers who spread false doctrines in order to ruin the faith. God's true servants will grieve over such things as they observe evil increasing to the point that the whole building seems ready to collapse, that nothing remains of what had once been built—built moreover with success. Those active in this work might well lose heart. Nevertheless we should look to God, hoping that he will so work that all will be accomplished, and that these interfering rascals will no longer be able, as in the past, to corrupt sound doctrine. Their wickedness will be disclosed and we will see that their only motive was pride and malice. Some will act with more restraint, but others will show that they deserve to lose all sense and reason. They are dogs and swine who defy God and all religion, but their shame will be uncovered. All the same God's servants must continue on. Even though all may seem lost and hopeless they must believe that God can by a miracle safeguard a remnant, so that they know that their efforts have not been wasted.

Such is Paul's message. While the wicked may prosper for a time and seem about to sweep everything away, to erase God's memory from the world and to completely banish his word, we must in every trial and extremity hold our ground and patiently await what we are promised here—that after those times when the darkness is so complete that we can see nothing, God will bring in the day when his truth will prevail. Then we will see how much he cares for his church and how well he can heal those ills which we thought incurable. This is what Paul meant by saying that the wicked will go no further.

The same is said in the Psalm, though in a different context where the theme is persecution. If God leaves the wicked free, they will so cruelly mistreat the innocent and so oppress them that the good will be forced to hide. These rogues will therefore be free to act for a time, justice will be corrupt, right and equity will cease and the strong will seize others as their prey (Psa. 94:3-7). If such chaos and confusion reigned forever, God's children would be badly shaken and tempted to go astray. That is why we read in the Psalm that God will cut the cords of the wicked who have driven the plough over the back of God's church, when God allowed his children to suffer affliction without his help (Psa. 129:3-4). He will cut their cords, he says. Why? So that the good will not put forth their hands to do evil. Thus when we are prompted to envy evildoers or to hunt with the hounds, as the proverb says, we must come back to God's promise that he will cut the cords of the wicked, will frustrate their undertakings and will see that those who climb high fall headlong to their doom. The so-called learned will be shamed, hated and exposed as poisoners of men's souls. This is the outcome we should expect, and we should not doubt that God will give certain victory to us who have steadfastly served him.

In saying that 'their folly will be uncovered', the apostle does not mean only that their evil will be made known. Their folly will be uncovered and disclosed. Why does he say this? There are many who willingly allow themselves to be deceived, because they do not care to judge. They prefer false doctrine because that is what they want. In the end God forces them to see that men will find them to be liars, men without substance who will be brought to shame for having defended so bad a cause. God's truth for a while may be considered foolishness, an object of contempt to the proud who have no time for it. They think it crude in its naivety, or else they will not submit to it because it is too demanding, too hard to digest. So even though the world thinks so little of God's truth, men will finally realize that behind its so-called foolishness there is deep and wonderful doctrine, such as the angels in heaven worship. Thus, however much God's enemies delight in their falsehoods and think themselves most wise, their wisdom will bring them down and our Lord will reveal their nothingness.

Nowadays when we think of abuses in the popish church, we know them to be childish and utterly silly errors, so that even infants laugh at them. Forty years ago, however, these things were thought the height of wisdom, possessing more than angelic perfection! No one would have dared to be so bold as to doubt the rightness of all the monkey-tricks they do; they were regarded as high and sacred mysteries which we were all obliged to worship. For since the most eminent scholars had passed that way, nothing could be rightfully set aside. So all this popish foolishness was judged to be truth which conveyed the loftiest secrets of heaven and which called for our worship. How is it now that the papists have been uncovered? Today we can scarcely credit that we were so bewitched as to believe such things. Let us therefore praise the grace of our God who rescued us from this, senseless as we were.

Paul is right to insist that the folly of all who fought against God has been uncovered in the sight of all. By 'all', he does not mean everyone in general. He seeks to teach both great and small that God has so illumined the uneducated that even they can judge the papists' greatest teachers. I do not mean to crow, but they are forced to concede what I say. If, for example, some poor artisan is imprisoned for the gospel's sake, and if he is brought before the greatest experts in the world, they will surely be confounded. Cruelty will be their sole resource as they send God's servant to the stake, but their disgrace will be apparent. Having this, then, as our witness and our proof, would we not be far too thankless if we did not stick to God's sure truth which triumphs over the world and over those teachers who, as we say, want to reach for the moon? God brings them down, but gives both speech and wisdom to his children—yes, to the most ignorant who have no education or anything else. He gives them, I say, strength and wisdom to refute all their enemies. When we see such things, should we not praise God all the more and obey his will? Let us in any case so arm ourselves with God's truth that, though the whole world rises against us and a great many troubles come our way, we nevertheless go on. We do well to be mindful of this.

We cannot discuss what remains for now, but a word or two needs to be said. Whenever we face trials which upset us, we must look for support to God's truth. Let it serve as our firm foundation, even as Timothy, in Paul's words, followed his example of patience, teaching, faith, love, good works and courage in persecution. We must therefore devote ourselves to the service of our God and be taught by him in his school. Let us rest assured that God is our teacher, so that when we meet some new doctrine we are able to stand firm, knowing that we have been faithfully instructed. This is why so few people benefit from sound teaching. When God's word is preached to them they show no interest. It is enough if they can say: 'We get sermons, and we have the gospel.' They are mere novices, and many of us are simply learners of whom Paul spoke this morning, who never come to knowledge of the truth. They are too caught up in the business of this world, or else they think they can always find a way of making up for lost time. 'Well,' they say, 'though I missed a sermon, am I not still a Christian?' Indeed we do not lose our Christianity because of one sermon, but when we scorn God's word this way he might well withdraw from us. And when we gradually cease to want to follow his word, we will find to our surprise that the devil has taken us so far away that we have no means of coming near again. While, therefore, God is close to us and while he offers us his truth, let us make sure that we are grounded and built up in it, so that more and more we may withstand men's slanders and the obstacles which Satan and his servants put in our way.

Now let us cast ourselves down before the face of our good God, acknowledging our faults and praying that he may help us so to feel them that we may attain the true remedy for all our ills. Let us, that is, be strengthened by his word, and to have such liking for it that it may truly serve to feed us. May we meanwhile be cleansed of all the corruptions of our flesh and of all that would turn us from the path he shows us. May we therefore cling all the more to him until we reach the perfection to which he calls us.

# 22

---

# FOREWARNED AND FOREARMED

*But you fully observed my teaching, my conduct, my purpose, my faith, my patience, my love, my endurance and the things done to me in Antioch, Iconium and Lystra, <sup>11</sup> the persecutions and afflictions which I suffered; from all these the Lord delivered me. <sup>12</sup> And all who desire to live faithfully in Jesus Christ will suffer persecution, <sup>13</sup> but evil-doers and impostors will grow worse and worse, deceiving and being deceived.* (2 Timothy 3:10-13)

G iven how weak we are when we are involved in serious and difficult fights, we have to be armed and equipped well in advance so that we are not afraid of sudden or unexpected events. That is why it is very necessary for us to be always prepared, lest we be taken unawares. If God, however, should give us rest, we become neglectful and forget what conflict is; we do not even like to be disturbed or to have our ears assailed by appeals to think carefully about ourselves. This is why so very many people are overcome by quite minor trials and hardships. Let us make the most, then, of what we are taught here.

Paul, having urged Timothy to stand firm and not to flinch, adds that he should have long since been prepared, because he had been taught in an excellent school. He tells him that he was closely taught as someone who should follow step by step. This is the sense of the word which Paul uses. 'You know full well,' he says, 'the manner of life I lived.' Teaching thus comes first, but the apostle is not content with that. He therefore adds conduct, purpose, kindness, faith, patience, love and so on. His aim is therefore to show Timothy that already he ought to be fit and seasoned, as we say, and that he must not be a novice. When the devil stirs up trouble in the church, Timothy should not lose his way or show any sign of fear. Why? 'Because,' says Paul, 'you saw how I lived. You did not see me only for a day, but as you got to know me you found out all about my manner of life.'

The first thing we learn is that no one will ever be a good or effective teacher if he cannot offer himself as an example of all that he teaches. If we preach only with our lips but if our life fails to match, God's truth is no less valid nor is his authority diminished. Our actions, however, expose his truth to abuse and reproof. If I were preaching about steadfastness and the need to be resolute, while I myself was known to be fainthearted and to avoid all blows when courage was called for, would anything I said ever succeed in moving my hearers? If I preached about sobriety but was known to be a drunkard, or about chastity when I was known to be a fornicator—in short, if my life was inconsistent, what would I achieve by all my preaching except to discredit the doctrine I preached? At the very least no one would be greatly edified! So would we give authority to what we teach, so that it is accepted and our people deeply moved? Then let us make sure that our life matches our lips, that we speak in earnest and that we do not intend to send others out without keeping them company. We cannot tell them: 'Christians, be courageous', while we ourselves scuttle away like crayfish! Let us be careful, then, and endeavour to prove that we speak from the heart.

Notice also that if someone who is responsible for instructing us demonstrates that he is not pretending but that he is truly zealous to show us the right way, we are all the more rebuked if we are reluctant to follow what he says. If what he teaches is not powerful enough to prompt us to do good, our ingratitude is even less excusable. So let us resolve to make good use of the examples which God sets before our eyes. When there are men who not only tell us with their lips what we must do but who actually show us how we are to live, let us be ready and quick to act, so that we are not ungrateful to God who offers us the means and such sound, practical aids.

In this passage the apostle has more than Timothy in mind. What he says should also work for us, for although Paul is no longer living on earth, and although we have not seen, as Timothy did, how he lived, this testimony should be enough. Paul is not only a faithful messenger of God to us but his life confirmed all that his teaching contained. Let us therefore rouse ourselves, since God has set his seal on the words recorded here, not only giving us ears to hear Paul's voice but showing us the power present in him, as God's Spirit led and directed him. In him we have a pattern and model of all that he taught.

*You know*, Paul writes, *my teaching, my conduct and my purpose.* It is right that teaching is mentioned first, and the apostle gives it pride of place. For although a man's probity and virtues should impress us, what is taught should always come first, and not without reason. Everything which we observe in a human being has nothing like the power of God when he speaks, and when we know that it is he who calls us and who puts us to work. So in weighing up a man's virtues let us learn not to overlook or ignore what it is he teaches. This is most important, for we sometimes put the cart before the horse when we think that someone is outstanding, and when we try to copy him exactly but without discernment. Thus in every age simple souls have erred when they have tried unwisely to copy what they see. God's word must bring us light, and then to stop us acting thoughtlessly it must guide us so that we can judge what is good and what is bad. We must not say, 'So-and-so did this.' No, we must follow God and the example of those who keep his word. That is why we have much to learn from the priority which Paul gives to God's word, in preference to all those virtues which deserve our praise. These must follow, but God must have the authority to decide what is good and what is acceptable to him.

We see, then, that it is not enough for a pastor who leads God's church to be a man of many virtues and to live a holy life. He must also speak, for if he is dumb all his virtues achieve nothing and he shows that he does not deserve to be counted as God's servant. All who call themselves pastors in the church must engage in teaching. Not only must they live in such a way as to edify others by their virtues, but God's truth must sound forth from their lips and they must strive to instruct those committed to their care. That is one point.

As well as teaching, Paul mentions conduct and purpose. By 'conduct' he means an even and regular manner of life; by 'purpose' he means consistency. In essence, to call oneself God's servant, to chatter and to be eloquent are not what matters. We must also have a settled aim and purpose, so that people say: 'There's a determined man; he doesn't just work by fits and starts.' When a man is in the pulpit he may speak like an angel, but when he gets down he may be merely a chatterbox or a pleasure-seeker. Some may think him a marvel, but when it comes to the test he is capable of nothing. He is shown to be a hypocrite, having neither the disposition nor the consistency required of a servant of God. That is the lesson for us here.

If we had eyes enough to see what God tells us, when troubles come we would surely not err and stray as easily as we do. We would already have thought about things at leisure, so that when God supplied us with a worthy model we could say, 'This is the way to behave.' We would already have this as our aim and would have committed it to memory. The opposite, alas, is the case: we seem to want to shut our eyes. Anything which might strengthen our faith or any helping hand that God might give us, we refuse. We look instead for pretexts which will clear us of all wrong. If we deliberately transgress, provided we can say that we are not the first and that many are doing the same, lo and behold we think we are blameless and absolved! All we are doing is making a bad bargain worse, since we are defying God. By nature we are already prone to all kinds of sin, and by persisting are we not conspiring with Satan and hardening ourselves against God? Yet this is common today. That is why God allows so many people to lure us from the right path, and why there are so few who can say with Paul that to copy their behaviour is to lead an upright life.

Among those whose task is to proclaim God's word there are those who are cold and apathetic. Many, even, live dissolute lives: they scorn God and are out to enjoy themselves. Would that such things were not so common! It is all because of our malice, for then God lets Satan have his head, and the affliction we suffer is well deserved. If we think of what most people want, it is preachers after their own heart, people steeped in all sorts of villainy and evil and who revile God's word. This, I say, is what most people want nowadays. So when God gives us examples who can help us live better lives, let us learn from them. Let us also arm ourselves against all the trials which lie ahead. If the devil stirs up troubles let us be ready to meet them; we should not feel fearful or defeated. This is what Paul means to convey by speaking to us of teaching, conduct and purpose.

As to the other qualities he mentions, we have already said in what way they are relevant. They are intended to urge preachers of

God's word to behave in such a way that, when they exhort the people in their care and cite this very text, they should demonstrate faith if that is what they have taught; if love, it should be mirrored in their lives; or if patience, let it be seen that this is what they strive to practise. In sum, all whose lips are meant to utter God's word must try to give proof of it by their entire manner of life. And may their people also make sure that they do not waste the means which God provides. Only let us take care, for all that God gives us can help us live as we ought. Let us use it to help us grow, for we are weak and cold.

In referring to the persecutions which he suffered, and especially to those known personally to Timothy, Paul implies that he not only walked in godly fear when he had been left in peace and when there were no enemies to fight, but that he did the same when involved in bitter struggles. He neither stumbled nor changed direction. This is a text we ought particularly to note, for someone who is at rest may seem disciplined and happy to serve God; but although he shows no sign of weakness, when trouble strikes he becomes distraught, a different man from the one we knew before, completely changed! Thus Paul rightly makes the point that not only was he faithful to God's word when it was accepted, but in time of persecution he was never seen to alter, for he did not spare his life. Just as he withstood evil when God's truth had to be defended, so he was ready, if necessary, to seal it with his blood. He was not at all fainthearted, but was a good soldier of Jesus Christ. This is something we should not forget.

To follow up my earlier remarks, note, first, that when times are peaceful we must be taught to live in godly fear and in all holiness; and, second, that if God takes us further we must be ready to risk our lives for our testimony to the gospel. If affliction and suffering should come we should face them steadfastly. We should be willing to go on when the road ahead is smooth; but we should jump ditches and find a way among thorns and brambles too!

This is how all the faithful and all of God's children are placed. And because the flesh finds these things hard, Paul adds a word of comfort: *God always delivered me*, he says. 'You saw,' he might have said, 'how staunchly I behaved; but you also knew that God did not fail me. His grace always sustained me. You may hope, then, that when you do as you should God will always be with you. You will feel his help close by. When you call upon him he will always be ready to show himself your Saviour.' That is the apostle's meaning.

Now we must first realize that because we are weak, if our Lord shows us models of courage and strength we should make the most of them. Today, for example, there are many who are suffering for God's word. We may not always see the fires lit before our eyes, but our ears must certainly ring. For very often we hear how our Lord has called on people we know to die. If we do not want to be condemned as utterly ungrateful, we must accept this help which God gives and make use of it. How so? I see not merely one but a whole host of people who have suffered for the sake of God. Neither prison nor torture more cruel than death dissuaded them. But did not my God show me by this means that in time of need he will not abandon those who call upon him, and that he will strengthen them so that they are more than conquerors? If we plead our weakness, it is nothing. Was there any more iron or steel in them than there is in us? So since we know that they persisted because God's Spirit guided and upheld them, let us do the same, and let us not indulge in silly excuses by pleading that we are only human. These people were frail like us, yet God gave them strength when needed. We should not doubt that he will do the same for us when we call upon him, when we trust him and when we turn to him for refuge.

Having committed to memory the examples that are laid before us, we note that God so leads his faithful people that he never fails them. Paul, it is true, declares that God delivered him because he still had work for him in this world. God, however, has different ways of saving his own. Sometimes he delivers them by prolonging their life and by rescuing them from the hands of the wicked, despite themselves. But sometimes he delivers them through death. This kind of deliverance means little of course to unbelievers and to the children of this world who are wholly bound to the earth and to the life of the body. They have no idea what it means to be delivered through death by the hand of God. As for us, we see that God's children have no fear of death, that God is glorified in them and that he triumphs through them. Although despised by the world they put their enemies to shame. Those who were as nothing show that God has clothed them with wonderful grace and that they possess what no one could expect. God gives them victory over every trial and displays in them an unaccustomed wisdom surpassing any human power. When we see such things should we not grow stronger in the faith? Is this not ample cause for the comfort which Paul offers here?

So being fortified by the steadfast example of God's servants, their worthy conduct and the holiness of life we see in them, let us also remember the gifts which God has given them. He has always held them with his strong arm and has never failed them in time of need. He has drawn them from the pit of death and has been in every way a merciful Father to them. This is the very first thing to bear in mind if we are determined to overcome whatever trials Satan puts before us. If we choose to ignore the sound examples which are meant to build us up, then we go badly wrong. We ought to feast our eyes, as it were, on the many proofs which God gives us of his power and help, yet we think nothing of them. Then too we tell ourselves: 'What am I to make of this or that? What's likely to happen to me?' This is because the devil has blindfolded us and we are content to let him keep us in the dark, though God has clearly shown us how things stand. Let us therefore take careful note, as we should, of the gifts which God lavishes on his people, so that they serve as proofs, giving us fresh heart. May we not only be zealous and willing to walk uprightly, but though heaven and earth are turned upside down may we still press on. Why? Because we know that God is unchanging and that he will complete what he has begun. Thus in every age he has delivered his own. We should not fear, then, that he will abandon us in time of need or fail to help even us.

To show that Paul is not speaking only about himself, he states a general fact: *All who would live holy lives in Jesus Christ will be persecuted.* What he taught earlier thus concerns more than two or three. All who are members of Jesus Christ and who want to be part of his flock must prepare for this eventuality. Paul's case was not exceptional, for what he says is relevant to all of us. True, not all will suffer persecution in equal measure. God, we know, spares many of the faithful. For every believer who is burned a hundred or more will die in their beds. God has not laid down a sure, fixed rule that we will all be persecuted in the same way. The fact remains that we cannot serve God without being his soldiers, for the world is invariably hostile to Jesus Christ and to all his members. Men are driven by the spirit of Satan so that cruelty is bound to accompany the hatred of which we spoke. Believers will never therefore be at rest or ever be free of troubles or harassments.

This truth is doubly useful to us. We may first apply it personally, and then, when we see God's servants being persecuted by the wicked, we must never doubt their good name. I should perhaps explain this further, since it may not be clear. I began by saying that we must each be ready to suffer persecution if, as Paul writes, we wish to lead faithful Christian lives. The devil, as we have seen, is our deadly foe, and he has countless people in this world who serve him. If we wish to be on the side of Jesus Christ and to be loyal to him, we are in a state of war. Unless believers wish to deceive themselves they cannot be at peace. Even if we give no one cause to complain, we should not think that everyone does the same, for God will not have us live a life of repose. A man who has no other enemies will be anxious in himself. In any event God will always prod us to spur us on, even if only to rouse us from our lethargy. He will also test our endurance, and we must learn to long for the peace of heaven so that we do not go to sleep in this world. In a word, it is time for war.

Having determined, then, to resist Satan's attacks and in time of persecution to suffer patiently and not to fall away, we must come to this second point, that when one of God's servants is unjustly persecuted we are not to think any the less of him. This happens all the time. There are many who, as we say, twist and turn in every wind. They may applaud a man while he is held in high esteem, but if the wind changes they tell themselves: 'What's this? What was I thinking of?' As a result they condemn a believer straight away, like blind men, without wondering whether he was wrongly harassed or not. Now if all this meant that someone was personally harmed, that would be bad enough, but in persecuting him men do not scruple to condemn God's truth as well. Naturally there are people who pretend to accept the gospel as long as no one objects to its being preached. If troubles come, however, they show that it never took real root in them; they appeared to assent to the faith as readily as an ass will drop its ears! They do not even wait until things get painful before abandoning the lot. If God's word is in any way derided and called into question, how many there are who immediately choose evil and rebel! If one of God's servants is unfairly afflicted, men spit in his face. Why is that, if not because we have not remembered Paul's teaching that the sufferings of the blameless are more honourable—and are judged to be so—than all earthly triumphs. Otherwise we lose sight of the difference between virtues and vices.

See, here is one of God's servants being persecuted because he has faithfully done his duty, and there is an evildoer who is punished for his crimes. Both are persecuted, but one deserves to be hated and the other deserves our praise. Men's ingratitude should not stop us from honouring those who are persecuted for the truth. Let us above all not condemn them out of hand as we are all too inclined to do. Paul was right, then, to warn that all who would live holy lives in Jesus Christ will be persecuted.

What then should we do? First, each of us should take a hard look at himself. And because God has chosen and enlisted us as his soldiers, let us learn to fight. Although for a time God may bear with us and give us rest, we should not fail to have our weapons ready and to pray to him who gives us strength to keep us from faltering in time of need. If we do not happen to be persecuted with unsheathed swords, or if the fires have not been lit for us, we should know that God is sustaining us and we should thank him for it. But whether we are in danger or at rest, we do not know what God has in store for us. We must therefore resolve that when he allows us to be persecuted we will be ready to offer ourselves as a sacrifice to him. In addition each of us should consider his calling, so that we do not say, 'That person is not as badly off as I am!' It is for God to grant to each of us his portion, and since he knows how he wants to use us, let us allow him to lead us. So when we see some who are persecuted more than we are, let us acknowledge God's goodness to us; and when we see others who are untroubled and at their ease, let us not feel jealous or grumble at God as if he were pressing us too hard. Let us each bear our own burden, bow our shoulders and ask God to strengthen us. This is what we must do.

Consider also that persecution takes different forms. We will not always be dragged off immediately to death. Our neighbours may trouble us or we may be made to suffer unfairly. We may be threatened, or Satan may contrive other forms of injury. In short, whatever devices are used to attack us in this world will be employed, and whenever rest eludes us this saying will be fulfilled: we are obliged to fight.

Paul writes of those who wish to live holy lives in Jesus Christ. We should ponder his words. Without a doubt the wicked who shun the cross suffer much distress, as we all know. For the enemies of God, people who love evil, take their executioner with them. Though no one may challenge them, their iniquities continually torment them; they have a fire within, or are like the stormy sea when the waves crash against each other. Such are the worries of the wicked. No one can put up with them, for they are proud, cruel and grasping; they are untrustworthy and disloyal, so that everyone is their enemy. We even see those who are consumed by ambition, greed and suchlike fighting like cats and dogs, or spying on rivals in order to thwart them. Ours is a divided world, and those who are bent on mischief are justly pursued and punished. However, Paul expressly urges us to suffer the antagonism which Satan stirs up because we live godly lives in Jesus Christ. Peter, similarly, appeals to us to suffer not as thieves, murderers, fornicators or abductors (1 Pet. 4:15). The afflictions we bear should be for our witness to the gospel and for the glory of God. Let us therefore see that we do not suffer for our misdeeds. At the same time we should not lose heart if we are unfairly maligned, for Paul has already told us that we will not only suffer violence but that the world will revile us and will blacken our name with its slanders and abuse. All this we must bear patiently, yet we must do our best to walk in the sight of God and to live soberly with our neighbours, so that we can protest our innocence and demonstrate it in practice. Let it always be clearly known that we are persecuted because we live a holy life.

Paul adds the words 'in Jesus Christ'. This might at first glance seem superfluous, but there are good reasons why Paul uses this expression. It is to show that our Lord Jesus Christ is fulfilling the words he uttered when he said that he had not come to give peace to the world but to light a fire which will go on burning, and to stir up a conflict which will not die down until the devil and all who are his are wholly vanquished (Matt. 10:34). As a result the devil will continually strive for as long as possible to hinder the progress of the gospel. This is what the wicked in their madness are out to do. So how can we find rest and peace if we follow Jesus Christ? He has raised his banner high to signal that we must join battle. He calls us to arms, so we must follow him if we would be his disciples. Sometimes we see people who make a show of great strength and godliness, yet the world leaves them undisturbed. Why is this? Because it is easy to get on with unbelievers when we do not really follow Jesus Christ. But when the gospel is proclaimed, and when our religion tells us to worship the living God and to serve only him, then we must renounce the superstitions found among unbelievers, who at once become incensed and who burn with fury.

This is why Paul insists that if we remain true to our Lord Jesus Christ we will be attacked and sorely troubled. He came into the world to bring division, so that if we would obey the message of the gospel we must be the mortal enemies of those who would tolerate us if only we were not Christians. How many there are who would happily live with us if we were prepared to sit on the fence! We would not have to flee far provided we were willing to disguise ourselves! But since God's word is on our lips, and since by our lives we must show that we sincerely claim him as our teacher and instructor—since, then, we must confess our faith, the sparks will fly and storms will gather with all who would be at peace with us, except that Jesus Christ has called us to war. Let us therefore learn that it is not enough to live, as we say, like a philosopher, above reproach and free of the taint of robbery, immorality, drunkenness or other faults. No, that is not enough. We must follow our commander, the

Son of God. So when he raises his standard, calls us to arms and commands that battle be joined against all who cannot abide him and who furiously oppose his rule, each of us must accept these terms. That, in brief, is what this passage teaches us.

We are all familiar with this teaching. All we have to do is put it into practice! The times require this of us, and in fact compel it. The world today is so evil that we cannot lead upright lives without attracting enemies, for we are mixed in with many who despise God. Yes, the gospel is preached and a certain order prevails among us. None of this, however, will rid us of corruption. We know how bold and spiteful they are who fight against God. We are sure to meet opposition on every hand. The gospel is profaned and God's children do not know which way to turn. The world has no time for them. All this we know. So unless we have completely lost our senses, let us resolve to put this teaching to good use. Let us not wait until we are openly attacked, but let us continue to train, so to speak. Let us reflect all the time on Paul's warning, and because persecution from which we naturally shrink is bitter and hard for the flesh, let us not fear to side with Jesus Christ on these terms. Let us remember, as I said before, that if we die with him, life is prepared for us in heaven.

Hence, since victory for us is certain, and since for every three-day conflict we have abiding and imperishable fruit in heaven, let us take heart. And although the word 'persecution' might first make us want to withdraw, let us rise above it and so follow our Lord Jesus Christ that while insults and abuse may well-nigh banish us from human society, we may cleave to him until he brings us to the heavenly glory which he has promised us, and which he has won for us by his own blood.

Finally, in order to teach us that persecution is not only a matter of sword or fire but may take different forms, Paul writes: *Evildoers will grow worse and worse, being deceived and deceiving others also.*

This is a form of persecution we need to note. When Satan is left free to spread his lies, when many bitterly rail against the truth, defiling everything, and when in addition the wicked grow worse and worse, God's servants are sorely tried. In seeing such things might not God's servants be tempted to stray unless they had long been armed against them? Paul therefore urges us not to feel distressed when we see death at hand, prison, torture and so on, and when the wicked gnash their teeth against us. We must show ourselves to be steadfast and invincible. And when we see enemies in our very midst who seek to gain by injuring the church, when error and abuse are accepted more readily than sound teaching, when evildoers cry victory and openly revile and blaspheme while God's word goes backwards, let us persevere nevertheless in the face of all these scandals. This is the action which Paul urges on us here.

Now since there is no time for further explanations, let us determine to be ready for all kinds of battle, otherwise we will never be able to serve God and our Lord Jesus Christ and to oppose Satan, his deadly foe. He will not cease, and he has an infinite number of helpers in this world. We know that he is the father of lies; he is bent on cruelty and has the spirit of murder. Accordingly in living Christian lives we must always be exposed to much suffering and many tribulations. It is not for us to choose our portion; it is for God to give us the portion he pleases. So let us trust to his goodwill. It is for him to dispose of us, whether in life or death. Whenever he chooses to call us out of this world, let us be ready to follow him.

We should nevertheless take comfort when God does not allow us to be punished for the wrongs we do, although he might well destroy us, and rightly so. For who is there among us, however just he is, who does not deserve to die a hundred thousand deaths? But because God leaves our sins hidden and does not punish us for them, but wants us instead to suffer for our witness to his truth which is most worthy and precious, should we not take heart and give him thanks for the blessing and honour he bestows? For by delivering us from the disgrace which we deserved he desires us to bear his insignia and his coat of arms and to be his heralds. In sum, let us suffer for his sake. Let the cause that we defend be his, and may he call our enemies his. That being so, do we not have reason to be comforted? We know also that in all our afflictions we have a faithful protector in heaven, for our Lord Jesus Christ is the one to whom all power has been given by God the Father. Strengthened, therefore, by his Spirit, we cannot doubt that we will overcome all trials and obstacles and whatever troubles may come. Despite our many weaknesses we will be victorious, for nothing can hinder the triumph reserved for us in heaven.

Now let us cast ourselves down before the face of our good God, acknowledging our faults and praying that he may make us feel them better than before. May he open our eyes, so that we may hate our sins and our defilement and seek to be healed of them. And since we must walk in this world amid much wickedness and opposition, may he also give us both strength and power to battle bravely against all hindrances, so that we are not delayed nor tempted by the devil's wiles to do wrong. May our Lord Jesus Christ so reign in us that what was true of him may also be true of us—that we should be victorious over our enemies, until he makes them a stool for his feet, and calls us out of this world to that eternal life kept for us in heaven.

# 23

## GOD'S WORD MAKES US WISE

*But as for you, abide in the things which you have learned and which are entrusted to you, knowing from whom you learned them, <sup>15</sup> and how from childhood you have known the holy Scriptures which can make you wise to salvation, through faith in Jesus Christ.*

(2 Timothy 3:14-15)

Although we are sorely tried when we see the world wilfully following Satan's evil ways rather than God's truth, we must remain steadfast, especially now that God has made it clear that he expects us to stand firm and immovable. We believe lies more readily than the truth because we are wicked and corrupt. We follow our own natural inclinations and we do not see our own futility. So when Satan works his deceits in order to confuse us we rush to accept them; we do not need to be pushed! God must therefore work in us by the power of his Holy Spirit when he wants to draw us to him to remake us and to change us completely. Let us overcome these trials, then, so that when men turn out badly we remember that it comes from their evil nature and defilement.

We will better understand how to fight through to victory, however, if we consider Paul's command to Timothy: *Persist in the things which you have learned.* We see first of all that we would be immediately swept away if we were not equipped and armed with God's truth. Do we have wisdom enough to follow the good and to flee evil? Has nature endowed us with the power to discriminate so that we lean more to the truth than to falsehoods? The opposite is the case! As I have said before, we do not need to go to school to learn how to lie, cheat or deceive; we are all our own teachers and instructors in this regard. Thus when the devil contrives to do his very worst and uses his helpers to trick and seduce us, to dazzle our eyes and to turn everything upside down, evil only increases. We must therefore have the resources to resist it.

This is Paul's message to us in this passage. He tells us that if we have made good progress in God's school and have allowed his word to take real root in us, however much Satan resorts to his tricks and guile, and however much he tries to ruin everything and to blot out God's truth, we must nevertheless hold our ground. For God's truth is powerful enough to make us invincible against all lies, provided we accept and honour it as we should. That is Paul's first point. He does not only tell Timothy to be brave and not to believe the errors and untruths which the world holds dear; he tells him also to continue in the things that he has learned. It is as if Paul were saying: 'If you were ignorant and had never tasted God's truth, it would be pointless for me to urge you to be firm. But since God has graciously chosen to draw you to himself and since you have his word, you must boldly take up the fight.' Here we see the grace God shows us when he is pleased to give us the light of his truth. He does so to assist us not only to know what is good but to learn to discern evil and so to be on our guard. We must not let Satan poison us with his lies, but we must be wise so that we overcome every trial. And when he puts some obstacle in front of us or in our way, we must never be taken unawares. We are therefore urged to make the most of God's word. However much confusion and turmoil we see in the world, and however many deceivers there are who thrive and who because of our itching ears make many converts, we should not stop.

There is, however, another point which the apostle makes. Timothy had not only been taught the pure word of the gospel, the law and the prophets; he had also been made their keeper in order to impart them to others. True, we are all obliged according to our ability to teach our neighbours. But Timothy was a special case because of the office he held. Having been appointed by God as minister of his word, he was as it were the treasurer and steward of the message of salvation. He had thus all the more incentive to show the care and concern of which Paul spoke earlier. Believers, then, are not to flinch when they see men turning away from God. There will always be rebellious and stubborn people, but our faith must overcome. Ministers of God's word, in particular, who have the task of teaching publicly, must show the way, and their condemnation will be all the harsher if, in the face of trouble, they are erratic, fearful or distraught. Such is the lesson of our text.

What Timothy had learned is said *to have been committed to him, since he had learned holy Scripture from his childhood.* Timothy thus had a greater advantage than if he was a novice who had been only recently drawn to God or who was a convert from paganism. His father, it is true, was a pagan, but God in his goodness had allowed him to follow the faith of his mother and grandmother, as we have already seen. He had been faithfully instructed and had more or less imbibed God's word and religious faith with his mother's milk.

Now this is something we should really require in all ministers of God's word. In a well-ordered church those who show promise should be taught so carefully that they not only learn the liberal arts but are made familiar with the Scriptures, so that when they reach the age of twenty they can read them in church and acquire greater confidence.[21] All this was ruined when the devil won the day, and when with the advent of popery the most dreadful confusion prevailed. At any rate Christians ought to observe this practice, so that to preserve good seed for the church those who seem fittest to teach are made familiar with holy Scripture and are trained in it from early childhood.

Paul's words, we should note, are addressed to all who, from the very beginning, have been privileged to be taught God's pure truth. This is an important point, for if a man of sixty who is already old and with failing health comes to know the gospel, he must work hard to make up for lost time, since he has been in error all his life. But what of those who from earliest times have received sound and faithful instruction? Do they not owe God an even greater debt? Of course they do! See, here is a child who has been baptized in the name of Jesus Christ, who has no idea of popish abominations, who has heard the gospel, has had it drummed into him and has been constantly taught even before the age of discrimination. Must he not be vile and thankless if he ignores God's grace to him, and if he does not receive the truth more earnestly? Paul is therefore critical of all who have been properly taught from childhood but who then go astray. They have much less excuse and they deserve to be twice condemned, for they have forsaken what has long been taught to them, and which ought to have helped them grow.

Now regarding those who when young were instructed in the gospel, I would say this. Many have long since erred, but they must not remain indifferent if God should call them now that they have reached adulthood or when most of their life is past. As I said, they

---

[21] The need for a well-trained pastorate was never far from Calvin's mind. In place of the *ad hoc* arrangements then prevailing, he argued for the creation of a properly funded school in which students would proceed via a liberal arts curriculum to the study of disciplines relevant both to civil government and to the ministry of the church. The Reformer's wish was fulfilled in 1559, five years before his death, with the opening of the Geneva Academy, under the leadership of his colleague and eventual successor, Théodore de Bèze.

must stir themselves to much greater effort to make up for time lost or misspent. Whatever the case, young people who have never been fed false teaching or who have never acquired bad habits, but whom God in his prevenient grace has trained always to follow the way of salvation—is it not true that if they turn aside from the truth and allow the devil to claim them, they are unutterably miserable, having lost so priceless a blessing? Yet we see how it is. Those who have had no knowledge of popish superstition ought to be like little angels. It is clear, however, that they have almost no religious faith, that they scorn God and are so profane that they seem never to have heard one word of the gospel. They mean to spite God as if he had never drawn near to them; the closer he has been to them, the more disposed they are to defy him in their devilish rage. What are the young folk like whom we see today? Were they ever as infernally godless as they are now? It is all too clear. Terrible condemnation hangs over those who have been soundly taught the way of salvation since childhood, but who have made no response. That is what this verse implies.

Paul speaks of the things Timothy has learned *knowing from whom he learned them*. We cannot, that is, be firmly grounded in doctrine unless we are assured of its truth. If we try to be steadfast and not to falter but lack assurance, we are simply being obstinate. That is no virtue. So before we make up our minds about something it must be sealed and settled for us. It must be certain, so that we can say, 'This is genuine, beyond all doubt. This is not just a matter of opinion, about which I can say, "I think", "It seems to me". This is utterly and absolutely true.' If this is not the case all we will do is dig in our heels when we try to hold our ground. This is why Paul tells Timothy that he knew from whom he learned these things, and this is how we know that we have a stable faith—one, that is, which God approves. For the papists boast of having faith, just as the Turks and heathen do. What then? It is only an opinion, a belief that they happen to hold. Yes, they hold to it firmly. They are stubborn, which is no credit to them. No one can regard as sound an idea which cannot be tested or proved. So we must learn to discriminate if we want a well-ordered faith, one we know to be true. We must distinguish between light and darkness. That is one point.

At the same time we are urged not to be too hasty in accepting teaching we know nothing about. As soon as someone says something we become excited about what we hear. This is sheer recklessness. It is true that we must allow God to teach us, and we must show such readiness that as soon as he opens his mouth we are attentive and obey without reserve. But this is because we know that it is God who speaks. Let us be discerning in all such things. We should not be stupid or thoughtless in accepting outright everything we are told, for those who are too quick to believe are also too ready to err, and in next to no time it is impossible to tell whether we have won or lost them. This, then, is a most useful admonition. We should be discerning in the choices we make, and to be discerning we must first know whether what we choose is true or false. On the other hand we are urged not to resist stubbornly when there is something we are not quite sure about. To want to defend a dubious opinion is like shutting the door to God. For example, there are many ignorant people who are ashamed to be taught. 'Oh,' they say, 'I know what life is all about. I've lived a long time on this earth. I'm not a child any more.' That is what these dimwits say—people who have never thought about anything in their lives. Yet it is devilish folly when men are stubborn and when they rebel, for they madly resist God and do all they can to stop his grace from reaching them. So let us not be obstinate when matters are in doubt.

According to Paul's rule, then, we ought not to be unyielding when we know that this is God's word to us and that we have his infallible truth. If we have erred through ignorance let us turn around, and if God graciously stretches out his hand and warns us that we have gone wrong, let us be ashamed of our mistake and be ready to be corrected if need be. May we be meek enough to be conciliatory and to obey what we know to be good, since we were not wise enough at first to keep to the way of salvation.

There remains the question of where assurance comes from. I said that we must know that what we accept is the truth. But from where do we get such knowledge? Paul appears to suggest that a man who is good and well attested should teach us. After all, he taught Timothy, saying to him, 'You know from whom you learned these things.' Even so, our faith would be much too weak and shaky if it relied on one man's point of view. God alone must be the author of our faith. How then can Paul ask Timothy to consider none but him? Observe that Paul is not praising any wisdom, integrity or some such thing which might be found in him. Nor does he say that these things are enough. The essential thing is that he was made an apostle, that his was a heavenly calling and that he had been sent by God. It is on this that Timothy is expected to rely. True, Paul gave thorough proof that God had not called him in vain, for we know how faithfully he did his duty and how he lived an upright and holy life. He could well have been a mirror of all perfection. Nevertheless what came first was the knowledge that God had chosen him for his service, and that the teaching he dispensed was not earthly in origin but was the pure truth of our Lord Jesus Christ. Thus, to be fully assured and to be steadfast in the faith, we must be persuaded that God has spoken to us and has taught us, though through the agency of men. So if we say, 'I have a wise teacher, one who is highly skilled and who leads a holy life', that is no more than a lesser aid. We must be able to say that it is God who illumines us by his word and that those who instruct us are his servants; that they teach us purely, adding nothing of their own and conveying to us what they have received from his own lips.

How, it may be asked, can we be so certain? It is not the result of our own efforts or wisdom. We must ask God to seal his truth in our hearts by his Holy Spirit, so that we have a guarantee allowing us to be sure about his truth, as if it were a business deal we had transacted. That is why the Spirit of God is said to be the guarantee of our adoption and the seal by which God confirms his word and attests its truth in our heart (Rom. 8:15; 2 Cor. 1:22; 5:5). That too is why he is called the Spirit of wisdom and discernment (Isa. 11:2). We see, then, that we need assurance from God as a firm foundation for our faith, so that the devil can never vanquish it however much he tries. We may continue on our way, and emerge at last victorious from the conflicts by which God tests us in this transitory life.

Now if we ask the papists on what grounds they hold stubbornly to their beliefs, what can they say in their defence? Yes, they will say that they are following their fathers and their forebears, and they will cite their holy mother, the church. But when all is said and done, what else are their fathers and forebears but poor wayward beasts? And as for their so-called mother, the church, it is a synagogue of Satan which has banished and driven Jesus Christ from its midst. So although they hotly reject all sound doctrine and have been bewitched by the devil so that they follow their age-old delusions, there is no firmness in them. If in all conscience they seriously asked whether they had real assurance, they would be completely lost. This should not surprise us, for the papists are in a hopeless muddle and their foundation descends to the deepest hell. What a shame it is, then, that here where the gospel is preached and is most clearly understood, where God calls us to himself and where the voice of the great Shepherd, Jesus Christ, is heard, there are some who are fickle and unstable, uncertain whether it is God who speaks or not! How many are there who so believe the gospel that they do not worry when troubles and difficulties arise? This is because they have never sent down roots.

Admittedly they think that what they hear is sound and they approve. Yet they are far from having resolved to stay steadfast to the end because it was God they trusted and not the counsel of men. They have not heard God's assurance that they cannot go wrong if they obey his word. There are very few who make this their goal. Accordingly God leaves them troubled and uncertain, hanging as it were by a thread. Their faith does not last. Paul's reminder, then, that we must know from whom we have learned, is timely.

Next we are told that *Timothy was made wise through the holy Scriptures, according to the faith which is in Jesus Christ*. Here Paul assigns a fine and splendid title to Scripture. In it, he says, there is true and complete wisdom. He also makes the point that if we think we have a wise head on our shoulders we will never make progress in God's school, and our arrogance will defeat us. Thus there are those who presume to make their own unaided judgments and who do not deign to ask God for answers, thinking that they are smart enough to know the difference between good and evil. God laughs at their presumption. 'So you think you are great teachers who do not need to be taught? Run, run if you must to your doom and destruction!' That is how God deals with those who trust in their own understanding. So here Paul insists that wisdom is found only in Scripture, and that we should never think we can perfectly distinguish right from wrong. We must rid ourselves of such folly and never think of ourselves as wise.

Where, then, does wisdom begin? We must become foolish, Paul says in the first chapter of First Corinthians (1 Cor. 1:23-25). To be foolish in order to be wise may at first seem an impossible idea. Yet if anyone with the merest drop of self-confidence thinks that he has wit enough to act aright, God scorns and disowns him as his pupil. All we can do therefore is confess our foolishness. We do not know how to live until God stretches out his hand and opens our ears, as is said in Psalm 40, in order to instruct us (Psa. 40:6). This is what the apostle means when he says that Scripture can make us wise. Let us honour God's word by humbling ourselves before it and by attending to what it contains, knowing that when we have learned it we need nothing more. No more can be added to it, for we are well and truly wise when we learn from God. If, however, we try to go beyond it, the devil becomes our teacher. For what, as I said, can we grasp by ourselves? Nevertheless God blesses us by being our teacher. He accommodates himself to our ignorance in the most personal and intimate of ways, affirming that if we listen to him we will lack nothing but will be perfectly taught. If, however, we have such itching ears that we cannot accept God's pure, unvarnished word but want something new, is it not right that Satan should have us and lead us into error, so that we wander aimlessly about like lost beasts? So I say again, let us honour God's word, remain obedient to it and ascribe to it all wisdom.

'We have been taught,' says Paul, 'by the faith which is in Jesus Christ.' This is rightly said, for it is not enough simply to read holy Scripture; we must have faith in God and be persuaded of his truth if we are not to stray. The Jews have the law and the prophets always in their hands and they read them in their synagogues, but they remain forever blind. Why? Because they have not kept to the right path and do not know the proper use of Scripture. The same is true of those who read Scripture out of curiosity. Many do so hoping that they can learn a great deal about which they can talk. They simply thumb the pages, but on the last day of their life they are no wiser than on the first; they have no settled purpose or method. Others read out of self-interest, with the aim of twisting Scripture to their own ends. They act out of spite, like those who are embittered and who want to spread corruption. They writhe like snakes, hoping to pervert simple faith. Do such as these ever get anything from holy Scripture? They do not! Even so Scripture does not lose the function which Paul attributes to it: it continues to teach us the most perfect wisdom.

Why does Paul say 'faith in Jesus Christ'? Remember that in the third chapter of Second Corinthians Jesus Christ is called the soul of the law, so that, when separated from him, the law is likened to a corpse without vitality or strength (cf. 2 Cor. 3:6). What then must we do? To make the most of holy Scripture we must learn to go straight to Jesus Christ. And just as Paul here calls him the soul or spirit of the law, so elsewhere he says that he is its end (Rom. 10:4). Would we then spare ourselves the trouble of reading Scripture to no avail, and thus wasting time and effort? Let us go straight to Jesus Christ in whom are hidden all the treasures of wisdom and knowledge (Col. 2:3). What else is holy Scripture if not a mirror to help us behold our God? We know that our highest good, our happiness and glory is that God should reveal himself to us. Now Jesus Christ is the living image in whom God shows himself, as Paul writes in the fourth chapter of Second Corinthians (2 Cor. 4:4).

It follows therefore that although we may read holy Scripture, we will wander and stray as long as we live unless we follow the teaching given here—unless, that is, we know Jesus Christ and the benefits which he freely bestows on us, since he possesses the infinite treasures of wisdom, righteousness, holiness of life and, in a word, salvation. Paul does well then to remind us that if Scripture is to make us wise, we must use it to discover all about Jesus Christ and to put our trust in him. It is because the world has ignored this rule that so little benefit has been got from Scripture. Most people, it is true, have had little concern to learn about God's truth, or else they thought Scripture was the preserve of the church's experts, and that married folk like noblemen, merchants, farmers or artisans could leave it all behind. 'We are laymen,' they said, 'we follow worldly callings.' As a result they lost their heavenly Father's will and testament, and were excluded as far as possible from his inheritance.

Such was the terrible ingratitude which existed among men. The treasure given to us in holy Scripture was not accepted; no one paid any attention to it. Worse, however, was the fact that those who thought they were exceedingly clever and who were recognized teachers did not bother to look at Scripture. Hence thirty years ago there was no question of reading the Bible in order to become a serious teacher. If, in the whole of Italy, France and everywhere else we had asked great scholars what truth was or whether they had read the entire Bible, they would have answered 'No'. They had weightier matters to occupy them. They considered the Bible as nothing compared with the decrees of the holy Councils. They had rubbish of their own to which they gave attention, and they considered the Bible as more or less theology for the simple and for minor clerics. That, then, is how this treasure of wisdom was despised, and how those responsible for leading others were themselves wretched and blind. If they read Scripture they gave it their agreement, but they had no idea of searching in it for Jesus Christ and for the endless blessings given by God to us in him. They looked instead for a thousand useless subjects for debate. Holy Scripture was wrenched this way and that, and there was dreadful confusion and sacrilege when something so holy became man's plaything. In fact they did not hesitate to call it 'a nose of wax' in order to profane it utterly and to show contempt for God.[22] Nor is 'nose of wax' the only thing they say. They argue that there

---

[22] The 'nose of wax' image appears to be medieval in origin, and was often used by Roman Catholic apologists to demonstrate the need for a fixed and visible source of authority in the church, namely the pope and his councils. Calvin, in turn, taxes his opponents with indifference to Scripture and with contempt for the Holy Spirit who inspired it.

is nothing fixed in holy Scripture, that we do not know how to interpret or explain it, and that we must abide by the holy Councils and by their determinations. They say that since Scripture is a nose of wax it can be turned any way we like.

So we see just how free a hand the devil has had in this accursed and abominable thing called popery. Let us pay close attention to our text, for here the Holy Spirit has sought to remedy this hellish confusion. 'My friends,' he says, 'in the law and prophets you have the treasure of all wisdom. Yet you need direction, for if you act on your own whim and follow your own inclinations, our Lord will see that you lose your way and will never reach your goal. There are learners who never get ahead and who fall back. What should you do? You should seek Jesus Christ, and when you have found him you should rest content, knowing that if you trust in his gospel you have all you need.' This is the lesson for us here.

Consider also the word 'faith'. It is not enough to know Jesus Christ as unbelievers do. Our faith must rest firmly on him. We must accept him as the one whom God has made our teacher, and we must cling to his pure truth. And because we know that in him we have all righteousness, that through him we are reconciled to God, having obtained remission of our sins, and that in him we are sanctified in order to lead holy lives, let us stick to him, for he is our Mediator and Advocate who intercedes for us, and in whose name we call upon God. Let us turn to him alone for refuge and seek the least drop of goodness only in him, for he is its source and origin. It is from his fullness that we must all draw, as we read in the first chapter of John (John 1:16). That is why Paul speaks of the faith which is in Jesus Christ. In him we may truly behold God and be transformed into his glory. Even while we are here on earth and in this transitory life, God will cause his image to shine in us, until he gathers us into his eternal kingdom, having freed us from the misery and wretchedness of this world.

Now let us cast ourselves down before the face of our good God, acknowledging our faults and asking to be made so conscious of them that in sorrow we may wholly turn to him. May we, renouncing all our thoughts and feelings, allow him to teach us by his word, so that it corrects, encourages and rebukes us. And that we may know how much the Son of God has blessed us, may we come to him as members of his body, cleave to him and attain at last the heavenly life and the kingdom which God his Father has promised us.

# 24

---

# THE USES OF SCRIPTURE

*All Scripture is given by inspiration of God, and is useful for teaching,*
*for rebuke, for correction and for instruction in righteousness, [17] that*
*the man of God may be whole, being made ready for every good work.*

(2 Timothy 3:16-17)

Seeing that God's word is called our spiritual sword (Eph. 6:17), we must be armed with it, because the devil never ceases to fight against us in this world in order to deceive us and to ensnare us in his lies. To help us do this, Paul encourages us to give God's word all due reverence. We must all give it our obedience and heed it meekly and without dissent. Paul then outlines the benefits we receive from it, and which should stir us up to receive it reverently and submissively. It is of holy Scripture that he speaks, for in every age there have been hotheads who have tried to question all that Scripture contains, though they may have blushed to say that God's word should not be implicitly accepted. In every age there have been wicked men who on the surface affirmed that God's word possessed such majesty that all should bow before it, yet that did not stop them from blaspheming it.

Where is God's word to be found, except in the law, the prophets and the gospel? It is there that God has revealed to us his will.

To remove every objection, then, so that no one can excuse himself by saying that one may believe God's word without accepting holy Scripture, Paul makes this point: if we want to honour God and give him our obedience, we must accept what is contained in the law and the prophets. And to stop people choosing at will whatever they like, he declares that the whole of Scripture has the majesty he describes and that it is profitable. What he really means is that we cannot take bits and pieces of what we like best or fancy most in Scripture. We must unreservedly make up our minds that since God has spoken in the law and prophets we must hold to it. Paul's purpose, then, is clear. By 'holy Scripture' Paul does not mean the writings we have from him or from the other apostles and evangelists. The only written record in those times was the Old Testament. So he intended the law and prophets to be preached in the Christian church, for what they teach endures forever. Thus we see that those who today want the law to be rejected and nothing more said about it are like dogs or swine, just like certain villains who recently bawled out *'Consummatum est'* in every tavern in the town.[23] I myself had to forcefully resist them in my sermons, so much so that in their synagogues and taverns these rascals had a common cry, 'No more law! No more prophets!' So often did this happen that we might have taken them for Turks!

Yet here, as we see, Paul pulls Christians up short, and shows them that if they want to prove their faith and obedience to God, the law and the prophets must prevail and must guide them, so that they are seen to be permanently and eternally true; they do not change and are never out of date. God does not teach things which are valid only for a time; he intends them to remain in force, even today. Better that the world should perish, and that earth and sky should decay, than that the law and prophets should cease to

---

[23] *Consummatum est*: 'It is finished' (John 19:30). The preacher's critics would doubtless have relished the double barb in their parroting of the biblical text.

have authority. According to Paul, therefore, we must allow Scripture to guide and direct us; we must turn to it and look for wisdom nowhere else. Remember also, as I said, that we are not at liberty to choose as we like. We are to be obedient to God and to approve all that Scripture contains.

Two things are said here in praise of holy Scripture: *it is inspired by God, and it is useful.* Paul wants us to find it pleasurable and worthy of our acceptance. The fact that it is inspired by God is meant to stop mere man from inveighing against God. To resist him by refusing Scripture is to do battle with him, since it is not something devised by men; there is nothing earthly about it. If we do not want to be rebels against God and to defy him we must submit to holy Scripture. Such, then, is its authority. In the second place, as well as reverencing and honouring God as we ought, we must recognize what he has done to secure our welfare and salvation by teaching us the truth of Scripture. God is not out to waste our time with trifles. When we read Scripture with due care we discover that God has written nothing which is not fit and proper for us or which is of no practical use. That being so, how ungrateful would we be if we did not accept the benefits which he so liberally offers us! Paul, then, does more than praise Scripture by showing how it displays God's majesty. He wants us also to get to like it, to come eagerly to it and to profit by it, since that is the end which God had in view.

Now concerning the first point, we must see that Scripture will never serve us as it should if we are not convinced that God is its author. If we read Moses or one of the prophets merely as a human story, will we feel the warmth of God's Spirit stirring within us? Far from it! We will find Scripture more or less inert and lifeless until we are sure that God is speaking in it and revealing to us his will. This must be our starting point whenever we read that Scripture is inspired by God.

The pope indeed will boast that everything he declares is from God. If our miserable world has been continually deceived it has been under cover of God's name, for no worse poison or false teaching was ever put into this golden cup—that is, was more thoroughly disguised by the worthy claim that God had spoken thus to men. However, as we said this morning, as long as we are willing to be guided by God, we will have a sufficient seal of faith to show that what Scripture says is no devilish delusion or some man-made fiction, but that God has spoken and that he is its author. We will know this for a fact. If unbelievers, then, are ignorant of this and rail against the authority of Scripture, let us recognize God's infinite kindness to us in sealing for us his truth and in allowing us to feel its power. Let us acknowledge that our faith derives from him so that we can say that he has spoken, for this is what the prophets too confessed.

From Paul's words we may also conclude that the only firm authority in the church is God's. So if we would test a doctrine, its authority cannot rely on the wisdom of men; we must be sure that it comes from God. Everything else is useless. This is a point we need to observe, for in seeking to prove whether or not we are his people, God demands that he should be our King and the source of all our laws and ordinances. He must be master of our souls and we must bear his yoke, otherwise we cannot show that it is he who governs us. The rest is pretence, however much we invoke his name.

Thus, in order to show that we cannot doubt the truth of Scripture, Paul will not call Moses an outstanding man, or Isaiah an eloquent preacher. He makes nothing of men's personal qualities but describes them as instruments of God's Spirit. Their tongues were so controlled that they said nothing of their own accord, but it was God who spoke by their lips. We must not judge them simply as mortal creatures but as men whom the living God used and who, we may be sure, were faithful stewards of the treasure committed to them. If men had kept to this rule things would not have ended in such awful chaos as prevails today in popery. On what do the papists base their faith if not on men? Hence the dreadful confusion we see among the ignorant. No one in popery would dream of saying, 'This is the word of God', or of endorsing its majesty. It is all a sham. Of course they claim the name of God, but it is their dreams and fantasies they promulgate, nothing more.

The apostle, for his part, tells us to stick to holy Scripture, because it is there that God speaks, not men. He thus rules out all human authority, for God must be pre-eminent over all his creatures. All, both great and small, must submit to him, and no one must intrude, saying, 'I will speak.' Peter also insists that we be sure when going into the pulpit that we have been sent by God and that the message we bring is the one entrusted to us. 'Let him who speaks,' he writes, 'speak the word of God' (1 Pet. 4:11). In other words he must prove that he has not stepped in with his own ideas, but that he has God's pure truth. He must so set forth the word he preaches that God is honoured. Hence since all man-made doctrines are here thrown down, let us never give them entry; may they be banished from the Christian church. Let us make sure we keep to the simple truth by which God reveals his will to us in the law and the prophets. Let us hold fast to it, and let no man be raised so high as to command our consciences or to invent whatever articles of faith he pleases.

What, then, of the usefulness which Paul ascribes to Scripture? His purpose as we saw is that Scripture should be pleasurable to us and that we should be zealous in our use of it, since it is given to us not only to display God's majesty but to edify and to save us. If Scripture is useful, therefore, we are all too thankless if we do not attend most carefully to it, for who does not naturally desire his own good and salvation? And where else can these be found except in holy Scripture which imparts them to us? Woe to us, then, if we do not hear God speaking, seeing that he only wants what is best for us! It is not his own benefit he seeks, for what need has he of that? We are taught in any case that when we read Scripture, we are not to twist it to suit ourselves or to search it for answers to idle questions. Why not? Because, as the apostle says, it is useful for salvation. Thus when I expound holy Scripture, it must be my constant rule that those who hear me should benefit from my teaching and should be edified to their salvation. If this is not my motive and if I do not edify my hearers, I wickedly profane the word of God.

Again, if those who read Scripture or who come to church to hear the sermon are seeking only empty speculation, wanting simply to be entertained, they too are guilty of profaning this holy thing. So it is sinful of us to make Scripture serve our personal whims and to look for puzzles and problems in it, but to overlook its usefulness. So in urging us to be enthusiastic scholars in God's school—for God seeks only our good and our salvation—Paul warns us not to defile holy Scripture by making it serve our own ends. Instead, knowing that God meant it to be profitable to us, let us come to it to be instructed—instructed, that is, in everything relevant to our salvation.

Consider in what particular ways Scripture is useful to us. Paul could have stopped at his initial statement, but by making his meaning clearer he avoids the need for further interpretation. *Scripture*, he writes, *is useful for teaching, for rebuke, for correction and for instruction in righteousness, so that the man of God may be whole, trained—or prepared—for every good work.* Paul attributes more than one use to Scripture, for after 'teaching' he mentions 'rebuke, correction and instruction'. It is not enough for God to show us what is right, for we are pitifully cold. He must therefore prod us and be forceful, so that we know that he is speaking seriously to us and that we cannot trifle with him. This is why what Scripture teaches is never dry and soulless. In order to impel us to come to God we need reproof and correction. That is one thing to notice. Note also the order which Paul follows. He says that Scripture is useful for teaching before he speaks of reproof and correction. He mentions teaching first because that is the natural order. Unless we have been taught to recognize the truth, all the urging in the world will do no good. We must first acknowledge that what is laid before us is sound, correct and true. The word 'teaching' thus implies that we have been taught the truth beyond a shadow of a doubt, and have been edified to the point that no uncertainty remains.

Remember in this connection what was said before about Paul's teaching. This very morning we saw that our aim must be to know Jesus Christ, so that by putting our faith in him we become wise in God's sight. Earlier still we spoke of prayer and intercession, of the need to place our hope in God, to look to the eternal life to which he calls us, to mortify our natural feelings and to be remade according to God's righteousness. In sum, we are taught by Scripture to put our whole trust in God, to turn to him for refuge and to know him as our Father and Saviour in the person of his Son, our Lord Jesus Christ. God gave him up to death for us; through him we are reconciled to God and cleansed of all our spots; in him we are counted righteous; from him comes the confidence we have to call upon God, who will not refuse us if we come in the name of him who is our Advocate. Again, recall that in us there is only sin and the curse. We must learn to hate ourselves, knowing that God deserves to be served and honoured by us. And we must understand what God requires of us and what he approves, so that we may act accordingly.

This is the message, as we said before, contained in holy Scripture. Now although doctrine comes before everything else, it is not effective in itself because of our sloth and coldness. We need the spur to urge us on, which is why the next thing Paul mentions is reproof. His meaning is that to be well taught in God's school we must be exposed to judgment, stung, rebuked and condemned. The same is said in the fourteenth chapter of First Corinthians, where it is shown that when God's word is properly explained and when prophecy is fully employed, not only are the faithful edified but any unbeliever who enters the church and hears God's message will be rebuked and judged (1 Cor. 14:24). By 'rebuked and judged' Paul means that whereas before an unbeliever was wrapped in darkness, was happily ignorant and in his confusion had no idea of God, once God has enlightened him he acknowledges his past misery, evil and unhappiness, and sees heaven opened if he attends to God's truth. He learns that we are not created merely to pass through this world, so he looks higher up. In this way the faithless are convicted.

To put it even better Paul declares that the secrets of the heart are also revealed (1 Cor. 14:25), for as long as God's word lies buried no one thinks about himself; our hearts are hopelessly ensnared. So what must we do? We must apply God's word. We must wake up from our sleep and take more thought to ourselves; we must no longer forget about God and our soul's salvation. We must think hard about these things. On this foundation, then, let us honestly examine the whole of our life and feel ashamed of our wickedness. We must be our own judges if we would forestall the condemnation reserved for us before God. Thus by 'rebuke' or 'reproof' we understand that it is not enough to be told, 'This is what God wants.' No, we must be roused to earnest thought and must look closely at ourselves, so that when we approach God it is as if we were being called before him for judgment. Let all be brought to light, and let us be dismayed when we see our former misery and foulness. Then let us look longingly toward the heavenly life and resolve never to turn from it.

Nevertheless it is not enough to suffer reproof: correction must accompany it. We must be chastened by God's word in order to amend our lives. We must forsake our sins, and if we have been steeped in them we must be compelled to uproot them and to rid ourselves of them. In this way, then, having been awakened so that we think of God, let us be put on trial and convicted, so that when our offences are laid before us all we can do is condemn ourselves. We must be driven by force to do this, for if we have been given to our own pleasures and to the empty follies which deceived us, our punishment should be severe, sharp and strong if we are to give God the honour we owe him, and allow him to remake us and to turn us back to him. It is as when a father sees his children doing wrong. He is not content to say to them, 'What are you up to, children? What you are doing is not very nice!' No, he will tell them, 'You wretches, have I fed and brought you up only to be rewarded this way? Must you so disgrace me after I have been so good to you? Out of my sight, you wretches, you deserve to be delivered to the hangman since you are so worthless! Should I be feeding such villains in my house?' This is what happens when God, who has put up with much from us, sees that we are far more disobedient than children are to their earthly fathers. Should he not be angry with us, and should we not be cut to the quick when we see how hot he is against us? Not that he is swayed by passion, but he treats us harshly in order to tame us and to stop us bolting like a runaway horse. When we have strayed from him he must forcibly restrain us and we must learn what it is to obey him. That is why Paul describes these various functions in our text.

We may therefore judge whether it is sufficient to expound holy Scripture as if we were simply telling a story. If that were the case what Paul attributes to Scripture would make no sense. It would be enough to say, 'These are God's words to us.' On the contrary, Paul says that the spur needs to be applied in order to stir and goad us.

So the work of a good pastor is not simply to say when explaining Scripture, 'There you have it.' He must also be insistent and sharp so as to give power and energy to God's word. Accordingly in another place the apostle declares that pastors in the church must be forceful to the point of importuning their hearers (2 Tim. 4:2). They must not merely urge what is right but reprove and rebuke. True, we are told to do so in a gentle and kindly way, and with patience. Nevertheless chastisement is required, and no one should say, 'This is too much to bear! You shouldn't go on like that!' Let those who will not be reproved go and look for a teacher other than God, for they do not deserve to hear one word from his mouth!

Of course we would like to be spared and we have sensitive ears. There are many, as we know, who are incensed when threats and punishments are employed. 'Look here, is this any way to teach? Win us over by gentleness!' Is this what you want? Then go and teach God how it's done! These thin-skinned people cannot bear to hear one word of rebuke uttered against them. Why? 'We want to be talked to differently!' Go off to the devil's school, then! He'll oblige you handsomely, but to your own loss! Believers, on the other hand, should quietly accept what is taught and should humble themselves, being ready to be reproved and admonished when they have done wrong. Let their sins and offences be revealed and let the knife be produced to lance the boil, so that the pus can come out and they can be cleansed and properly healed. This, I say, is what is involved if we would be truly instructed in God's school.

Paul, as we saw, completes this verse by stating that 'Scripture is useful for instruction in righteousness, that the man of God may be complete and ready for every good work'. In saying that Scripture perfectly instructs us in righteousness, the apostle excludes anything that men may want to add. That is, we are no more righteous for having kept some observance or other devised by mortal man. Here we see just how pointless are the troubles to which the poor papists go. They are continually obeying whatever is recommended to them. What kind of righteousness do they attain? On what is it based? 'Oh, this is what the church commands!' Paul, however, never speaks of religion or of doctrine which lies outside of holy Scripture. There is no other righteousness than this. So do they follow God's commands? On the contrary! Thus if we want to lead a well-ordered life we must never build on what men have invented to suit themselves; we must do the things approved by God.

If we attend to the teaching of Scripture we will find our righteousness there. God rules out all the rest, declaring that it is mere foolishness and smoke. So Paul does well to speak of instruction in righteousness. In addition, he shows us that to be good theologians we must be holy of life. God's word is not a matter for idle talk, nor is it meant to make us eloquent, clever or anything like that. It is meant for amendment of life, so that we are willing to serve God, to give ourselves without reserve to him and to pattern our wills on his. Thus to know whether someone has gained much from the gospel we must look to his life. Many, it is true, jump quite high and have a ready tongue. But if we cannot see in their lives a righteousness of God matching that which Paul demands, we can be sure that the rest of their lives will be defiled because they are not governed by God's word. So we must use and employ God's word in order to reform our lives and to walk uprightly. The man of God when properly instructed will thus be complete, prepared for every good work.

This statement makes even more explicit the phrase 'instruction in righteousness', for it at once excludes anything which men might invent. In our desire to serve God as we choose we try to make God subject to us, and we have our own ideas about what good works are. God, however, refuses to acknowledge them. Paul, then, knowing that in our boldness we prize our own works and cannot keep within the bounds which God has set, puts his finger on the problem so that it may be more readily fixed. He tells us that as long as we have God's word we will be people who are whole, lacking nothing and being ready for every good work. By 'wholeness' he means that we will be fit and equipped, as when a body has all its parts and is missing nothing. The word he uses has the sense of 'without fault'. We therefore understand that because we are utterly sinful God must repair his image in us by means of his word, to help us attain the wholeness of which Paul speaks. Then we will be fully formed for every good work.

Let men boast as much as they like that they live good and holy lives and that their works are virtuous. Once they come before the heavenly Judge it will all be as wind. Paul speaks advisedly of 'every good work', for he might simply have said that we are 'prepared for good works'. We might quibble that whatever notion we might have of good works is not to be condemned. No, 'every good work' is what the apostle says, implying that we muddle and mar everything when we add ideas of our own to God's commands.

The main teaching in this passage is thus that all that is man-made is corrupt. In popery the word 'good works' describes fasting on the eve of holy days, abstinence from meat on Fridays, keeping Lent, worshipping the saints, gadding about from altar to altar and from chapel to chapel, hearing Mass, having it sung and going on pilgrimages. Such nonsense is an endless maze, and no one can get to the bottom of the many laws and statutes forged by the devil. What then? One day we will have to appear before the Judge and account for ourselves. He has already spoken, and we must not think that the truth he has given us here is not his full and final word. Here, then, we learn that if we have profited from holy Scripture we are prepared for every good work. What, then, of the man-made traditions and practices which in popery have almost buried God's word? If we took a pair of scales to weigh human traditions alongside God's word, God's word would not weigh a hundredth part compared with the host of traditions we see. The papists may speak of God's commands and they cannot deny that he must be served, but they value tradition much more. Where will it end? Let us not be knowingly deceived, for we find the fullness of our perfection and of all good works in holy Scripture. God rules out everything else and declares that nothing else matters or is acceptable in his sight. Men number their works in vain: they simply double their condemnation.

We might ask, since wholeness is found in both the law and the prophets, what use the gospel is to us. We may think that Paul's teaching is unnecessary, but there is an easy answer. The gospel was not given to us in order to add anything to the law and the prophets. Read and leaf through everything contained in the New Testament. We will find that not a single syllable has been added to the law and the prophets. All we have is an explanation of what was already taught there. It is true that God has given more grace to us than to the fathers who lived before the coming of our Lord Jesus Christ, and that things are now made much clearer for us. Still, nothing has been added. So when Paul tells us that we will find full righteousness in the law and the prophets, it does not diminish the gospel in any way. There is in Scripture complete agreement between the Old and New Testaments. Hence today we have less excuse than Old Testament believers had, for besides the teaching contained in the law, the apostles who followed Jesus Christ have explained things so intimately to us, and God draws us to himself in such a way, that we are in no doubt as to what we should do. We need do only what he has commanded in every age.

Since, therefore, God has made things clear to us and has shown us all that he had in mind, we must yield to his kindness, otherwise we are like monsters bent on defying nature itself. In sum, if we would practise what this passage teaches and make best use of

Scripture, we must strive for holiness of life and recognize that God will not be served according to our wishes, but that he has given us a sure rule, one which is perfect for us and which indeed is. faultless. Our task, then, is to bring all our thoughts, feelings and energies to bear on holy Scripture, so that we may have the heavenly Judge's commendation. And may we do so all the more when we see that our gracious God has drawn close to us, and has so revealed his will to us that we have no excuse if we fail to cleave to him.

> Now let us cast ourselves down before the face of our good God, confessing our faults and begging him to make us feel them more and more. And since he urges and exhorts us to come to him, and calls to us with outstretched arms, let us not turn wilfully away, but may he draw us by his Holy Spirit so that we cling to him with ever greater fervour. To this end may we learn to live in full conformity with his will and to forsake our own ideas and fleshly wisdom, asking for grace to attend meekly to his word, and so to profit that it becomes more pleasing to us each and every day.

# 25

## PRESSING HOME GOD'S WORD

*I charge you therefore before God and the Lord Jesus Christ, who will judge the quick and the dead at his appearing and in his kingdom: ² preach the word, persist in season and out of season, convict, threaten and admonish with all patience and teaching.* (2 Timothy 4:1-2)

What was said in the previous sermon was meant to encourage each of us to read holy Scripture, since it is so useful to us and since God has included in it everything necessary for our salvation. God, however, was not content simply to lay Scripture before us so that we could study it. In his infinite goodness he devised a second means for our instruction: preaching, which expounds the teachings of Scripture. To this end he appointed pastors in his church whose office is to teach. This is an aid which God added because of our ignorance. It was already enough that he should have offered us his word in written form for each of us to read and learn. We see how extraordinarily generous God was in this regard. Yet when we understand that he deals with us according to our infirmity, and that he ensures that the pieces are chewed over to make them more digestible for us, when, in short, he feeds us like little children, we must see that we have no excuse if we prove to be poor scholars in his school.

We might have objected that Scripture was too hard for us when it was not explained. But since God has put two means at our disposal, allowing us to read and seek the truth as we find it in the law, the prophets and the gospel, and giving us messengers we can hear who make the truth much plainer—since God shows himself so intimately to us, should it not melt our hearts? Would we not be much too slack if we did not take care to receive what is preached to us in God's name? Accordingly Timothy is told to preach. Paul had already described Scripture as profitable, thus in a sense inviting us to read it. At the same time, however, he says that God desires to stir us up, and because we are rough and ignorant, someone is needed to show us the way, to guide us, to give us a helping hand, to bring to us the message of the gospel and to reveal God's will to us. For although we may have read holy Scripture and found it profitable, God still desires to help us understand it more easily, thanks to the second means he has devised.

Such is the main theme of this passage. Each of us must be moved to read and study what is contained in Scripture, and we must do this not only in our homes but when we come together to receive the doctrine which is preached to us. We must respect the order which God has appointed among us. Those whose task is to teach must likewise perform their duties carefully and must do as Paul bids them.

It is important that we weigh the words Paul uses. Already we have noted that Timothy was an outstanding man, diligent in building up the church and unsparing in his efforts. We might think that Paul had only to remind him of his duties. Since he had proved so zealous there was no need to prod him further. Nevertheless Paul speaks most forcefully here, not only outlining Timothy's duties but summoning him, as it were, before the heavenly Judge. *I charge you*, he says, *before God and before the Lord Jesus Christ*. So Timothy is called before God to answer for how faithfully he has discharged the duties entrusted to him. Clearly, to preach God's word is no small or insignificant task: it is the treasure of life and salvation. Just as God once and for all in giving up his only Son rescued us from the pit of death, so, when the gospel is proclaimed, he allows us to share in the costly gift of life obtained for us. Hence Paul calls the gospel God's power for salvation to all who believe (Rom. 1:16). When God chooses to draw us to himself and to make us his inheritance, he employs the gospel. It is a most precious thing to him, for the benefits of the death and passion of our Lord Jesus Christ are conferred on us. We receive their fruit so that we do not find them void or ineffective. This is how we attain salvation and are made whole again, becoming partners with the angels in paradise. This too is how God reigns in our midst and has dominion over us. Paul is therefore right to urge Timothy to speak, reminding him that he is answerable to the Judge in heaven, and that he must do his utmost to preach the word of God.

Further, he bids Timothy preach *in season and out of season.* It is as if Paul said: 'You should not choose only the times which suit your hearers; you must be urgent and insistent.' We might think this insistence out of place, for since men are naturally very sensitive they get annoyed when pressed too hard. Unless we relent it seems that all we do is weary them; they become disgusted with God's word. But supposing we did nothing but tried to please them. Or supposing we stopped whenever they said, 'That's enough!' What would happen then? They would cease to look for God with any enthusiasm. If we tried to satisfy everyone's wishes, people would receive the preaching of God's word reluctantly and coldly. Thus God desires that those who preach his word should be insistent, and if those who hear them become upset and even sated, they should not be left to wallow in their sloth or to turn so quickly from God's word. We must press them hard even when they are unwilling.

Again, the apostle declares that it is not enough to preach as if we were in school, teaching God's law, his promises or the truths of holy Scripture. We must, he says, *convict, threaten and exhort.* In other words, if we left men free to follow what they are taught, they would never move a foot! Teaching itself is not effective unless reinforced by exhortations, threats and various goads to prick and nettle us. Like ill-tempered animals when left alone in idleness, we are not easily made to take the path to salvation. Nevertheless to preserve a balance Paul also says that this must be done *with teaching.* That is, our exhortations must be based on sense and reason, otherwise we are simply beating the air. Teaching, then, is the foundation, and threats, rebukes and all the rest help to raise the edifice. Paul wants us to mingle gentleness with these, so that hearers are not repelled by too much sharpness which often makes them defiant and inflames them against God. They must be warned wherever possible, since our sole aim is to draw them to God. This is the gentleness of which Paul speaks, and which he asks us to use along with reproofs and threats. Now since this is Paul's meaning, or rather the meaning of the Holy Spirit who speaks through him, let us make the best use we can of this short summary.

Concerning the first point, God sets particular store on our being properly instructed in his word, for the Holy Spirit so directed Paul's tongue that he said not one word too much. God attaches the highest importance to the teaching of holy Scripture, so that the people are appropriately instructed. In not sparing his only Son, God has shown how dear our salvation is to him. Paul therefore summons Timothy before God's judgment seat to remind him of Ezekiel's words, that preachers of his word are like watchmen, and that if they do not cry aloud when danger is near, men's souls will be required at their hand (Ezek. 3:17-18; 33:7-8). If, then, people perish through our indolence when God has made us his messengers, their blood will be required of us; we will be condemned before God as responsible for the loss of those we failed to teach. Such is the summons which Paul issues and which confirms Ezekiel's earlier prophecy. He makes it clear that those chosen to be teachers are more tightly bound, and will be liable for the death not of men's bodies but of their souls when they fail to turn sinners from the path of destruction.

We should thus feel encouraged when we see how well God has provided for our salvation, and we would be utterly ungrateful if we resisted the goodness of our God who seeks to keep us safe in him. However unconcerned we are, however sleepy, God cares for our welfare and wants to preserve us for the heavenly inheritance. Should this not give us strength and confidence? On the other hand we will bring dreadful condemnation on our heads if we do not take care to walk in fear and in obedience to God, and if we do not profit when he holds out his hand and draws so close to us.

Notice also that the best means of waking us up is to bring us before the bar of God. Now if Timothy, who was like an angel in this world, had to be roused this way, how much more do we who are creatures of flesh, whose minds and feelings flit to and fro and who understand so little of this short-lived world! Do we not need much more to be reminded of God's judgment? So let each of us reflect that if we are too tied to this world and have too little heart for God, we must, once our earthly pilgrimage is past, appear before the Judge in heaven. All will then be brought into the light. This is how we may be truly roused if the world keeps us too closely bound.

Why is the coming of our Lord Jesus Christ important for us? We need not dread it, although at first glance it might seem daunting. No one can wean us from this world unless we are made to fear. As long as we are confident we indulge ourselves and bask happily in our pleasures. We must therefore feel some fear or else we will never seek to come to God. There are, however, two kinds of fear. The first is terror which makes us flee from God and stops us ever drawing near to him. The second simply forces us to think about ourselves. Whereas once we were sleepy and careless and had random, wandering thoughts, fear teaches us to gather them in and cures us of our idle fancies. Thus it is said that we must appear before the judgment seat of God (Rom. 14:10). Yet the mention of judgment is not meant to frighten us, to dismay us or to make us lose heart. It is meant to instil in us a measured fear, which wakes us up and helps us see that we must so live as to appear one day before our appointed Judge. Who is this Judge? The Son of God, our Redeemer—and our Advocate too.

Hence Paul speaks of our Lord Jesus Christ *who will judge the quick and the dead*. When we are told that the Son of God intercedes for us, do we fear to come before his judgment seat? No! We may approach boldly and with full confidence, for he will not allow his death and passion to be fruitless or powerless to do us good. He has also taken the title of Advocate and Intercessor, and will so judge us that he will preserve our salvation and will stand surety for us. Remember, then, that Scripture does not set God's judgment before us in order to terrify us but to lead us to our Lord Jesus Christ, and to assure us that God does not desire to judge us harshly. (What would happen if he did? We would be utterly crushed!) No, while keeping us in check he would not have us doubt his mercy toward us, as we try to serve and honour him and as we do the work entrusted to us. This is something we must remember.

In describing Jesus Christ as the Judge of the world, Paul wants Timothy to know that any who forsake the flock, who do not protect it from wolves or who leave the sheep hungry for the food of life, must expect vengeance from our Lord Jesus Christ. Why? Because he claims for himself the office of Judge: it is before him that we must appear. He therefore honours us by making us his representatives, so that the man who goes into the pulpit to preach speaks with the authority of God's Son and in his name. Paul thus declares that God has appointed us his ambassadors, so that we may exhort the church in his name and proclaim the gospel on his authority (2 Cor. 5:20). Since he honours us who are mere earthworms by allowing us to represent him, to speak as through his lips and with such authority that he might seem to be present among us—since, then, our Lord Jesus Christ honours us this way, if we fail to do as he commands how can he be merciful to us? Do we not deserve awful retribution from him for our faithlessness and ingratitude?

Think, on the other hand, of the treasure entrusted to us, with God his Father ruling us by his Holy Spirit, for his word is the instrument he uses to that end. Moreover he allows us to share in the eternal salvation which he has won for us by his death and passion. If, then, there is no preaching, his death and passion are blotted out and he is no longer acknowledged as the world's Redeemer. His being given up to death is of no advantage to us. If all this is lost because of our infidelity, can we be excused? When we appear before him, must he not rise up against us to shame and confound us?

This is Paul's way of sharply prodding Timothy so that he duly performs his office. Note, however, that although Timothy is urged to do these things, he might well have come before the heavenly Judge freely and with a clear conscience, having striven to edify the church and to rule the flock entrusted to him. Why? Because Jesus Christ sustains us when he sees our weaknesses and makes up for what we lack. We should not think that he intends to treat us harshly. He covers our faults; his righteousness will answer for us before God his Father; his death and passion are the payment which frees us from all our debts; his is the office of Advocate, though he is still our Judge. This is true for all of us, despite the fact that it is Timothy who is being addressed. Whenever we are summoned before the judgment seat of the Son of God, we must know that he will not permit us to scorn so priceless a gift which he offers us, namely the redemption which he has purchased for us. The gospel is too sacred a thing to be dismissed; otherwise we profane and defile what God has intended for our salvation. Be assured, therefore, that although the remembrance of the judgment committed to our Lord Jesus Christ should make us tremble, if we will not hear him when he speaks, quietly receive what he tells us and accept him as our Shepherd, he will be our Judge, whether we like it or not.

But consider the way in which God's Son seeks to win us for himself. He entreats us, as Paul says elsewhere (2 Cor. 5:20). How can this be? He who is head of the angels, everlasting God, in whom the fullness of deity dwells, before whom every knee must bow—yes, even the devils in hell—and whom all creatures honour and revere—how can such a one speak so softly, as a man to his friend, while we do not deign to hear him? What can we say? We must therefore stand amazed when we see with what uncommon gentleness the Son of God stoops to entreat us—worthless carrion as we are, steeped in iniquity, defiled, deserving only to be spurned like foul lepers and cast into the depths of hell—to entreat us, I say, in order to bring us to salvation! Know, then, that it will cost us dear if today we turn a deaf ear to the entreaties of God's Son. We will hear the dreadful trumpet sounding our doom, and the sentence of condemnation will be uttered over us if we refuse to hear that gentle, loving voice which invites us to share in the salvation won for us.

Therefore whenever mention is made of the judgment of Jesus Christ, we should be seized with fear and trembling. We are not meant, however, to be filled with dread and to flee from his presence; we are meant to wake up. If today we obey our Shepherd's voice, despite our many failings our Lord Jesus Christ will not forget that he is always our Advocate. He will welcome us and cover our faults so that we may look to his coming with joy and expectation. For in his earlier letter the apostle spoke of the mark common to all believers, that they rejoice as they await the coming of Jesus Christ (1 Tim. 6:14-15). Let us bear this thought in mind.

In declaring that Jesus Christ will judge the quick and the dead, Paul points out that those who are found alive at his coming will not die as we do, but will be changed in an instant, as we saw in Thessalonians (1 Thess. 4:17), and as is also said in the fifteenth chapter of First Corinthians (1 Cor. 15:51-53). We will then be rid of our flesh which will decay; we will be consumed as if nothing of us remained. Yet our souls will be safely and securely protected until the day when all will be restored. Those, however, who are alive at the coming of Jesus Christ will be changed so that all that is mortal in them will vanish; they will not experience natural death as we do today. This is why it is said in our creed that our Lord Jesus Christ will come to judge the quick and the dead, just as Paul confirms in this verse. What he means is that we cannot promise ourselves one day or many days, but that we must always have one foot raised in the happy expectation that when the trumpet sounds we will meet the Son of God. Though we are alive now we do not know when Jesus Christ will come, for he will come in a moment, in the twinkling of an eye, as Paul says (1 Cor. 15:52). This is the image he uses when he speaks of an unexpected coming. Let us therefore keep careful watch and be on our guard; let us not sleep as the faithless do, for, as we read in Thessalonians, we are not in darkness, since the Lord Jesus Christ gives us the light of his gospel (1 Thess. 5:5). He is the Sun of righteousness, so it is right that we should be alert. It is not surprising if the children of this world are asleep, for God has not given them his grace and brought them to the light. Let us, then, continue on, and run fast lest we be taken unawares, for our Lord will come as a thief (Matt. 24:43; 2 Pet. 3:10). But if, as I said, we are watchful, we will always be ready to answer when our Lord Jesus calls us, because we will have been expecting him. So much for that point.

In addition we learn that even though we die we have not wasted our time by serving God. True, we will return to dust, but let us look forward to that day. Although our life is hidden and although we see death everywhere beneath our feet, know that our Lord Jesus Christ did not rise in vain. He rose not only for himself but in order to gather us to himself as members of his body. So when someone is old and frail he should not think that in serving God his efforts have come to nothing, as if death swept everything away. Let him despise what he sees immediately in front of him and let him hope in the promise of the Redeemer's coming. In this way we can take heart, and be firm and resolute in our service to God and in our battles for him, wherever he should use us.

The Son of God at his coming will judge the dead as well as the living. This article of faith is thus consonant with what Paul teaches, for he seeks to show that when we do as we are bidden God takes us under his protection. We need not fear if Jesus Christ does not immediately appear to us, since we do not know the time of his coming. It could as well be today as tomorrow. Let us be ready, then, so that we are not taken by surprise. Further, although we do not know how imminent his coming is, and although we see no sign of it, while we may be on the brink of the grave or think that we will rot in the earth a hundred times over before Jesus Christ comes to restore us fully, we must not think that we are any the worse for that. Jesus Christ has been ordained Judge not only of the living but of the dead, and he will bring our dust forth from the tomb. Although the resurrection may seem commonplace to us, when the last trumpet is heard, just as Jesus Christ raises our souls from death whenever the gospel is preached, so we will experience a full and finished resurrection; then he will come in person to make all things whole again and perfect.

The apostle says that this will be *when he appears in his kingdom.* Not that he is not King now, for we read in the second chapter of Philippians that God has given him a name above all other names, before which all must bow the knee and confess that he is in the glory of God his Father. Jesus Christ already took possession of his kingdom when he rose from the dead and ascended into heaven, for when we confess in the creed that he is seated at the right hand of the Father, no fixed place is meant. It is an image borrowed from kings who have their lieutenants sit beside them. Thus God desires to rule the world through the agency of his Son and by his hand. In a word, today our Lord Jesus Christ has dominion over all creation, but because this is not visible, Paul says that he will come in his kingdom, as he himself foretold: 'The Son of man will come in the majesty of God his Father' (Matt. 19:28). The kingdom of God was indeed established as soon as the gospel began to be preached in the world. Even so we do not see it in its fullness; it is not yet ours to enjoy. At present our salvation lies in hope, and what we hope for must be hidden from us, as Paul writes in the eighth chapter of Romans (Rom. 8:24). By the same token it is said in Colossians that our life is hidden in Jesus Christ, and will not be revealed until Jesus Christ, who is our life, appears (Col. 3:3-4).

Understand, then, that God governs us through his Son, and that our Lord Jesus Christ has already taken up the sovereign rule which has been given to him. If we know this to be true we can place our faith in him, knowing that he has all power in his hand. For why would he raise us from the dead if we were not in his care and under his protection? How wretched we would be if it were otherwise! Would we not risk becoming Satan's prey every minute of the day? Where would our trust and assurance be, and rest for our conscience? But since we know that God's power is given to our Lord Jesus Christ in order to uphold us, to preserve us from all ill, to beat back our enemies and to keep us safe in his shadow, then even in the midst of conflict we may already sense victory; in the midst of storm and whirlwind we are in the haven of salvation and may boldly take our rest, nothing doubting. This is what we get by knowing that Jesus Christ has already entered into his kingdom. Because, however, we await his coming which is concealed from us, his kingdom is not yet known to us. We enjoy it only by faith and hope. We have the first fruits of it, but our thoughts must reach further ahead, and we must be patient until the things which we do not now see are revealed to us at the right time. We must embrace them with assurance, as if we could already touch them with our hand and experience them directly. Paul uses the word 'kingdom' to convey all this to us.

We come now to Paul's command to Timothy: *Preach the word in season and out of season, and with insistence.* We cannot therefore be too diligent in our teaching, because men are by nature far too cold when it comes to seeking God's kingdom. Scripture does well to urge us to seek the kingdom of God, and the rest will be added to us (Matt. 6:33). If we try to seek first the things which pertain to this present life, we put the cart before the horse for these are only incidentals. Yet who does not do this? We know how wrapped up we are in ephemeral things so that no one can tear us from them. Force and violence must be used to get us to draw near to God! What if we waited for people to come asking for spiritual food? Some might settle for once a week, others less often. To listen to a single word is more than enough, supposing we are not in a hurry! So there are good reasons, as I said, for Paul to use the word 'insistence'.

Although this is a message for Timothy, it is also a message for all believers. Just as ministers of God's word must obey Paul's instructions—that is, must be urgent and insistent if they are to do their duty—all of us must follow suit. For not only are hearers slow to heed God's word, but the one who preaches will never be as zealous as he ought to be unless he is ruthless with himself and is driven to ask: 'What am I doing here? What charge has been given to me? If it is an honourable one and if I fail to do my duty, it will cost me dear.' Anyone who does not do his duty and who does not even try, merely goes through the motions, as we say, as if it were forced labour. Now since the minister of God's word has to force himself to preach with urgency, he must certainly be insistent with those he knows are indolent and who would rather retreat than advance. People are sensitive and are easily vexed when they hear sound teaching. We should nevertheless persist with our preaching. We should remember too to insist not only with those who care nothing for God and who refuse his word, but even with the faithful. Above all let us be mindful of the reproofs and threats of which Paul speaks. Why? Because while we react mildly if what we hear does not upset us much, when a sore spot is touched or a sharp rebuke uttered, or when we are told that we need to do better than before, we flare up, feeling we are being pressed too hard. Even the best will sometimes say, 'I'm doing all I can. Why are you so hard on me?'

Ministers want people to be always doing more, because they are God's agents and are mindful of the Master they serve; they want men to submit to God's majesty. Now if we need to speak urgently even to the good, who want to be spared and to hear that what they have only half or partly done is quite sufficient, what of those who scoff at God and who are determined to throw off every yoke? We must be more insistent with them than with the good, who as we said are merely weak.

This, then, is how we can make best use of the text before us. Time does not allow us to go further, but we should at least review what has been said. Ministers of God's word must, on the one hand, rouse themselves if they see their zeal and fervour flagging; they must first and foremost be insistent with themselves. On the other hand, when they see that their message is upsetting and annoying their hearers who do not want a hundredth part of it, they should not stop but should persevere regardless. If they see the wicked gnashing their teeth as though they were fit to burst, they should keep on, conscious that they cannot serve God without that urgency of which the Holy Spirit speaks here. Although the good sometimes like to be spoiled a little, to be treated more gently and not to be reprimanded for their faults, ministers must nevertheless insist, knowing that urgent appeal must be made even to the good. This is not something which applies only to some; it applies to all without exception. Experience itself teaches us that those who have a heart for God must be urged to come to him, for there is always some reluctance in us. We would dearly love to rest every step of the way, like travellers who drag their feet and wings unless they are made to hurry on. 'Keep on walking!' is the cry, but they prefer to sit down in every place they meet and loll upon the grass or in the shade.

That is how we are. Our motives may be good but they do not last. We tire in an instant and soon grow cool. We may endure a few bad blasts but we quickly get depressed and are tempted to stay where we are unless someone prods us and eggs us on. So as experience shows we need to be aroused. We should not think it strange if people awaken us from sleep and goad us to go on. All will be lost if we are simply left to wallow; we will die in our sleep. Let us allow ourselves, then, to be stirred up, and let us keep running until we reach our goal.

> Now let us cast ourselves down before the face of our good God, acknowledging our faults and praying that he may be pleased to forgive them. May he so correct them that we may forsake our

sins and all the seductions which enslave our nature and which turn us away from him. May he graciously stretch forth his hand to support us in our weaknesses, until we are brought at last to that perfection which can only be ours when he gathers us into his everlasting kingdom.

# 26

---

# DECEIVERS AND DECEIVED

*Preach the word, persist in season and out of season, convict, threaten*
*and admonish with all patience and teaching. ³ For the time will come*
*when they will not accept sound teaching, but having itching ears they*
*will gather up teachers to suit their own desires, ⁴ and they will turn*
*away from hearing the truth and will turn instead to fables.*

(2 Timothy 4:2-4)

We saw this morning that it is not enough for the word of God to be preached when we are inclined to hear it or when it suits us to listen. Because we are so slack we must each rouse ourselves and allow ourselves to be spurred on as God commands. Moreover it is not enough that we should be taught to know God's will, but we must be reproved for our failings and must patiently endure whatever chastisements come our way, for they are the medicines we need. If we were perfectly sound and had no faults God would be content to give us the food we liked, so that his word would have only the sweetest and most wholesome taste. But since we cannot profit from God's instruction unless he cures the evil in us, it is this that must be done.

This is the purpose of the threats and punishments contained in holy Scripture, and which we must lay every day before the people if we are to do our duty properly. What Paul says here about *convicting, threatening and admonishing* is entirely in accord with what he said before about Scripture. It is not for us to devise as we will one means or another for serving God and his church. We must always attend to what it is that God commands. There is no dominion other than the one given by God to his Son, our Lord Jesus Christ. Thus anyone who wants to be a good and faithful teacher must teach in the manner laid down by God.

In Scripture we have more than a bare statement of the law of God. There is strong insistence on reproofs, exhortations and admonitions, so that in a sermon it is not enough to say, 'This is a word from God.' No, there must be goads as well. This shows that those who get upset when they are rebuked for their offences have no idea of what Christianity is about. 'Why don't you preach the gospel?' they say. Really? Just think of what the gospel contains. We are not told only that God is our Father, that he showed himself our Saviour in Jesus Christ, that we must call upon him, hoping that he will be favourable to us, relying on his free grace and looking to him for salvation and for the remission of sins, as we serve him according to his commands. The gospel contains more than this. God rebukes us every time he warns us; he summons us to appear before him; he threatens us. In short, the gospel is rightly called a sharp sword to sacrifice us to God (cf. Heb. 4:12). We will never make progress until we are entirely humbled, and until our nature is so mortified that God may quietly claim us as his.

None of this can happen unless we are urgent and insistent. God must thunder, as it were, and hurl his lightning bolts at us. Thus those who cannot bear to be threatened and chastised show that they have never really tasted God's word, and that they are only hypocrites who merely jest when they pretend to be religious. Yet this is a far too common grievance. Let us in any case learn to apply the lesson God gives us here, and may all the objections we hear not stop us from freely serving him as he commands. For if an envoy is sent by a powerful lord, he will have courage enough to speak even if his message is most unwelcome. He will say: 'I am not speaking for myself, but am on official business. I have written authority to state my case.' If this is allowable in mortal men, how much more must it be true of God who puts chastisements and threats in our mouth, and intends us to use them daily in his church? Must we refrain because they are not to men's liking? The first lesson of our text is that we must never approach God's word lightly, so that we give God a hearing only in our spare time. This is far from giving God the obedience he deserves. We must each do our best to work hard and profitably.

Now God tells us that night and day he stretches forth his arms not only to receive us but to call to us from afar, and that all he wants is to shelter us beneath his wings, to rule us and to treat us gently. We, for our part, should be quick to run to him when we hear his invitation and to set aside whatever gets in the way, for we all think that we are excused if we are busy with our own affairs. 'Of course,' we say, 'I'd gladly come to church, but I can't. I have other business to attend to.' Do not think that by such trivial evasions we can settle accounts with God. Our Lord Jesus Christ makes this clear when he derides those who claim that they have married, have bought a farm or are off to work in a vineyard or in a field (Matt. 22:3-4; Luke 14:18-20). We all say that sort of thing, but the Son of God tells us that it counts for nothing so far as he is concerned. So when the devil spreads his nets without quite separating us from God, when he hinders or obstructs us so that we do not run as fast as we should, let us learn to break his nets and to press on, even if we have to force ourselves as the Holy Spirit urges us to do. But if the faithful have to strive so hard to put God's word ahead of their own desires and wants, what of us who are bent on mindless fun and pleasures? Must we not heed Paul's word even more?

When we come to hear God's word, remember also that we do not only come to learn something new or unfamiliar which we can then take home with us. Though we may already know what God wills for us, we should come to receive the medicine which is prepared for us. Since we are so slow, let us allow God to rouse us and to dig the spur in hard. May we be patient all the while and learn to profit. We should not be like some people who will not hear about their failings; they turn a deaf ear, and donkey-like are quite unmoved.

It is not enough to refrain from resisting God bitterly, stubbornly and openly: we must put the warnings he sends us to good use. If we have been sleepy for a time or, worse, hardened in our sins; if we have abused God's goodness and failed to walk in godliness as we ought, we should be cut to the quick, knowing that our life is short and that we are answerable to God for having ignored his punishments. God is most gracious to us when he chastises us only with words, and when he threatens us before he lays his hand on us. This is how we should feel if we want to make good progress in God's school. We must not only learn what God's will is; we must also be roused by punishments and threats, conscious that our ills require such remedies.

So Paul speaks of both *patience and teaching*. By 'teaching' he is suggesting that those who are meant to rebuke and denounce sin should have reason on their side. What would be the point of sourly condemning everything we did not like? We would all be passing judgment and God would cease to have authority. No man should think himself so mighty that he rejects whatever does not take his fancy. God's truth is what we need to give substance to what we say, and to assure us that we do not threaten men in vain. There is, as Scripture says, only one lawgiver who has authority to save and to destroy (James 4:12). So if a preacher denounced whatever he liked, he would be usurping the authority of God.

Thus teaching must always come first if we would build on a sure and firm foundation.

By 'teaching' the apostle means that, as a first and logical step, we must set forth the grace which God has shown us in our Lord Jesus Christ. We must know where to look for assurance of salvation and how we may pray with confidence to God; we must also know the rule for good living—all this as taught by holy Scripture. If, though knowing this, we go to sleep amid the pleasures of the world, we must be prodded awake and made to see that these are only smoke and shadows which keep us bound to the earth. If our flesh rebels against God we must be subdued by means of threats. We must see God as our Judge if we will not have him as our Father and if we abuse the loving-kindness which he shows us in his Son. When we swell with pride God must humble our arrogance, and make us conscious of our sins so that we are ashamed of them. We should have no liking for the world and should learn that but for God's care we would always be at risk. Finally, we should be moved to pray to him and to turn to him for refuge. This is how sound teaching must always be the basis of all our threats and admonitions. We should, that is, be taught nothing which God himself has not spoken and which Scripture does not attest and confirm. Whatever we teach must come from God; he must be its author.

If this is the case we are free to exhort and rebuke. Indeed we must do so, as long as we observe the principle laid down here by Paul, and which is a rule no one can lawfully change. As for the word 'patience' or 'mildness', Paul does not mean that in reproving people we should try to charm them, for there are those who would love to be offered sugar and honey! He is thinking of the mildness which should be found in all who preach God's word. They should desire the salvation of those they teach, even though their thanklessness might irritate them and make them feel like giving them up as lost and hopeless.

Paul therefore uses the word advisedly, for we know that the prophets, although filled with the Spirit of God, became so upset and bitter when they saw men's obstinacy and malice that they were ready to throw it all up, to hate their very lives and to feel almost like blaspheming. 'Why has God put me here? Must I be compelled to do this work? I would rather die a hundred deaths than toil for nothing!' Their anger, thus, was kindled when they saw no signs of improvement and when their work proved fruitless. Since the holy prophets endured such trials, it is clear that we need patience to keep us in check, and to help us go on when we see people who not only resent God but are full of venom and arrogance, or who are so stupid or unstable that we do not know how to win them over. And though occasionally we may draw them to God, they will forsake him and turn against him. That being so we must arm ourselves with patience, otherwise we would have to abandon the work committed to us. This is why Paul uses the word.

This is not to say that the reproofs which we have to make should never be sharp or should never upset those who hear. We see how the prophets and apostles behaved, and the example of Jeremiah provides a clear illustration of this passage. Jeremiah is as severe as any of the prophets. He does not cease to insist on God's judgment and retribution; he speaks with a voice of thunder and pours forth such stinging rebukes that he seems to want to crush the people utterly, to blacken them and to make them as loathsome as possible. Jeremiah's manner is, as we see, extremely sharp, or at least so forceful as to make us tremble. Nevertheless there is in him the mildness of which Paul speaks. For the word implies a measure of self-restraint which stops irritation from going too far. Ezekiel, too, immediately exhibits the same virtue when he says that God made him eat the scroll with which he was to threaten the city of Jerusalem and the whole of Judaea (Ezek. 3:1). Here we have God about to indict the Jews. He orders Ezekiel to proclaim the fact, to trumpet it abroad and to announce the news. But before anything else Ezekiel has to swallow the scroll, so that it is impressed not only on the tip of his tongue but on his heart, giving him the zeal and energy to deliver his message. Such is his inner turmoil that he is quite distraught, yet he does not spare himself. Thus we see both things at work in him. He reproves and rebukes as he goes about his mission. He is unyielding and does not flinch in the face of men, but he is not devoid of pity or kindness. Jeremiah also felt like weeping: his eyes were like a fountain in his head; all was changed to tears because he had compassion on this doomed, unhappy people (Jer. 9:1). We understand, then, why Paul should speak of patience or mildness.

Reproof and rebuke are indeed necessary, even though we have cause to grieve and fret when we gain almost nothing, when people grow worse because of our teaching and when the wicked who once defied God still laugh at him, reject his word and tread it underfoot. Although, I say, we might well give up, let this word act as a restraint. It is God's intention that we persist, not despite ourselves—we should not, that is, feel compelled to obey him to whom we belong—but that we should patiently wait for him to touch the hearts of those we think incorrigible, that he may convert them, tame them and lead them to the way of salvation. Or else let this message serve to condemn men when they are determined to defy God. They will have no excuse, and God, having waited for so long, will finally give vent to his wrath.

To confirm this word of warning, the apostle writes that men will much prefer to turn aside to vanities and falsehoods than to receive sound and worthwhile teaching. *The time will come*, he says, *when there will be heaps of teachers who will so fill men's ears with fictions*—that is, with idle, useless things—*that they cannot abide God's truth*. It is as if we said to a physician who had an unruly patient: 'Hurry up, this man can't contain himself. He's been muttering this and that. Unless you provide a quick remedy, it will be too late. Something bad will probably happen.' In the same way Paul urges Timothy to be quick and zealous in making his appeal to men, and to be insistent, as we said before. Why? Because, says Paul, Satan is stirring up such mischief that most are already infected, and what is worse they are heaping up teachers, piles of them, who tell false tales—impostors, who are out to deceive them.

Paul's meaning is clear, but let us look more closely at what he says. In speaking of the ruin and disaster which will follow, he blames people for having itching ears. What he refers to is the itch which comes from mindless curiosity and which makes us fussy and demanding, so that we want to be indulged and to be regaled with pleasant speech. From time immemorial, as we know, men have always longed to hear things new and entertaining, just as Paul said earlier. So whenever men turned their attention to something, it was to foolishness, and they ignored what was necessary for their salvation. It is serious indeed when we forget the best gift God has given us, and when we spurn and spoil it. For what is the highest treasure we have? Is it not reason and understanding, which make us different from the brute beasts? Here we see God's image stamped upon us, the gift of reason and intellect. What do we do with it? Instead of making proper use of so precious and noble a gift, we corrupt it, we flutter aimlessly about and rack our brains in search of rubbish, inconsequential nonsense, so much so that if animals had an ounce of intelligence they would rightly condemn us. 'What?' they would say. 'God has made you in his image and given you wisdom and understanding, yet you waste your time on follies which bring no profit! You make no attempt to remember that God has made you in the expectation of a better life, that he calls you his children and would make you his heirs! You forget the God who placed his image in you so that you might behold his majesty and glory!' Truly, we need no

# Deceivers and Deceived

other judges than oxen or asses to condemn us when they see how wilful we are.

Given that we are so inclined to evil, or rather so addicted to it, we ought to heed Paul's warning all the more when he tells us that people will turn away from God, and that those who began so well will be taken by the devil from the flock and will end up as apostates. This will happen, he says, because they have itching ears. Let us therefore shun this absurd curiosity like the plague, since it robs us of the chief blessing which God has given us, making us swerve from the truth in which our salvation lies and is contained. There is also another failing. It is when we want to be handled gently and to be gratified. Hence Micah tells us that the Jews of his time would willingly have accepted those who announced good grape harvests and successful crops, and who brought nothing but welcome news (cf. Mic. 2:11). In the same way, are there not today those who want preachers who will tell them what they want to hear, people who will say: 'Live well, my friends, for God is not as severe or unfeeling as some say. To be told that he has ceased to be merciful is so depressing! We ought, of course, to confess our faults, but we can still have a good time. If we believed these trouble-makers who are always on about God's judgment, God must be our deadly enemy, ready at any moment to strike us down. Can he be so cruel? Doesn't he want his children sometimes to be at rest?'

Such, then, are those who announce good grape harvests and successful crops, and who deceive their hearers by promising that God will send them plenty of food to eat. Yet this is what Ezekiel says: 'Woe to those who slay the souls which should live, and who give life to the souls that should die' (Ezek. 13:19). He declares that deceivers do not cease their work until they have killed those who were once healthy and who had a fair knowledge of God. They abandon those who might have been led to the right path and

379

they refrain from making mention of it. So when we have itching ears—when, that is, we merely want plasters to be put on the sores we have and thus to cover them up—when we want to be soothed with flattery, God will give us what we want, but it will not be for our good.

What should we therefore do? We should first acknowledge that there are good reasons why the dreadful ruin we see nowadays should have come upon us. Some say that this is because ordinary folk are helpless if they are deceived and badly led. This does not take us, however, to the real source. The fact is that such destruction could not have happened if God had not paid men the wages they deserved for having itching ears and for pursuing falsehoods, for preferring to go to their doom instead of being led to God. Thus Paul in Second Thessalonians says that when error is rife, it is because men have disobeyed the one who made and formed them; they refuse to accept the truth of his gospel and are bound to fall into all kinds of superstition (cf. 2 Thess. 2:10).

So knowing that the gospel has been marred because men refuse to be taught by God but choose instead to please themselves, let us look to ourselves and resolve not to give in to our foolish curiosity. We must not burden our minds by endless inquiry into this or that, but must allow God to teach us what he knows is pertinent to our salvation. Nor should we look to others to gratify or indulge us, since we cannot bear to be chastised. While those who are content to wallow in their iniquity have itching ears, let us be stung so that we sense our failings. May God's fear so fill us that we never cease to tremble and to be ashamed of ourselves, until God should lay his hand on us, heal us by his word and be a physician to us. That, in brief, is what we need to bear in mind.

It is no accident that Paul should speak of *people who collect teachers for themselves.* He is not content to say that they look for teachers who will suit them and will refuse those whom God has sent. He speaks of a pile, a large number of teachers. Why? Because when it comes to being deceived our appetite is enormous! Accordingly the prophets liken the fanaticism with which hypocrites strive to serve God to the frenzy of stallions lusting after mares (Ezek. 23:20). They appear to be beside themselves, devoid of reason and understanding. Such an image at first seems odd to us. It is because once we turn away from God the devil moves and drives us so that nothing satisfies us. We love lies, we long for them and we do not care if we are duped. We would like to be duped a hundred times over! This is why hypocrites never come straight to God, but pretend to approach him by roundabout ways. Yet all the while they draw further and further apart from him, so that we end up with heaps of teachers, as Paul says.

We have seen this happen among the papists, and we still see it today. What scum all these monks, priests and clerics are! They fill the world with their stench, as even the blind can see. Yet people are happy to put up with them. If in some town we had to feed good and faithful pastors who were only one twentieth of what these rascally priests and monks are, what a fuss there would be! It only takes two pastors for people to get irritated and annoyed.[24] So as usually happens we have these heaps of teachers who are mentioned here. If all we had was Paul's word of warning, would that not be enough? But as experience shows, and as our Lord himself teaches, what was foretold by the apostle has been fulfilled. What then are we to do, except hold fast to the simplicity of the gospel and ask God to grant us the Spirit of meekness, so that we are open to his teaching and attend patiently to what he says? Let us resist our restless appetites so that we do not make a new heap for ourselves. That is Paul's word to us.

---

[24] It was the city authorities who paid the stipends of Geneva's pastors, so that the question of their maintenance on occasion proved contentious. The Ecclesiastical Ordinances of 1541 allowed for five full-time ministers and three assistants to serve the city's three parishes.

To recall what was said earlier, Paul urges Timothy to be increasingly watchful because he sees the world growing worse. Why? So that at least we are not so lazy and cowardly that we dissemble and say nothing when God's truth is attacked, and so that we are as careful to defend it as Satan's ministers are to destroy it. True, it is harrowing and painful for one man to withstand a whole host. Even so, there is nothing surprising about this. Satan will find any number of allies who are ready to veil the truth, to decry sound teaching and to dilute it—in other words, to bring in falsehoods and distortions and to lead souls to perdition. He will therefore find plenty of seed. And as I said before, when it comes to self-deceit we are all past masters supposing we never went to school! Nevertheless there will be a small number of people, a handful perhaps, who uphold God's truth and who endeavour to lead his church in all sincerity. Thus when God's servants are only two or three against a hundred, they might first be overcome by dread. They must therefore be armed with strength from on high to battle continually on. For God's truth will finally triumph, even though it finds few defenders in this world and is mostly banished to the point of vanishing altogether. For all that, it will win the day. Let us take courage, then, and be strong when we see the devil raising up people whose only aim is to overturn Scripture. Let us determine never to falter or run from the fight, but to be brave soldiers to the end.

Now if this appeal was necessary in Timothy's time, it is as necessary now, or even more! Do we not see people with itching ears? The gospel upsets many who would much prefer some kind of worldly wisdom. If they do not like what they are given, they want it to be forgotten and immediately removed from God's register. The same was true of the teaching of our Lord Jesus Christ. Was it not rejected by those who were completely arrogant and who trusted in their own judgments? Did they not say, 'This is a hard saying' (John 6:60)? If, however, our hearts were more pliant, nothing in God's word would seem hard or strange to us. There are many today, it is true, who would like a counterfeit gospel, because its sheer simplicity displeases them. Then there are the curious who only want the chance to prattle on and to raise one question after another. God therefore seeks to rein us in; he will not have us wander or stray as we please. What he wants is for us to follow simply what he knows is most expedient and useful for our salvation. Our minds, however, are never at rest: we want the kind of teaching which suits us. Further, we know that most people cannot bear to be warned or corrected, still less are they open to plain teaching. When we speak, not too harshly, of people's failings, they think that the end has come!

The world is thus as wicked as ever it has been, and those who have professed the gospel seem bent on doing away with God's grace if they possibly can. For it is not only the papists who fight furiously against us, but those who claim to be reformed according to the gospel. They act like calves which have broken free and which will not hear of yoke or discipline or anything else. They want to be allowed to do as they choose, so that disobedience is sanctioned, blasphemy is unchecked and immorality condoned. As for drunkenness and similar things, they have no care as long as there is some form of church observance, and as long as scorn is heaped on the pope and on idolaters. This is how many who pretend to adhere to the gospel want to be led, all because they have itching ears. We should fear lest our Lord withdraws the grace which he has placed among us. Let those, then, who are accounted teachers be all the more alert when they see men becoming so inured to evil that they want everything to be allowed them. When we see such mindlessness we should be moved to cry all the louder, and to be sharp when warning and chastising those who rebel against God and who are out to ruin everything.

That is one thing to notice. For the rest, we should each profit from Paul's admonition and make the most of it while God gives us the opportunity. It is certain that if things go on as they are, God will bring worse confusion upon us than he has on the papists. They are poor blind souls who have never given God such extreme offence as we do today. It is as if we had made up our minds to run full tilt at him and to erase all trace of his majesty.

Therefore, as I have said, let all of us with one accord wake up and learn to walk in fear, since there are so few who are content with the simple gospel. Let us set firm limits to all our thoughts and feelings, so that we do not desire more than God permits and imparts to us through his word. When these others indulge in evil let us be more careful to walk in godly fear. His yoke will be gentle and pleasant when we get used to it, but we must not have ears which itch to hear mere flattery. Those who only want to be beguiled must go off to the devil. He will flatter them indeed, for he is only too happy to humour those he wants to damn along with him. He will cajole and spoil them—in a word, he will treat them the way they like. But in the end he will make them pay most dearly for their share.

Let none of this appeal to us. It is a deadly poison, as I said before. Let us rather give God thanks for providing remedies which purge us of our evil appetites, and let this be proof to us that he has us in his care. Let us be all the more diligent, then, in receiving his gift with all due reverence. May we be submissive and obedient to his good will, and may his word and the message of salvation continue among us, that by this means we may enjoy them forever.

Now let us cast ourselves down before the face of our good God, acknowledging our faults and begging him to make us feel them so that we are led to firm and true repentance. May we condemn ourselves for the disobedience and misery within us, and beseech him to guide and govern us by his Holy Spirit, granting us to renounce this world. And may he sustain us in our infirmities until he remakes us in his glorious image, and brings us to that perfect righteousness for which we aim.

# 27

## TAKING LEAVE OF LIFE

*But be watchful in all things, endure afflictions, do the work of an evangelist and prove your ministry. ⁶ For I must be sacrificed, and the time of my departure is at hand.* (2 Timothy 4:5-6)

When we see others who go wrong, the danger is that we also will feel insecure. Paul nevertheless concludes from this that the faithful ought to grow even more confident when they see the less firm and steadfast drifting away from God and abandoning the right path. They should be all the more encouraged to follow God's holy calling. Accordingly, having described the world as so evil that it cannot abide sound teaching but wants only to be deceived, the apostle appeals to Timothy *to be watchful in all things.*

God therefore tells us that the worse the confusion around us, the more we should be on our guard. So although it is Timothy who is called to carry the lamp which will give light to the whole church, we are all meant, each in his own place, to follow Paul's admonition. In the same way we are commanded not to go to sleep when we see danger approaching. Now we are alert enough when it comes to worldly affairs and to this present life. Will we take less care where the salvation of our souls is concerned? So we reason this way: if Satan is troubling God's church, fomenting scandals, deceiving folk, scattering and putting all to flight, we must be all the more vigilant so that nothing takes us by surprise. For this to happen we must be armed with patience, because when things go bad God's children are bound to feel stricken and distressed, being held up to mockery, shame and abuse. Even if they are not personally injured they suffer painfully when they see God's name blasphemed, his worship spurned and whatever is good ridiculed and tossed aside. So when they see such things, although they remain unharmed, they feel such distress that rest escapes them and they grieve night and day. When, therefore, the devil sets up his standard and when scandals and troubles are rife, we can only succeed in defending ourselves if we are strengthened by patience, and if we do not lose heart because of the afflictions which we must suffer.

Now if ever this warning was useful, necessity shows us that we need it now. Has not the world reached the height of iniquity? Most people furiously oppose the gospel. Others pretend to accept it, but how obedient are they? People are so proud and contemptuous that they show their defiance as soon as faults are reproved, or as soon as too sharp a word is said to those who want to sin with impunity and to bring everything down. The papists allow their friars to rail and inveigh against them, even though they feed them lies which will finally damn them. Yet those who loudly claim to want reformation according to the gospel cannot bear to be chastised if they are at fault; they gnash their teeth at God and fulfil Paul's words to the Corinthians (2 Cor. 11:3-4). If there were false teachers who deceived them they would tolerate their tyranny; if they slapped them they would hold their peace; but if they are purely taught in God's name and for their salvation, they are so thin-skinned that one word is enough to spark resistance, and if the preacher even partly does his duty, it is open war!

Would to God these things were not so obvious! So what are we to do, except obey Paul's warning and be on our guard? And because we must put up with complaints and arguments, and because the wicked are free to do as they like, either spitting in our faces or harassing us in more indirect ways, let us steel ourselves, as it were, through patience. Let nothing deter us but let us continue along the path to which God has called us. This is how we are to persevere in the midst of such confusion. Though adversity may make us weep, we must not lose heart.

Addressing Timothy again, the apostle commands him *to do the work of an evangelist, and to complete (or confirm and fully prove) his ministry.* Here Paul encourages Timothy by reminding him of the work to which he has been called. God has conferred an exceptional gift on him by putting him in a place of honour in his church. For as we learn from the fourth chapter of Ephesians, evangelists came next after apostles and are named ahead of pastors and teachers (Eph. 4:11). A group of twelve was not enough to take the gospel throughout the world; God therefore appointed other helpers. This was Timothy's position, for as we saw earlier Paul had chosen him to oversee the pastors and to establish order and discipline in all the churches. Since God had bestowed so great an honour on him, it was only right that he should toil all the harder. How ungrateful we would be if we did not work with all our might when God not only adopts us as his children but chooses us to manage and superintend his household. As was said before, if the task of preaching has been entrusted to us, God makes us stewards of his amazing mysteries in order to build up his kingdom in this world.

When we reflect that God appeared to us in the flesh and revealed to us his heavenly glory, that he who was clothed with our own nature is worshipped by the angels, honoured by every creature, given supreme dominion in both heaven and earth, and all for our salvation—when, I say, we reflect on these things, should we not be carried away by feelings of deepest awe? For we are frail vessels—yes, broken, worthless jars!—yet God wills that this precious treasure should be borne by us. So it is only right that we should do our very best to perform our duties faithfully, and that those whom God has made ministers of his word should be all the more accountable than ordinary believers. This is why Paul tells Timothy to do the work of an evangelist and to prove or fulfil his ministry. It is as if he said to him: 'It is not enough for you to have the title. You must know that the one who called you expects you to be his servant to the very end.'

From Paul's words we may derive a general rule. We learn that each must take thought to himself, should consider his standing and the kind of life to which God has called him. A man who is married must recognize his responsibilities. He is to manage his household, to live peaceably with his wife, to be her head and to guide her well, to support her and to try to instruct his children in the fear of God; he must work and must patiently bear the family troubles which God sends to test and train us. If someone should also have servants, he must understand that God is their master, and he should employ them in such a way as to set a good example. Those who hold public office should look to themselves and remember that they are not merely serving men but must one day appear before God, who claims dominion over men of all conditions. We must all conclude, then, that whatever our station in life God would have us serve him. We must faithfully fulfil the duties of our calling, or else we are guilty before God. Whatever our responsibilities and obligations toward men, God is the one with whom we have most to do. It is to him that we must look.

It is not enough to have shown for a time that we are willing to do what is right. We must continue to the end. We must prove our ministry, that is, our service to God. We must show that we do not bear the name under false pretences like those who boast of their standing, but who only defile the place where they are and who defy God. They would do much better, alas, to bow their heads, to hide from men's eyes and to feel thoroughly ashamed. The honour to which they lay claim will cost them dear when they fail to serve God in the place where he has put them. Above all, if he has entrusted us with worthy responsibilities we should burn with all the more zeal. We know that in the household of a king or prince no office is lowly or contemptible. So if our Lord calls us to serve him in his house, should we not consider it an honour a hundred thousand times greater than if we served an earthly ruler? Again, each of us should say to himself: 'Here am I, a useless creature, yet God is willing to employ me in his service. And although I am worthless, he wants to get from me some pleasing service. I can bring him nothing of my own, so how can he be gracious enough to have me glorify him through his Holy Spirit?' If there were no more to it than that, should this not rouse us to prove our ministry—to show, that is, that God has not chosen us in vain, but has made room for us in his house and has taken us into his employ? That is Paul's meaning here.

Notice what he says next: *As for myself, I go to be sacrificed, and the time of my departure (or my loosing) is at hand.* This is Paul's way of bidding Timothy to be strong from now on, since he will not have the help and support he had before. Paul rightly called Timothy his true and natural son (1 Tim. 1:2). Not that he had begotten him according to the flesh, but he wants us to know that he was a child who was content to copy his father in every way. That was the kind of man Timothy was, and Paul had not failed to be a father to him. As long as the apostle was alive Timothy had a sound and fitting helper. If he felt weak, Paul could encourage him; if he needed advice, he could direct him; if he was under attack, he could shield him and, as we saw, arm him with his authority. Now, writes Paul, all this will cease. 'God desires to take me out of the world,' he says. 'You must therefore be ready, for you will have struggles more bitter than any you have had before. I will not be here to help you or to defend our cause as once I did. There will be no one to sustain you. You will have to take charge for the sake of others and to direct everything yourself. Make up your mind, then, to call upon God and to trust him as you steadfastly press on, for there are fierce battles you will have to face.'

Paul's aim, as we see, is to urge us not to lose faith when all aid has been withdrawn—I mean the lesser helps which we find useful and which God is sometimes pleased to give us. Naturally if we have good pastors to lead us we stand doubly condemned if we are no longer fervent in the faith. But even if we lack the support we would like, even when all is shaky, when the devil is breathing down our neck and when we do not rebuff him as bravely as we should, we should not lose hope. God will aid us from on high and will stretch out his hand to help us if we look to him. What, then, must we do? If God gives us people who set a good example, who are zealous for his glory and who want nothing more than to aid us in time of need, let us make the most of them, and thank God for taking pity on us and for upholding us in our weakness. Let us make as much use as we can of the means which God supplies.

In any case, when we are bereft of what the world calls help and when the wicked run hard at us, when obstacles mount up and when floods seem to carry all before them, let us nevertheless look to heaven and beg God by the secret power of his Holy Spirit to make us invincible against all that the devil tries to do. What we must do, then, is to take advantage of the helps which are at hand, and if God deprives us of them let us still remain steadfast and continue on our way. Why? Because God will make up for all that we lack in the sight of men. That is Paul's message to us here.

Observe also that Paul seeks to reinforce his appeal by leaving us, so to speak, his last will and testament, as a father might do when speaking to his child. 'While I was alive on earth,' he might have said, 'I tried always to show you the way so that we could both serve God with one accord. Up until now you have behaved just as I would wish. Once I have departed this world you must keep pressing on. I am about to die, but remember my words as if I were drawing up a genuine will and testament. The best inheritance I can leave to you is that you should continue to serve God.'

How exactly does Paul speak about his death? 'I go to be sacrificed,' he writes, 'and the time of my departure is at hand.' In speaking of sacrifice, he is referring to the kind of death which had been prepared for him. The word he uses is the same as that used of sacrifices normally offered when covenants were made. If nations or rulers sealed alliances, a sacrifice was made in order to ratify them. By this means they testified that anyone who broke the pact should be torn to pieces and struck down by God. When Paul speaks of the message he brings, he calls it the word of reconciliation (2 Cor. 5:19). In other words, God sent him to make peace between himself and men. Thus whenever the gospel is preached, it is as if God were making a covenant with us, declaring that he is our Father and that he regards us as his children. To bring this about he undertakes not to impute our sins to us, although we are cursed creatures who deserve to be destroyed. Nevertheless he is willing to wash and cleanse us by the blood of his Son, and to accept the death and passion which he suffered to make up for the righteousness we lacked. This is the essence of the gospel which we preach to everyone.

Paul says that he is to be sacrificed, by way of confirming the covenant which God has made with men. His death will seal the message which he preached, and the truth which he proclaimed with his lips will gain in authority with believers when they see that he has not spared himself, nor that his life was so dear to him that he would not risk it for the sake of the inerrant truth he had taught. As he writes in the second chapter of Philippians, 'If I am offered upon the sacrifice of your faith, I rejoice and will rejoice, knowing that it will all work for your salvation' (Phil. 2:17). From this we learn, first, that if our God graciously allows our blood to be spilt as a testimony to his truth, it is a fragrant sacrifice; so we should surmount all trials and accept death willingly. Although our flesh is weak, if we really savour the fact that our Lord wills to accept us as a sacrifice which will seal the truth of his gospel, we will be helped to overcome whatever regrets we feel.

May God therefore impress on our souls the importance of this word 'sacrifice'. If he should choose and call us to bear witness to the gospel, let us come forward freely and with brave hearts, cherishing the honour he does us in counting us worthy to suffer for his sake, as we read in the fifth chapter of Acts (Acts 5:41). There is, however, more. Just as each believer must be encouraged to offer himself to God, let us use the deaths of those who staunchly defended the gospel cause to strengthen our faith. There are those whom God calls to be martyrs for the gospel's sake. Though the wicked may offer to spare their lives if they recant, they remain defiant and do not yield an inch. When we see such things, is this not proof of God's truth? So let us make the most of those who show how earnest was their belief, and whose faith was the same as ours. We share the fruit of it with them.

God's enemies admittedly do all they can to suppress the gospel and to wipe out all remembrance of our Lord Jesus Christ. This is why they burn with such fury, why they light their fires and try to swallow up the message of salvation. Yet God has another use for his servants' deaths: he makes them seed which will continually multiply the number of his people. He wants us to be watered like soil which lies half parched. When he discovers such dryness and barrenness in us so that we do not bear fruit in sufficient abundance, he sprinkles us with the blood of the martyrs. Hence we should rightly glorify our God when we see such divine steadfastness in mortal men, and as we glorify him we should be mindful that he desires to seal our faith, and that the witness which we have already received from his Holy Spirit should be stamped upon us. That is the second thing to remember about this verse.

Our faith, it is true, should not rest upon men. Even if they rebel and are so seized with fear that, to save their lives, they forsake and deny the gospel, we should not be shaken, because God's truth abides forever. However frail and changeable we are, God's truth remains untouched. So our faith can never be based on either men's steadfastness or their fragility. Nevertheless the helps we receive are not to be despised. This is what Scripture urges us to do, as does the apostle when he speaks of a great cloud of witnesses, of whom some were sawn in two, some stoned, some were stretched tight like drums, some were flayed and some made to answer in other ways—so many and such dreadful torments (Heb. 11:36-37; 12:1). God's power, however, triumphed over all these cruelties, and they attained the crown and were victorious over their enemies. Should not such examples be plain as day for us, and would we not feel disgraced if we were to fail or falter? Paul was therefore right to describe his death as a sacrifice, for his teaching has far greater weight when we see his very blood before us. And when we hear him speaking, we recognize that this is not someone discussing his death at leisure, but a man who could already see his executioner close by, and who was expecting to be dragged off soon to the gallows and to be shamefully killed. With every word he uttered there was not one drop of blood in his veins which did not serve to seal his witness to the gospel. When we think of this, should we not say with utter amazement: 'These are not the words of a mere man. It is the Spirit of God who makes himself known in such frail and tiny vessels, and who displays in them his extraordinary power'?

May we be strengthened, then, and may we draw a useful lesson not only from Paul's death but from the deaths of those today who give us greater assurance of the truth which we are taught here. We are bound of course to feel pain when we see our poor brethren suffer. If they are in prison, our hearts, as the letter to the Hebrews says, must be captive with them as we share their distress (Heb. 10:33). Nevertheless we should glorify God when we see how he sends them into battle so that they triumph over their enemies. Since what they gain through their struggle is also ours, let us give praise to him who has made them strong. For God chooses to arm them with steadfastness and to use them to uphold his truth, in order that we too should be edified. In this way the death of martyrs—that is, witnesses to God—is a sacrifice.

What then? We are so far from taking this to heart that we let it all pass by. Scripture says that the tears of the faithful are precious in God's sight, as if he held them in a bottle of ointment (Psa. 56:8; Isa. 25:8; Rev. 7:17; 21:4). What therefore of their blood, when we let it flow but are not ourselves sprinkled by it in order to glorify our God? This is the last thing on our mind. Those who boast that they are pillars of the gospel find the very name 'martyr' repulsive to them; they cannot abide it. They thus prove that they are merely curs, having no more Christian faith in them than swine, since they are ignorant of even the most common words of Scripture.

We for our part should understand why Paul spoke this way. He was not driven by self-interest but wanted his death to serve a useful purpose. He made it an enduring memorial, not for a short time only but to the end of the world. Although God does not honour all of us by calling us to die by fire or the sword for our witness to the gospel, we must be a sacrificial offering to him whether in life or in death. In life we must do as Paul says in the twelfth chapter of Romans, and be living sacrifices to our God (Rom. 12:1). Whatever belongs to our nature must die and be cast away. And even what we think is our greatest asset, reason, must be put to death in us so that God's Spirit may have control and make us living sacrifices. This is how Christians must strive to offer them-selves to God and to consecrate their whole lives to him.

But how in death may we be living sacrifices? By being ready to depart this world whenever God is pleased to take us, and by not opposing him but by quietly confessing: 'Lord, you have made us, fed us and sustained us up until now. Dispose of us as you will, and let us not resist you in any way at all.' This is what will give us cou-rage. Although we do not suffer for the gospel, we know that God accepts our life and death as a holy offering when we readily obey him in this as in all else. The same point is made in the fourteenth chapter of Romans: 'Whether we live or die, we live or die to him' (Rom. 14:8). We are not, that is, to live selfishly, according to our likes and fancies. Nor should we think to bring death forward or to shorten it. We are to commit everything into God's hands. Dying, let us live by taming all earthly thoughts and feelings; living, let us die by being willing to depart whenever he calls us. And all the while, as I said, let us learn to commit ourselves into his hands, so that with David we may confess that if our spirit is in his hands, it will be safely and securely kept (Psa. 31:5). May we entrust our spirit to him and make him master of it, so that none may take it from him.

To emphasize what he has said Paul adds that 'the time for his departure is at hand'. He means that he is taking leave of earthly things, for from what does death separate us? We will lose the company of the living, to be sure, and within us we will suffer the parting of soul from body. But he who believes is not destroyed by death: his soul remains whole, for it has been made in the image of God. It remains immortal. That being so, we should not find death troublesome or worrying as is usually the case. Why does death terrify us so? It is because of our unbelief: we think that death is the end of everything for us. Many entertain this idea since they think of themselves merely as animals. We do indeed share a common life, but we bear the marks of immortal life since God has endowed us with sense and reason, and given us knowledge enough to call him our Creator. Although we are ensnared in ignorance and error without end, some trace remains to make us feel that we have been created, not for this present, transitory life but for one on high to which God calls us. But because we do not know that our destiny lies there we shrink from death as much as possible, and when there is talk of it we are overcome by dread, thinking that all is lost. So if we are to accept death calmly and to face it with such steadfastness that we promptly offer ourselves to God when he calls, let us attend to what Paul says.

What, then, is death? A loosening of bonds, so that though our body undergoes change we do not perish. We are not destroyed; we remain whole. True, our bodies decay, but there is resurrection promised to us at the last day. Let this be our confidence. More is certainly needed, for we may still have misgivings, just as unbelievers do who do not know what will become of them, even if they know that their souls are immortal. 'How do we know what will happen?' they say. Since we, however, have the promise of salvation, and since we know that God is the guardian of our souls, let us put an end to all doubt and distrust. To do this we must come back to David's words which we quoted earlier: 'Into your hands I commit my soul' (Psa. 31:5). This was his cry throughout his life, for he was continually in danger: 'Lord, you will keep me. Though a hundred deaths surround me I will be safe in your hands.' We must therefore follow his lead, confident that God will not leave us helpless and that he will gather us to himself, for we are, above all, members of our Lord Jesus Christ, to whose care he has entrusted us. The heavenly Father was not content simply to declare himself the guardian of our souls. He assigned this office to Jesus Christ, and made him our keeper and defender. So when we are in his hand we can never doubt that he will preserve us by his infinite power, however many the troubles which confront us. He assures us that the Father who has entrusted us to him is mightier than all (John 10:29). By this he means that if we dread the fierce storms and tempests which may assail us, we should be mindful of God's all-surpassing power, knowing that because of it we can surmount everything which we might fear.

We must stop. For the present we can go no further. After dinner we will say more about this passage, in which Paul speaks of the crown of righteousness which has been prepared for him. We ought, at any rate, to understand why we are called to be heirs of the kingdom of heaven. For the sole reason why God takes us out of this world is that he may bring us to that heavenly glory which is now hidden from us, as are our salvation and the fullness of the blessings for which we hope.

> Now let us cast ourselves down before the face of our good God, acknowledging our faults and asking him to make us feel them better than before. May we be touched to the quick, so that being led to true repentance we may come to him, and may more and more direct our steps toward the path of salvation. And may he all the while sustain us in our weaknesses until we are wholly free of them, and are able to enjoy his perfect righteousness.

# 28

---

# THE VICTOR'S CROWN

*I have fought a good fight, I have finished my race, I have kept the faith.*
*⁸ As for the rest, a crown of righteousness is prepared for me, which the*
*Lord, the righteous judge, will give me on that day, and not to me only*
*but to all who love his coming.* (2 Timothy 4:7-8)

If someone sets us a good example and convinces us that he has virtues which are not to be despised, we gain a great deal simply by observing him. As we know, things can go smoothly when there is present in a town or district someone to whom God, through his Spirit, has imparted grace. Therefore since Paul knows that his absence might impede the work of others, he tells us that, though he has finished his race, no one should falter in mid-course or think that he has achieved anything worthwhile until, like him, he has persevered to the end. We see Paul, then, as a man who has endeavoured all his life to build up God's church. His example had kept many people from going astray, but in quitting this world he fears that they may do just that. So he anticipates the danger by saying that, just as he has shown others how he has run his race, never tiring until he reached the end, they must do the same, and not lose heart before they reach the goal to which God is calling them.

We will understand his meaning better if we consider the image of combat, as it was then practised, or of the wrestling match. For just as now there are archery and firearms contests, in those times there were foot, horse and especially chariot races. *I have fought the good fight*, Paul tells us. That is, he was wholehearted in his desire to offer himself for God's service. Nor were his efforts frustrated, since he was successful in his fight. Lest, however, we think that his was only a momentary enterprise, he introduces a second image: *I have finished my race.* It is as if he were saying: 'I did not merely raise my shield to test my strength. I persisted, running steadily the course traced out for me.' Now races were measured over certain distances, as are our lists: so many feet long, so many feet wide. Foot-runners had to run fast over a given number of paces, and when they had finished, the one who came first was clearly the bravest and the best. It was the same with chariot racing.

Paul uses these metaphors advisedly. He speaks of course of idle, useless entertainments, but his aim is to shame us all the more if we are slow to run or fight when God summons us, and when he presides, so to speak, watching us and promising us the richest of prizes. If, then, we are sluggish or reluctant to persevere, or if we falter mid-way, have we any excuse? Think of what Paul writes in Corinthians (1 Cor. 9:25): 'In the contests where men struggle to the bitter end, what is it they hope for? Nothing but a laurel wreath.' (For the wreath was considered an outstanding prize.) Here, however, we have a very different reward: our Lord calls us to the inheritance of the heavenly kingdom, and wills that we should share in his glory and immortality. Yet we do not deign to lift a foot, nor do we move an arm without great difficulty. Do we not show that we pay God scarcely any honour, that we do not trust his promises, that we are faithless, in a word?

In those days those who intended entering a contest ate only biscuit; in fact they did not dare do more than half satisfy their hunger. So here are these poor fools—that is clearly how Paul regarded them—who, to win fame as an athlete or wrestler, and to earn one word of praise, fasted and put their lives at risk. For though living they wasted away, not even eating wholemeal bread or drinking their fill of water. They abstained from all rich foods and dieted rigorously as though they had another life to live. It was all for the sake of a little acclaim, so that people might clap and say, 'What a brave fellow! He deserves to win a dozen wreaths. He competed well. Let him be crowned!'

Here, on the other hand, is our God who calls to us, not so that we might get a little praise in this life, but in order to choose us for himself. He tells us our reward is ready—the crown of glory which will never fail. We know that the angels in paradise applaud us, and that at the last day we will be welcomed by the holy patriarchs, the holy prophets, the apostles and martyrs. Should this not inspire us to walk loyally on and to fight steadfastly to the very end? This is why Paul, in speaking of the good fight which he has fought, employs these metaphors. He might well have said: 'Let those who have toiled for the sake of worldly ambition, for greed or for reputation, be glad and boast as much as they like about their struggles. For my part I have cause to be content that I have served my God. I did not take a step which did not count in his sight. Let the angels in heaven applaud me for having been the tool God used to help advance the kingdom of his Son. I gladly rejoice in this.' As for the second image, Paul is right to say that he has finished his race. We will see many who want to be let off once they have done one good deed! They think that God should therefore grant them leave and allow them to relax for the rest of their lives. On the contrary, the apostle insists that nothing has been achieved unless we persist to the end.

It is important here to remember Paul's personal circumstances. He was in prison, awaiting the hand of his executioner. From a human point of view he was to die a shameful death. Unbelievers were opening their mouths to blaspheme and were heaping abuse on him. In the eyes of the Jews he was a renegade, and many false Christians spoke evil of him throughout the churches. The whole world was his deadly enemy. One might have thought that he had wasted his time by struggling as he had done. He might have been a leading teacher, a man esteemed, having a front row seat, judging others, famous and immensely popular. He might have been revered in Jerusalem as a holy man, for there were none who excelled him in integrity of life. He might have been rich and welcome in every place. Who would not have said that he was out of his mind and exceedingly blind to risk disgrace, to lose reputation and to arouse the fury of everyone against him—the fury of his own people and of every nation, even those who did not know him—only to die ignominiously in the end? Who would not have said that he would have done better to take things quietly?

Nevertheless the apostle defies and scorns the opinions of all men. Why? Because he has his Judge in heaven, and he is content to be absolved by him, though the entire world should condemn him. Punishment and death are common to criminals and martyrs. The only thing which distinguishes them is motive. Thus, when we hear of a martyr who is burned and of a robber who suffers the same fate, the death they undergo looks no different. When, however, we think about their motive, the robber, we see, is suffering for his crimes and offences, whereas the martyr has his inner testimony, being able also to demonstrate that he has walked uprightly and is suffering for God's cause. Thus Paul defies the judgments of the faithless. He does not care whether the world reviles him, as long as he has the approval of the Judge in heaven.

See, then, how important it is to have these two things which I have briefly mentioned. For those who are most wicked are sometimes the most brazen. Those who deserve to be hanged a hundred times over spew forth abuse against their judges, as we well know. The point, however, is this. We can always claim before God and his angels that we have lived a decent life, but we must prove it. When our life is judged we must be found to be honest and true, so that those with eyes to see can testify that we are unjustly made to suffer. These two things were characteristic of Paul and all the prophets, and of all who have ever suffered for their witness to the gospel. Thus he is able to say, with every justification, that he has fought the good fight.

Hence, following his exhortation, let us make sure that we do not suffer for our own offences—neither for murder, immorality or theft, nor for disloyalty, subversion or any other crime. No, when we have to answer for God's truth our position will be more than honourable if God deigns to allow us to defend him, and to show through us his power to triumph, just as he displays the relentless might of his Holy Spirit in those who are obedient to his word. When, therefore, God uses us to bear witness to his name and wishes to be glorified in us, let us bravely follow and not think that our efforts are in vain. The world may mock our simplicity and unbelievers may loathe us and spit in our faces. Let us nevertheless so value God's approval that we emerge victorious, and let us like Paul defy all that is said and done to us as we suffer for the truth.

We see how Paul withstood the Corinthians, who claimed to be believers and who thought highly of themselves. Yet Paul derides their foolish opinions when he sees how full they are of conceit, how drunk with pride and how much wiser than the gospel (1 Cor. 4:3-5). 'Well now,' he says, 'I beg to differ, for you judge in darkness, but the day of the Lord is coming when all will be made clear.' If the apostle could thus defy those who hypocritically gloried in the name of Jesus Christ, how should we act toward the deadly enemies of our salvation, who mindlessly rage against the Son of God and who plainly oppose the religion which we hold? Should we tremble when we have to suffer at the hands of these tyrants? Let us learn from Paul's example to lift our eyes heavenward and to press on. If the world rejects us, if we suffer much affliction and endure insults and shame for having done what is right, let us learn to look up, otherwise we will be like reeds shaken by the wind.

If once we can fix our eyes on God we will be hardened, for that is the word which Hebrews uses of Moses (Heb. 11:27). 'Having beheld God,' we read, 'he was hardened against all wickedness.' Moses is depicted as a rock which holds out against the waves. Since he was brought up in the royal court, how could he not have been tempted to desire the crown, being the king's adopted son? Yet he preferred the reproach of Jesus Christ. At the cost of a hard and difficult struggle, he suffered for many years in a foreign land and laboured to earn a living. Finally he was required to confront the king, listening to his many threats and experiencing much humiliation and abuse. It was necessary for him to be hardened. So too it is for us. The apostle to the Hebrews shows us how. If we can fix our eyes on God we will be immovable and steadfast. However much the devil tries to undermine our faith he will never succeed, for we know that we are only happy when we fight under the banner of our Lord Jesus Christ. This inevitably means that when God is the one to whom we look, the world will mock and reproach us. We must therefore be armed in order to persevere. If all we do is raise our shields, what will we achieve? So let us go on, conscious that God does not accept us in his service only for a little time, but to our life's end. Whoever, then, is not ready and determined to glorify God by his life and death, does not know what it is to fight.

First, then, we must reckon with the fact that God calls us to be sacrificial offerings to him, not for one day only but for the rest of our lives. However much we may languish and fear to perish in our wretchedness, we must persevere regardless. And when the time comes for us to die, we must summon up even more courage and keep moving on, like wearied sailors who, when nearing shore, rejoice on catching sight of the harbour ahead. 'Wonderful!' they tell themselves. 'Two or three hours from now we will be able to rest and relax.' So if the sight of the harbour injects new strength into these poor men, fatigued and worn out as they are, what should we do when we approach our goal and when our race is done? Has not our God held us with a strong hand, and although we have taken many false steps and have sometimes fallen, has he not put us on our feet again before we reach our end? Should we not strive to come ever closer to him? Thus when Paul says that he has run his race, this is the lesson we must learn.

Paul writes that *he has kept the faith*. Here he explains how we may fight and win. The word 'faith' may, it is true, have the sense of 'faithfulness', meaning that he has been loyal to our Lord Jesus Christ, has never strayed but has always done what was required of him. We may, however, take the word in its usual sense, so that Paul is understood to say that he has never swerved from the pure and simple gospel, and has trusted the promise of salvation which it contains. Having preached to others, he makes it clear that he spoke in all sincerity. For this is the source of the loyalty which God demands of us: we are to stand firmly upon his word, and to be so grounded in it that no storm or whirlwind can ever shift us from it. Remember, therefore, that having fought our battles, to be successful we must keep the faith.

Now as we saw before, a good conscience is the key to success. For those who give themselves to evil—those, that is, who scoff at God and who have no more reverence for the gospel than for anything else—deserve to be destroyed by God and to die the most fearful of deaths. So, as Paul says, they must go to the bottom of the sea, like a ship which sinks and perishes (1 Tim. 1:19). Those who do not keep the faith in all good conscience are lost, and God would have them perish miserably to demonstrate how precious his gospel is to him. For when he is thus avenged it is a sign that we are not to make light of the doctrine of salvation.

Notice, therefore, that we must be true and upright, having a clear conscience, walking in God's fear and holding to his promises of grace and goodness, or we will never be willing to run our race to the end. A good conscience will safeguard our faith. And although we may be hindered by our own inherent weakness, and so dismayed by the fierce assaults and alarms which come our way that we fail to advance, we will nevertheless win through, for God will not forsake us. Let us not forget the verse we quoted earlier from First Corinthians. There Paul reproaches those who do not run as hard as they should, telling them: 'Those who compete for a prize—or to cite the sport most popular today, those who go in for wrestling—have no guarantee that they will get a reward' (1 Cor. 9:24). In Paul's day two or three hundred runners might have competed. They would have come fully equipped from two or three hundred miles around, but it was only to win a laurel crown. They willingly went to much expense and took great trouble over a thing of no importance; and when they had done their best, only one of them, the fittest, was crowned. Even when two prizes were awarded, or three or four, the crown went only to the bravest; the rest returned home shamefaced, the butt of mockery: 'This man had high hopes, but look, he lost!' There were other competitions too, no holds barred, designed to beat the opponent into the ground. They held lead weights in their hands to strike and pound, so that men would be carried off bloody and badly beaten. When such as these had fought as hard as they could, there was a prize to win, but not for everyone—only for one, two or three among so great a number.

When God, however, calls on us to run, is there a prize which only one can win, while all who trail behind lose out? Not at all!

Together we help each other, so that even if I come a hundredth, or rather a millionth, as long as I am looking to God those who have already finished will hold out their hands to welcome me into the company of the holy martyrs who have gone before, and of the holy prophets who have waited longer still. Since God summons us to this kind of race and on such terms, would we not be villains indeed if we failed to take heart and to walk or run, according to our Lord's command? This is what keeping the faith should mean to us.

The next verse reinforces the point which has just been made. There Paul says this: *As for the rest, the crown of righteousness is prepared for me, which the Lord, the righteous judge, will give me on that day.* He reminds us, then, that he has not run in vain. He says the same thing elsewhere, for just as we have a proverbial saying 'to beat the water', so Paul speaks of 'beating the air', to show that his fight has not been in vain (1 Cor. 9:26). He knows, as he says, that the crown cannot be taken from him, for it was promised by him who is sure and infallible truth. Thus when we have the promise of our God, when in his infinite goodness he binds himself to us, what have we to fear? What excuse can we plead if we fail to take heart? Do we not show that we fail to honour God, and that instead we wrong him, believing that he is neither faithful nor reliable? Those who stake their all on what God says will surely overcome every hindrance in the world. We therefore judge that all who grow weary in mid-course, or who cannot move an arm or a leg, are faithless, and that they seek to make God a liar if they possibly can. They may not utter this blasphemy out loud, but by their life they demonstrate that they have no faith in God. They do not honour him by relying on him as on the one who can never disappoint us.

Let it be clear, then, that we can never boast with Paul that we have fought bravely and successfully unless we are sure that our

God has not called us in vain. We must also possess the promises by which we are led to hope in the eternal salvation which is reserved in heaven for us. We must always keep these promises in view and be always mindful of them. So when Paul says, 'As for the rest', he is saying in effect, 'It is true that I am in terrible distress and that I know I am a weak creature. Even so my God, who has hitherto aided me, will not fail me now. I therefore trust him for the future, just as I experienced his grace in days gone by, and throughout my life.' This is also what we must do. We must not only set our sights on what is present but we must look above and beyond the world. That is why the apostle to the Hebrews calls faith a vision of things not seen and the ground of things not yet present (Heb. 11:1).

Naturally all this seems strange to us. What? How can we see what is invisible? It can't be done! True, but God does not give us eyes which discern what the world sees, but the eyes of faith which see into heaven itself. Thus, although according to reason and common sense the hope which God gives us is hidden, we may nevertheless be sure of it when we have the mirror of his word and when we direct our faith to him. This is where we cast our anchor, not just a hundred feet or yards out but right up to heaven, as we read in the letter to the Hebrews (Heb. 6:19). Notice that if we are to be steadfast in our walk and not turn back but keep moving on when we are on the right path, we must know for sure that God will not fail us. However much the troubles we meet may prevent us from coming to him, from hiding under the shadow of his wings and from calling upon him as our Father, we must be absolutely certain that the crown of righteousness is made ready for us. How can we be certain? Because in putting us to work God had no intention of abandoning us to see how we would cope. He has promised to give us strength and confidence. Let us expect him, then, to give us victory, and let us not fear that it is not prepared for us: it is as if we already held it in our hands. God wants us to honour him by hoping in what we do not see—in what indeed exceeds our comprehension. That is the significance of the phrase, 'As for the rest'.

Let us see that we lay hold of God's gracious gifts which we have previously received. Let this be our firm resolve: 'God must complete what he has begun.' These are Paul's words in the first chapter of Philippians (Phil. 1:6). To the Corinthians he writes that God has poured out his riches on them and will deny them nothing necessary for their salvation, until the coming of our Lord Jesus Christ (1 Cor. 1:5-7). We are therefore taught that we should not thank him simply for what we already know of his goodness, but that we should leave the world behind and never doubt that because he has adopted us, he will lead us to the eternal inheritance of the kingdom of heaven. Although we may meet much adversity, lose heart and see chasms opening all around us, although we may have one foot in the grave and be assailed by many dangers, although the devil himself is prince of the air, let us nevertheless hope in our God and believe that he will give effect to our adoption, until we possess the things for which we now hope and which are not yet present.

When Paul declares that the crown of righteousness is made ready for him, he seems at first glance to be claiming merit for himself. Accordingly the papists, to prove the truth of their free will and their works of merit, quote this passage. 'See,' they say, 'Paul claims that the crown of righteousness is prepared for him. He must therefore have been a man whose works were just. So we are not saved by faith alone, but when we have earned merit God rewards us as those who have done well.' Now the first thing to ask is where these great and noble deeds come from. Is there anyone who can boast that he has power enough to fight his own battles? When Paul speaks of those who share his calling—those, that is, who preach the gospel—he affirms that no one is sufficient

(2 Cor. 3:5). Sufficient for what? Paul is not talking about persevering or about being brave in time of persecution, nor about building a church. He is not thinking about withstanding evil for a time, or of courting death and of taking leave of life. No, he means that we are incapable of one good thought—incapable, he says, unless our sufficiency comes from above. Let men, then, exult and play the hero as much as they like; let them flaunt their free will. Since they are incapable of one good thought, how can they achieve anything? How can they be staunch enough to persevere in God's truth or to overcome everything the devil does to thwart them? If they cannot have one good thought even for a second, what are they to do for the rest of their lives?

Thus when Paul refers, as here, to the crown of righteousness which is prepared for him, he is not thinking of anything noble he has done as if it were his own achievement. The righteousness of which he speaks is something he has received from the grace of God. It is as he says in another place: 'What do you have that you have not received? If you received it, it is a debt which you owe. And if it is a debt, why do you boast about it?' (1 Cor. 4:7). With one word, then, Paul throws down all the arrogance we display whenever we claim credit for ourselves. 'All that you have,' he says, 'has been given to you. You are thus blaspheming when you try to assert yourselves. You usurp what God has given you—given you on the understanding that it is his and that he should have the praise which he deserves. Otherwise what else are you but a thief who is out to steal the honour of your God?' That is one point.

Furthermore, the papists especially should note what was said by one of their own whom they call their teacher: 'How could God grant the crown as a righteous judge unless he had first given us grace as a merciful Father? And how could there be righteousness in us unless grace had gone before to justify us? And how could this crown be given as something due unless it had been given as something not due?' These are Augustine's words.[25] So if the papists insist on not following holy Scripture, at least they should not wickedly deny something they are supposed to believe!

Yet that is not all. It is certainly true that God cannot be the righteous Judge who saves us unless he first shows himself to be a merciful Father. We have no righteousness apart from that which he has placed in us, and the only reward God can give is to crown us with his gifts. In addition, however, although God has given us grace to serve him, and although we may have striven hard and done our very best, the good we do can never meet with God's acceptance. He will find much to reprove even in our best endeavours; the finest virtue which people see in us will prove to be defiled. For although we are sure that we serve God willingly, there is always something or other which holds us back—some worldly consideration or some momentary temptation which means that we fail to call upon God as we ought, that we are not as keen, as earnest or as warm as we should be, and that we are not as ready to serve our neighbours as duty demands. Instead we work to benefit ourselves; it is our advantage that we have in mind. These flaws are found in all our works. They would be rightly condemned if God did not have pity on us and did not bear with us. As he says through the prophet, he accepts our service as a father accepts his child's attempts to please him; they are far from perfect and amount to nothing, yet the father is content because he loves his child (cf. Psa. 103:13). By the same token God displays his sheer goodness when he accepts our works, giving no thought to their worth or merit but accepting them because he loves us, and counting them as righteous and above reproach, despite their many imperfections.

---

[25] It is rare for Calvin in his sermons to cite any authority by name. The reference is to Augustine's work *On Grace and Free Will*, VI.14. Cf. *Inst*. III.18.5, which records Augustine's words and adds the comment made here, that our works are pleasing to God only through his goodness and forbearance.

This text, then, is so far from helping the papists prove that works have merit in God's sight and that we are not saved by faith alone, that it rather gives the lie to them. For when we look closely at Paul's words this verse leads to the inevitable conclusion that we are saved by faith alone because, as we have said, God cannot crown our works unless his pure grace has enabled us to do them. Since this is so, when the papists speak of their works of merit, they first make themselves God's partners, and believe that they cooperate with him—that is the word they use—that is, they bring some worthy inclination, a certain good will, so that God aids them when they mean well and gives them a helping hand. Complacency therefore goes to their head, for they think that they will always manage to do good whenever they choose. Hence they give themselves to all kinds of evil and are full of uncleanness; they are swept away by abominable passions and are so bewitched and blinded that they shut their eyes to everything. They pride themselves on their free will, their virtues and their merits. And since they do not dare to deny that they are sinful and accountable to God, they add their works of satisfaction, asserting: 'I may have failed to do right here, but there is another way for me to make amends.' That is how it is with these poor wretches. Yet when they have done all they can, what rest is there for their consciences? They are bound to be always anxious and troubled because they have no assurance of salvation. In fact it is one of their chief articles of faith to say that it is presumptuous for men to be sure of their salvation.[26] This is God's just judgment on them, since like wild beasts they have risen up against him. So these poor wretches are left in limbo, that is, in unbelief, for they have no hope of salvation.

[26] In its decree on justification (January 1547), the Council of Trent had condemned 'the vain confidence of heretics', affirming in its ninth chapter that 'no one can know, with the certainty of faith which cannot be subject to error, that he has obtained the grace of God'.

For our part, however, once we know that God in his unmerited goodness has called us and acknowledged us to be his children, not for our own merits but for the sake of Jesus Christ, we may be sure that our works are agreeable to him. Why? Because of some worth in them? Not at all! Because he does not impute their faults to us. Flawed though they are, he nevertheless accepts us as if we had rendered full and complete service. It is on the remission of our sins that we rely, so that we may call to him, saying: 'Lord, since you are pleased to bear with us and to be merciful to us, we owe you all the more. And if you choose to accept our works which are imperfect and defiled, it is because of your unmerited goodness.' That, I say, is how this thought ought to humble and abase us. The papists, however much they laud their works and merits, are forced to shut their mouths, for God confounds them in their pride when they seek to war against him.

Thus if this were the only verse of its kind in the whole of Scripture, it is enough to show that we are saved by faith alone when we place our trust in God's sheer goodness, not only because he has mercy on us but because he accepts our works, unworthy as they are. Because of their many blemishes they ought to have been putrid to him, yet he accepts them since he is pleased to treat them as pure and unblemished, and to receive them for the sake of our Lord Jesus Christ.

> Now let us cast ourselves down before the face of our good God, acknowledging our faults and begging him to make us feel them more. And since he is pleased to test us in this world, let us not be so fainthearted that we fail to struggle bravely against Satan and all who serve him. Although we see ourselves attacked on every side, with God's enemies so many as to fill the world and his poor church assailed by foes within, let us take heart and battle on until, with victory won, we are led in triumph to our appointed goal.

Yet may he also give us grace to be humble before him, presuming nothing of ourselves or of our virtues, but relying instead on his pure goodness. May we know that every blessing and all our worldly necessities come to us from him, and that we must look to him for everything else. Above all, may we receive pardon for our trespasses and sins, through the perfect holiness and righteousness of our Lord Jesus Christ.

# 29

---

# HANDS ACROSS THE SEA

*As for the rest, a crown of righteousness is kept for me, which the Lord, the righteous judge, will give to me on that day, and not to me only but to all who love his coming. ⁹ Do your best to come to me soon, ¹⁰ for Demas has forsaken me, having loved this present world; he has gone to Thessalonica, Crescens to Galatia and Titus to Dalmatia. ¹¹ Only Luke is with me. Take Mark and bring him with you, for he can be useful and of service to me. ¹² I have also sent Tychicus to Ephesus. ¹³ When you come, bring with you the cloak that I left at Troas with Carpus, and the books and especially the parchments.*

(2 Timothy 4:8-13)

W e saw before that, if we would courageously serve God, we must always have the coming of our Lord Jesus Christ in mind. Without it we are sure to falter every minute of the day, for we are frail, needing little to make us go astray, and the temptations which Satan sets before us are many. The only way we can have strength enough to follow the right path is by knowing that our Lord Jesus Christ will come to restore the things which are now amiss. We seem to be labouring in vain when the world mocks us and when we are reproached for doing good. We know, however, that at his coming Jesus Christ will overturn all of the world's false judgments, and will show that we have not misspent our time serving him. Even so, we must remember that we cannot hope for the crown of righteousness at his coming unless God in his mercy accepts what we have done. Not that we bring him anything worthwhile or deserving of praise. It is because he has once and for all received us in his mercy and loves us as his children. This too is why our works are acceptable to him. We must therefore rely on the pure word of our God if we hope for anything from his hand.

We turn now to Paul's mention of 'that day'. *On that day*, he says. He might have said, more explicitly, 'at the coming of our Lord Jesus Christ'. But the phrase he uses is very much stronger and should touch us more. Here he reveals the firmness of his faith, describing the day of Jesus Christ's coming as if it were already present. It is true that, according to our fleshly powers of reason, we cannot know how soon our Lord Jesus Christ will come. Our salvation is necessarily enclosed in hope and, as Paul says, what we hope for is hidden (Rom. 8:24). However, because we know that God's Son came down to save us from the miseries of this world and to obtain for us the kingdom of heaven, we cannot doubt that he will give effect to the death and passion he suffered for our salvation. We can therefore enjoy all the benefits he won for us and experience the fruit and consequences of his first coming. So when Paul refers to judgment day, he points directly to it, assuring us in the power of the Holy Spirit that there is nothing uncertain about the second appearance of the Son of God. However incomprehensible it is to the flesh, we must see it with the eye of faith. That is, because the promise of his coming is given to us as in a mirror, it is there that we must direct our gaze.

Sadly, those who call themselves Christians are far from putting this lesson to proper use. We cannot see three inches beyond our face, so that as soon as God delays to help us when we need him we become distraught, uncertain of what will happen to us. How then could we climb so high as to see the Son of God seated in majesty and heavenly glory, hidden from human view? Nevertheless Paul does not write in vain. When Jesus Christ calls us to himself and commands the trumpet to sound in our ears, as if it were already audible to us who stand before his judgment seat, we ought certainly to be roused. Nor is it only here that Paul speaks this way, for in mentioning earlier the help he had received from Onesiphorus, he asks the Lord to reward him 'on that day'(2 Tim. 1:18). Remember also that Paul already knew that death was close at hand when he spoke about the crown of righteousness. We should therefore not be alarmed when all seems lost and hopeless: it is then that we are led to raise our heads on high, since our redemption is near. We can be sure that we will not be disappointed, for we have placed our trust in the Son of God who is changeless truth, and who reveals God to us, giving us knowledge of his eternal counsel. This, then, is what we need to grasp concerning the coming of our Lord Jesus Christ.

Lest, however, we think that Paul has only been speaking about himself, he adds that *it is for all of God's children to enjoy*, and he goes on to describe believers as *those who love the appearing of our Lord Jesus Christ*. Do we want to share in this priceless blessing of which Paul speaks—the knowledge, that is, that God in his goodness always receives us, and that what we offer him is never lost but is like a fragrant sacrifice to him? Do we want to behold life in the midst of death? When we are reviled and abused in the sight of men, do we want to be able to bear it patiently and to be sure that the crown of glory is ours? Then let us love the coming of the Son of God. Such a love is impossible without knowledge. As the popular saying goes, 'Know first, love afterwards.' So if we are not convinced by God's word that our Lord Jesus Christ has been made Judge of the world, and that he will prove it when he gathers us to himself in the company of the angels—if this is not firmly rooted in our hearts we cannot love his coming, for it will have no attraction for us.

We see indeed how carried away we are by this world's vanities, which so enthral us that we give no thought to the spiritual kingdom to which God daily invites us. True, whenever we come to church this truth is drummed into us, and we cannot open holy Scripture without coming across some word of encouragement. Yet we quickly tire, because our empty, foolish liking for the world so fills our mind that we do not know what it is to love the coming of our Lord. So let us stir up our faith. Let us awaken it so that it is no longer stifled by worldly pleasures and the corrupt cravings of our flesh. Let us tear up the weeds which stop the good seed of faith from bearing fruit. And once we lay hold of all that the coming of God's Son means for our redemption, may it arouse that love which Paul describes here.

For good reason, then, we are told that if we would have the crown of righteousness we must yearn for it, with such love and fervour that nothing here below should hold us back. Let us see that we obey what Jesus Christ has taught, that where our treasure is, there will our heart be also (Matt. 6:21). Let us not seek our happiness in perishable things: they will always deceive us. We should know that the chief good which we must seek is the heavenly life prepared for us, and which will be revealed at the coming of God's Son. Let this be the thing for which we long with all our heart.

'But how,' someone may ask, 'can we await the coming of our Lord Jesus Christ, given that we are sinners and will be put to shame if we appear before his majesty? For when we compare the Son of God with the wretchedness which is in us, should it not fill us with utter despair?' Now it is not possible for us to love his coming unless we are persuaded that he will come for our salvation. Admittedly when God speaks to the wicked who resist his word and who scorn his righteousness, and to the hypocrites who falsely claim his name, he says to them: 'Woe to you who hope in the coming of the Lord. For when I come it will be in darkness and in gloom, in storm and whirlwind. I will bring you anguish and distress. You should not therefore look for my coming' (Joel 2:2). Although this prophecy is not about the final coming of our Lord Jesus Christ, it does refer to his coming whenever he chooses to show himself. Hypocrites, however, pretend to trust God and humbly to obey him, yet they reject his word and are hostile to him. That is why the prophets tell them: 'You ask to see the day of the Lord and you claim to desire it above all else. When he does come in judgment do not think that it will not be to your shame and ruin.' Now as for us, we know that our Lord Jesus Christ will not come to destroy the members of his body; he will not be severe, but will show them instead the fruit of the redemption he has purchased for them. Thus although we are poor, miserable sinners who labour under the curse, we may nevertheless boldly rejoice at the coming of the Son of God. He does not forget his office, which is to be our Advocate; and as Judge of the world he will cover us with the obedience which he rendered to his Father, so that it is credited to us as if it were our own. Our Lord Jesus Christ, then, will not come with such awful majesty that he will treat us as we deserve. He will pardon our offences and allow us to taste the fruit of what is daily preached to us—that God in his sheer goodness is truly reconciled to us. Since this is so, we can truly love his coming.

How few there are who can say with Paul that the crown of righteousness is prepared for them! We all confidently boast that we are Christians, but do we go to our deaths fully persuaded that God is the keeper of our souls, that he has them in his care and that we may rest until the final coming of our Redeemer? Who lives in such a way that death has no terrors for him, because he knows that in committing his soul to God he is putting it in so safe a place that he has nothing to fear? On the contrary, having loudly professed our Christian faith, when there is talk of death we are so terrified that it is pitiful to see. It is as if we had never heard one word of the gospel—had never heard that Jesus Christ went down to hell to free us from it, and had ascended into heaven to open the gate for us. We have no taste for any of that; our unbelief is clear. It is disgraceful if we glory in the word 'Christianity' when there is not an ounce of it in us. This text is therefore a warning to us that we cannot be counted as God's children unless we so live in this world that, the closer death comes to us, the more we learn to rejoice, knowing that though the outward man perishes we will be fully restored by the power of him who can do all things. So may God's promises be so etched upon our hearts, and may they so bear the Holy Spirit's seal, that there is nothing in his word which we have cause to doubt.

Let us also open our eyes to understand that whenever the gospel is preached to us, it is as if Jesus Christ were crucified before us. We should never doubt that his death and passion will have their full effect. If we are unsure of ever attaining his glory, we are guilty in a sense of pulling him from his throne. Yet we confess that he is seated at the Father's right hand, that he rules with might and is sovereign over all. So if we doubt whether our inheritance is kept for us in heaven, we deny this very article of our faith. We deny that it is his death which redeems us, and we renounce the death and passion of our Lord Jesus Christ. Let us not forget these things. Let us correct that accursed unbelief which so controls our flesh, and let us learn what it means to love the coming of the Son of God.

Turning to Timothy, the apostle says to him: *Do your best to come quickly to me*. It is true that Timothy had a busy ministry in the city of Ephesus where there was much business to be done. Still, we cannot doubt that Paul thought that his presence would profit the whole church much more. He does not forget the church of Ephesus, however, for he sends Tychicus there as Timothy's replacement. And he tells us why. *Demas has left me*, he says, *having loved this present world; he has gone to Thessalonica, Crescens to Galatia and Titus to Dalmatia. Only Luke is with me.* Here Paul reveals that he needed Timothy's presence to help him defend the gospel. Being in prison and expecting only death, he foresees great troubles, because the weak soon stumble unless they are made strong in the faith. Paul anticipates these things and thus wants to have Timothy with him at the time of his death, or for some other work which God might have him do and which he cannot accomplish on his own. That is what this verse tells us.

In case, however, we think that these are simply personal details of no concern to the church at large, or that the Holy Spirit has here set down things unrelated to the message of salvation, notice that in begging Timothy to come soon, Paul shows how important it is for the church's edification to anticipate the difficulties and troubles which the devil stirs up in times of change and alteration. This is a most useful lesson, for every day we see God's servants being harassed. The whole edifice seems in danger of collapsing when the wicked are free to act and when God's children are so cruelly oppressed by the enemies of the truth. When change is in the air the faith of the godly might well be shaken. We should thus be warned so that we do not suddenly panic. It is something we should foresee well in advance, so that whatever happens we remain firm and do not falter. Our faith should be immovably steadfast, able to overcome whatever attacks the devil may make.

That is one point. When, therefore, we read that Paul summoned Timothy to come to him across the sea to defend the gospel, we see how vital it is that God's word should be upheld. If anyone is persecuted, he should tell himself: 'This is a heavy load I bear on my shoulders, but it is a worthy one. To defend the gospel and to confound the wicked is the greatest sacrifice I can make to God. I will uphold God's name, then, and I shall do so to the very end.' So although Paul is speaking personally to Timothy, he is pointing to a truth which is important to all of us, provided we are able to apply and use it profitably.

Look, in particular, at what Paul says about Demas: 'He has left me, having loved this world.' He does not accuse him of having given the gospel up and of having become an apostate and an enemy of God. He does not mean that he has cut himself off from the church like a rotten limb. Rather, Demas has gone away, either for his own benefit or because it suits him better, or because he shrinks from the cross and the trials which he endured while in Paul's company. Nevertheless Paul discredits him, for to say that because a man loved the world he went away, is to do more than simply shame him. It is as if Paul said that he preferred the world to God. Such an exchange is never proper, but it is for our instruction that Paul pronounced so harsh a judgment on Demas. We know that in other passages he praises him highly, calling him his partner and helper in upholding the gospel (Col. 4:14; Philem. 24). Yet here Paul discredits him for all time, for to the very end of the world, whenever the name of Jesus Christ is proclaimed, Demas will be pilloried and will have a sentence of condemnation on his head, because he shrank from the pain he suffered with Paul. He was too fainthearted, too fond of his own ease.

Bear in mind, then, that though in our own eyes we may have done much, it amounts to nothing unless we keep on to the end. For as we saw, Demas was held in high regard and with his own lips Paul bore splendid witness to him. Was it a small thing that he was called the partner of an apostle whom God had richly endowed and to whom he had given so great a reputation that he was called a chosen vessel to bear the name of Jesus Christ throughout the world (Acts 9:15)? Together with him, Demas is called, exalted, as it were, above the clouds! Not that men applaud him, but the Holy Spirit in a sense has honoured him and might have raised him up to be a burning lamp in the midst of the church. Yet having been assigned so high a place of honour, he is disgraced for all time, since Paul tells us that he loved the world better. Thus if God has given us grace to serve him and has used us to bear witness to his gospel, if we have set a good example and are respected in his church, if we have been leaders of others and have been ranked, so to speak, among the best, let us take care how we walk, and not think that God has hired us only for a while but will let us go when our time is up. We must recognize that we serve God on one condition only: that we dedicate our life and death to him.

All who have faithfully sought to build God's church and to promote the gospel of Jesus Christ should see in Demas a mirror of themselves. Since he was reproached for preferring the world to God, they should know that unless they persevere to the end, while every man on earth may forgive them their fault, God reckons it up. For we will be judged by the same standard by him who is no respecter of persons and whose sentence is always just. We gain nothing, then, though the whole world may favour us and though no one sees this fault in us or knows about it. We will finally be condemned, just as Demas was, if we do not obey God's call or reject the blandishments which Satan offers to make us love the world. This is not to say that we should not take thought for our own life and obtain the things we need—but only if we do not draw back or turn aside from our calling. We must each consider what God commands us to do and what our responsibilities are.

If our Lord gives us rest and allows us to serve him without much strife, we should give him thanks for bearing with us in our weakness. Yet we should not let our ease and pleasures lull us to sleep or stop us moving forward, even if we are not assailed by suffering. God who sees our weakness will not leave Satan free to act or allow him to hound us to the end. Yet should he allow us to suffer so that we do much less than we would like, let us not take this as an excuse to say: 'I have no wish to give the gospel up or to forsake my duty. But look, things have never been so hard. I can enjoy my comforts while still serving God.' Really? God calls us to go one way, while we go the other! We think we can turn tail and abandon the path traced out for us. We must all, then, take a close look at ourselves and learn what is meant by this love of the world of which Paul speaks.

What, then, does it mean? It means that we are so engrossed by present realities that we grow cold and no longer desire the kingdom of heaven and the life to which God calls us. Thus when Paul talks about 'this present world', he intends to reproach those who are so dazzled by transitory things that they forget that the world will be restored. We speak about the world, not knowing what we say. The world in its present state is like a woman in travail, as Paul says in the eighth chapter of Romans (Rom. 8:22). The creation is not complete: because of Adam's sin all is subject to misery. There is no sun or moon which is not marred by corruption. Whether we look high or low, the world we see is in decay. Nothing is sure or certain and we see the evidence of sin before our very eyes. We must therefore weep and groan. In sum, says Paul, all creatures, including those devoid of feeling, are like women in labour. Even we who are God's children and who, having received the first fruits of his Spirit, yearn for completion, must take our place beside the insensate, lifeless creatures and suffer along with them. At least, he says, let us not be so stupid as not to see that the world is imperfect and incomplete.

In speaking of this present world, Paul is comparing the world as it now is with the consummate world which we will see at the coming of our Lord Jesus Christ. Let us learn, then, to love both our God and him whom he sent to be our Redeemer. Let not this world stop us always longing for spiritual blessings. As Peter writes in his first letter, although believers have not seen Jesus Christ, they love him, and are so thrilled by his love that they tremble with joy (1 Pet. 1:8). 'You have heard,' he says, 'that Jesus Christ has redeemed you from death and has brought you into his heavenly glory. Therefore you love him, for he gave himself up for your salvation and by the sacrifice of his death and passion he has reconciled you to God his Father. It is in him that you seek blessing, and not coldly, for you leap for joy.' If we do not have this, it is a sign that we are without faith. So when love for the Lord Jesus Christ and for his coming is impressed on our hearts, we will not be so wrapped in worldly things that we cannot move beyond them. We will remember to do the duties entrusted to us and will follow the path laid out for us. We should always look to the coming of Jesus Christ, which we now know by faith.

These are things we should think about when the example of Demas is set before us. As I said before, all who are preoccupied with this world's honours, wealth and pleasures must take their place alongside this poor wretch who is here discredited. Nor should they excuse themselves by claiming that they have not forsaken Jesus Christ. For as we said, Paul does not accuse Demas of being an enemy of the gospel or of having cut himself off from the church. He accuses him of having withdrawn to a more peaceful spot in order to escape the blows, and of having shirked the battles prepared for him. So when a man, for his own ease or comfort, seeks to leave the flock, and when, seeing the church about to suffer persecution, he retreats, he is reckoned among those who love the world. If we knew what it was to love Jesus Christ, we would certainly be willing to suffer along with everyone else when called to do so.

In any case, it should be clear that Paul, while greatly in need of Timothy's presence, was not so preoccupied with himself that he failed to provide for the needs of the churches. We note, then, that he sent Titus who was with him to Dalmatia, a country a long way off; and he sent another to Asia. So he has those who might have been of service to him set sail across the sea. He is willing to part with all these helpers since he knows the church's urgent needs. That is why I said that in calling Timothy, Paul did not want to deprive Ephesus of a good pastor. It was because things were calmer now that Timothy could come to Rome, without the risk of trouble occurring in his absence. In addition he sent Tychicus to take his place. That was his motive in wanting Timothy to join him. Although, therefore, the apostle is in dire straits, he does not forget what is happening a long way from him. He continues to show a fatherly concern for all of God's church, so that if in some small corner of the world help is needed, he is only too ready to supply the remedy if he can do so.

Accordingly we should learn not to be so busy with our own affairs that we do not think about the church in general. This is a lesson worth remembering, given the sluggishness we see in us. If all is well with us we hardly spare a thought for our brethren who are in distress. Everywhere the fires are lit; we know what is done to God's children; we see problems and troubles and there is always talk of them. They do not have to be three hundred miles away; they are almost at our gates. But are we moved? If this is all the kindness we can muster, do not think that God will own us as his children, for we should feel compassion for all his church. We should share both good and bad with them. Let each of us, then, learn from Paul's example to think less of self, to be concerned for the whole church and to correct the wrongs he sees as his position and resources allow. Not all of us, it is true, will have the means which were given to Paul, but we should try according to our ability to assist all of God's church. If we cannot do more, let God at least be witness to our love when we intercede for our poor brethren who suffer; and when he gives us rest and leisure may it encourage us to think of those who are more hard pressed than we are.

To conclude, Paul asks Timothy *to bring when he comes the cloak—or the book chest—together with the books and especially the parchments which he had left behind in Troas.* Here we see that although death was coming close, Paul was still keen to learn, so that he might be better able to teach others. As for the word 'cloak', some assume it to be a kind of coat to give protection against the rain. If we interpret it this way, it is a sure sign that Paul was deprived of worldly comforts and had to ask from so far away for a cloak to cover him. Since, however, he mentions also books and parchments, it is probable that the word means a case or box in which books are kept. At all events Paul, as I said, still desires to use his time profitably, even though he has one foot in the grave.

Now this is the man who was taken up into the third heaven, who had seen things incomprehensible to men and about which he dared not speak (2 Cor. 12:2-4). So Paul, who had had more revelations than any other apostle, asks for books which he requires for study. He is still a prisoner who has more or less laid his body aside and who sees death close at hand. Already he has half left the world behind him, his soul not so much dwelling in his body as being taken up on high. Yet when we see him still intent on studying, what are we to do? Cursed, then, be our laziness when, as we see, the ignorant have no desire to profit from the gospel! There are those who are unimaginably stupid and who are incapable of saying what the gospel is about. If urged to give themselves to reading and to listening, they reply: 'I'm no scholar! That's not my job!' That is how some think they can escape by pleading ignorance. Others, as soon as they acquire some knowledge of God and are ready to argue about Scripture, become so conceited that they think they know everything and have no further need to study.

It would even detract from their good name, for they affect to be experts. If they think that they are held in high regard as teachers, they close their books; they have no further use for them, they have served their purpose. Yet here we have Paul—whom none of us can ever approach however long we live—who, having reached full maturity, does not fail to keep on studying.

He does it not out of hypocrisy or false humility but because he knows that we can never be too fit to teach God's church. Thus whenever we seek to be good and effective teachers we must begin by being good students—and not only begin, but continue to be diligent all the days of our lives. Since Paul sets us so fine an example, would it not be shameful if, having cast a passing glance at what Scripture contains, we thought we knew more than enough? Here, then, is a lesson for every one of us. We are urged as long as we live to grow strong in our knowledge of salvation. To do this we should not sit with mouths agape, but must make sure we use the means which God provides. Let us listen to sermons and value the reading of God's word; let us hear wholesome, reverent speech which will edify us. Let us not cease, morning and evening, to learn some useful text which will bring to mind the things we have forgotten, and which will add to our appreciation of God's truth.

Above all, let those who are responsible for teaching others look to themselves, for however clever they may be they are far from being as good as Paul. Let them therefore commend themselves to God, that he may graciously give them fuller knowledge of his will, so that they may impart to others what they have received. And when they have been faithful teachers all their lives, when it is their turn to die, let them still wish to be useful by sharing their knowledge with those around them. Thus great and small, teachers and the folk who hear them, the wise and the simple, rich and poor, young and old—let all be encouraged, as we are taught here, to grow continually and not to be weary, until we no longer see in part as in a mirror, but behold the glory of God, face to face.

Now let us cast ourselves down before the face of our good God, acknowledging our faults and praying that it may please him not to impute them to us. May he remake us for himself, so that our one desire is to please him and to devote our lives to his holy law. And since we are all the time hindered by our many infirmities, may he sustain us until, being wholly rid of them, we are clothed with the perfection for which we now yearn.

# 30

---

## WHO IS ON THE LORD'S SIDE?

*Alexander the smith did me much harm; may the Lord repay him according to his works. ¹⁵You also should beware of him, for he greatly resisted our words. ¹⁶No one aided me at my first hearing, but all abandoned me. I pray that it may not be charged against them. ¹⁷But the Lord assisted me and strengthened me, that I might do the work of preaching and that all the Gentiles might hear. I was delivered from the mouth of the lion. ¹⁸The Lord will deliver me from all evil and will save me in his heavenly kingdom. To him be glory for ever. ¹⁹Greet Prisca and Aquila and the house of Onesiphorus. ²⁰Erastus remained in Corinth, and I left Trophimus sick in Miletus. ²¹Try hard to come before winter. Eubulus, Pudens, Linus, Claudia and all the brethren greet you. ²²The Lord Jesus Christ be with your spirit. Grace be with you. Amen.* (2 Timothy 4:14-22)

At first sight we might think that Paul was too swayed by emotion when he prayed that God would repay Alexander the smith for his deeds. He has no such feelings toward those who did not do what they should have done to aid him; on the contrary he prays that God will forgive them. It seems that here we have two prayers which cannot be reconciled. Paul speaks of one man who has opposed him, and of a number of others who were lax and cold in their defence of the gospel. Of the first, he says: *May God repay him according to his demerits*. That is, may God punish him severely, meaning that God should show him neither favour nor mercy but should cast him headlong into hell. Of the second, he says: *May God have compassion on them*. Even though they had been disloyal and had betrayed him, he asks that God might pardon them for their misdeeds. All things considered, however, we will see that the apostle was motivated by right and proper zeal in the case of Alexander the smith, and that God was so leading him that he had gentler feelings toward the others, however unworthy they were.

To understand the whole passage, note that Alexander the smith—or coppersmith—had from the outset given much evidence of Christian faith, and was thought to be among the most mature. But he is not content to become a turncoat, as we say: he is openly hostile to the gospel and does all he can to combat God's truth. So incensed is he that he withstands Paul and falls to fighting with him. It is not, then, a question of human weakness, as when we see people who falter through fear and who prove less staunch than we would like. Those who give in when overcome by weakness deserve pity. Anyone, however, who behaves so badly that he resists God, tramples on his word, blasphemes against the doctrine of salvation and tries hard to suppress it, can only be possessed by Satan, and bears more or less the mark of the reprobate. That is why Paul denounces the smith in such terms, for he was not weak in any way as God's children sometimes are, but he was moved by diabolical frenzy. For he must have thrown all hope away to display such enmity against the gospel.

It is clear, then, that here as everywhere else Paul maintains a balance. He had compassion on those poor weak souls who had not done as they should: they were like straying sheep. In their case he asked God not to impute it to them. This is love over which the

Holy Spirit has full control. On the other hand he did not spare a man who was a complete renegade. Seeing no remedy, for he was past correction, Paul was utterly zealous and prayed not for forgiveness but that God would bring him down. There is a lesson in this for all of us. First, God chose to humble Paul by raising up this man to oppose him. If we compare the two, we see an artisan, a man without much schooling or intellect. The highest title Paul gives him is 'smith', yet he is forced to engage in argument with him. If he had been a most learned and clever man, we might have said that it was a fairly even match. Nevertheless God chose to try Paul in this way. The lesson, therefore, is that sometimes we will have to do battle with worthless people. We should not have to dignify their chatter with a reply, for they are no more than curs who yap and bark. Even so God's servants must take the fight to them. If they think that this may harm their reputation, they must sooner or later see that, when in serving God we think our work pointless or insignificant, we should be content to know that God approves. So when we are faced with ignorant and unintelligent people, we must nevertheless hold our ground as we struggle for the truth. We should not care what the world may think or say, but should rather look to God who wills to test us in this way.

See how necessary it was for the prophet Ezekiel to fight against women who were witches, but who mimicked the prophetesses of the time; he had no choice but to confront such people (Ezek. 13:17). In men's eyes this was scarcely fitting for so noble a prophet, but he concluded that since these women were prey to Satan, he had to defend God's truth against the devil's errors and lies. We must do the same. It is not for us to choose our opponents, so that in winning an argument with someone of note and reputation we might impress by our brilliance. It is not for us to choose. Let us instead be happy for our Lord to enter us for the fray and to test us in the process. And when we have striven to serve him, we should know that what we have done is acceptable to him, although the world may not agree.

Our point is, then, that we must never be ashamed to have to battle sometimes against the rude and boorish, as we might say. Remember also, however, that it is only the most ignorant who are really brazen. A man of learning and intelligence, however ill-willed he may be, will be more moderate than someone who has never learned a thing. That man will be quite shameless! The smith who is referred to here is like a mirror to us of the insolence we see in ruffians who know nothing of honour, and who have no qualms about resisting God and men. It's all one to them, and it is useless to try to make them see reason; they are quite deaf and cannot be made to blush in the slightest. Let not those, then, who oppose God's servants think so highly of themselves that they complain about being vexed and upset. We should send them off to keep company with this man of whom Paul speaks.

Nowadays we see a good many rascals who are drunkards, inveterate boozers and so on, and who come out with miserable things. They think that by reviling God's servants they have gained a point or two. Now if that is their proud boast, what honour is it for Alexander the smith to have had his name recorded in God's word, except that, as I said before, our Lord chose him to be a model of that reckless boldness typical of the ignorant who war against God foolishly, without discernment and with the utmost fury? When we see such examples in our own time, we should not think them new or novel, for God from the beginning sought in this way to test his church and to make us more resolute today.

We notice too that when Satan is given his head, he uses all kinds of tools and will set them to work, so that we wonder how those devoid of wit or cleverness can be so skilled in mischief. This shows that when Satan is left free to act he will always find suitable allies. We are thus encouraged to recognize how good God is to us when he reins the wicked in. When it comes to doing good, we are pitifully slow; but when it comes to evil, we are much too keen and quick! So when we see the world full of evildoers and of despisers of God whose aim is to reduce all to chaos, we should acknowledge God's exceptional grace in not leaving them free to act and in holding them back. Otherwise there would be many smiths in the world, intent on resisting the truth!

Notice moreover that those who once savoured the gospel are far worse enemies, and a hundred times more bitter, than the poor blind souls who did not know true teaching. Those, I say, are much cleverer at making mischief, as we well know. There are apostates who have been mixed in with us and who have been taught along with us. When, however, they rise up and defy God, they are much better equipped to overturn the truth and to corrupt everything than are the wretched papists, despite their reputation for learning. Hence we should not think it strange today if those who once appeared to belong to Christ's flock and church wander off, and like half-devils attempt to disguise the truth. After all, we see what occurred in Paul's day. Yet it is a comfort to know that though God may allow Satan a free hand, he always makes sure that his truth triumphs in the end—not only over the ignorant with their brazen impudence but over the most gifted experts in the world.

Let us have truth, therefore, on our side. Let us call upon God and walk in all sincerity, never doubting that we will be victorious over our enemies. To be sure we will be troubled and tormented. As Paul rightly says, Alexander the smith showed him much evil. Those are his words, for that was the common style of speech, equivalent to 'did him much harm'. So although Paul was upheld by the Holy Spirit's power, and although with one word he could have silenced all the wicked who opposed the truth, he nevertheless found this to be a most difficult fight. Why? Because God meant to humble him. Thus although the wicked may sometimes seem to do as they please and to enjoy men's applause, and although we may be oppressed, we should not be surprised, since Paul himself complains that a smith gave him much trouble.

It is no different today. When some ruffian objects to sound teaching he will attract a large and important following, because while everyone makes profession of the gospel hardly one in ten is not content to see things muddled, with the result that no one can tell who are the winners and who the losers. Why is this? It is because most think that they will be free to live dissolute lives and to mock God as they like. Because religion serves as a curb to restrain us and to stop us acting like wild animals, many people welcome conflict and controversy from which the wickedest always come out on top. When we see such things we should bear them patiently, being persuaded that God will give us the same happy outcome as he gave Paul. For the apostle's own example shows how God continually guides and governs his own, and how he gives them victory, though they may suffer for a time.

Notice again that Paul is not complaining that Alexander the smith has personally harmed him by hounding him to death or by insulting him. He says that he has resisted his teaching. So when we are God's children we should be more deeply hurt and saddened if God himself is blasphemed, or his truth twisted and marred, than if we suffered all the abuse and injury in the world. If indeed God's truth is not so precious to us, where is our zeal? When God's word is vilified we must take it to heart. The words of the Psalm, although fulfilled in the person of Jesus Christ, are applied by Paul to all believers: the zeal they feel should consume their heart, so that they know no peace (Psa. 69:9; Rom. 15:3). If this is not true of us, we show that we have neither zeal nor love for our God, and thus that we are not worthy to be called his children. Who, after all, allows men to mock his father? Yet a father is an earthly being, worth nothing in himself. Who would dare to boast that he was a child of God, yet show no concern when God's word was ridiculed and his truth blasphemed?

Let us always remember that when people rise up against God and the simple gospel, we should be more upset and troubled than if we ourselves suffered all the abuse and wrongs under the sun. Accordingly Paul writes that Isaac was persecuted by Ishmael (Gal. 4:29). It was not that Ishmael beat or struck his brother Isaac or that he robbed him of his inheritance or drove him by force from home. Instead he made fun of him. Yet this tiny bit of sarcasm Paul calls persecution. Why? Because it ought to make us feel incensed. When we see men maligning God's majesty, when we see vermin and scum who boldly rebel against their Creator and who heap abuse on the truth—which is the sceptre of God's universal rule and the ground of our salvation—must we permit these things without one sign of sorrow or distress? That, in sum, is what Paul means when he makes the one complaint that 'he resisted my words'. He plainly shows that it was not he who was injured; it was God's truth which was attacked.

We come now to the prayer which Paul made concerning him: 'May he be repaid according to his deserts.' As we said, Paul was not moved by anger or by a surge of resentment against the smith. The zeal he showed was controlled by the Holy Spirit, so that his request may be seen as a genuine sentence passed upon this wretched man who had dared to challenge the gospel. We perceive, then, how precious God's truth is to him, for we see how he bears with the offences men commit against him, and with what patience he tries to bring them to repentance—yes, even those who have gravely sinned against him. As he says through his prophets, what man will accept a woman who has left her husband and played the harlot? 'But,' says God, 'you have been untrue and have utterly offended me, yet I am ready to be reconciled to you' (Jer. 3:1, 12).

Here our Lord testifies that he will not only pardon us for the small offences which we commit through ignorance or weakness before quickly returning to the right and proper path. Even when we have long been lost and helpless and have led vile and vicious lives, he still has mercy on us. When, however, we blaspheme against his truth, it is an unpardonable sin if it is done out of sheer spite, as was the case with this accursed man on whom the Holy Spirit pronounces dreadful condemnation. Observe therefore that although all sins are abominable in God's sight, the very worst is when we revile and speak ill of God's word and of true religion. In God's eyes murder, cruelty, poisoning or anything else is not to be compared with rebellion against him.

If we think hard about it, should we consider a man's life to be as precious as God's truth? A man's life is circumscribed by time. Here what is at stake is the salvation not only of our souls but of the whole world. It is all about God's kingdom and of how he is to be served and glorified among us. So if men decide to rise up against God's majesty, to end the rule and dominion which he has given to our Lord Jesus Christ, or if they mean to crush poor souls and lead them to perdition, what shall we say, except that these should be much more hateful to us than any other crime? It is no wonder, then, that Paul should speak so forcefully against this wretched tool of Satan who, knowing the truth, having been taught the gospel and having professed it, proceeds in hellish rage to blot out the majesty of Jesus Christ, to subvert all truth, to ruin poor souls, to rob them of their salvation, to shut the gate to paradise and to deny men all contact with God and their Creator. When someone goes to these extremes, must not God arise and treat him with the utmost severity? Let us learn, therefore, first of all, to honour the truth of the gospel which is so precious and sacred to God. And since he values his holy word more than anything else which men esteem, let us receive it with all humility and reverence, and let each of us obey it. If we would do homage to God, let us show it by being subject to his word. It must be our focus, for it is there that God most clearly manifests to us his glory. That is one point.

Let us be careful not to resist God's holy truth and genuine religion. That would be to challenge God openly and to go to war against him. We might not say so out loud but our actions would reveal it. If we would guard against this evil, let us make sure that we do not sport with God, for there are scoundrels who merely laugh at the mention of God's word and who speak derisively about it. God is bound to cast them off if they continue to despise him. It is then that the devil will seize them, making them angry and spiteful so that they blaspheme against the Holy Spirit. Do we want God, then, to restrain us and to keep us from breaking out in awful blasphemies against him and from fighting against his truth? Then let us resolve to accept the message which is preached to us or which we read, cherishing it as sacred and as a treasure beyond all price.

Moreover when we see these wretches who are so bad that they defy even God, know that it is the fruit of their hypocrisy. Having chosen to make light of so great a teacher as God, they are sure in the end to fall headlong to their deaths, as we well know. Would to God these things were less in evidence than they are! But when God reveals them to us we must learn from them, so that we may fear and honour him with utmost patience. We should be horrified to see such things and we should detest the people who do them. As Paul says of Alexander: *Beware of him.* Timothy is to shun the coppersmith like the plague. So when we see these wretched creatures who oppose God and his word, let us depart from them, lest God's vengeance engulf us too.

Now there are people who complain when they are shunned. They are God's worst enemies, yet they claim that they are gravely wronged when we point them out and urge the ignorant to avoid them, showing how dangerous it is to associate with them. So they complain: 'What's going on? What are we accused of? Why do you blacken our name?' But do not those who oppose their Creator bear the mark of Satan? Do they not make open war on God? The devil, after all, is our enemy, and when we see his lackeys and side with them, do we not conspire with them against God? Do we not plainly defy God, even if we are not so bad as to take up arms immediately against the gospel? Nevertheless we try God sorely when we have close dealings with such people. We are much too weak, and all the while we court defilement. Hence when we see the enemies of God's truth we must look on them with abhorrence; we must shun them, having nothing to do with them if we want to avoid their poison. The fact is that they corrupt everything else at the same time, making it impossible to associate with them or to draw near to them without becoming infected. That is the sense of Paul's warning.

As we said before, in asking God to repay the smith according to his deserts, Paul is not thinking about himself. We cannot, therefore, excuse ourselves by falsely appealing to his example as many people do. They are keen to be admired for their intense zeal, but the fervour they display is for their own private purposes. Paul in this text has no thought for himself; he forgets everything except the need to uphold God's truth. Accordingly, if we set out to ask God to cleanse the world and especially his poor church, to wipe out all who scorn his majesty, who overturn true religion and who falsify his word—if that is our aim, we must not be driven by fleshly considerations, but by the sole wish to see God glorified. And even if this is our goal, we must beware of adding our own motives to the mix. If we did, it would be one step too far. For it is not enough to be rightly zealous: wisdom must moderate our zeal so that the Spirit of God is fully in control.

Do not forget, either, that we are to show pity toward those who, we know, are not yet outcasts. As long as there is hope for men, we must always pray that God will have pity on them and will be merciful. We should continue to hope until such time as God reveals that he has cut off those who have risen against him—has cut them off, I say, like rotten limbs. Without doubt, this is the sort of certainty which Paul had concerning the smith of whom he speaks. He did not rush to judgment ahead of time, but was absolutely sure that this man was a reprobate. This is the evidence we must have before we ask God to bring the wicked down. Such things are rare, however, and we must not make them a common rule. Let us instead learn to restrain ourselves, and not be too headstrong in entreating God to ruin and scatter those who are opposed to us. Recall what our Lord Jesus Christ said to his disciples: 'You do not know what kind of spirit leads you' (Luke 9:55). For they had cited the example of Elijah, and wanted fire to descend from heaven to consume the enemies of the gospel. Yes, but it was not the spirit of Elijah who was inspiring them! They went much further than they should. We must guard against such things.

This is why I said we cannot derive a general rule from Paul's words about one man. We must weigh everything with care, and determine whether those who blaspheme against the truth do so out of settled malice, and whether they are renegades who, having forsaken Jesus Christ, mean to fight with him, to take his kingdom and his majesty from him and to erase the memory of his name. When we see people like that who are strangers to all religion, the devil has them and they suffer God's punishment, showing that they are utterly cast out and have forfeited all hope of salvation. Yet while we can make no general rule, there will be signs or marks supplied by God. Otherwise what is said about Alexander the smith, or what we read in John, would make no sense, namely that there is a sin which leads to death (1 John 5:16). If we did not sometimes know that God had cast men out and had closed the door of salvation to them, showing them to be incapable of correction and to be slaves to Satan, why would John have spoken of a mortal sin which cannot be forgiven?

We return, then, to our earlier point. If people simply succumb to weakness, falter in the face of the gospel and fail to attest their faith as they ought; or if they err in one way or another because Satan takes them unawares, however grave their faults we should feel pity for them and do all we can to bring them back to the right way. We should ask God to stretch out his hand and to draw them back by the grace of his Holy Spirit. But when, on the other hand, we see men openly defying God, resisting his word and keen to destroy religion if they can, this is a God-given sign that he has cast them off and wants us to have nothing to do with them. As Paul rightly declares, when men out of set and conscious malice oppose the truth of God which once they knew, when they attempt to abolish his worship and to extinguish the light of his word, they must be condemned without pity. It is no longer a question of love. God separates us from such people; he will not have us view them as men, but as already part of the devil's crew.

Since this is God's view of them, we should ask him to crush those who cannot be corrected, and to demonstrate how dear his truth is to him and how much he cherishes the kingdom which he has established in and through his Son. We should have compassion on all poor sinners, even on those who, overcome by fear or feigning death, retreat when they should be defending God's cause. Though they are less brave than might be wished, we should pity them, following the example of Paul who could have felt indignant about being so foully abandoned. Who abandoned him? His brethren, who pretended to make common cause with him—and who indeed did! Yet they withdrew and left him without help. Despite their cowardice he forgives them and prays to God for them. We must do the same. If we could see ourselves as we are, we would not be so hasty in passing judgment on our fellows. We would bear more gently with each other, whatever our faults. 'See that you are not also tempted,' says Paul (Gal. 6:1). So when we see others failing, what else should we do but pray for them, since we need the same to be done for us? This is a point worth noting.

At the same time we see how wonderful it is when God gives us strength to persist in firmly defending the gospel. Paul is speaking here about those whom we might call the first fruits of God's church, the flower of the elect. God had begun to call them and even to make them ministers. The believers in Rome numbered more than three or four. The church, admittedly, was but a handful compared with the many inhabitants of that great city. It was as populous as a whole country. Even so believers were numerous enough, yet not one thought to assist Paul. He had Luke with him but was without any of the rest. We should therefore bow our heads, knowing that unless God aids us from on high we will betray him in time of need. When it comes to defending his truth we will abandon him and ask to be exempt. This is a grievous, monstrous sin, but we must face the fact that we cannot trust ourselves. We are not strong enough to hold our ground. Where would we be if God did not support us? We know the dreadful sentence passed by our Lord Jesus Christ: 'Whoever denies me before men, I will deny before my Father in heaven' (Matt. 10:33). If God had not shown exceptional mercy to those of whom Paul speaks, they would have all been lost. Left to themselves they would have been banished from God's kingdom, and would have forfeited the salvation which had before been offered to them in the gospel. We have every reason, then, to shut our mouths and to lament the misery within us. Without the strength which God gives us we would risk disaster every minute of the day. With one false step we could fall and break our necks. That is what this passage teaches us.

Consider, here, what little truth there is in the papists' claim that Peter was the first bishop of Rome. If their chronicles are to be believed, he and Paul were contemporaries. They hold that they both died on the same day: one was put to death on the same day as the other, but twelve months apart. In this text Paul refers to his first hearing. So Peter must have already been in Rome, for the papists say that he was pontiff for seven years. It follows, then, that Peter must have abandoned the faith of our Lord Jesus Christ, have given up his inheritance and the hope of salvation promised by the gospel, and have drawn away from the apostles, having no further fellowship with them! This shows just how false and mythical is the papists' story about Peter's seat being in Rome.

As to the other names mentioned by Paul, they are recorded here to teach us to be humble and to be careful when we pray, asking God to keep us from being fainthearted should we be called to witness to his truth. The conclusion to which Paul is led is this: 'God did not fail me.' So even if men forsake us and leave us completely alone, all is not lost. Though we are abandoned, God has ample power to aid us. This is a good test and trial of our faith. We may be greatly alarmed when we see no earthly help. Let us nevertheless look to our God and rest solely on him. Until we learn to honour him this way and to be content with him and with his aid alone, we surely see him as no better than men. For when men are strong enough to help us, we place our trust in them. And when God tells us that he is powerful but gives no immediate proof of it, we become fearful and distrustful. Do we not, then, make him equal to the creatures, and ascribe fewer powers to him than to mortal men?

The lesson for us here is that when we are bereft of human help, we must continue to rely on God, knowing that he is mighty to save us. And when we have experienced his help, we can affirm with Paul that *he will deliver us from every evil work*. The apostle does not say that God will deliver him from death. He has already reckoned on the fact that he must be a sacrificial offering to God. He is content for God to strengthen him by his Holy Spirit so that by his death he may bear witness to the gospel. He does not worry about persecution or about the anguish he must endure, as long as he is obedient to God and triumphs over the trials and afflictions he must face. This is something that we must also do.

*May the Lord Jesus Christ be with your spirit.* Such is the apostle's final prayer. It is true that if we are in God's care our bodies, too, will be preserved. He will come to our aid whenever it is useful for us. Still, we should never feel so concerned for our bodies that we deny the soul its pre-eminence. It should be enough for us that God is with our spirit, that he preserves us and that our Lord Jesus Christ has us under his protection, leading and guiding us not only through this fleeting, perishable life but through death and beyond. May we seek only to glorify our God until he grants us to share in his glorious immortality.

Now let us cast ourselves down before the face of our good God, acknowledging our faults and beseeching him to make us feel them more and more, and to lead us to true repentance. Since he has been pleased to reveal his truth to us, may we receive it with all reverence, and may we grow ever stronger in it. If Satan's allies should rise up against it, let us not be troubled; such things are common, for thus was the faith of our fathers tested. Let us pray to God for strength to fight bravely and constantly for his glory, being always confident that with his aid we will triumph, and that victory is already prepared for us. May we never allow the wicked to win, and when they come forth let them be put to shame. Let us also be willing to live and die in obedience to our God, and may he dwell in us by his Holy Spirit, delivering us from every evil work and from all of Satan's trials. And though we must pass through much hardship and affliction, may he so preserve us that, knowing that we are under his protection, we may rejoice that he has always aided and assisted us, and has kept us from falling into evil ways.


## PRAISE BE TO GOD

End of John Calvin's sermons on the two epistles
of Paul the Apostle to Timothy, which were
simply taken down by the regular recorder
and never reviewed by the author
nor changed in any way.

# PRAYERS BEFORE AND AFTER
# THE SERMON

The Genevan liturgy of 1542 specified for the Sunday morning service a prayer for illumination said by the minister before the sermon, and a set prayer of intercession said after the sermon. Calvin modelled his prayer for illumination on the one which he had already used in the French church of Strasbourg. The intercessory prayer followed the brief extempore prayer with which he concluded his sermons, and was introduced by the words 'Thus we will all say …'. (Texts in *CO* 23: 741-42; 6: 175-78.)

## PRAYER FOR ILLUMINATION

Let us call upon our good God and Father, since all fullness of wisdom and light is found in him, mercifully to enlighten us by his Holy Spirit in the true understanding of his word, and to give us grace to receive it in true fear and humility. May we be taught by his word to place our trust only in him and to serve and honour him as we ought, so that we may glorify his holy name in all our living, and edify our neighbour by our good example, rendering to God the love and obedience which faithful servants owe their masters, and children their parents, since it has pleased him graciously to receive us among the number of his servants and children.


# PRAYER OF INTERCESSION


Almighty God and heavenly Father, you have promised to hear and answer our requests which we make to you in the name of your beloved Son, Jesus Christ our Lord. We are further taught by him and his apostles to gather together in his name, with the promise that he will be among us and will intercede for us before you, that we may receive and obtain all things on which we are agreed on earth.

You bid us pray, first, for those whom you have set up over us, our leaders and governors; and next, for the needs of all your people, and of all men everywhere. Therefore, trusting in your holy truth and in your promise, being assembled here before you in Jesus' name, we lovingly beseech you, our God and Father, in your infinite mercy freely to pardon our transgressions, and so to lift our thoughts and desires to you that we may earnestly call upon you according to your good will and pleasure.

We therefore pray, heavenly Father, for all princes and lords, your servants to whom you have committed the rule of justice. Most particularly do we pray for the rulers of this city, that you will clothe them with your Spirit, who alone is gracious and sovereign, and daily increase his gifts in them, that they, acknowledging your Son Jesus Christ to be King of kings and Lord of lords, with full power in heaven and on earth, may seek to serve him and exalt his reign in all their dominions, and may according to your will guide and govern their subjects, who are the work of your hands and the sheep of your pasture. And may we, your people, here and everywhere, being kept in peace and tranquillity, serve you in holiness and righteousness; and, free from the fear of our enemies, may we give you praise all our days.

We pray also, true Father and Saviour, for all whom you have appointed to be pastors to your people, who have the care of souls and the stewardship of your holy gospel. May you lead and direct them by your Holy Spirit, that they may be found faithful and true ministers of your glory, always striving to bring home the erring and wayward sheep to the Lord Jesus Christ, our chief Shepherd and supreme Bishop, that they may daily prosper and grow in him in all righteousness and holiness. Grant, moreover, that all churches may be delivered from the mouths of ravenous wolves and hirelings, who follow their own designs and ambitions and who have no care for the honour of your holy name and the welfare of your flock.

Next we pray, most gracious God and merciful Father, for all men generally. Since you desire all men to acknowledge you as Saviour of the world, through the redemption won by our Lord Jesus Christ, may those who do not know him, being in darkness and captive to ignorance and error—may they by the light of your Holy Spirit and the preaching of your gospel be led into the way of salvation, which is to know you, the only true God, and Jesus Christ whom you have sent. May those whom you have already visited with your grace and enlightened by the knowledge of your word, grow in all goodness, enriched by your spiritual blessing, so that together we may all worship you with heart and voice, giving honour and homage to Christ, our Master, King and Lawgiver.

Likewise, O God of all comfort, we commend to you all whom you visit and chastise with cross and tribulation, whether it be through poverty or prison, sickness or exile, or affliction of body or mind. May you make known to them your fatherly love, and assure them that their chastisement is for amendment of life. And may they with willing hearts turn to you and, having turned, receive your comfort, being delivered from every distress.

Finally, O God and Father, grant also that we, who are gathered here in Jesus' name to hear his word, may, without dissembling or hypocrisy, acknowledge that by nature we are lost, that we deserve your punishment and daily heap up condemnation to ourselves by our wretched and unruly lives. Help us to see that in us there is nothing good, and that flesh and blood can never inherit your kingdom. May we gladly and with steadfast trust submit to our Lord Jesus Christ, our only Saviour and Redeemer. And may he so live in us that, our old Adam being put to death, we may rise to a new and better life, to the praise and glory of your name.

# INDEX OF
# SCRIPTURE REFERENCES

# INDEX OF SUBJECTS

Other John Calvin titles
translated by Robert White and
published by the Trust

*Sermons on First Timothy*

ISBN: 978 1 84871 799 2, Clothbound, 864pp.

*Sermons on Titus*

ISBN: 978 1 84871 569 1, Clothbound, 312pp.

*Sermons on the Beatitudes:*
*Five Sermons from the 'Gospel Harmony'*
*Delivered in Geneva in 1560*

ISBN: 978 0 85151 934 0, Clothbound, 128pp.

*Songs of the Nativity:*
*Selected Sermons on Luke 1 & 2*

ISBN: 978 1 84871 010 8, Clothbound, 280pp.

*A Guide to Christian Living*[1]

ISBN: 978 1 84871 040 5, Soft cover gift edition, 168pp.


*Faith Unfeigned:*
*Four Sermons Concerning Matters Most Useful for*
*the Present Time, with a Brief Exposition of Psalm 87*

ISBN: 978 1 84871 086 3, Clothbound, 208pp.


*The Institutes of the Christian Religion:*
*A New Translation of the 1541 Edition*

ISBN: 978 1 84871 463 2, Clothbound, 920pp.


[1] Also known as *The Golden Booklet of the True Christian Life*.

## ABOUT THE PUBLISHER

THE Banner of Truth Trust originated in 1957 in London. The founders believed that much of the best literature of historic Christianity had been allowed to fall into oblivion and that, under God, its recovery could well lead not only to a strengthening of the church, but to true revival.

Inter-denominational in vision, this publishing work is now international, and our lists include a number of contemporary authors, together with classics from the past. The translation of these books into many languages is encouraged.

A monthly magazine, *The Banner of Truth,* is also published. More information about this and all our publications can be found on our website or supplied by either of the offices below.

### THE BANNER OF TRUTH TRUST

3 Murrayfield Road  PO Box 621, Carlisle,
Edinburgh, EH12 6EL    Pennsylvania 17013,
UK    USA

banneroftruth.org